THE ESSENTIALS OF RISK MANAGEMENT

THE ESSENTIALS OF RISK MANAGEMENT

MICHEL CROUHY

DAN GALAI

ROBERT MARK

McGraw-Hill

New York   Chicago   San Francisco   Lisbon   London
Madrid   Mexico City   Milan   New Delhi
San Juan   Seoul   Singapore
Sydney   Toronto

11 12 13 14 15 16 17 18 DOC/DOC 1 5 4 3 2 1 0

ISBN 0-07-142966-2

This publication is designed to provide accurate and authoritative information in regard
to the subject matter covered. It is sold with the understanding that the publisher is not
engaged in rendering legal, accounting, or other professional service. If legal advice or
other expert assistance is required, the services of a competent professional person
should be sought.

> —*From a declaration of principles jointly adopted by a committee of the*
> *American Bar Association and a committee of publishers.*

McGraw-Hill books are available at special quantity discounts to use as premiums and
sales promotions, or for use in corporate training programs. For more information, please
write to the Director of Special Sales, Professional Publishing, McGraw-Hill, Two Penn
Plaza, New York, NY 10121-2298. Or contact your local bookstore.

Library of Congress Cataloging-in-Publication Data
Crouhy, Michel.
    The essentials of risk management/by Michel Crouhy, Dan Galai, Robert Mark
       p.   cm.
    ISBN 0-07-142966-2 (hardcover : alk. paper)
    1. Risk management. I. Galai, Dan. II. Mark, Robert. III. Title.
HD61.C773 2005
658.15'5—dc22   2005015628

Contents

FOREWORD

Growth and *profitability* are exciting words for investors and stakeholders in companies all over the world. Yet they can be illusory and destructive measures of performance in the absence of risk control and risk management.

At IXIS Corporate and Investment Bank, the investment banking division of Groupe Caisse d'Epargne, one of France's leading universal banks, we have a tradition of understanding the critical relationship between risk and reward.

On the one hand, we are a long-established banking organization that is proud of its continuity, long-lasting business relationships, and conservative sense of discipline, all of which combine to offer the considerable business advantage of robust credit ratings from the leading agencies.

On the other hand, over the last few years, the company has actively restructured and positioned itself to play a leading role in the consolidation of the banking industry and in new banking activities. Not least, our investment banking division is recognized as a leading player in some of the world's most innovative risk management and derivative and structured products markets, such as inflation-indexed securities, securitization of residential and commercial mortgages in the United States, and collateralized debt obligations.

In a dynamic and competitive world, companies cannot manage either strategic or tactical risks by adopting a passive stance. They need to develop the mindset and tools to explore the many dimensions of risk associated with each activity and opportunity so that they can balance these against the more obvious signs of reward.

This is something we tell our investment banking clients, but it's also something we practice ourselves.

Over the last few years, we've invested heavily in our risk management expertise by providing advanced training for our associates in sophisticated risk modeling, financial engineering, the implications of new regulations such as Basel II, improvements in corporate governance, and so on. We've developed proprietary risk models to better assign counterparty credit ratings, and we've developed a comprehensive set of stress-test scenarios to help us take into account the effect of credit and market risks (such as a sharp movement in credit spreads) and business risks (such as variations in the prepayment speeds of mortgages).

All this has strengthened our belief that investing in intellectual capital in the area of risk management is at least as important as investing in other areas of bank expertise.

This isn't only a matter of improving the capabilities of specialist risk managers and risk modelers. The challenge for senior executives of large financial institutions is also how to make sure that the enterprise assesses risk in a cohesive way along clearly established lines of authority and accountability, with each bank activity pursuing the interests of the enterprise as a whole.

Risks must be not only measured, but efficiently communicated and managed right across the firm.

I welcome the way in which this book brings together many of the most sophisticated approaches to risk management, and particularly the way in which it endeavors to make these new ideas accessible to a wide audience.

Anthony Orsatelli
CEO of IXIS Corporate and Investment Bank
Member of the Executive Board
of Groupe Caisse d'Epargne

PROLOGUE

This book draws on our collective academic and business experience to offer a user-friendly view of financial risk management. We've tried to keep the book's language straightforward and nonmathematical so that it is accessible to a wide range of professionals, senior managers, and board members in financial and nonfinancial institutions who need to know more about managing risk. In turn, we hope this means that the book is also suitable for college students, for those in general MBA programs, and for any layperson who is simply curious about the topic of modern financial risk management.

Although largely a new work, this present book draws to some extent on *Risk Management*, a volume that we published with McGraw-Hill in the year 2000. That earlier book offers a detailed and technical discussion of the techniques employed to manage market risk, credit risk, and operational risk, and is aimed primarily at those who are already proficient in risk analytics to some degree.

We were fortunate that *Risk Management* turned out to be highly popular among risk management practitioners in the financial industries and also used extensively in specialized MBA courses on risk management. But it seemed that the time was right for a book that was accessible to a wider range of readers. Over the last five years, there has been an extraordinary growth in the application of new risk management techniques in financial and nonfinancial institutions around the world. The need for a sophisticated understanding of risk management methodologies is no longer confined to the risk management or derivative specialist. Many managers and staff whose jobs are to create, rather than simply conserve, shareholder value are now required to make sophisticated assessments of risk, or to play a critical part in the formal risk management process.

Meanwhile, in the aftermath of the millennial corporate scandals and the resulting efforts to strengthen corporate governance practices and regulations (such as the Sarbanes-Oxley Act in the United States), a broad community of stakeholders such as shareholders, bondholders, employees, board members, and regulators is demanding that institutions become increasingly risk-sensitive and transparent. In turn, this means that stakeholders themselves, as well as a larger tranche of staff in each organization, must improve their understanding of approaches to financial risk management. There can't be a meaningful dialogue about risk and risk management if only one party to the conversation understands the significance of what is being said.

We hope this book is a useful tool in the education of this broader community of company employees and stakeholders on the essentials of risk management. We believe that such an educational effort is now a necessary part of achieving best-practice risk management.

This book should also serve to update readers of our earlier volume, *Risk Management,* on the continuing evolution of best-practice risk policies, risk methodologies, and associated risk infrastructure. Readers of that earlier volume will find that *Essentials of Risk Management* has filled many gaps and offers entirely new chapters on important topics such as corporate governance, economic capital attribution and performance measurement, asset-liability management, and credit scoring for retail portfolios, as well as an updated treatment of the new Basel Accord. We also try to communicate the rich variety of new financial products that are being used to manage risk, such as the dramatic increase in the use of credit derivatives. We hope this treatment will allow readers without formal analytical skills to appreciate the power of these new risk tools.

Modern approaches to financial risk management are today implemented across many industries. Readers won't be surprised, however, to find that we draw many of our examples from the banking industry. The banking industry demands a sophisticated approach to financial risk management as a core skill, and it has spawned most of the new risk management techniques and markets of the last decade. In particular, our discussion is substantially enriched by the new regulatory approaches originating from the Basel Committee on Banking Supervision, the closest approximation the banking industry has to an international regulatory body. Although the committee's new Accord on risk and capital in the banking industry, published in the summer of 2004, has drawn criticism as well as praise, the huge amount of research and industry discussion that underpinned the committee's efforts has yielded many insights. That research and discussion, as well as the implementation of the Accord itself over the next few years, will have a global impact on best-practice risk management well beyond the banking industry.

The more analytically inclined reader may wish to use our earlier volume, *Risk Management*, to drill down into the detailed arguments and notation that support our discussion of market, credit, and operational risk management. Also, as we did not want to burden the reader of this book with too elaborate an academic apparatus, we would refer researchers to our earlier book for a very detailed set of technical footnotes, references, attributions, and bibliography.

In contrast, Chapter 1 of this present book offers a wide-ranging introductory discussion that looks at the many facets and definitions of "risk" as a concept, while also making clear the structure of this book and the relationship between the various chapters on specialized topics.

Finally, we would like to thank Rob Jameson, our editor, for his tremendous efforts to keep us diligent and ensure that we made progress on the book. His contributions went well beyond the call of duty. We also thank colleagues, friends, and users of our earlier volume, *Risk Management,* for their encouragement, comments, and suggestions. We consider this book, too, to be a living document, and we welcome your comments and suggestions on any items or improvements that you feel might interest or benefit readers of future editions.

Michel Crouhy

Dan Galai

Robert Mark

THE ESSENTIALS OF
RISK MANAGEMENT

CHAPTER 1

Risk Management—A Helicopter View[1]

The future cannot be predicted. It is uncertain, and no one has ever been successful in forecasting the stock market, interest rates, or exchange rates consistently—or credit, operational, and systemic events with major financial implications. Yet, the financial risk that arises from uncertainty can be managed. Indeed, much of what distinguishes modern economies from those of the past is the new ability to identify risk, to measure it, to appreciate its consequences, and then to take action accordingly, such as transferring or mitigating the risk.

This simple sequence of activities, shown in more detail in Figure 1-1, is often used to define risk management as a formal discipline. But it's a sequence that rarely runs smoothly in practice: sometimes simply identifying a risk is the critical problem, while at other times arranging an efficient economic transfer of the risk is the skill that makes one risk manager stand out from another. (In Chapter 2 we discuss the risk management process from the perspective of a corporation.)

To the unwary, Figure 1-1 might suggest that risk management is a continual process of corporate risk reduction. But we mustn't think of the modern attempt to master risk in defensive terms alone. Risk management is really about how firms actively select the type and level of risk that it is appropriate for them to assume. Most business decisions are about sacrificing current resources for future uncertain returns.

In this sense, *risk management* and *risk taking* aren't opposites, but two sides of the same coin. Together they drive all our modern economies: the capacity to make forward-looking choices about risk in relation to

---

1. We acknowledge the coauthorship of Rob Jameson in this chapter.

FIGURE 1-1

The Risk Management Process

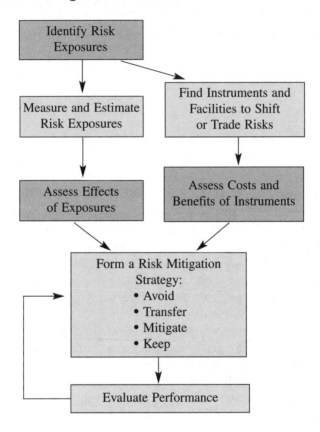

reward lies at the heart of the management process of all enduringly successful corporations.

Yet the rise of financial risk management as a formal discipline has been a bumpy affair, especially over the last 10 years. On the one hand, we've seen an extraordinary growth in new types of institutions that earn their keep by taking and managing risk (e.g., hedge funds), as well as some extraordinary successes in risk management mechanisms: the lack of financial institution bankruptcies during the violent downturn in credit quality in 2001–2002 is often claimed to be the result of better credit-risk management processes at banks.

Risk management is also now widely acknowledged as the most creative force in the world's financial markets. A striking recent example is the development of a huge market for credit derivatives, which allows institutions to obtain insurance to protect themselves against credit default (or, alternatively, to get paid for assuming credit risk as an investment). Credit derivatives can be used to redistribute part or all of an institution's credit-risk exposures to banks, hedge funds, or other institutional investors, and they are a specific example of a broader, beneficial trend in financial markets summed up by Alan Greenspan, chairman of the U.S. Federal Reserve Board:

> The development of our paradigms for containing risk has emphasized dispersion of risk to those willing, and presumably able, to bear it. If risk is properly dispersed, shocks to the overall economic system will be better absorbed and less likely to create cascading failures that could threaten financial stability.[2]

On the other hand, the last 10 years have seen some extraordinary and embarrassing failures of risk management in its broadest definition. These range from the near failure of the giant hedge fund Long-Term Capital Management (LTCM) in 1998 to the string of financial scandals associated with the millennial boom in the equity and technology markets (from Enron, WorldCom, Global Crossing, and Qwest in the United States to Parmalat in Europe).

Unfortunately, risk management has not consistently been able to prevent market disruptions or to prevent business accounting scandals resulting from breakdowns in corporate governance. In the case of the former problem, there are serious concerns that derivative markets make it easier to take on large amounts of risk, and that the "herd behavior" of risk managers after a crisis gets underway (e.g., selling risky asset classes when risk measures reach a certain level) actually increases market volatility.

Sophisticated financial engineering, supplied by the banking, securities, and insurance industries, also played a role in covering up the true economic condition of poorly run companies during the equity markets' millennial boom and bust. Alongside rather simpler accounting mistakes and ruses, this type of financial engineering was one reason that some of these companies violently imploded after years of false success (rather than simply fading away or being taken over at an earlier point).

---

2. Remarks by Chairman Alan Greenspan before the Council on Foreign Relations, Washington, D.C., Nov. 19, 2002.

Part of the reason for risk management's mixed record here lies with the double-edged nature of risk management technologies. Every financial instrument that allows a company to transfer risk also allows other corporations to assume that risk as a counterparty in the same market—wisely or not. Most importantly, every risk management mechanism that allows us to change the shape of cash flows, such as deferring a negative outcome into the future, may work to the short-term benefit of one group of stakeholders in a firm (e.g., managers) at the same time that it is destroying long-term value for another group (e.g., shareholders or pensioners). In a world that is increasingly driven by risk management concepts and technologies, we need to look more carefully at the increasingly fluid and complex nature of risk itself, and at how to determine whether any change in a corporation's risk profile serves the interests of stakeholders. We need to make sure we are at least as literate in the language of risk as we are in the language of reward.

The nature of risk forms the topic of our next section, and it will lead us to the reason we've tried to make this book accessible to everyone, from shareholders, board members, and top executives to line managers, legal and back-office staff, and administrative assistants. We've removed from this book many of the complexities of mathematics that act as a barrier to understanding the essential principles of risk management, in the belief that, just as war is too important to be left to the generals, risk management has become too important to be left to the "rocket scientists" of the world of financial derivatives.

WHAT IS RISK?

We're all faced with risk in our everyday lives. And although risk is an abstract term, our natural human understanding of the trade-offs between risk and reward is pretty sophisticated. For example, in our personal lives, we intuitively understand the difference between a cost that's already been budgeted for (in risk parlance, a predictable or expected loss) and an unexpected cost (at its worst, a catastrophic loss of a magnitude well beyond losses seen in the course of normal daily life).

In particular, we understand that risk is not synonymous with the *size* of a cost or of a loss. After all, some of the costs we expect in daily life are very large indeed if we think in terms of our annual budgets: food, fixed mortgage payments, college fees, and so on. These costs are big, but they are not a threat to our ambitions because they are reasonably predictable and are already allowed for in our plans.

The real *risk* is that these costs will suddenly rise in an entirely un-expected way, or that some other cost will appear from nowhere and steal the money we've set aside for our expected outlays. The risk lies in how *variable* our costs and revenues really are. In particular, we care about how likely it is that we'll encounter a loss big enough to upset our plans (one that we have not defused through some piece of personal risk management such as taking out a fixed-rate mortgage, setting aside savings for a rainy day, and so on).

This day-to-day analogy makes it easier to understand the difference between the risk management concepts of *expected loss* (or expected costs) and *unexpected loss* (or unexpected cost). Understanding this difference is a task that has managed to confuse even risk-literate banking regulators over the last few years, but it's the key to understanding modern risk man-agement concepts such as economic capital attribution and risk-adjusted pricing. (However, this is not the only way to define risk, as we'll see in Chapter 5, which discusses various academic theories that shed more light on the definition and measurement of risk.)

The main difference betweeen our intuitive conception of risk and a more formal treatment of it is the use of statistics to define the extent and potential cost of any exposure. To develop a number for unexpected loss, a bank risk manager first identifies the risk factors that seem to drive volatility in any outcome (Box 1-1) and then uses statistical analy-sis to calculate the probabilities of various outcomes for the position or portfolio under consideration. This probability distribution can be used in various ways; for example, the risk manager might pinpoint the area of the distribution (i.e., the extent of loss) that the institution would find wor-rying, given the probability of this loss occurring (e.g., is it a 1 in 10 or a 1 in 10,000 chance?).

The distribution can also be related to the institution's stated "risk appetite" for its various activities. For example, as we discuss in Chapter 4, the senior risk committee at the bank might have set boundaries on the institution's future risk that it is willing to take by specifying the maxi-mum loss it is willing to tolerate at a given level of confidence, such as, "We are willing to countenance a 1 percent chance of a $50 million loss from our trading desks on any given day."

The formality of this language and the use of statistical concepts can make risk management sound pretty technical. But the risk manager is simply doing what we all do when we ask ourselves in our personal lives, "How bad, within reason, might this problem get?"

What does our distinction between expected loss and unexpected loss

BOX 1-1

RISK FACTORS AND THE MODELING OF RISK

In order to measure risk, the risk analyst first seeks to identify the key factors that seem likely to cause volatility in the returns from the position or portfolio under consideration. For example, in the case of an equity investment, the risk factor will be the volatility of the stock price (categorized in the appendix to this chapter as a market risk), which can be estimated in various ways.

In this case, we identified a single risk factor. But the number of risk factors that are considered in a risk analysis—and included in any risk modeling—varies considerably depending on both the problem and the sophistication of the approach. For example, in the recent past, bank risk analysts might have analyzed the risk of an interest-rate position in terms of the effect of a single risk factor—e.g., the yield to maturity of government bonds, assuming that the yields for all maturities are perfectly correlated. But this one-factor model approach ignored the risk that the dynamic of the term structure of interest rates is driven by more factors, e.g., the forward rates. Nowadays, leading banks analyze their interest-rate exposures using at least two or three factors, as we describe in Chapter 6.

Further, the risk manager must also measure the influence of the risk factors on each other, the statistical measure of which is the "covariance." Disentangling the effects of multiple risk factors and quantifying the influence of each is a fairly complicated undertaking, especially when covariance alters over time (i.e., is *stochastic*, in the modeler's terminology). There is often a distinct difference in the behavior and relationship of risk factors during normal business conditions and during stressful conditions such as financial crises.

Under ordinary market conditions, the behavior of risk factors is relatively less difficult to predict because it does not change significantly in the short and medium term: future behavior can be extrapolated, to some extent, from past performance. However, during stressful conditions, the behavior of risk factors becomes far more unpredictable, and past behavior may offer little help in predicting future behavior. It's at this point that statistically measurable risk threatens to turn into the kind of unmeasurable uncertainty that we discuss in Box 1-2.

mean in terms of running a financial business, such as a specific banking business line? Well, the *expected* credit loss for a credit card portfolio, for example, refers to how much the bank expects to lose, on average, as a result of fraud and defaults by card holders over a period of time, say one year. In the case of large and well-diversified portfolios (i.e., most consumer credit portfolios), expected loss accounts for almost all the losses that are incurred. Because it is, by definition, predictable, expected loss is generally viewed as one of the costs of doing business, and ideally it is priced into the products and services offered to the customer. For credit cards, the expected loss is recovered by charging the businesses a certain commission (2 to 4 percent) and by charging a spread to the customer on any borrowed money, over and above the bank's funding cost (i.e., the rate the bank pays to raise funds in the money markets and elsewhere). The bank recovers mundane operating costs, like the salaries it pays tellers, in much the same way.

The level of loss associated with a large standard credit card portfolio is predictable because the portfolio is made up of numerous bite-sized exposures and the fortunes of customers are not closely tied to one another—on the whole, you are not much more likely to lose your job today because your neighbor lost hers last week (though the fortunes of small local banks, as well as their card portfolios, are somewhat driven by socioeconomic characteristics, as we discuss in Chapter 9.)

A corporate loan portfolio, by contrast, is much "lumpier" (e.g., there are more big loans). Furthermore, if we look at industry data on commercial loan losses over a period of decades, it's apparent that in some years losses spike upward to *unexpected* loss levels, driven by risk factors that suddenly begin to act together. For example, the default rate for a bank that lends too heavily to the technology sector will be driven not just by the health of individual borrowers, but by the business cycle of the technology sector as a whole. When the technology sector shines, making loans will look risk-free for an extended period; when the economic rain comes, it will soak any banker that has allowed lending to become that little bit too concentrated among similar or interrelated borrowers. So, correlation risk—the tendency for things to go wrong together—is a major factor when evaluating the risk of this kind of portfolio. The tendency for things to go wrong together isn't confined to the clustering of defaults among a portfolio of commercial borrowers. Whole classes of risk factors can begin to move together, too. In the world of credit risk, real estate–linked loans are a famous example of this: they are often secured with real estate collateral, which tends to lose value at exactly the same time that the default rate for property developers and owners rises. In this case, the "recovery-rate risk" on any defaulted loan is itself closely correlated with the "default-rate risk." The two risk factors acting together can sometimes force losses abruptly skyward.

In fact, anywhere in the world that we see risks (and not just credit risks) that are lumpy (i.e., in large blocks, such as very large loans) and that are driven by risk factors that under certain circumstances can become linked together (i.e, that are correlated), we can predict that at certain times, high "unexpected losses" will be realized. We can try to estimate how bad this problem is by looking at the historical severity of these events in relation to any risk factors that we define, and then examining the prevalence of these risk factors (e.g., the type and concentration of real estate collateral) in the particular portfolio under examination.

A detailed discussion of the problem of assessing and measuring the credit risk associated with commercial loans, and with whole portfolios of loans, takes up most of Chapters 10 and 11 of this book. But our general point immediately explains why bankers are so excited about new credit-risk transfer technologies such as credit derivatives, described in detail in Chapter 12. These bankers aren't looking to reduce predictable levels of loss. They are searching for ways to put a cap on the problem of high unexpected losses and all the capital costs and uncertainty that these bring.

The conception of risk as unexpected loss underpins two key concepts that we'll deal with in more detail later in this book: value at risk (VaR) and economic capital. VaR, described and analyzed in Chapter 7, is a statistical measure that defines a particular level of loss in terms of its chances of occurrence (the "confidence level" of the analysis, in risk management jargon). For example, we might say that our options position has a one-day VaR of $1 million at the 99 percent confidence level, meaning that our risk analysis shows that there is only a 1 percent probability of a loss that is greater than $1 million on any given trading day.

In effect, we're saying that if we have $1 million in liquid reserves, there's little chance that the options position will lead to insolvency. Furthermore, because we can estimate the cost of holding liquid reserves, our risk analysis gives us a pretty good idea of the cost of taking this risk (we look at some of the uses of, and wrinkles in, this simple assertion in Chapter 15).

Under the risk paradigm we've just described, risk management becomes not the process of controlling and reducing expected losses (which is essentially a budgeting, pricing, and business efficiency concern), but the process of understanding, costing, and efficiently managing unexpected levels of variability in the financial outcomes for a business. Under this paradigm, even a conservative business can take on significant amount of risk quite rationally, in light of

- Its confidence in the way it assesses and measures the unexpected loss levels associated with its various activities
- The accumulation of sufficient capital or the deployment of other risk management techniques to protect against potential unexpected loss levels
- Appropriate returns from the risky activities, once the cost of risk capital and risk management is taken into account
- Clear communication with stakeholders about the company's target risk profile (i.e., its solvency standard once risk taking and risk mitigation are accounted for)

This takes us back to our assertion that risk management is not just a defensive activity. The more accurately a business understands and can measure its risks against potential rewards, its business goals, and its ability to withstand unexpected but plausible scenarios, the more risk-adjusted reward the business can aggressively capture in the marketplace without driving itself to destruction.

As Box 1-2 discusses, it's important in any risk analysis to acknowledge that some factors that might create volatility in outcomes simply can't be measured—even though they may be very important. The presence of this kind of risk factor introduces an uncertainty that needs to

BOX 1-2

RISK, UNCERTAINTY ... AND TRANSPARENCY ABOUT THE DIFFERENCE

In this chapter, we discuss risk as if it were synonymous with uncertainty. In fact, since the 1920s and a famous dissertation by Chicago economist Frank Knight,[1] thinkers about risk have made an important distinction between the two: variability that can be quantified in terms of probabilities is best thought of as "risk," while variability that cannot be quantified at all is best thought of simply as "uncertainty."

---

1. Frank H. Knight, Risk, *Uncertainty and Profit,* Boston, MA: Hart, Schaffner & Marx; Houghton Mifflin Company, 1921.

(continued on following page)

B O X   1 - 2 *(Continued)*

In a recent speech,[2] Mervyn King, governor of the Bank of England, helped to point up the distinction using the example of the pensions and insurance industries. Over the last century, these industries have used statistical analysis to develop products (life insurance, pensions, annuities, and so on) that are important to us all in looking after the financial well-being of our families. These products act to "collectivize" the financial effects of any one individual's life events among any given generation.

Robust statistical tools have been vital in this collectivization of risk within a generation, but the insurance and investment industries have not found a way to put a robust number on key risks that arise *between* generations, such as how much longer future generations might live and what this might mean for life insurance, pensions, and so on. Some aspects of the future remain not just risky, but uncertain. Statistical science can help us to only a limited degree in understanding how sudden advances in medical science or the onset of a new disease such as AIDS might drive longevity up or down.

As King pointed out in his speech, "No amount of complex demographic modelling can substitute for good judgement about those unknowns." Indeed, attempts to forecast changes in longevity over the last 20 years have all fallen wide of the mark (usually proving too conservative).[3]

As this example helps make clear, one of the most important things that a risk manager can do when communicating a risk analysis is to be clear about the degree to which the results depend on statistically measurable risk, and the degree to which they depend on factors that are entirely uncertain at the time of the analysis—a distinction that may not be obvious to the reader of a complex risk report at first glance.

In his speech, King set out two principles of risk communication for public policy makers that could equally well apply to senior risk committees at corporations looking at the results of complex risk calculations:

> First, information must be provided objectively and placed in context so that risks can be assessed and understood. Second, experts and policy makers must be open about the extent of our knowledge and our ignorance. Transparency about what we know and what we don't know, far from undermining credibility, helps to build trust and confidence.

---

2. Mervyn King, "What Fates Impose: Facing Up to Uncertainty," Eighth British Academy Annual Lecture, December 2004.

3. We can't measure uncertainties, but we can still assess and risk-manage them through worst-case scenarios, risk transfer, and so on. Indeed, a market is emerging that may help institutions to manage the financial risks of increased longevity: in 2003, reinsurance companies and banks began to issue financial instruments with returns linked to the aggregate longevity of specified populations, though the market for these instruments is still very immature.

be made transparent, and perhaps explored using the kind of worst-case scenario analysis we describe in Chapter 7. Furthermore, even when statistical analysis of risk *can* be conducted, it's vital to make explicit the robustness of the underlying model, data, and risk parameter estimation—a topic that we treat in detail in Chapter 14, "Model Risk."

THE CONFLICT OF RISK AND REWARD

In financial markets, as well as in many commercial activities, if one wants to achieve a higher rate of return on average, one often has to assume more risk. But the transparency of the trade-off between risk and return is highly variable.

In some cases, relatively efficient markets for risky assets help to make clear the returns that investors demand for assuming risk. For example, Table 1-1 illustrates the risk/return relationship in the bond markets. It shows data on yields from seven-year bonds with different risk ratings over a period of four weeks in February 2004. The ratings are provided by Moody's and the yield data by CIBC. (In Chapter 10 we discuss rating agency procedures and how they relate to default risk.) Looking at the table, it is clear that the market demands a higher yield on riskier bonds. On February 4, 2004, the yield on the best-quality Aaa-rated bonds was 3.80 percent, just 13 basis points (bp) above the yield on government bonds, which are usually assumed to be entirely free of the risk of default. The yield on the lowest-rated investment-grade bonds, the Baa bonds, was 4.76 percent. But at the riskiest end of the credit spectrum, bonds with very low CCC ratings yielded a striking 11.02 percent.

Even in the bond markets, the "price" of credit risk implied by these numbers for a particular counterparty is not quite transparent. Though bond prices are a pretty good guide to relative risk, various additional factors, such as liquidity risk and tax effects, confuse the price signal (as we discuss in Chapter 11). Moreover, investors' appetite for assuming certain kinds of risk varies over time. Sometimes the differential in yield between a risky and a risk-free bond narrows to such an extent that commentators talk of an "irrational" price of credit.

However, in the case of risks that are not associated with any kind of market-traded financial instrument, the problem of making transparent the relationship between risk and reward is much more profound. A key objective of risk management is to tackle this issue and make clear the potential for large losses in the future arising from activities that generate an apparently attractive stream of profits in the short run.

Ideally, discussions about this kind of trade-off between future

TABLE 1-1

Credit Spreads by Rating for Seven-Year Corporate Bonds (February 2004)

Credit Spreads By Rating	02/04/04	Change	02/11/04	Change	02/18/04	Change	02/25/04	Change	03/03/04
Investment Grade									
Moodys Aaa Index[2] (YTW)	3.80%	(7)	3.73%	0	3.73%	(9)	3.64%	4	3.68%
7 Year Treasury (YTM)	3.67%	(10)	3.57%	(3)	3.54%	(4)	3.50%	5	3.55%
Bps Spread (STW)	**13**	**3**	**16**	**3**	**19**	**(5)**	**14**	**(1)**	**13**
Moodys Aa Index[2] (YTW)	4.12%	(11)	4.01%	5	4.06%	(3)	4.03%	3	4.06%
7 Year Treasury (YTM)	3.67%	(10)	3.57%	(3)	3.54%	(4)	3.50%	5	3.55%
Bps Spread (STW)	**45**	**(1)**	**44**	**8**	**52**	**1**	**53**	**(2)**	**51**
Moodys A Index[2] (YTW)	4.39%	(13)	4.26%	3	4.29%	(2)	4.27%	5	4.32%
7 Year Treasury (YTM)	3.67%	(10)	3.57%	(3)	3.54%	(4)	3.50%	5	3.55%
Bps Spread (STW)	**72**	**(3)**	**69**	**6**	**75**	**2**	**77**	**0**	**77**
Moodys Baa Index[2] (YTW)	4.76%	(14)	4.62%	3	4.65%	(7)	4.58%	4	4.62%
7 Year Treasury (YTM)	3.67%	(10)	3.57%	(3)	3.54%	(4)	3.50%	5	3.55%
Bps Spread (STW)	**109**	**(4)**	**105**	**6**	**111**	**(3)**	**108**	**(1)**	**107**

Credit Spreads By Rating	02/05/04	Change	02/12/04	Change	02/19/04	Change	02/26/04	Change	03/04/04
Speculative Grade									
CIBC Hymark[TM] (YTW)	7.74%	(11)	7.63%	6	7.69%	8	7.77%	(3)	7.74%
Weighted Treasury (YTM)[1]	2.84%	(19)	2.65%	2	2.67%	(3)	2.64%	7	2.71%
Bps Spread (STW)	**490**	**8**	**498**	**4**	**502**	**11**	**513**	**(10)**	**503**
BB Index (YTW)	5.92%	(9)	5.83%	2	5.85%	(4)	5.81%	(7)	5.74%
Weighted Treasury (YTM)[1]	2.98%	(18)	2.80%	2	2.82%	(5)	2.77%	5	2.82%
Bps Spread (STW)	**294**	**9**	**303**	**0**	**303**	**1**	**304**	**(12)**	**292**
B Index (YTW)	7.09%	(8)	7.01%	3	7.04%	5	7.09%	(9)	7.00%
Weighted Treasury (YTM)[1]	2.81%	(20)	2.61%	1	2.62%	(3)	2.59%	7	2.66%
Bps Spread (STW)	**428**	**12**	**440**	**2**	**442**	**8**	**450**	**(16)**	**434**
CCC Index (YTW)	11.02%	(21)	10.81%	18	10.99%	32	11.31%	(17)	11.14%
Weighted Treasury (YTM)[1]	2.81%	(17)	2.64%	1	2.65%	(3)	2.62%	10	2.72%
Bps Spread (STW)	**821**	**(4)**	**817**	**17**	**834**	**35**	**869**	**(27)**	**842**

[1] Made up of a weighted treasury yield that reflects the underlying duration of the YTW.
[2] Based on corporate bonds and Treasuries with an average maturity of 7 years. Uses an average of all industries.
Source: CIBC World Markets High Yield Research and Moodys

profits and opaque risks would be undertaken within corporations on a basis that is rational for the firm as a whole. But organizations with a poor risk management and risk governance culture sometimes allow powerful business groups to exaggerate the potential returns while diminishing the perceived potential risks. When rewards are not properly adjusted for economic risk, it's tempting for the self-interested to play down the potential for unexpected losses to spike somewhere in the economic cycle and to willfully misunderstand how risk factors sometimes come together to give rise to severe correlation risks. Management itself might be tempted to leave gaps in risk measurement that, if mended, would disturb the reported profitability of a business franchise.

This kind of risk management failure can be hugely exacerbated by the compensation incentive schemes of the companies involved. In many firms across a broad swathe of industries, bonuses are paid today on profits that may later turn out to be illusory, while the cost of any associated risks is pushed, largely unacknowledged, into the future.

We can see this general process in the banking industry in every credit cycle as banks loosen rules about the granting of credit in the favorable part of the cycle, only to stamp on the credit brakes as things turn sour. The same dynamic happens whenever firms lack the discipline or means to adjust their present performance measures for an activity so that they are in line with the future risks that the activity generates. It is particularly easy for trading institutions to move revenues forward through a "mark-to-market" process, for example. This process employs estimates of the value the market puts on an asset to record profits on the income statement before cash is actually generated; meanwhile, the implied cost of any risk can be artificially reduced by applying poor or deliberately distorted risk measurement techniques.

This collision between conflicts of interest and the opaque nature of risk is not limited solely to risk measurement and management at the level of the individual firm. Decisions about risk and return can become seriously distorted across whole financial industries when poor industry practices and regulatory rules allow this to happen—the most famous example being the U.S. savings and loan crisis in the 1980s and early 1990s (see Box 8-1). History shows that, when the stakes are high enough, regulators all around the world have colluded with local banking industries to allow firms to misrecord and misvalue risky assets on their balance sheets, out of fear that forcing firms to state their true condition will prompt mass insolvencies and a financial crisis.

Perhaps, in these cases, regulators think they are doing the right thing, or perhaps they are just desperate to postpone any pain beyond their term of office (or that of their political masters). For our purposes, it's enough to point out that the combination of poor standards of risk measurement with a conflict of interest is extraordinarily potent at many levels—both inside the company and outside.

THE DANGER OF NAMES

So far, we've been discussing risk in terms of its expected and unexpected nature. We can also divide up our risk portfolio according to the *type* of risk that we are running. In this book, we follow the latest regulatory approach in the global banking industry to highlight three broad risk types:

> *Credit risk* is the risk of loss following a change in the factors that drive the credit quality of an asset. These include adverse effects arising from credit grade migration, including default, and the dynamics of recovery rates.
>
> *Market risk* is the risk of losses arising from changes in market-risk factors. Market risk can arise from changes in interest rates, foreign exchange rates, or equity and commodity price factors.
>
> *Operational risk* refers to financial loss resulting from a host of potential operational breakdowns that we can think of in terms of people risks, process risks, and technology risks (e.g., frauds, inadequate computer systems, a failure in controls, a mistake in operations, a guideline that has been circumvented, or a natural disaster).

Understanding the various types of risk is important because each category demands a different (but related) set of risk management skills. The categories are often used to define and organize the risk management functions and risk management activities of a corporation. We've added an appendix to this chapter that offers a detailed family tree of the various types of risks faced by corporations. It can be applied to any corporation engaged in major financial transactions, project financing, and providing customers with credit facilities.

The history of science, as well as the history of management, tells us that classification schemes like this are as *valuable* as they are *dangerous*. Giving a name to something allows us to talk about it, control it, and assign responsibility for it. Classification is an important part of the effort to make an otherwise ill-defined risk measurable, manageable, and transferable. Yet the classification of risk is also fraught with danger because as soon as we define risk in terms of categories, we create the potential for missed risks and gaps in responsibilities—for being blind-sided by risk as it flows across our arbitrary dividing lines.

For example, a sharp peak in market prices will create a market risk for an institution. Yet the real threat might be that a counterparty to the bank that is also affected by the spike in market prices will default (credit risk), or that some weakness in the bank's systems will be exposed by high trading volumes (operational risk). We are missing a trick if we think of price volatility in terms of market risk alone.

We can see the same thing happening from an organizational perspective. While categorizing risks helps us to organize risk management, it fosters the creation of "silos" of expertise that are separated from one another in terms of personnel, risk terminology, risk measures, reporting lines, systems and data, and so on. The management of risk within these silos may be quite efficient in terms of a particular risk, such as credit risk, or the risks run by a particular business unit. But if executives and risk managers can't communicate with one another across risk silos, they probably won't be able to work together efficiently to manage the risks that are most important to the institution as a whole.

Many of the most exciting recent advances in risk management are really attempts to break down this natural organizational tendency toward silo risk management. Risk measurement tools such as VaR and economic capital are evolving to facilitate integrated measurement and management of the various risks (market, credit, and operational) and business lines. We can also see in many industries a much more broadly framed trend toward what consultants have labeled *enterprisewide risk management,* or ERM. ERM is a concept with many definitions, usually tied to a particular consultancy service or software product. Basically, though, an ERM system is a deliberate attempt to break through the tendency of firms to operate in risk management silos and to ignore enterprise risks, and an attempt to take risk into consideration in business decisions much more explicitly than has been done in the past. There are many potential ERM tools, including conceptual tools that facilitate enterprisewide risk measurement (such as economic capital), monitoring tools that facilitate enterprisewide risk identification (such as control self-assessment schemes where business lines take a structured approach to defining and tracking their risk profiles), and organizational tools such as senior risk committees with a mandate to look at all enterprisewide risks. Through an ERM system, a firm limits its exposures to a risk level agreed upon by the board and provides its management and board of directors with reasonable assurances regarding the achievement of the organization's objectives.

As a trend, ERM is clearly in tune with a parallel drive toward the unification of risk, capital, and balance sheet management in financial institutions. Over the last few years, it has become increasingly difficult to distinguish risk management tools from capital management tools, since risk, according to the unexpected loss risk paradigm we outlined earlier, increasingly drives the allocation of capital in risk-intensive businesses such as banking and insurance. Similarly, it has become difficult to distinguish capital management tools from balance sheet management tools, since risk/reward relationships increasingly drive the structure of the balance sheet.

But we shouldn't get too carried away here. ERM is a goal, but it is clear from financial industry surveys that most institutions are a long way from fully achieving that goal. A recent survey by management consultant Deloitte observes:

> Enterprise Risk Management continues to generate interest among risk managers, executives, the board of directors and shareholders. Given the core role of risk management in financial institutions, it seems intuitive that ERM might be the final "destination" for companies wanting to demonstrate advanced capabilities. For all the hype, however, ERM continues to be an elusive concept that varies widely in definition and implementation, and reaching full maturity may take several years.[3]

NUMBERS ARE DANGEROUS, TOO

Once we've put boundaries around our risks by naming and classifying them, we can also try to attach meaningful *numbers* to them. A lot of this book is about this problem. Even if our numbers are only judgmental rankings of risks within a risk class (Risk No. 1, Risk Rating 3, and so on), they can help us make more rational in-class comparative decisions. More ambitiously, if we can assign absolute numbers to some risk factor (a 0.02 percent chance of default versus a 0.002 percent chance of default), then we can weigh one decision against another with some precision. It is interesting to note in this context that Professor Daniel Kahanman, the Nobel laureate in economics, warns us that people tend to misassess extreme probabilities (very small ones as well as very large ones).

---

3. Deloitte, *2004 Global Risk Management Survey*, p. 17.

And if we can put an absolute cost or price on a risk (ideally using data from markets where risks are traded or from some internal "cost of risk" calculation based on economic capital), then we can make truly rational economic decisions about assuming, managing, and transferring risks. At this point, risk management decisions become fungible with many other kinds of management decision in the running of an enterprise.

But while assigning numbers to risk is incredibly useful for risk management and risk transfer, it's also potentially dangerous. Only some kinds of numbers are truly comparable, but all kinds of numbers tempt us to make comparisons. For example, using the face value or "notional amount" of a bond to indicate the risk of a bond is a flawed approach. As we explain in Chapter 7, a million-dollar position in par value 10-year Treasury bonds does not represent at all the same amount of risk as a million-dollar position in a 4-year par value Treasury bond.

Introducing sophisticated models to describe risk is one way to defuse this problem, but this has its own dangers. Professionals in the financial markets invented the VaR framework as a way of measuring and comparing risk across many different markets. But as we discuss in Chapter 7, the VaR measure works well as a risk measure only for markets operating under normal conditions and only over a short period, such as one trading day. Potentially, it's a very poor and misleading measure of risk in abnormal markets, over longer time periods, or for illiquid portfolios.

Also, VaR, like all risk measures, depends for its integrity on a robust control environment. In recent rogue-trading cases, hundreds of millions of dollars of losses have been suffered by trading desks that had orders not to assume VaR exposures of more than a few million dollars. The reason for the discrepancy is nearly always that the trading desks have found some way of circumventing trading controls and suppressing risk measures. For example, a trader might falsify transaction details entered into the trade reporting systems, by using fictitious trades to (supposedly) balance out the risk of real trades, or by tampering with the inputs to risk models, such as volatility estimates that determine the valuation and risk estimation for an options portfolio.

The likelihood of this kind of problem increases sharply when those around the trader (back-office staff, business line managers, even risk managers) don't properly understand the critical significance of routine tasks, such as an independent check on volatility estimates, for the integrity of key risk measures. Meanwhile, those reading the risk reports (senior executives, board members) often don't seem to realize that unless they've asked key questions about the integrity of controls, they might as well tear up the risk report.

While the specialist risk manager's job is an increasingly important one, a broad understanding of risk management must also become part of the wider culture of the firm.

THE RISK MANAGER'S JOB

First he sat in the back seat and then he had his foot on the brake, now he's got one hand on the steering wheel! Is there no end to the risk manager's advancement into every aspect of risk-taking in a financial firm? Next he'll be right there in the driving seat, with traders, salesmen, corporate financiers and chief financial officers doing his bidding. So, is the risk manager turning into something else?[4]

As this breathless quotation from *Euromoney* magazine makes clear, risk managers have played an increasingly important and active role in banks and other financial and nonfinancial enterprises over the last decade. Risk managers are traditionally involved in risk avoidance and risk reduction. But the risk management function has also developed tools so that the potential returns and the potential losses associated with those returns are measured and (as far as possible) made economically transparent. This aspect of the risk manager's role is easily misunderstood.

First and foremost, a risk manager is not a prophet! The role of the risk manager is not to try to read a crystal ball, but to uncover the sources of risk and make them visible to key decision makers and stakeholders in terms of probability. For example, the risk manager's role is not to produce a point estimate of the U.S. dollar/euro exchange rate at the end of the year; but to produce a distribution estimate of the potential exchange rate at year-end and explain what this might mean for the firm (given its financial positions).

These distribution estimates can then be used to help make risk management decisions, and also to produce risk-adjusted metrics such as risk-adjusted return on capital (RAROC) (see Chapter 15). RAROC helps make it clear that the risk manager's role is not just defensive—it also offers firms the information about balancing risk and reward that they need if they are to compete effectively in the longer term (see Chapter 15). Implementing the appropriate policies, methodologies, and infrastructure to risk-adjust numbers and improve forward-looking busi-

---

4. *Euromoney,* February 1998, p. 56.

ness decisions will be an increasingly important element of the modern risk manager's job.

But the risk manager's role in this regard is rarely easy—these risk and profitability analyses aren't always accepted or welcomed in the wider firm. Sometimes the difficulty is political (business leaders want growth, not caution), sometimes it is technical (no one has found a best-practice way to measure certain types of risk, such as reputation or franchise risk), and sometimes it is systemic (it's hard not to jump over a cliff on a business idea if all your competitors are doing that too).

This is why defining the role and reporting lines of risk managers within the wider organization is so critical. If risk is not made transparent to key stakeholders, or those charged with oversight on their behalf, then the risk manager has failed.

Perhaps the trickiest balancing act over the last few years has been trying to find the right relationship between business leaders and the specialist risk management functions within an institution. The relationship should be close, but not too close. There should be extensive interaction, but not dominance. There should be understanding, but not collusion. We can still see the tensions in this relationship across any number of activities in risk-taking organizations: between the credit analyst and those charged with business development in commercial loans, between the trader on the desk and the market-risk management team, and so on. Where the balance of power lies will depend significantly on the attitude of senior managers and on the tone set by the board. It will also depend on whether the institution has invested in the analytical and organizational tools that support a balanced decision—a risk-adjusted decision.

As the risk manager's role is extended, we must increasingly ask that difficult question: "Who is checking up on the risk managers?" Out in the financial markets, the answer is hopefully the regulators. Inside a corporation, the answer includes the institution's audit function, which is charged with reviewing risk management's actions and its compliance with an agreed-upon set of policies and procedures (Chapter 4). But the more general answer is that the firm as a whole has to have a much firmer grip on risk management practices, concepts, and tools.

THE RISK MANAGEMENT LEARNING CURVE

The authors of this book have been privileged to work in banks and other financial institutions since almost the beginning of the modern revolution in risk management in the 1980s. The authors' experience includes portfolio management, where the primary focus is on generating revenues, as well as roles such as chief risk officer, where the primary responsibility is clearly to manage risk.[5]

In the early days, risk management as a specific function was fragmented and lacked analytic rigor. Yes, there were pockets of deep expertise in a few financial institutions. But there was a pervasive sense, in most financial institutions, that risk managers played a relatively unimportant role in the business as a whole.

For example, the head of credit was someone whose views were respected, but not necessarily rewarded. In part, that was because traditional credit officers typically had strong fundamental credit analysis skills that allowed them to say yes or no to individual transactions, but did not have the kind of analytical skills and tools that would have helped them to make more complex risk/reward judgments. Typically, credit officers acted as gatekeepers for, rather than active managers of, whole portfolios of credit risky assets.

Market-risk expertise often either was present mainly on the trading floor, giving rise to a potential conflict of interest, or resided in personnel outside the trading organization who had limited trading experience. Even at large banks, a trading floor risk management team might consist of a small quantitative team plus a small risk comptroller function. Organizations as a whole had no concerted program to control operational risk, which was managed at the line level, where the priority was often to reduce costs (expected losses that reduced line profitability) rather than enterprise risk (unexpected loss levels that might threaten the whole organization).

Through the 1980s and 1990s, there were huge advances in risk management tools and techniques within specialized areas. But as we mentioned earlier, these advances came at the cost of silo risk management, i.e., a tendency to consider the risks of activities or business lines in isolation, without considering how those risks interrelate and affect other business lines and the enterprise as a whole. The problem was often compounded by an overarching organizational culture that rewarded business leaders on the basis of short-term returns, such as growth in business volume, as opposed to the more appropriate philosophy of rewarding them on the basis of long-term, risk-adjusted returns.

---

5. The authors have also benefited from being active advisory members of boards for profit and not-for-profit institutions, and from serving in senior strategic and tactical roles, e.g., as members of a bank management committee.

The risk management function has changed dramatically over the past 10 years. Across the financial industries, we can now see many highly skilled and well-compensated risk functions, particularly in the domains of market risk and credit risk. The measurement of market risk has evolved from simple indicators, such as the face value or "notional" amount for an individual security, through more complex measures of price sensitivities such as the duration and convexity of a bond, to the sophisticated combination of the latest VaR methodology, stress testing, and scenario analysis that we describe in Chapter 7.

Recently, there has been a broad-based attempt to overcome the barriers between the risk specialists and other key risk management actors in a firm (business line, board, and stakeholders). The chief risk officer (CRO) is a relatively new role that brings together an institution's risk disciplines under one person. The CRO is usually a member of the management committee. That means that risk management now has a seat at the executive top table. The world's major financial institutions are implementing sophisticated ERM programs that embrace a dramatic growth in tools aimed at controlling operational risk.

There are certainly some growing pains here. ERM has become a buzzword for management consultants with a confusing variety of definitions, CROs sometimes struggle to define a meaningful role for themselves with the power to effect real change in their organizations, and the industry is struggling to find out which operational risk management tools are most useful. But the fundamental trend toward a "joined up" conception of risk management is surely a move in the right direction.

A significant remaining challenge is how to deal with risks that can't be measured—not just the risk of uncertain events, but also the so-called soft risks such as failures of business ethics and reputation risk. The most powerful forces in risk management over the last decade have been progress in the quantification of risk and developments in markets that help us price and trade risk. As a result, risk management as a discipline has tended to focus on things that it can measure (e.g., the risk of a foreign exchange transaction) and to sideline those risks that it cannot. Yet, while it is difficult to put a number on the risk from a conflict of interest, or to score the "risk culture" of an organization, these risks also have to be assessed, prioritized, and managed. Otherwise, as financial industries around the world have discovered over the last few years, juries and judges will surely succeed in putting a number on the risk exposure at some time down the road!

All of the trends we've just mentioned are important, and Table 1-2 summarizes a few of the broad ups and downs of risk management. But we believe that the most radical shift in risk management is the way in which risk metrics have started to provide information for day-to-day business systems and to inform forward-looking strategic decisions. Risk management is no longer a rather passive attempt to manage risks that have already been assumed. Instead, risk tools and risk metrics have become

TABLE 1-2

Ups and Downs in Risk Management

Ups

- Dramatic explosion in the adoption of sophisticated risk management processes, driven by an expanding skill base and falling cost of risk technologies
- Increase in the skill levels and associated compensation of risk management personnel as sophisticated risk techniques have been adopted to measure risk exposures
- Birth of new risk management markets in credit, commodities, weather derivatives, and so on that are the most innovative and potentially lucrative financial markets in the world
- Birth of global risk management industry associations as well as a dramatic rise in the number of global risk management personnel
- Extension of the risk measurement frontier out from traditional measured risks such as market risk toward credit and operational risks
- Cross fertilization of risk management techniques across diverse industries from banking to insurance, energy, chemicals, and aerospace
- Ascent of risk managers in the corporate hierarchy to become chief risk officers, and in best-practice organizations to generally become members of the top executive team (e.g., part of the management committee)

Downs

- Risk managers continue to find it a challenge to balance their fiduciary responsibilities against the cost of offending powerful business heads
- Risk managers do not generate revenue and therefore have not yet achieved the same status as the heads of successful revenue-generating businesses
- It's proving difficult to make truly unified measurements of different kinds of risk
- Quantifying risk exposure for the whole organization can be hugely complicated and may descend into a "box ticking" exercise
- The growing power of risk managers could be a negative force in business if risk management is interpreted as risk avoidance: it's possible to be too "risk averse."

critical to decisions about all kinds of transactions, in an effort to achieve the appropriate risk-adjusted return target ratios for an institution. Even in the difficult area of operational risk and soft risks, new approaches are helping to "red flag" key risk areas and trends for senior management and board members and to prioritize risk management initiatives in a more rational way than in the past.

THE PAST, THE FUTURE—AND THIS BOOK'S MISSION

We can now understand better why the discipline of risk management has had such a bumpy ride across many industries over the last decade. The reasons lie partly in the fundamentally elusive and opaque nature of risk—if it's not unexpected or uncertain, it's not risk! As we've seen, "risk" changes shape according to perspective, market circumstances, risk appetite, and even the classification schemes that we use.

The reasons also lie partly in the relative immaturity of financial risk management. Practices, personnel, markets, and instruments have been evolving and interacting with one another continually over the last decade to set the stage for the next risk management triumph—and disaster. Rather than being a set of specific activities, computer systems, rules, or policies, risk management is better thought of as a set of concepts that allow us to see and manage risk in a particular and dynamic way.

Perhaps the biggest task in risk management is no longer to build specialized mathematical measures of risk (although this endeavor certainly continues). Perhaps it is to put down deeper risk management roots in each organization. We need to build a wider risk culture and risk literacy, in which all the key staff members engaged in a risky enterprise understand how they can affect the risk profile of the organization—from the back office to the boardroom, and from the bottom to the top of the house. That's really what this book is about. We hope it offers nonmathematicians an understanding of the latest concepts in risk management so that they can see the strengths and question the weaknesses of a given decision. Nonmathematicians must feel able to contribute to the ongoing evolution of risk management practice.

Along the way, we can also hope to give those of our readers who are risk analysts and mathematicians a broader sense of how their analytics fit into an overall risk program, and a stronger sense that their role is to convey not just the results of any risk analysis, but also its meaning (and any broader lessons from an enterprise risk management perspective).

TYPOLOGY OF RISK EXPOSURES

In Chapter 1 we defined risk as the volatility of returns leading to "unexpected losses," with higher volatility indicating higher risk. The volatility of returns is directly or indirectly influenced by numerous variables, which we called risk factors, and by the interaction between these risk factors. But how do we consider the universe of risk factors in a systematic way?

Risk factors can be broadly grouped into the following categories: market risk, credit risk, liquidity risk, operational risk, legal and regulatory risk, business risk, strategic risk, and reputation risk (Figure 1A-1). These categories can then be further decomposed into more specific categories, as we show in Figure 1A-2 for market risk and credit risk.

In this figure, we've subdivided market risk into equity price risk, interest-rate risk, foreign exchange risk, and commodity price risk in a manner that is in line with our detailed discussion in this appendix. Then we've divided interest-rate risk into trading risk and the special case of gap risk; the latter relates to the risk that arises in the balance sheet of an institution as a result of the different sensitivities of assets and liabilities to changes in interest rates (see Chapter 8).

In theory, the more all-encompassing the categorization and the more detailed the decomposition, the more closely the company's risk will be captured. In practice, this process is limited by the level of model complexity that can be handled by the available technology and by the cost and availability of internal and market data.

Let's take a closer look at the risk categories in Figure 1A-1.

FIGURE 1A-1

Typology of risks

FIGURE 1A-2

Schematic presentation, by categories, of financial risks

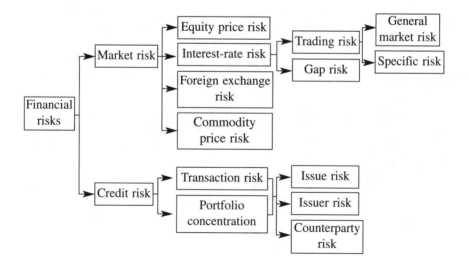

MARKET RISK

Market risk is the risk that changes in financial market prices and rates will reduce the dollar value of a security or a portfolio. Price risk for fixed-income products can be decomposed into a general market-risk component (the risk that the market as a whole will fall in value) and a specific market-risk component, unique to the particular financial transaction under consideration, that also reflects the credit risk hidden in the instrument. In trading activities, risk arises both from open (unhedged) positions and from imperfect correlations between market positions that are intended to offset one another.

Market risk is given many different names in different contexts. For example, in the case of a fund, the fund may be marketed as tracking the performance of a certain benchmark. In this case, market risk is important to the extent that it creates a risk of tracking error. *Basis risk* is a term used in the risk management industry to describe the chance of a breakdown in the relationship between the price of a product, on the one hand, and the price of the instrument used to hedge that price exposure, on the other. Again, it is really just a context-specific form of market risk.

There are four major types of market risk.

Interest-Rate Risk

The simplest form of interest-rate risk is the risk that the value of a fixed-income security will fall as a result of an increase in market interest rates. But in complex portfolios of interest-rate-sensitive assets, many different kinds of exposure can arise from differences in the maturities, nominal values, and reset dates of instruments and cash flows that are assetlike (i.e., "longs") and those that are liability-like (i.e., "shorts").

In particular, as we explain in more detail in Chapter 6, "curve" risk can arise in portfolios in which long and short positions of different maturities are effectively hedged against a *parallel shift* in yields, but not against a change in the *shape of the yield curve*. Meanwhile, even when offsetting positions have the same maturity, basis risk can arise if the rates of the positions are imperfectly correlated. For example, three-month Eurodollar instruments and three-month Treasury bills both naturally pay three-month interest rates. However, these rates are not perfectly correlated with each other, and spreads between their yields may vary over time. As a result, a three-month Treasury bill funded by three-month Eurodollar deposits represents an imperfectly offset or hedged position.

Equity Price Risk

This is the risk associated with volatility in stock prices. The general market risk of equity refers to the sensitivity of an instrument or portfolio value to a change in the level of broad stock market indices. The specific or idiosyncratic risk of equity refers to that portion of a stock's price volatility that is determined by characteristics specific to the firm, such as its line of business, the quality of its management, or a breakdown in its production process. According to portfolio theory, general market risk cannot be eliminated through portfolio diversification, while specific risk can be diversified away.

Foreign Exchange Risk

Foreign exchange risk arises from open or imperfectly hedged positions in a particular currency. These positions may arise as a natural consequence of business operations, rather than from any conscious desire to take a trading position in a currency. Foreign exchange volatility can sweep away the return from expensive cross-border investments, and at the same time place a firm at a competitive disadvantage in relation to its foreign competitors.[1] It may also generate huge operating losses and, through the uncertainty it causes, inhibit investment. The major drivers of foreign exchange risk are imperfect correlations in the movement of currency prices and fluctuations in international interest rates. Although it is important to acknowledge exchange rates as a distinct element of market risk, the valuation of foreign exchange transactions requires knowledge of the behavior of domestic and foreign interest rates, as well as of spot exchange rates.[2]

Commodity Price Risk

The price risk of commodities differs considerably from interest-rate and foreign exchange risk, since most commodities are traded in markets in which the concentration of supply in the hands of a few suppliers can magnify price volatility. Fluctuations in the depth of trading in the market (i.e.,

---

1. A famous example is Caterpillar, a U.S. heavy equipment firm, which in 1987 began a $2 billion capital investment program. A full cost reduction of 19 percent was eventually expected in 1993. During the same period, the Japanese yen weakened against the U.S. dollar by 30 percent, which placed Caterpillar at a competitive disadvantage vis-à-vis its major competitor, Komatsu of Japan, even after adjusting for productivity gains.
2. This is because of the interest-rate parity condition.

market liquidity) often accompany and exacerbate high levels of price volatility. Other fundamentals affecting a commodity's price include the ease and cost of storage, which varies considerably across the commodity markets (e.g., from gold, to electricity, to wheat). As a result of these factors, commodity prices generally have higher volatilities and larger price discontinuities (i.e., moments when prices leap from one level to another) than most traded financial securities. Commodities can be classified according to their characteristics as follows: hard commodities are nonperishable commodities, the markets for which are further divided into precious metals (e.g., gold, silver, and platinum), which have a high price/weight value, and base metals (e.g., copper, zinc, and tin); soft commodities, or commodities that have a short shelf life and are hard to store, which are mainly agricultural products (e.g., grains, coffee, and sugar); and energy commodities, which consist of oil, gas, electricity, and other energy products.

CREDIT RISK

Credit risk is the risk that a change in the credit quality of a counterparty will affect the value of a security or a portfolio. Default, whereby a counterparty is unwilling or unable to fulfill its contractual obligations, is the extreme case; however, institutions are also exposed to the risk that a counterparty might be downgraded by a rating agency.

Credit risk is an issue only when the position is an asset, i.e., when it has a positive replacement value. In that situation, if the counterparty defaults, the firm loses either all of the market value of the position or, more commonly, the part of the value that it cannot recover following the credit event. (The value it is likely to recover is called the *recovery value*, or the *recovery rate* when it is expressed as a percentage; the amount it is expected to lose is called the *loss given default*.)

Unlike the potential loss given default on coupon bonds or loans, the one on derivative positions is usually much lower than the nominal amount of the deal, and in many cases is only a fraction of this amount. This is because the economic value of a derivative instrument is related to its replacement or market value rather than to its nominal or face value. However, the credit exposures induced by the replacement values of derivative instruments are dynamic: they can be negative at one point in time, and yet become positive at a later point in time after market conditions have changed. Therefore, firms must examine not only the current exposure, measured by the current replacement value, but also the profile of potential future exposures up to the termination of the deal.

LIQUIDITY RISK

Liquidity risk comprises both funding liquidity risk and asset liquidity risk, although these two dimensions of liquidity risk are closely related (see Figure 1A-3). Funding liquidity risk relates to a firm's ability to raise the necessary cash to roll over its debt; to meet the cash, margin, and collateral requirements of counterparties; and (in the case of funds) to satisfy capital withdrawals. Funding liquidity risk can be managed by holding cash and cash equivalents, setting credit lines in place, and monitoring buying power. (Buying power refers to the amount that a trading counterparty can borrow against assets under stressed market conditions.) In Chapter 14 we discuss in detail the liquidity aspects of the Long-Term Capital Management crisis in August 1998, after Russia defaulted on its debt obligations.

Asset liquidity risk, often simply called liquidity risk, is the risk that an institution will not be able to execute a transaction at the prevailing market price because there is, temporarily, no appetite for the deal on the other side of the market. If the transaction cannot be postponed, its execution may lead to a substantial loss on the position. This risk is generally very hard to quantify. (In current implementations of the market value-at-risk, or VaR, approach, liquidity risk is accounted for only in the sense that one of the parameters of a VaR model is the period of time, or holding period, thought necessary to liquidate the relevant positions.) Asset liquidity risk may reduce an institution's ability to manage and hedge market risk as well as its capacity to satisfy any shortfall in funding by liquidating its assets.

OPERATIONAL RISK

Operational risk refers to potential losses resulting from inadequate systems, management failure, faulty controls, fraud, and human error.[3] As we

FIGURE 1A-3

The dimensions of liquidity risk

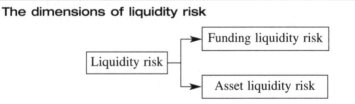

---

3. The Basel Committee has identified the following event types as having the potential to result in substantial operational risk losses: internal fraud, e.g., intentional misreporting of positions,

discuss in Chapters 13 and 14, many of the large losses from derivative trading over the last decade are the direct consequence of operational failures. Derivative trading is more prone to operational risk than cash transactions are because derivatives, by their nature, are leveraged transactions. The valuation of complex derivatives also creates considerable operational risk. Very tight controls are an absolute necessity if a firm is to avoid large losses.

Operational risk includes fraud—for example, when a trader or other employee intentionally falsifies and misrepresents the risks incurred in a transaction. Technology risk, principally computer systems risk, also falls into the operational risk category.

Human factor risk is a special form of operational risk. It relates to the losses that may result from human errors, such as pushing the wrong button on a computer, inadvertently destroying a file, or entering the wrong value for the parameter input of a model.

LEGAL AND REGULATORY RISK

Legal and regulatory risk arises for a whole variety of reasons and is closely related to reputation risk (discussed later). For example, a counterparty might lack the legal or regulatory authority to engage in a risky transaction. In the derivative markets, legal risks often become apparent only when a counterparty, or an investor, loses money on a transaction and decides to sue the provider firm to avoid meeting its obligations (for an example, see Box 6-3). Another aspect of regulatory risk is the potential impact of a change in tax law on the market value of a position. For example, when the British government changed the tax code to remove a particular tax

---

employee theft, and insider trading on an employee's own account; external fraud, e.g., robbery, forgery, check kiting, and damage from computer hacking; employment practices and workplace safety, e.g., workers' compensation claims, violation of employee health and safety rules, organized labor activities, discrimination claims, and general liabilities; clients, products, and business practices, e.g., fiduciary breaches, misuse of confidential customer information, improper trading activities on the bank's account, money laundering, and sales of unauthorized products; damage to physical assets, e.g., terrorism, vandalism, earthquakes, fires, and floods; business disruption and system failures, e.g., hardware and software failures, telecommunication problems, and utility outages; and execution, delivery, and process management, e.g., data entry errors, collateral management failures, incomplete legal documentation, unapproved access given to client accounts, nonclient counterparty misperformance, and vendor disputes. Basel Committee on Banking Supervision, *Sound Practices for the Management and Supervision of Operational Risk*, February 2003.

benefit during the summer of 1997, one major investment bank suffered huge losses.

BUSINESS RISK

Business risk refers to the classic risks of the world of business, such as uncertainty about the demand for products, the price that can be charged for those products, or the cost of producing and delivering products. We've offered a recent example of business risk in Box 1A-1.

In the world of manufacturing, business risk is largely managed through core tasks of management, e.g., choices about channels, products, suppliers, how products are marketed, and so on. There is, of course, a

---

BOX 1A-1

NONBANKING EXAMPLE OF BUSINESS RISK: HOW PALM TUMBLED FROM HIGH-TECH STARDOM

Palm was a pioneer in hand-held computers in the early 1990s. In December 2000, annual sales were up 165 percent from the previous year. In March 2001, the first sign of slowing sales hit the firm. The top management of Palm decided that the appropriate response was to quickly launch its newest model of hand-held computers, the m500 line.

The CEO, Carl Yankowski, received assurances from his management that the m500 line could be out in two weeks. Palm unveiled the m500 line on March 19. Sales of Palm's existing devices slowed further as customers decided to wait for the new model. The problem was that the wait wasn't two weeks. Palm hadn't left enough time for the testing of the m500 before sending the design to be manufactured. Production of the m500 line kept hitting snags. Palm wasn't able to ship the new model in volume until May, more than six weeks after the announcement.

Inventory of the older product began to pile up, leading to a huge $300 million write-off of excess inventory and a net loss of $392 million for the fiscal quarter ended June 1, compared with a profit of $12.4 million a year earlier. The firm's stock price plummeted, and, as a consequence, an acquisition that was key to Palm's strategy collapsed—the deal was for $264 million in Palm's stock. The company cut 250 workers, lost key employees, and halted the construction of a new headquarters.

Palm's rivals, such as RIM (BlackBerry) and Microsoft, increased their efforts to capitalize on Palm's mistakes.

very large general business literature that deals with these issues, so for the most part we skirt around the problem of business risk in this book.

However, there remains the question of how business risk should be addressed within formal risk management frameworks of the kind that we describe in this book and that have become prevalent in the financial industries.

Although business risks should surely be assessed and monitored, it is not obvious how to do this in a way that complements the banking industry's treatment of classic credit and market risks. There is also room for debate over whether business risks need to be supported by capital in the same explicit way. In the new Basel Capital Accord, "business risk" is excluded from the regulators' definition of operational risk, even though some researchers believe it to be a greater source of volatility in bank revenue than the operational event/failure risk that the regulators *have* included within bank minimum capital requirements.

Business risk is affected by such factors as the quality of the firm's strategy and/or its reputation, as well as other factors. Therefore, it is common practice to view strategic and reputation risks as components of business risk, and the risk literature sometimes refers to a complex of business/strategic/reputation risk. In this typology, we differentiate these three components.

STRATEGIC RISK

Strategic risk refers to the risk of significant investments for which there is a high uncertainty about success and profitability. If the venture is not successful, then the firm will usually suffer a major write-off, and its reputation among investors will be damaged. Box 1A-2 gives an example of strategic risk.

BOX 1A-2

NONBANKING EXAMPLE OF STRATEGIC RISK: HOW NOKIA, CHASING THE TOP END OF THE MARKET, GOT HIT IN THE MIDDLE

In 1999 Nokia launched a huge and costly effort to explore the new market for cell phones that allow users to get on the Internet, watch movies, and play video games. Nokia spent hundreds of million of dollars launching a

---

(continued on following page)

string of "smart phones," allocating 80 percent of its research and development budget ($3.6 billion a year) to software, much of it designed to give phones computerlike capabilities. Nokia was also racing to thwart the threat of Microsoft coming "first to market" with similar software for smart phones (which would set the standards for this new market).

In retrospect, it appears that Nokia focused on the wrong battle and picked the wrong competitor to worry about. Smart phones have proved too bulky and too expensive for many consumers, and at this time they maintain a tiny presence in the market.

Moreover, by concentrating on smart phones, Nokia has neglected one of the hottest growth sectors in cell phones, i.e., cheaper midrange models with sharp color screens and cameras, giving its competitors, such as Samsung Electronics and archrival Motorola, a rare opportunity to steal market share. The bet that phones would one day converge with computers was premature.

Nokia's global market share plunged to 29 percent from 35 percent by mid-2003. In 2003, Nokia sold 5.5 million smart phones, far short of its target of 10 million. In the first quarter of 2004, Nokia's sales fell 2 percent in a global cell phone market that grew 40 percent from the year before, as measured by the number of units sold.

Banks, for example, certainly suffer from business risks and strategic risks, as illustrated in Box 1A-3. Some of these risks are very similar to the kind of risk seen in nonfinancial companies, while others are driven by market or credit variables, even though they are not conventionally thought of as market risks or credit risks.

REPUTATION RISK

Reputation risk is taking on a new dimension after the accounting scandals that defrauded the shareholders, bondholders, and employees of many major corporations during the boom in the equity markets in the late 1990s. Investigations into the mutual fund and insurance industries by New York Attorney General Elliot Spitzer have also made clear just how important a reputation for fair dealing is, both with customers and with regulators. In a survey released in August 2004 by PriceWaterhouseCoopers (PWC) and the Economist Intelligence Unit (EIU), 34 percent of the 134 international bank respondents believed that reputation risk is the biggest risk

B O X   1 A - 3

EXAMPLES OF BUSINESS AND STRATEGIC RISK IN BANKING

- Retail banking
  - The advent of new business models such as Internet banking puts pressure on existing business strategies.
  - A major acquisition turns out to be much less profitable than forecast.
- Mortgage banking
  - A sharp rise in interest rates triggers a sharp fall in mortgage origination volumes.
- Wealth management
  - Falling or uncertain stock markets lead to lower investment fund sales.
- Capital market activities
  - The relative size of the bank may limit its ability to win large loan underwritings.
  - Higher exposure to capital markets creates earnings volatility.
- Credit cards
  - Increased competition has led some banks to offer credit cards to the new market segment of subprime customers, whose credit scores are worse and whose payment behavior is not well understood.
  - Competitors with sophisticated credit risk management systems may begin to steal genuinely profitable market share, leaving competitors that cannot differentiate between customers unwittingly offering business to relatively risky customers.

to market and shareholder value faced by banks, while market and credit risk scored only 25 percent each.

No doubt this was partly because corporate scandals like those involving Enron, WorldCom, and other such companies were still fresh in bankers' minds. Some experts, however, believe that reputation risk is a genuine emerging issue, and that the new Basel Capital Accord will help to shift the attention of regulators and investors away from quantifiable risks like market and credit risk and toward strategic and business risk.[4]

---

4. See Duncan Wood, "Reputation: The Banking Industry's Biggest Risk?" August 13, 2004, www.bankingrisk.com.

Reputation risk poses a special threat to financial institutions because the nature of their business requires the confidence of customers, creditors, regulators, and the general marketplace. The development of a wide array of structured finance products, including financial derivatives for market and credit risk, asset-backed securities with customized cash flows, and specialized financial conduits that manage pools of purchased assets, has put pressure on the interpretation of accounting and tax rules and, in turn, has given rise to significant concerns about the legality and appropriateness of certain transactions. Involvement in such transactions may damage an institution's reputation and franchise value.

Financial institutions are also under increasing pressure to demonstrate their ethical, social, and environmental responsibility. As a defensive mechanism, in June 2003 ten international banks from seven countries announced the adoption of the "Equator Principles," a voluntary set of guidelines developed by the banks for managing social and environmental issues related to the financing of projects in emerging countries. The Equator Principles are based on the policy and guidelines of the World Bank and the International Finance Corporation (IFC) and require the borrower to conduct an environmental assessment for high-risk projects to address issues such as sustainable development and use of renewable natural resources, protection of human health, pollution prevention and waste minimization, socioeconomic impact, and so on.

Banks should clearly monitor and manage risks to their reputation. But, as with business risk, there is no clear industry view on whether these risks can be meaningfully *measured* or whether they should be supported by risk capital. In the case of reputation risk, the problem is compounded: a bank that reserves money against the danger of damage to its reputation may be tacitly admitting in advance that its conduct is reprehensible.

CHAPTER 2

Corporate Risk Management—A Primer

Risk in the widest sense is not new to business. All companies are exposed to traditional business risks: earnings go up and down as a result of such things as changes in the business environment, in the nature of competition, in production technologies, and in factors affecting suppliers. Firms do not sit idle when they are confronted by such business risks, but respond in various time-honored ways, such as holding inventories of raw materials (in case of unexpected interruption in supply) or of finished products (to accommodate unexpected increases in demand), signing long-term supply contracts at a fixed price, or even conducting horizontal and vertical mergers with competitors, suppliers, and distributors. This is risk management, but it's also classic business decision making. In this chapter, we'll look at a more specific, and relatively novel, aspect of business risk management: why and how should a firm choose to hedge the financial risks that might affect its business by means of financial contracts such as derivatives?

This issue has captured considerable attention from corporate management in recent years, as financial risk management has become a critical corporate activity—and as regulators such as the Securities and Exchange Commission (SEC) in the United States have begun to insist on transparent disclosure of the exposure of a company to financial risk and its risk management policy principles. New legislation, regulations, and practices that seek to improve corporate governance standards have been proposed around the world. In the United States, in particular, the Sarbanes-Oxley (SOX) legislation enacted by the U.S. Congress in the summer of 2002 requires internal control certifications by chief executive officers (CEOs) and chief financial officers (CFOs). CEOs and CFOs in the United States now have to certify that financial statements filed with the SEC are "true and fair." Boards of directors cannot hide behind the defense of ignorance anymore. They need to be satisfied that best-practice internal management procedures and controls are in place and perform well—and they know that they may be held personally liable if the firm is exposed to undue risk through bad management practices.

The new rules were prompted, of course, by a rash of extraordinary corporate governance scandals that emerged between 2001 and 2003 as a result of the 1990s equity boom. While some firms had been using risk management instruments overenthusiastically to "cook the books," others had not involved themselves sufficiently in analyzing, managing, and disclosing the fundamental risks of their business.

In this chapter, we'll take a look at the practical decisions a firm must make if it decides to engage in active risk management. These include how the board sets the risk appetite of a firm, the specific procedure for mapping out a firm's individual risk exposures, and the selection of risk management tactics. We'll also sketch out how each exposure can be tackled using a variety of risk management instruments such as swaps and forwards, and take a quick look at how this kind of reasoning has been applied by a major pharmaceutical company (Box 2-2). We'll use manufacturing corporations as our examples, since the arguments in this chapter apply generally to corporate risk management.

We've set quite an ambitious agenda. But before we launch into the practicalities of hedging strategies, we must first confront a theoretical problem that continues to cause confusion in the world of risk management. The problem is that, according to the most fundamental theoretical understanding of the interests of shareholders, executives should not actively manage the risks of their corporation at all!

WHY *NOT* TO MANAGE RISK IN THEORY

Among economists and academic researchers, the starting point for this discussion is a famous analysis by two professors, Franco Modigliani and Merton Miller (M&M), laid out in 1958, which shows that the value of a firm cannot be changed merely by means of financial transactions.[1] The M&M analysis is based on an important assumption: that the capital markets work with absolute perfection. (The markets are assumed to be "perfect" in the sense that they are highly competitive and that participants are

---

1. F. Modigliani and M.H. Miller, "The Cost of Capital, Corporation Finance, and the Theory of Investment," *American Economic Review* 48, 1958, pp. 261-297.

not subject to transaction costs, commissions, contracting and information costs, or taxes.) Under this assumption, M&M reasoned that whatever the firm can accomplish in the financial markets, the individual investor in the firm can also accomplish or unwind on the same terms and conditions.

This line of reasoning also lies behind the seminal work of William Sharpe, who in 1964 developed a way of pricing assets that underlies much of modern financial theory and practice: the capital asset pricing model (CAPM).[2] In his work, Sharpe establishes that in a world with perfect capital markets, firms should not worry about the risks that are specific to them, known as their idiosyncratic risks, and should base their investment decisions only on the risks that they hold in common with other companies (known as their systematic or beta risks). This is because all specific risks are diversified away in the investors' portfolios, and, under the perfect capital markets assumption, this diversification is assumed to be costless. (See Chapter 5 for an elaboration of these models.) Therefore, firms should not engage in any risk-reduction activity that individual investors can execute on their own without any disadvantage (caused by economies of scale, for example).

Those who are opposed to active corporate risk management often argue that hedging is a zero-sum game that cannot increase earnings or cash flows. Some years ago, for example, a senior manager at a U.K. retailer pointed out that, "Reducing volatility through hedging simply moves earnings and cashflows from one year to another."[3] This line of argument is implicitly based on the perfect capital market assumption that the prices of derivatives fully reflect their risk characteristics; therefore, using such instruments cannot increase the value of the firm in any lasting way. It implies that self-insurance is a more efficient strategy, particularly because trading in derivatives incurs transaction costs.

We've listed some theoretical arguments against using derivatives for risk management, but there are also some important practical objections. In particular, active hedging can distract management from its core business. Risk management requires certain skills and knowledge; it also requires infrastructure and data acquisition and processing. Especially in small and medium-sized corporations, management often lacks the skills and time necessary to engage in such activity. (Empirical evidence indicates that small firms indeed engage in hedging less than larger

---

2. W. Sharpe, "Capital Asset Prices: A Theory of Market Equilibrium under Conditions of Risk," *Journal of Finance* 19, 1964, pp. 425-442.
3. J. Ralfe, "Reasons to Be Hedging-1,2,3," *Risk* 9(7), 1996, pp. 20-21.

corporations.) Furthermore, a risk management strategy that is not carefully structured and monitored is a double-edged sword: if it goes wrong, it can drag a firm down even more quickly than the underlying risk.

As a final point, following the new U.S. SEC disclosure requirements and new accounting standards in the United States and around the world, it can be argued that firms may avoid trading in derivatives in order to reduce the cost of compliance, or to protect the confidential information that might be revealed by their forward transactions (e.g., the level of sales in certain currencies that they envisage). In some cases, given the new standards, hedging that reduces volatility in the true economic value of the firm might still act to increase the firm's earnings variability as communicated to the equity markets through the firm's accounts.

AND SOME REASONS *FOR* MANAGING RISK IN PRACTICE

The theoretical arguments against hedging might seem powerful, but the assumption that capital markets operate with perfect efficiency makes the theoretical case vulnerable to counterarguments based on the realities of the corporate environment. One common approach to explaining why corporations manage financial risks is to claim that firms hedge in order to reduce the chance of default and to reduce the cost of financial distress. This argument arises out of a crucial and undeniable market imperfection: the high fixed costs associated with financial distress and bankruptcy.

A related argument is that managers act in their own self-interest, rather than in the interests of shareholders. Since managers may not be able to diversify the personal wealth that they have accumulated (directly and indirectly) in their company, they have an incentive to reduce volatility. In a twist to this argument, it can also be argued that managers have an interest in reducing risks, whether or not they have a large personal stake in the firm. This is because the results of a firm provide signals to its board and to the equity markets concerning the skills of its management, and it is not easy for shareholders to differentiate between volatility that's healthy and volatility that's caused by management incompetence. It might be that managers prefer to manage their personal exposure to the equity price of their firm (their managerial "performance indicator"), rather than to risk the confusion of managing their firm in a way that corresponds more exactly to the long-term economic interests of a fully diversified shareholder.

Another line of argument in favor of hedging rests on the effect of progressive tax rates, under which volatile earnings induce higher taxation than stable earnings. The empirical evidence for this as a general argument is not very strong. Certainly, many firms use derivatives for tax avoidance rather than risk management purposes, but this is a separate issue.

More important, perhaps, is that engaging in risk management activities allows management to have better control over the firm's natural economic performance. Each firm may legitimately communicate to investors a different "risk appetite," confirmed by the board. By employing risk management tools, management can better achieve the board's objectives.

Furthermore, the theoretical arguments do not condemn risk-reduction activity that offers synergies with the operations of the firm. For example, by hedging the price of a commodity that is an input to its production process, a firm can stabilize its costs and hence also its pricing policy. This stabilization of prices may in itself offer a competitive advantage in the marketplace that could not be replicated by any outside investor.

As a side argument, it's worth pointing out that individuals and firms regularly take out traditional insurance policies to protect property and other assets at a price that is higher than the expected value of the potential damage that may occur if the risk materializes (as assessed in actuarial terms). Yet very few researchers have questioned the rationale of purchasing insurance with the same vigor that they have questioned the purchase of newer risk management products such as swaps and options.

Perhaps the most important argument in favor of hedging, however, is that companies may be trying to reduce the cost of capital and enhance their ability to finance growth. Without hedging, the volatility of a firm's cash flows might lead it to reject investment opportunities. This is likely to be particularly expensive for the firm if it is forced to ignore profitable opportunities that are related to its special comparative advantages or to private information that it possesses. The debt capacity and costs of the firm may be also adversely affected by high cash flow volatility—no one is happy to lend money to a firm that looks likely to suffer a liquidity crisis.

An empirical study in the late 1990s investigated why firms use currency derivatives.[4] Rather than analyze questionnaires, the researchers

---

4. C. Geczy, B. A. Minton, and C. Schrand, "Why Firms Use Currency Derivatives," *Journal of Finance* 82(4), 1997, pp. 1323-1354.

looked at the characteristics of Fortune 500 nonfinancial corporations that in 1990 seemed potentially exposed to foreign currency risk (from foreign operations or from foreign currency–denominated debt). They found that approximately 41 percent of the firms in the sample (of 372 companies) had used currency swaps, forwards, futures, options, or combinations of these instruments. The major conclusion of the study was, "Firms with greater growth opportunities and tighter financial constraints are more likely to use currency derivatives." They explain this as an attempt by the firms to reduce fluctuations in cash flows, so as to be able to raise capital for growth opportunities. In Box 2-1 we review some more attempts to discover the empirical reasons why firms have shown such a thirst for risk management instruments since the 1980s.

The theoretical argument about why firms might legitimately want to hedge may never produce a single answer; there are a great many imperfections in the capital markets and a great many reasons why managers want to have some control over their firm's results. But the theoretical argument against hedging has one important practical implication: It tells us that we should not take it for granted that risk management strategies are a "good thing," but instead should examine the logic of the argument in relation to the specific circumstances and aims of the firm (and its stakeholders).

HEDGING OPERATIONS VERSUS HEDGING FINANCIAL POSITIONS

When discussing whether a particular corporation should hedge its risks, it is important to look at how the risk arises. Here, we should make a clear distinction between hedging activities that are related to the operations of the firm and hedging that is related to the balance sheet.

If a company chooses to hedge activities related to its operations, such as hedging the cost of raw materials (e.g., gold for a jewelry manufacturer), this clearly has implications for its ability to compete in the marketplace. The hedge has both a size and a price effect, i.e., it might affect both the price of the firm's products and the number of products sold. Again, when an American manufacturing company buys components from a French company, it can choose whether to fix the price in euros or in U.S. dollars. If the French company insists on fixing the price in euros, the American company can opt to avoid the foreign currency risk by hedging the exposure. This is basically an operational consideration and, as we

BOX 2-1

WHAT REAL-WORLD EVIDENCE IS THERE
ABOUT WHY FIRMS HEDGE?

While academics discuss whether nonfinancial corporations *should* manage
financial risk, many corporations are already engaged in risk management
activities. Nance, Smith, and Smithson (1993) surveyed 169 large firms to
find out what determined their hedging policy.[1] The study found a significant relationship between the use of derivatives and tax and dividend policies. Dolde (1993) also surveyed Fortune 500 companies, and found that
85 percent of the responding firms had used derivatives.[2] Larger firms
tended to use derivatives more than the smaller firms in the sample.

A survey conducted by the Wharton School in partnership with CIBC
World Markets found that 50 percent of the responding companies used derivatives.[3] The percentage of usage increased sharply among larger firms
(those with a market value greater than $250 million), with 83 percent of
this group responding positively. Of the firms using derivatives, foreign exchange risk was the risk most commonly managed by means of derivatives
(83 percent of all derivatives users). Interest-rate risk was the next most
commonly managed risk (76 percent). Commodity risk was managed by
means of derivatives by 56 percent of derivatives users, while equity risk
was the least commonly managed risk at just 34 percent. While this survey
has not been updated since 1998, the relative use of derivatives across asset classes is likely to have remained about the same.

---

1. D. R. Nance, C. W. Smith, and C. W. Smithson, "On the Determinants of Corporate Hedging," *Journal of Finance* 48(1), 1993, pp. 267–284.
2. W. Dolde, "The Trajectory of Corporate Financial Risk Management," *Journal of Applied Corporate Finance* 6, 1993, pp. 33–41.
3. G. M. Bodnar, G. S. Hayt, and R. C. Marston, "1998 Wharton Survey of Financial Risk Management by U.S. Non-Financial Firms," *Financial Management* 27(4), 1998.

outlined earlier, lies outside the scope of the CAPM model or the perfect
capital markets assumption.

In a similar way, if a company exports its products to foreign countries, then the pricing policy for each market is an operational issue. For
example, suppose that an Israeli high-tech company in the infrastructure
business is submitting a bid to supply equipment in Germany over a period of three years, at predetermined prices in euros. If most of the high-
tech firm's costs are in dollars, then it is natural for the company to hedge
the future euro revenues: why should the company retain a risky position

in the currency markets? Uncertainty requires management attention and makes planning and the optimization of operations and processes more complicated. It is generally accepted that companies should concentrate on business areas in which they have comparative advantages, and avoid areas where they cannot add value. It follows that reducing risk in the production process and in selling activities is usually advisable.

The story is quite different when we turn to the problem of the firm's balance sheet. Why should a firm try to hedge the interest-rate risk on a bank loan? Why should it swap a fixed rate for a variable rate, for example? In this case, the theoretical arguments we outlined earlier, based on the assumption that capital markets are perfect, suggest that the firm should not hedge.

Equally, however, if we believe that financial markets are in some sense perfect, we might argue that investors' interests are unlikely to be much harmed by appropriate derivative trading. The trading, in such a case, is a "fair game." Nobody will lose from the activity, provided that the firm's policy is fully transparent and is disclosed to all investors.

If one argues that financial markets are not perfect, then the firm may gain some advantage from hedging its balance sheet. It may have economies of scale or have access to better information about a market than investors.

This all suggests a twofold conclusion to our discussion:

- Firms should risk-manage their operations.
- Firms may also hedge their assets and liabilities so long as they disclose their hedging policy.

In any case, whether or not it makes use of derivative instruments, the firm must make risk management decisions. The decision not to hedge is also, in effect, a risk management decision that may harm the firm if the risk exposure turns into a financial loss.

In most cases, the relevant question is not whether corporations should engage in risk management, but rather how they can manage and communicate their particular risks in a rational way. In Box 2-2 we can see an example of how Merck, a major pharmaceutical company, chose to describe one part of its hedging policy to investors in a particular financial year. We can see that the firm has adopted a particular line of reasoning to justify its hedging activities, and that it has tried to link some of the specific aims of its hedging activities to information about specific programs. As this example illustrates, each firm has to consider which risks to accept and which risks to hedge, as well as the price that it is willing

BOX 2-2

HOW MERCK MANAGES FOREIGN
EXCHANGE EXPOSURE[1]

While the U.S. dollar is the functional currency of the Company's [Merck's] foreign subsidiaries, a significant portion of the Company's revenues are denominated in foreign currencies. Merck relies on sustained cash flows generated from foreign sources to support its long-term commitment to U.S. dollar-based research and development. To the extent the dollar value of cash flows is diminished as a result of a strengthening dollar, the Company's ability to fund research and other dollar-based strategic initiatives at a consistent level may be impaired. The Company has established revenue hedging and balance sheet risk management programs to protect against volatility of future foreign currency cash flows and changes in fair value caused by volatility in foreign exchange rates.

The objective of the revenue hedging program is to reduce the potential for longer-term unfavorable changes in foreign exchange to decrease the U.S. dollar value of future cash flows derived from foreign currency denominated sales, primarily the euro and Japanese yen. To achieve this objective, the Company will partially hedge anticipated third party sales that are expected to occur over its planning cycle, typically no more than three years into the future. The Company will layer in hedges over time, increasing the portion of sales hedged as it gets closer to the expected date of the transaction, such that it is probable the hedged transaction will occur. The portion of sales hedged is based on assessments of cost-benefit profiles that consider natural offsetting exposures, revenue and exchange rate volatilities and correlations, and the cost of hedging instruments.

The primary objective of the balance sheet risk management program is to protect the U.S. dollar value of foreign currency denominated net monetary assets from the effects of volatility in foreign exchange that might occur prior to their conversion to U.S. dollars. Merck principally utilizes forward exchange contracts which enable the Company to buy and sell foreign currencies in the future at fixed exchange rates and economically offset the consequences of changes in foreign exchange on the amount of U.S. dollar cash flows derived from the net assets. Merck routinely enters into contracts to fully offset the effects of exchange on exposures denominated in developed country currencies, primarily the euro and Japanese yen. For exposures in developing country currencies, the Company will enter into forward contracts on a more limited basis and only when it is deemed economical to do so based on a cost-benefit analysis which considers the magnitude of the exposure and the volatility of the exchange rate.

---

1. Extracted from Merck's Form 10-K filing with the Securities and Exchange Commission, March 21, 2003.

to pay to manage those risks. The firm should take into account how efficiently it will be able to explain its aims to investors and other stakeholders.

PUTTING RISK MANAGEMENT INTO PRACTICE

Determining the Objective

A corporation should not engage in risk management without deciding clearly on its objectives in terms of risk and return. Without clear goals, accepted by the board of directors, management is likely to engage in inconsistent, costly activities to hedge an arbitrary set of risks. Some of these goals will be specific to the firm, but others represent important general issues.

For example, is the firm concerned with managing the volatility in its economic profits or the volatility in its accounting profits? The two measures of profit do not necessarily coincide, and at times their risk exposure is vastly different. Imagine a U.S. firm that purchases a plant in the United Kingdom that will serve U.K. clients for a sum of £1 million. The investment is financed with a £1 million loan from a British bank. From an economic point of view, the sterling loan backed by a plant in the United Kingdom is fully hedged. However, if the plant is owned and managed by the U.S. company (that is, if it fails the "long arm test" that determines whether a subsidiary should be considered as an independent unit), its value is immediately translated into U.S. dollars, while the loan is kept in pounds. Hence, the company's accounting profits are exposed to foreign exchange risk: if the pound is more expensive, in terms of the dollar, at the end of the year, the accounts will be adjusted for these financial costs and will show a reduction in profits.

Should the U.S. company hedge this kind of accounting risk? If it buys a futures contract on the pound, its accounting exposure will be hedged, but the company will be exposed to economic risk! In this case, no strategy can protect the company against both the accounting and the economic risk simultaneously. (As we hinted earlier, while most managers claim that they are concerned with economic risk only, in practice many corporations, especially publicly traded corporations, hedge their accounting risks in order to avoid fluctuations in their reported earnings.)

It is senior management's prerogative, subject to local regulatory rules, to decide whether to smooth out the ups and downs of accounting profits, even at significant economic cost. But such a decision should be reviewed by the board, and should be conveyed to middle management as a guiding policy for management actions. If senior management is concerned with economic risk instead, this policy should also be made clear, and a budget should be allocated for this purpose.

Another important factor that should be made clear by senior management is the time horizon for any of the risk management objectives. Should hedging be planned to the end of the quarter or the end of the accounting year? Should it be set three years into the future? Hedging a future expected transaction with a long-term option or futures contract has liquidity, accounting, and tax implications. For example, should the firm hedge a sales order from a French customer that will be delivered two years from now? Remember that the income will be allowed to enter the firm's books only upon delivery, while the futures contract will be marked to market at the end of each quarter (see also Box 2-3). The derivatives contract may also incur a tax liability if, at the end of the tax year, it shows a profit.

The objectives that are set should not take the form of slogans, such as, "maximum profit at minimal risk." Senior management should declare whether the aim is to hedge accounting profits or economic profits, short-term profits or long-term profits. Senior management should also consider which of the corporation's many risks should be hedged, and which risks the company should assume as part of its business strategy. The objectives should be communicated in clear, executable directives. In addition, the criteria for examining whether the objectives have been attained should be set in advance. A jewelry company may decide to fully hedge its gold inventory, or it may insure the price of gold below a certain level. By following such a policy, the company can remove all or some of the risk stemming from raw material prices for a given period.

It may make sense for the board to approve certain "risk limits," i.e., to allow management to operate within a given zone of prices and rates, and be exposed to the risk within the zone, but to disallow risk exposure beyond those limits. In such a case, the limits should be set clearly. For example, a British company might decide to avoid dollar exposures above $5 million. It might also decide to tolerate fluctuations of the dollar within the exchange rate zone of $1.50 to $1.60 to the pound, but to hedge currency risks that fall outside these limits.

Mapping the Risks

After the objectives have been set and the general nature of the risks to be managed has been decided upon, it is essential to map the relevant risks and to estimate their current and future magnitudes.

For example, let us assume that management has decided to hedge *currency risks* arising from current positions and expected transactions in the next year. Now, the office of the firm's chief financial officer will have to map the specific risks that are likely to arise from exchange-rate fluctuations. It should make a record of all assets and liabilities with values that are sensitive to exchange-rate changes, and should classify all these positions in terms of the relevant currency. In addition, information should be collected from the sales or marketing division on firm orders from foreign clients in each currency that are due over the coming year, as well as on expected orders from foreign clients that will need to be filled during this period. (A decision must be made about whether to hedge unconfirmed sales. It might be decided, for example, to base the hedge on expected revenues.)

Then, all expected expenses over the coming year that are denominated in foreign currencies should be traced (with the help of the production division). Again, the firm will have to decide how it is going to distinguish between firm purchasing commitments and uncertain purchase orders. The timing of cash inflows and outflows for each foreign currency can then be matched.

The same sort of mapping can be applied to other risk factors and risky positions, starting with the business risk of the firm and moving to its market risks and credit risks. Operational risk elements should also be identified.

Since 1998, the SEC has required publicly traded companies to assess and quantify their exposure to financial instruments that are linked to changes in interest rates, exchange rates, commodity prices, and equity prices. However, the SEC does not require firms to assess their underlying or "natural" exposure to changes in the same risk factors. Management, needless to say, cannot ignore these natural positions, whether they are matched to derivative positions or not.

When mapping a firm's risks, it is important to differentiate between risks that can be insured against, risks that can be hedged, and risks that are noninsurable and nonhedgeable. This classification is important because the next step is to look for instruments that might help to minimize the risk exposure of the firm.

Instruments for Risk Management

The next step after mapping the risks is to find the relevant instruments for risk management. Some of the instruments can be devised internally. For example, a U.S. firm with many assets denominated in British pounds can borrow money in pounds, in a loan transaction with the same time to maturity as the assets, and thus achieve a natural hedge (at least, an economic hedge, though not necessarily an accounting hedge). Similarly, a division with a euro liability may be hedged internally against another division with euro-denominated assets. Internal or "natural" hedging opportunities like this sidestep the transaction costs and many of the operational risks associated with purchasing risk management contracts and so should be considered first.

Next, the company should collect any competing offers to manage the risks identified as transferable or insurable during the risk-mapping process. Management can then evaluate each decision based on the likely costs and benefits. The firm might decide to fully insure or offset some risks, partially insure others, and refrain from insuring some insurable risks. With regard to traditional insurance products, many large and well-diversified companies, operating in a variety of geographical areas, nowadays opt to self-insure their property (including cars, plants, and equipment). The same logic can sometimes be applied to financial risks.

There are plenty of financial instruments for hedging risks, as we can see in Figure 2-1 (and as we describe in more detail in Chapter 6). The most fundamental distinction is between instruments that are traded on public exchanges and over-the-counter (OTC) instruments that represent private contracts between two parties (often a corporation and a bank). Exchange-traded instruments are based on a limited number of underlying assets and are much more standardized than OTC contracts. For example, the strike prices and maturities of exchange-traded options are defined and set in advance by the exchanges in order to "commoditize" the risk management product and promote a thriving and liquid market.

Conversely, OTC products are issued by commercial and investment banks and thus can be tailored to customers' needs. For example, an OTC option on the British pound can be customized to have a size and maturity that fits the needs of the customer and a strike price that suits the client's strategy. OTC instruments can be made to "fit" a customer's risk exposure quite closely, but they tend to lack the price transparency and liquidity advantages of exchange-traded products. Another concern in the OTC market is the credit risk associated with the counterparty to each contract.

The active markets for exchange-traded instruments in the United States, for example, are mainly the Chicago Board Options Exchange (CBOE), which offers active markets in equity and index options; the Philadelphia Options Exchange, which is the leader in foreign exchange options; the Chicago Board of Trade (CBOT), which runs huge markets in futures on stock indexes, bonds, and major commodities; the Chicago

FIGURE 2-1

The Evolution of Financial Instruments for Hedging Risks

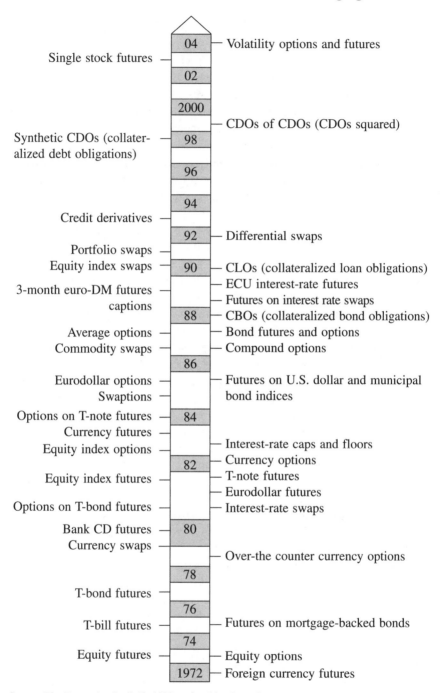

Single stock futures —

04 — Volatility options and futures

02

2000

— CDOs of CDOs (CDOs squared)

Synthetic CDOs (collater- — 98
alized debt obligations)

96

94

Credit derivatives —

92 — Differential swaps

Portfolio swaps —
Equity index swaps — 90 — CLOs (collateralized loan obligations)

3-month euro-DM futures — — ECU interest-rate futures
captions — — Futures on interest rate swaps
88 — CBOs (collateralized bond obligations)

Average options — — Bond futures and options
Commodity swaps — — Compound options
86

Eurodollar options — — Futures on U.S. dollar and municipal
Swaptions — bond indices
Options on T-note futures — 84
Currency futures —
Equity index options — — Interest-rate caps and floors
82 — Currency options
Equity index futures — — T-note futures
— Eurodollar futures
Options on T-bond futures — — Interest-rate swaps
Bank CD futures — 80
Currency swaps —
— Over-the counter currency options

78

T-bond futures —
76
T-bill futures — — Futures on mortgage-backed bonds
74
Equity futures — — Equity options
1972 — Foreign currency futures

Source: The Economist, April 10, 1993, updated by the authors.

Mercantile Exchange (CME), with major markets in currency futures; and the International Monetary Market (IMM), with options on futures on foreign currencies and on bonds and interest rates. There are also active markets for options and futures in London (LIFFE), Paris (MATIF), Frankfurt, and Zurich (Eurex) and in most major countries and financial centers.

The variety of exchange-traded and, especially, OTC instruments is huge. In fact, investment bankers are willing to price almost any possible derivative based on known, traded underlying financial instruments. This leaves the corporate hedger with the considerable problem of identifying the most suitable instruments to hedge the specific risky positions of his or her firm, taking into consideration cost and liquidity.

Constructing and Implementing a Strategy

The office of the CFO must have access to all the relevant corporate information, market data, and statistical tools and models before attempting to devise a hedging strategy. The firm will need to select certain pricing and hedging models to help in the formation of the strategy. A firm can opt to purchase statistical estimates and/or models from external vendors. However, the officers in charge of risk management must have a deep understanding of the tools they are about to employ to reach decisions.

A key tactical decision is whether to hedge risks by means of static strategies or whether to plan more dynamic strategies. In a static strategy, a hedging instrument is purchased that matches the risky position as exactly as possible, and the hedge is maintained for as long as the risky position exists; this kind of strategy is relatively easy to implement and monitor. Dynamic strategies involve an ongoing series of trades that are used to calibrate the exposure and the derivative position. With this strategy, implementing and monitoring the positions requires much greater managerial effort and may incur higher transaction costs.

For example, suppose that a U.S. company exporting to England is expecting to receive five million British pounds three months from today, and wishes to hedge the downside risk, i.e., the risk that the dollar will be devalued against the pound. It could simply follow the static strategy of buying a put option for the full quantity and term of the exposure. Alternatively, to hedge dynamically, the firm might buy a longer-term put option than the three-month maturity of the exposure (longer-maturity options often trade at a lower implied volatility, and thus cost less) and adjust the quantity of the put so that it simulates the three-month put option in the static strategy. The dynamic strategy may require the hedger to

adjust the put position on a daily or weekly basis and to increase or reduce the quantities of options, and possibly to switch to other options with
still lower relative risk premiums (maintaining the relevant hedge ratio over
time). To follow a dynamic approach, the firm must have sophisticated and
reliable models with which to trade in the markets and monitor its positions, and the staff and skills to put these tools to use. But even this will
not necessarily save the firm from making significant errors in communicating and implementing its risk management strategy. In Box 2-3 we take
a look at a dynamic corporate risk management strategy put in place by
a major U.S. energy trading company, Metallgesellschaft Refining &
Marketing, Inc. (MGRM)—a strategy that went seriously wrong. It's worth
noting that in this case there has never been any suggestion of fraud or
malpractice; problems arose purely through the nature, implementation,
and communication of the corporate risk management strategy.

Another fundamental consideration in the hedging strategy is the
planning horizon. The horizon can be fixed at the end of a quarter or the
end of the tax year, or it might be a rolling horizon. Investment horizons
should be made consistent with performance evaluations.

Other important considerations are accounting issues and potential

BOX 2-3

DYNAMIC RISK MANAGEMENT STRATEGIES CAN GO BADLY WRONG—THE MGRM EXAMPLE

In 1993, MGRM (MG Refining & Marketing), the U.S. subsidiary of
Metallgesellschaft (MG), entered into contracts to supply end-user customers with 150 million barrels of oil products (gasoline and heating oil)
over a period of 10 years, at fixed prices.

MGRM's fixed-price forward delivery contracts exposed it to the risk of
rising energy prices. In the absence of a liquid market for long-term futures
contracts, MGRM hedged this risk with both short-dated energy futures contracts on the New York Mercantile Exchange (NYMEX) and over-the-
counter (OTC) swaps. The derivative positions were concentrated in
short-dated futures and swaps, which had to be rolled forward monthly as
they matured. Each month, the size of the derivatives position was reduced
by the amount of product delivered that month, with the intention of pre-
serving a one-to-one hedge. According to Culp and Miller (1995),[1] "such
a strategy is neither inherently unprofitable nor fatally flawed, provided top
management understands the program and the long-term funding commitments necessary to make it work."

(continued on following page)

B O X   2 - 3   *(C o n t i n u e d)*

This rolling hedge strategy can be profitable when markets are in a state known as "backwardation" (oil for immediate delivery commands a higher price than does oil for future delivery), but when markets are in "contango" (the reverse relationship), it can result in losses. This is because when a company is rolling the hedge position in a backwardated market, the contract near expiration is sold at a higher price than the replacement contract, which has a longer delivery date, resulting in a rollover profit. The contrary applies when the market is in contango.

This meant that MGRM was exposed to curve risk (backwardation versus contango) and to basis risk, which is the risk that short-term oil prices might temporarily deviate from long-term prices. Over 1993, cash prices fell from close to $20 a barrel in June to less than $15 a barrel in December, leading to $1.3 billion of margin calls that MGRM had to meet in cash. The problem was further compounded by the change in the shape of the price curve, which moved from backwardation to contango. MGRM's German parent reacted in December 1993 by liquidating the hedge, and thus turned paper losses into realized losses.

Whether or not the cash drain from the negative marked-to-market value of the futures positions was sustainable, the decision by the supervisory board to liquidate the hedge might not have been the optimal one. According to Culp and Miller, at least three viable alternatives should have been contemplated to avoid the price impact of unwinding the hedges in the marketplace: securing additional financing and continuing the program intact, selling the program to another firm, or unwinding the contracts with the original customers.

---

1. C. Culp and M. Miller, "Blame Mismanagement, Not Speculation, for Metall's Woes," *European Wall Street Journal*, Apr. 25, 1995.

tax effects. Accounting rules for derivatives are quite complex and are constantly being revised. Under the current rules, derivatives used for hedging must be perfectly matched to an underlying position (e.g., with regard to quantities and dates). They can then be reported together with the underlying risky positions, and no accounting profit or loss needs to be reported. If the positions are not perfectly matched, the marked-to-market profit or loss on the hedge must be recorded in the firm's accounts, even though changes in the value of the underlying exposure are not. Accounting rules affect how derivatives are presented in quarterly or end-of-year financial reports, and how they affect the profit and loss statement.

Tax considerations can be very important, since they affect the cash flows of the firm. Different derivative instruments with different maturities may incur very different tax liabilities; tax treatment is also inconsistent from country to country. This means that a multinational corporation might find it advantageous to use derivatives in one country to hedge positions that are related to its business in another country. Professional advice on tax matters is a key factor when devising hedging strategies.

A strategy is only as good as its implementation, but, however skillful the implementation, some deviation from the plan can be expected. Prices in the marketplace can change adversely and make some hedges unattractive. Since different people within the firm are often responsible for establishing risky positions and hedging positions, special care should be taken to monitor the positions. For example, if the British client in our earlier example pays the firm after two, rather than three, months, then the three-month put must be liquidated before it matures.

Performance Evaluation

The corporate risk management system must be evaluated periodically. Crucially, the evaluation should assess the extent to which the overall goals were achieved—not whether specific transactions made a profit or loss. Whenever a risk is hedged, the party on one side of the hedge transaction inevitably shows a profit, while the counterparty inevitably shows a loss. The corporation can never know in advance which side will increase in value and which side will lose value; after all, that's why it is managing the risk in the first place. So if the goal is to eliminate risk, and risk is eliminated, then the risk manager has done the job well even if the hedged position has generated an economic or accounting loss (compared to the original, unhedged position).

Reducing earnings volatility may not be the only criterion, however. Risk managers can legitimately be evaluated in terms of how well they manage the transaction costs of hedging, including the tax payments that can arise when derivatives are employed. He or she should also act within a given budget; major deviations from the budget should be explored and explained.

When evaluating the performance of risk management, the board of directors should also decide whether or not to change the company's policy. There is nothing wrong with a firm's changing its objectives, so long as the changes are based on thorough analysis and are consistent with the other activities and aims of the firm. Local regulatory requirements for the disclosure of risks may mean that policy changes in market risk management should be made public if the changes are material.

CHAPTER 3

Banks and Their Regulators—The Research Lab for Risk Management?

In this chapter, we move on from our earlier discussion of corporate risk management to look at the special case of bank risk management and regulation, partly because it is so important in and of itself and partly because bank risk management techniques have had a huge influence on the more general world of financial risk management.

We'll take a look at how structural changes in the financial markets—including the internationalization of banking and the dramatic growth of derivatives—led to the key existing pieces of international bank regulation, the 1988 Basel Accord and its 1996 Amendment. We'll also examine the new Basel Capital Accord, commonly known as Basel II, which was finalized in June 2004 and which will begin to supplant the 1988 Accord at the end of 2007.[1] The plan is for some banks to implement the new Accord in parallel with existing regulation—so-called parallel runs—from year-end 2005 or later on in 2006, depending on the jurisdiction. Banks are very aware that the new rules require them to gather significant new risk data and to introduce many new systems and approaches; the implementation of Basel II is therefore a long-term process that is underway some years before the formal compliance dates.

Many aspects of Basel II remain controversial. But no one doubts that the risk management issues raised during the regulatory reform process, as well as the rules themselves, will prove hugely influential throughout the risk management industry for years to come. Basel II has also stimulated the thinking of nonbank financial institution regulators; e.g., the Securities and Exchange Commission (SEC) in the United States

---

1. Basel Committee on Banking Supervision, *International Convergence of Capital Measurement and Capital Standards* (Basel, Switzerland: Basel Committee on Banking Supervision, June 2004).

has adopted Basel II, which will allow securities firms to opt into the new regulatory capital regime. Further, the insurance industry is currently looking to apply more sophisticated regulatory capital standards.

As this implies, much of the impetus for banks to develop standardized risk management systems comes from their regulators, so let's start with some essential scene setting.

BANK REGULATION AND RISK MANAGEMENT

Regulators carefully watch over banks' activities, monitor their risk management standards closely, and impose a unique set of minimum required regulatory capital rules on them. Why do they do so?

There are two key reasons: banks collect deposits from ordinary savers, and they play a key role in the payment and credit system.

While bank deposits are often insured by specialized institutions (such as the Federal Deposit Insurance Corporation, or FDIC, in the United States and the Canadian Deposit Insurance Corporation, or CDIC, in Canada), in effect national governments act as a guarantor for commercial banks; some also act as a lender of last resort. National governments therefore have a very direct interest in ensuring that banks remain capable of meeting their obligations: they wish to limit the cost of the government "safety net" in the event of a bank failure. This is one reason why the amount of capital retained by a bank is regulated. By acting as a buffer against unanticipated losses, regulatory capital helps to privatize a burden that would otherwise be borne by national governments.

Furthermore, fixed-rate deposit insurance itself creates the need for capital regulation. As deposits are insured up to a given limit, there is no incentive for depositors who stay within the insured limits to select their bank cautiously. Instead, depositors may be tempted to look for the highest deposit rates, without paying enough attention to a bank's creditworthiness.

Regulators also try to make sure that banks are capitalized well enough to avoid a systemic "domino effect," whereby the failure of an individual bank, or a run on a bank caused by the fear of such a failure, propagates to the rest of the financial system. Such domino effects can cause other banks and financial companies to fail, disrupting the world economy and incurring heavy social costs. It was the fear of such a failure that led regulators in the United States to intervene to help Continental Illinois, the largest bank ever rescued by the FDIC, in 1984. More recently, a series of bank runs in Russia in the summer of 2004 led to significant fears of a domino effect in the Russian banking system, though this was averted. The underlying threat is that banks can act as a kind of transmission belt by which setbacks in the financial sector are rapidly pushed through to the wider economy.

THE PUSH TO STANDARDIZE
BANK CAPITAL MANAGEMENT

Prior to the implementation in 1992 of the 1988 Basel Accord, bank capital was regulated in some countries by imposing uniform minimum regulatory capital standards. These were applied to banks regardless of their individual risk profiles. The off-balance-sheet positions and commitments of each bank were simply ignored.

But from the mid-1980s, the Bank of England and the Federal Reserve Board became increasingly concerned about the growing exposure of banks to off-balance-sheet claims, coupled with problem loans to third-world countries. At the same time, regulators in the United Kingdom and the United States came under pressure from international banks with headquarters in the two countries. The banks complained of unfair competition from foreign banks, especially those from Japan and the Far East, that were subject to much more lenient regulations and, especially, were not subject to formal capital requirements.

The response of the Bank of England and the Federal Reserve Bank was, first of all, to strengthen the equity base of commercial banks by requiring that they set aside more capital against risky assets. As far as capital requirements were concerned, the approach was to demand more capital than before: at least 8 percent against risk-weighted assets. In addition, the regulators proposed translating each off-balance-sheet claim into an equivalent on-balance-sheet item, so that capital could be assessed against derivative positions.

Second, the regulators attempted to create a "level playing field." They proposed that all international banks should adopt the same capital standards and the same procedures. The Federal Reserve Board and the Bank of England assigned to the international Basel Committee the job of studying the positions of banks worldwide, planning the details of the proposition, and proposing a set of common procedures to the regulating bodies.

The Basel Committee on Banking Supervision (Basel Committee) has emerged as the nearest thing the international banking industry has to an international regulator, although it is really more of a coordinator of national regulators than an authority in its own right. On the committee sit senior officials of the central banks and supervisory authorities from the G-10 as well as officials from Switzerland and Luxembourg. (The G-10 is composed of Belgium, Canada, France, Germany, Italy, Japan, the Netherlands, Sweden, the United Kingdom, and the United States.) The Basel Committee meets four times a year, usually in Basel, Switzerland, under the patronage of the Bank for International Settlements (BIS).

It was the intention of the Basel Committee that its interim proposals should be adopted, tested, and later amended according to accumulated experience. Thus, the story of bank regulation since the 1980s has been one of an ongoing dialogue between the Basel Committee and commercial banks all over the world, with the active involvement of local central banks and local controllers of banks.

Few professionals in the banking industry believe that the systems proposed (or imposed) by the Basel Committee are, in any sense, perfect. Nevertheless, the role of the Basel Committee in forcing banks to appropriately quantify risks, evaluate risks, price risks, and monitor risks over the last two decades has proved invaluable.

The first results of this process were the 1988 Basel Accord and its subsequent amendments.

THE 1988 BASEL ACCORD

The 1988 Basel Accord, also referred to as the Accord or Basel I, established international minimum capital guidelines that linked banks' capital requirements to their credit exposures, divided into broad classes that grouped together similar types of borrowers such as OECD banks, non-OECD banks, and corporate borrowers. Each borrower type was then linked to specific capital requirements.

The Accord was intended to raise capital ratios, which were generally perceived to be too low, and to harmonize minimum capital ratios for banks in all major jurisdictions across the world. It focused on credit risk because credit risk was perceived at the time as the predominant risk factor in banking. As a standard, the 1988 Accord was strikingly successful and has now been adopted in some form in more than 100 countries.

Although the banking industry has now designed a new regulatory framework that will update the 1988 Accord, the 1988 Accord is a long way from being "old hat." The new Basel II regulations will not replace the 1988 Accord anywhere until year-end 2007, and it is uncertain how fully they will be adopted by national regulators around the world. In effect, many banks, including most smaller banks in the United States, will be allowed to continue to conform to the 1988 Accord standards for many years, and perhaps indefinitely.

So What Did the 1988 Accord Require of Banks?

The 1988 Accord is laid out in a document called *International Convergence of Capital Measurement and Capital Standards*, published in July 1988. It defines two minimum standards for meeting acceptable capital adequacy requirements: an assets-to-capital multiple and a risk-based capital ratio.

The assets-to-capital multiple is an overall measure of the bank's capital adequacy. The second and more critical measure focuses on the credit risk associated with specific on- and off-balance-sheet asset categories. It takes the form of a solvency ratio, known as the Cooke ratio, defined as the ratio of capital to risk-weighted on-balance-sheet assets plus off-balance-sheet exposures (the risk weights being assigned on the basis of the broad classes of counterparty credit risk that we mentioned earlier).

In the next sections, we review the main features of the 1988 Basel Accord as it stands today after several modifications.

The Assets-to-Capital Multiple

The assets-to-capital multiple is calculated by dividing the bank's total assets, including specified off-balance-sheet items, by its total capital. The off-balance sheet items included in this test are direct credit substitutes (including letters of credit and guarantees), transaction-related contingencies, trade-related contingencies, and sale and repurchase agreements. All of these items are included at their notional principal amount.

At present, the maximum multiple allowed is 20. It is conceivable that a bank with large off-balance-sheet activities might trigger this multiple as the minimum capital requirement, but in general the assets-to-capital multiple is not the binding constraint on a bank's activities.

The Risk-Weighted Amount Used to Compute the Cooke Ratio

The second and more critical measure takes the form of a solvency ratio, known as the Cooke ratio, that is defined as the ratio of capital to risk-weighted on-balance-sheet assets plus off-balance-sheet exposures, where the weights are assigned on the basis of counterparty credit risk.

In effect, the Cooke ratio requires banks to set aside a flat fixed percentage of their risk-weighted assets of various kinds (e.g., 8 percent for corporate loans and 4 percent for uninsured residential mortgages) as regulatory capital against default.

In determining the Cooke ratio, it is necessary to consider both the on-balance-sheet and specific off-balance-sheet items. On-balance-sheet items have risk weightings ranging from 0 percent for cash, revolving credit agreements with a term of less than one year, and OECD government securities to 100 percent for corporate bonds and certain other items. Off-balance-sheet items are first expressed as a credit equivalent, and then are appropriately risk-weighted by counterparty. The risk-weighted amount is then the sum of the two components: the risk-weighted assets for on-balance-sheet instruments and the risk-weighted credit equivalent for off-balance-sheet items.

Table 3-1 gives the full list of risk capital weights (WA) by asset categories, and Table 3-2 shows the weights that apply to credit equivalents by type of counterparty (WCE).

There is an apparent inconsistency between Tables 3-1 and 3-2, since the risk weight for corporate assets as they relate to off-balance-sheet instruments is half that required for on-balance-sheet assets. The Accord's rationale for this asymmetry is the superior quality of the corporations that participate in the market for off-balance-sheet products. It is true that there

TABLE 3-1

Risk Capital Weights by Broad On-Balance-Sheet Asset Category (WA)

Risk Weights (%)	Asset Category
0	Cash and gold bullion, claims on OECD governments such as Treasury bonds, or insured residential mortgages.
20	Claims on OECD banks and OECD public-sector entities such as securities issued by U.S. government agencies or claims on municipalities.
50	Uninsured residential mortgages.
100	All other claims, such as corporate bonds and less-developed country debt, claims on non-OECD banks, equity, real estate, premises, plant and equipment.

TABLE 3-2

Risk Capital Weights for Off-Balance-Sheet Credit Equivalents by Type of Counterparty (WCE)

Risk Weights (%)	Type of Counterparty
0	OECD governments
20	OECD banks and public-sector entities
50	Corporations and other counterparties

was a time when only the most financially sophisticated corporations entered the world of derivatives, but this is no longer the case.

Calculation of the Credit Equivalent for Off-Balance-Sheet Exposures

For nonderivative off-balance-sheet exposures, a conversion factor applies. This is because the notional or "face value" amount of these instruments is not always representative of the true credit risk that is being assumed. The value of the conversion factor is set by the regulators at somewhere between 0 and 1, depending on the nature of the instrument (Table 3-3).

TABLE 3-3

Credit Conversion Factors for Nonderivative Off-Balance-Sheet Exposures

Conversion Factor (%)	Off-Balance-Sheet Exposure Factor
100	Direct credit substitutes, bankers' acceptances, standby letters of credit, sale and repurchase agreements, forward purchase of assets.
50	Transaction-related contingencies such as performance bonds, revolving underwriting facilities (RUFs), and note issuance facilities (NIFs).
20	Short-term self-liquidating trade-related contingencies such as letters of credit.
0	Commitments with an original maturity of one year or less.

The resulting credit equivalents are then treated exactly as if they were on-balance-sheet instruments.

The Accord also recognizes that the credit risk exposure of long-dated financial derivatives fluctuates in value. The Accord methodology estimates this exposure by supplementing the current marked-to-market value with a simple measure of the projected future risk exposure.

Calculation of the risk-weighted amount for derivatives under the Accord proceeds in two steps, as shown in Figure 3-1. The first step involves computing a credit equivalent amount, which is the sum of the current replacement cost when it is positive (and zero otherwise) and an add-on amount that approximates future projected replacement costs. The current replacement value of a derivative is its marked-to-market or liquidation value. (When the value is negative, the institution is not exposed to default risk, as the replacement cost of the contract is zero.)

The add-on amount is computed by multiplying the notional amount of the transaction by the add-on factor required by the Accord.

Capital and the Cooke Ratio

Banks are required to maintain a capital amount equal to at least 8 percent of their total risk-weighted assets (as calculated in the previous sec-

FIGURE 3-1

Calculation of the BIS Risk-Weighted Amount for Derivatives

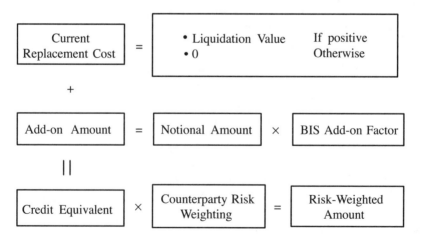

tion). Capital, as defined by the Cooke ratio, is broader than equity capital. It initially consisted of two components:

Tier 1, or core capital, which includes common stockholder's equity, noncumulative perpetual preferred stock, and minority equity interests in consolidated subsidiaries, less goodwill and other deductions.

Tier 2, or supplementary capital, which includes hybrid capital instruments, such as cumulative perpetual preferred shares and qualifying 99-year debentures. These instruments are essentially permanent in nature and have some of the characteristics of both equity and debt. Tier 2 capital also includes instruments with more limited lives, such as subordinated debt with an original average maturity of at least five years.

According to the original Accord, tier 1 and tier 2 capital should represent at least 8 percent of the risk-weighted assets, to protect the bank against credit risk. At least 50 percent of this amount must take the form of tier 1 capital.

In practice, capital levels of regulated banks tend to exceed these minimum requirements. There are various reasons why banks might want to retain capital in excess of the minimum required by regulators, but research suggests the most important reason is to create a buffer that prevents them from accidentally transgressing the regulatory rules. Other powerful reasons are peer pressure and the need for banks to maintain credit ratings and credit standings that allow them to access wholesale markets cheaply. The rating agencies take their own view of how well capitalized a bank is, and this may not be directly related to the bank's minimum capital requirement. This does not mean that minimum capital requirements are unimportant; they are very important drivers of overall capital levels, even if they don't determine those levels exactly.

Following the 1996 Amendment to the original Basel Accord, banks can use a third tier of capital to cover market risk in the trading book (but not credit risk in the banking book). Tier 3, or subsupplementary capital, consists of short-term subordinated debt with an original maturity of at least two years. It must be unsecured and fully paid up. It is also subject to lock-in clauses that prevent the issuer from repaying the debt before maturity, or even at maturity should the issuer's capital ratio become less than 8 percent after repayment.

Let's now take a closer look at the reasons behind this 1996 Amendment for market risk.

THE EXPLOSION OF BANK MARKET RISK
AND THE 1996 MARKET RISK AMENDMENT

When devising the 1988 Accord, regulators focused primarily on the credit risks that banks were exposed to, and ignored market risk and other risks. But this hardly reflected the reality of many banks' risk exposures, even during the 1980s.

Modern banks are engaged in a range of activities that extend well beyond lending and the credit risk that this generates. They trade all types of cash instruments, as well as derivatives, such as swaps, forward contracts, and options—either for their own account or to facilitate customer transactions.

This kind of bank trading activity grew exponentially in the 1980s and 1990s, so that by the time the Amendment was published in 1996, the Federal Reserve Bank estimated that U.S. banks possessed over $37 trillion of off-balance-sheet assets and liabilities, compared to approximately $1 trillion only 10 years earlier. According to a recent BIS publication, as of June 2004, banks worldwide had a total exposure to derivatives of approximately $220 trillion in notional value. The multitude and magnitude of these instruments, and their complexities, mean that it has become essential to measure, manage, limit, and control the market risk exposure of banks.

The rise in importance of risk management instruments over the last few decades has been driven by a rise in volatility in many of the principal financial markets, which has led banks to become both users and providers of risk management instruments.

The prime example of this change is the foreign currency market. From 1944, with the signing of the Bretton Woods Agreement, international foreign exchange rates were artificially fixed. Central banks intervened in their foreign currency markets whenever necessary to maintain stability. Exchange rates were changed only infrequently, and only with the permission of the World Bank and the International Monetary Fund (IMF). These bodies usually required a country that devalued its currency to adopt tough economic measures in order to ensure the stability of the currency in the future.

The regime of fixed exchange rates broke down during the late 1960s as a result of global economic forces. These included a vast expansion of international trading and inflationary pressures in the major economies. The shift to flexible foreign exchange rates introduced daily (and intraday) volatility to exchange rates. As the hitherto obscured volatility surfaced in traded foreign currencies, the financial market began to offer currency traders special tools for insuring against these "new" risks.

Figure 3-2 depicts the percentage change in the value of the German Deutsche mark relative to the U.S. dollar up until the early 1990s. The shift in the levels of volatility is very noticeable in the early 1970s, as the currency market moved to floating exchange rates. As indicated in the figure, the shift precipitated a string of novel financial contracts based on the exchange rates of leading currencies.

The first contracts tended to be various kinds of futures and forwards, though these were soon followed by foreign currency options. In 1972 the Mercantile Exchange in Chicago (CME) created the International Monetary Market (IMM), which specialized in foreign currency futures and options on futures on the major currencies. In 1982, the Chicago Board Options Exchange (CBOE) and the Philadelphia Stock Exchange introduced options on spot exchange rates. Banks joined the trend by offering over-the-counter (OTC) forward contracts and options on exchange rates to their customers.

The development of interest-rate volatility and derivative instruments

FIGURE 3-2

Month-End German Deutsche Mark/U.S. Dollar Exchange Rates

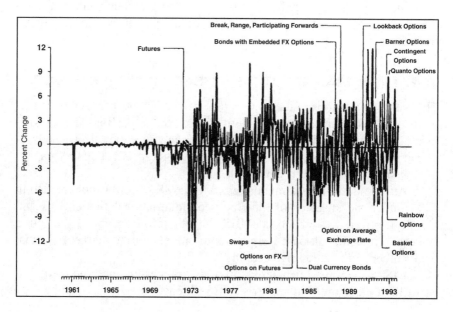

followed a similar path from the early 1970s, as we describe in Chapter 6. The equity and commodity markets also came to support significant derivatives markets, often actively developed by banking institutions. The end result of bank activity in these new derivative markets was that banks naturally became ever more exposed to volatile derivative instruments— and these exposures had to be carefully risk managed.

GROUP OF 30 (G-30) POLICY RECOMMENDATIONS

The 1996 Amendment to the Basel Accord had a notable precursor. In 1993, the Group of 30 (G-30) published a report that described best-practice price risk management recommendations for dealers in and end users of derivatives (as well as for legislators, regulators, and supervisors). The report was based in part on a detailed survey of industry practice among dealers and end users around the world.

The G-30 focused on providing practical guidance for managing derivatives businesses, offering an important benchmark against which participants could measure their own price-risk management practices. Its recommendations covered sound market-risk policies (e.g., the establishment of a market-risk function independent from trading decisions); credit-risk policies; enforceability policies; infrastructure policies, accounting and disclosure policies, and so on. These recommendations continue to act as the cornerstones of any modern bank risk management framework.

THE 1996 MARKET RISK AMENDMENT ("BIS 98")

The recommendations in the G-30 report helped establish qualitative standards for banks' management of derivative market risk. But the explosion in bank trading of derivatives and more mundane securities clearly had implications for how regulators calculated the amount of regulatory capital a bank should set aside to cover risk.

An important 1996 Amendment to the 1988 Accord (implemented in 1998 under the auspices of the Bank for International Settlements and therefore referred to widely as "BIS 98") therefore extended the initial Accord to include risk-based capital requirements for the market risks that banks incur in their trading accounts.

BIS 98 requires financial institutions to measure and hold capital to cover their exposure to market risk. BIS 98 encompasses debt and equity positions in bank trading books, and foreign exchange and commodity positions in both the trading and banking books. These positions include all financial instruments that are marked to market, whether they are plain vanilla products such as bonds or stocks, or complex derivative instruments such as options, swaps, or credit derivatives.

The authorities recognized the complexity of correctly assessing market-risk exposure, especially for derivative products. The Basel Committee therefore allowed institutions that met certain risk management standards to choose between employing their own internal value-at-risk (VaR) model, known as the *internal models approach*, or employing a standard model proposed by the Basel Committee, known as the *standardized approach*. (We explain the concept behind value-at-risk modeling in Chapter 7; it's also worth noting here that bank regulators in the United Kingdom implemented model-based market-risk capital charges some years earlier under the Amsterdam Accord.)

Market risk is not the only risk arising from instruments such as derivatives; they give rise to credit risk as well. Under BIS 98, off-balance-sheet derivatives, such as swaps and options, are subject to both the market-risk charge and the credit-risk capital charges stipulated in the original 1988 Accord.

By contrast, on-balance-sheet assets in the trading portfolio are subject to the market-risk capital charge only—a feature that helped offset the aggregate effect of the new rules on the amount of capital banks had to set aside.

Also, banks adopting the internal models approach tended to realize substantial capital savings, on the order of 20 to 50 percent, depending on the size of their trading operations and the type of instruments they traded. This is because internal models can be designed to capture diversification effects by realistically modeling the correlations between positions.

In addition to the market-risk capital adequacy requirements, the Basel Committee has set limits on concentration risks. Risks that exceed 10 percent of the bank's capital must be reported, and banks are forbidden to take positions that are greater than 25 percent of the bank's capital. Had these rules been effective in 1994, Barings Bank would have been prohibited from building up such huge exchange-traded futures positions, and the world's most famous example of rogue trading might have been avoided. (At the time the bank collapsed in February 1995, Barings' exposures on the SIMEX and OSE were 40 percent and 73 percent of its capital, respectively.)

1996 Amendment Qualitative Requirements

Before an institution can become eligible to use its own internal VaR model to assess the regulatory capital related to market risk, it must put sound risk management practices in place—largely in accordance with the G-30 recommendations we described earlier.

In particular, the institution should have a strong risk management group that is independent from the business units that it monitors, and that reports directly to the senior executive management of the institution.

Implementing a VaR model is a significant endeavor, as we describe in more detail in Chapter 7. An important part of setting up any VAR model for regulatory purposes is ensuring that the risk factor model inputs are reliable and accurate:

- A formal vetting system is needed to approve the models, any modifications to them, their assumptions, and their calibration.
- Model parameters should be estimated independently of the trading desks to avoid the temptation by the traders to "fudge" volatility numbers and other key parameters..

WHY DOES BASEL 1988 NEED REPLACING?

The rules of the original 1988 Accord are generally acknowledged to be flawed for five main reasons.

First, the risk-weighted ratios in the current rules don't differentiate adequately between the riskiness of bank assets, and are in some ways non-sensical. For example, they assume that a loan to a corporate counterparty generates five times the amount of credit risk as does a loan to an OECD bank, regardless of the borrowers' respective creditworthiness. That means that a loan to General Electric Corporation, an AAA-rated entity, has to be supported by five times as much regulatory capital as a similar loan to a Mexican (BB) or Turkish bank (B). General Electric is also considered to be considerably more risky than the sovereign debt of Turkey or Mexico. Clearly, this is the opposite of what one might think appropriate.

Second, regulatory rules assume that all corporate borrowers pose an equal credit risk. For example, a loan to an AA-rated corporation requires the same amount of capital as a loan to a B-rated credit. This is also clearly inappropriate.

Third, the 1988 Accord does not appropriately take maturity factors into effect. For example, revolving credit agreements with a term of less than one year do not require any regulatory capital, while a short-term facility with 366 days to maturity bears the same capital charge as any long-term facility. (A *revolver* is a facility that allows a corporation to borrow and repay the loan at will within a certain period of time.) The bank is clearly at risk from offering short-term revolver facilities, yet so long as the term is less than one year, no regulatory capital is required. This has led to the creation by many banks of a 364-day facility, in which banks commit to lend for 364 days only, but then continuously roll over the facility into the next year—a clear example of how banks alter their behavior to circumvent regulatory rules. (Such a facility attracts no capital, even if the terms of the facility are such that if the commitment is canceled, the obligor then has the right to pay back the amount drawn over a number of years.)

Fourth, the Accord does not provide any incentive for credit-risk mitigation techniques such as the use of credit derivatives—now one of the fastest-growing risk management markets.

Fifth, the Accord does not address complex issues such as portfolio effects, even though credit risk in any large portfolio is bound to be partially offset by diversification across issuers, industries, and geographic locations. For example, a bank is required to set aside the same amount of regulatory capital for a single $100 million corporate loan as for a portfolio of 100 different and unrelated (independent) $1 million corporate loans. While a single $100 million loan might go sour, it's extremely unlikely that 100 loans of a similar standing in a fully diversified portfolio will all go wrong at once.

These shortcomings have produced a distorted assessment of actual risks and have led to a misallocation of capital. The problem is that, as the definition of regulatory capital drifts further away from the bank's understanding of the true amount of risk capital necessary to support a position (i.e. economic capital), the bank faces a strong incentive to play a game of "regulatory arbitrage."

Regulatory arbitrage describes a bank's attempt to modify its behavior so that it incurs lower capital charges while still incurring the same amount of actual risk—a bit like tax avoidance, only with regard to regulatory risk capital. Banks often do this by using financial engineering constructs such as, for example, securitization through various types of collateralized debt obligations (CDOs) and the use of credit derivatives.

In the process, banks sometimes end up transferring high-grade exposures from their banking book to their trading book, or outside the banking system, so that these high-grade exposures do not attract regulatory capital. But that means that the quality of the assets remaining on the books deteriorates—exactly the reverse of the outcome sought by regulators.

The elimination of regulatory arbitrage can be achieved only by a better alignment of regulatory and economic capital—that is, by making sure that regulatory capital truly reflects the amount of economic risk that a bank is taking. That way, banks have little incentive to bend the rules in their favor.

Even if the 1988 Accord measured risk more accurately, it would still be inadequate for modern banks because of the rate of change and innovation in the banking industry. Improvements in internal risk management processes, the adoption of more advanced risk measurement techniques, and the increasing use of credit-risk mitigation techniques such as securitization and credit derivatives have changed banks' monitoring and management of exposures and activities to an extraordinary extent over the last couple of decades.

These problems with the 1988 Accord led larger banks to argue that banks should be allowed to develop their own internal credit portfolio models to determine VaR for credit in lieu of the overly simplistic standards set by the 1988 Accord. These credit VaR models would be approved by regulators and used by the industry to calculate the minimum required regulatory credit-risk capital associated with the traditional loan products in the banking book.

However, in working out the new rules for Basel II, regulators refused to go quite that far in the near term. Instead, they created a menu of increasingly advanced approaches to calculating credit risk that attempt to incorporate some of the sophistication of a true portfolio credit model. Let's take a brief look at some of the details.

BASEL II—A BANKING REVOLUTION?

In June 1999 the Basel Committee declared its intention to build a new capital adequacy framework, known as Basel II, to replace the 1988 Accord. Between 1999 and the summer of 2004, when the new rules were published, there ensued an extensive—and at times contentious—consultation process with banks and various industry groups.

The overarching goal for the Basel II framework is to ensure the adequate capitalization of banks and to encourage best-practice risk management in order to strengthen the overall stability of the banking system. The regulators have designed the system so that it's suitable for application to banks of varying levels of complexity and sophistication. More specifically, the objectives of Basel II are to:

- Promote safety and soundness in the financial system by maintaining at least the same level of capital as banks maintain with today's system.
- Enhance competitive equality. The new rules should not offer incentives for regulators in some countries to make their rules more attractive to banks in order to attract investment in the banking industry in their country. Two banks with the same portfolios should hold the same capital wherever they are located.
- Apply a more comprehensive approach to risks that takes into account more types of risk, such as operational risk and interest-rate risk. Operational risk, which we look at from a nonregulatory standpoint in Chapter 13, covers a whole range of events such as computer failures and fraud by staff.

The Basel Committee developed its comprehensive framework for capital regulation around what the regulators called their "three pillars": minimum capital requirements, supervisory review, and market discipline.

Pillar I concerns how regulators say banks must calculate their minimum regulatory requirements—this pillar most directly replaces the 1988 Accord and has attracted the most industry and media attention.

Pillar II concerns the supervisory approach to bank capital management. The objective here is to ensure that banks follow rigorous procedures, measure their risk exposures correctly, and have enough capital to cover their risks. This pillar allows regulators to scrutinize bank practices that look like attempts at regulatory arbitrage. Pillar II is also the route for supervisors to make sure that banks have considered risks that are not explicitly covered under Pillar I. For example, for the time being, interest-rate risk in the banking book, a significant form of bank risk, is treated under Pillar II and is not part of the Pillar I capital requirement calculations. Banks will face an interest-rate risk capital charge only when the interest-rate risks in an individual institution's banking book are significantly above average.

Pillar III introduces a radical new requirement for banks to disclose risk information to the equity and credit markets, in the hope that investors will be better able to exert discipline on bank behavior (i.e., discourage them from taking inappropriate risks).

The objective of Pillar I is to revise the 1988 Accord's capital ratios by aligning minimum capital requirements more closely to each bank's actual risk profile. The new minimum capital requirement framework encompasses three areas of risk: (1) credit risk (included in the 1988 Accord), (2) the market risk of trading activities (introduced in the 1996 Market Risk Amendment), and (3) operational risk (new).

In particular, Pillar I is designed to do a better job than the 1988 Accord of obliging banks to hold more capital for high-risk than for low-risk borrowers. To make the regulations sensitive to the varying degrees of sophistication among banking institutions, the regulators have laid out three options for the calculation of the minimum required capital for credit risk.

Under the standardized approach, risk weights are based on available external credit ratings, for example, those from rating agencies such as Standard & Poor's and Moody's. This option is really designed for banks engaged in less complex forms of lending and credit underwriting. More sophisticated banks will be allowed to use one of two internal ratings–based (IRB) approaches to credit risk. Under an IRB approach, banks are allowed to rely partly on their own assessment of their borrowers' credit risk to determine their minimum capital requirement, provided that they can satisfy the regulators on a number of topics such as the quality of the internal credit data available to them, the processes they use to set and validate the parameters used in the calculation, and the soundness of various control procedures. Perhaps the most critical problem here is how to validate a bank's internal risk ratings, and how to link risk weights to these internal ratings in a way that ensures an economically meaningful and reasonably consistent capital treatment of similar risks across banks. For many banks this implies significant changes in systems, processes, and data gathering. (The most sophisticated banks at some point may also be allowed to use portfolio credit models when data limitation and validation issues have been satisfactorily addressed.)

Credit risk is not the only risk that determines a bank's capital charge under the new rules. Controversially, Basel II introduces a new capital charge for operational risk. Working out a credible way of measuring operational risk proved to be one of the most formidable challenges faced by regulators.

Similar to the range of options available for assessing credit risk exposures, the regulators will allow banks to choose between one of three approaches for measuring operational risk exposures: (1) the Basic Indicator Approach, (2) the Standardized Approach, and (3) the Advanced

Measurement Approach (AMA). The first two approaches don't really try to measure operational risk accurately; instead, they apply regulator-defined proxy measurements that, under the Standardized Approach, are somewhat tailored to the kind of business lines that constitute the bank.

The AMA offers a more radical approach to the problem. Under the AMA, banks will be permitted to choose their own methodology for assessing operational risk, so long as it is sufficiently comprehensive and systematic. The extent to which specific standards and criteria are required when the AMA is used is minimal in an effort to spur the development of innovative operational risk approaches by the banking industry. The regulators say that any operational risk measurement system must have certain "key features," which include the use of "internal data, relevant external data, scenario analysis and factors reflecting the business environment and internal control systems." They will also insist that banks have a "credible, transparent, well-documented and verifiable approach for weighting these fundamental elements" in any operational risk calculations. (In Chapter 13 we describe the proposed Basel II approach to operational risk in more detail.)

Banks will be encouraged by their local regulators to move along the spectrum of available approaches for both credit and operational risks as they develop more sophisticated controls and validation techniques and build ever more comprehensive databases. But the rate of adoption of Basel II and its variant methodologies will vary considerably from regulator to regulator around the world. Most banks in Europe will be obliged to follow the new rules. But the U.S. regulators have declared that only the 10 largest banks in the United States must adopt Basel II, and that these banks must opt for the most advanced approaches for both credit and operational risks. (At least 10 other banks in the United States are expected to join this group of large, sophisticated players.) Those U.S. banks that are not involved in international activities will continue to report regulatory capital according to the 1988 Accord and won't have to invest the considerable amount of money that the major U.S. banks are spending to upgrade their credit and operational risk systems.

In Basel II, the Basel Committee recognizes the need to provide tangible incentives for banks to adopt the more advanced approaches to capital measurement. It has carried out a series of quantitative impact studies (QIS) to see what effect the new rules will have on the minimum capital requirements for banks, and to allow it to better calibrate some of the factors within the new formulas. Banks that invest in enhanced risk management and that can therefore adopt the most advanced methodologies for calculating minimum capital requirements look likely (on average) to gain some reductions in minimum regulatory capital; in any event, risk-sensitive minimum capital requirements should allow bank capital to be used more efficiently to protect against risk.

The scope of application of the Basel II Accord has been extended to include, on a fully consolidated basis, any holding company that is the parent entity within a banking group (to ensure that it captures the risk of the whole banking group). Banking groups are groups that engage predominantly in banking activities, and, in some countries, a banking group may be registered as a bank. Majority-owned or controlled banking entities, securities entities (where subject to broadly similar regulation or where securities activities are deemed banking activities), and other financial entities should generally be fully consolidated.

One remaining problem is the issue of consistency between the methodologies developed for the banking and trading books. The regulators will review the treatment of the trading account to ensure consistency with the methodologies developed for the banking book (in order to reduce the incentive for regulatory arbitrage). An interesting issue is how to harmonize an approach to incorporate liquidity risk into the risk measurement frameworks, so as to allow for a differing treatment of the various instruments in both the trading account and the banking book.

PILLAR I: MINIMUM CAPITAL REQUIREMENTS FOR CREDIT RISK – MORE DETAIL

Definition of Capital

The new framework maintains both the current definition of capital and the minimum capital requirement of 8 percent of the risk-weighted assets:

$$\frac{Total\ Capital}{Credit\ Risk + Market\ Risk + Operational\ Risk} = \frac{Capital\ Ratio}{(minimum\ 8\%)} \quad (3\text{-}1)$$

where risk-weighted assets are the sum of the assets subject to market, credit, and operational risk. Tier 2 capital cannot exceed more than 50 percent of total regulatory capital, which is the sum of tier 1 and tier 2 capital.

We should mention again that regulatory capital is broader than equity capital. It has three components: tier 1, or core capital, which includes common stockholders' equity, noncumulative perpetual preferred stock, and minority equity interests in consolidated subsidiaries, less goodwill and other deductions; tier 2, or supplementary capital, which includes hybrid capital instruments such as cumulative perpetual preferred shares; and tier 3, or subsupplementary capital, which consists of short-term subordinated debt with an original maturity of at least two years.

Under the Standardized Approach, Basel II incorporates both expected and unexpected losses (see Chapter 1 for their definition) into the calculation of capital requirements, in contrast to the 1996 Amendment, which is concerned only with unexpected loss for market risk in the trading book. The justification for including expected losses in the capital requirement is that loan loss reserves are already counted as tier 2 capital and are constituted to protect the bank against credit losses. However, in the current regulatory framework, loan loss reserves are eligible for tier 2 capital only up to a maximum of 1.25 percent of risk-weighted assets.

Under the IRB approaches, the option of including general loan loss reserves in tier 2 capital that was given by the 1988 Accord is withdrawn. Instead, banks need to compare the expected loss to the total eligible provisions. When expected loss is greater than the eligible provisions, banks have to deduct the difference from capital, with the deduction being on the basis of 50 percent from tier 1 and 50 percent from tier 2 capital. In the other instance, when expected loss is less than the eligible provisions, banks may recognize the difference in tier 2 capital up to a maximum of 0.6 percent of credit risk-weighted assets.

Now let's look in more detail at the Standardized, IRB Foundation, and IRB Advanced approaches to calculating minimum required capital for credit risk.

The Standardized Approach

The Standardized Approach is conceptually the same as the 1988 Accord, but it has been designed to be more risk sensitive. The bank allocates a risk weight to each of its assets and off-balance-sheet positions and produces a sum of risk-weighted asset values.

For example, a risk weight of 50 percent means that an exposure is included in the calculation of risk-weighted assets at 50 percent of its full value, which then translates into a capital charge equal to 8 percent of that value, or equivalently to 4 percent (= 8% × 50%) of the exposure.

Individual risk weights depend both on the broad category of borrower (that is, whether it is a sovereign, a bank, or a corporate) and on the rating provided by an external rating agency (Table 3-4). For banks'

TABLE 3-4

Standardized Approach—New Risk Weights

Claim		AAA to AA$^-$	A+ to A$^-$	BBB+ to BBB$^-$	BB+ to BB$^-$ (B$^-$)^a	Below BB$^-$ (B$^-$)^a	Unrated
		Credit Assessment					
Sovereigns		0%	20%	50%	100%	150%	100%
Banks	Option 1^b	20%	50%	100%	100%	150%	100%
	Option 2^c	20%	50%	50%	100%	150%	50%
	Short-term claims^d	20%	20%	20%	50%	150%	20%
Corporates		20%	50%	100%	100%	150%	100%
Securitization tranches^e		20%	50%	100%	350%	Deduction from capital	

^{a} B$^-$ is the cutoff rating for sovereigns and banks. It is BB- for corporates and securitization exposures.
^{b} Risk weighting based on risk weighting of sovereign in which the bank is incorporated. Banks incorporated in a given country will be assigned a risk weight one category less favorable than that assigned to claims on the sovereign, with a cap of 100% for claims to banks in sovereigns rated BB+ to B-.
^{c} Risk weighting based on the assessment of the individual bank.
^{d} Short-term claims in option 2 are defined as having an original maturity of three months or less.
^{e} The risk weights for short-term ratings are 20% for A-1/P-1, 50% for A-2/P-2, and 100% for A-3/P-3; for all other ratings or unrated, there is capital deduction.
Source: Basel Committee on Banking Supervision, 2004.

exposures to sovereigns, the Basel Committee applies the published credit scores of export credit agencies..

For claims on corporations, the new Accord proposes to retain a risk weight of 100 percent except for highly rated companies (that is, those rated AAA to A-) and non-investment-grade borrowers rated below BB-. Highly rated companies would benefit from a lower risk weight of 20 to 50 percent. Non-investment-grade companies are given a risk weight of 150 percent. Short-term revolvers, with a term less than a year, would be subject to a capital charge of 20 percent, instead of zero under the current 1988 Accord. Basel II puts highly rated corporate claims on the same footing as the obligations of bank and government-sponsored enterprises.

Shortcomings of the Standardized Approach

How successful is the Standardized Approach at mending the gaps in the original 1988 Accord? Our view is that the Standardized Approach is an improvement, but that it has flaws that are rather similar in kind to those of the 1988 Accord. Banks will have the same incentive as before to play the regulatory arbitrage game for the following reasons:

- There is not enough differentiation among credit categories— six credit categories (including unrated) are not sufficient. For example, the same risk weight (100 percent) is attributed to a corporate investment-grade facility rated BBB and a non-investment-grade facility rated BB-.

- The unrated category receives a risk weight of 100 percent, which is less than that attributed to non-investment-grade facilities rated below BB-. This does not make much sense, since it removes any incentive for high-risk institutions to pay for a rating. So long as they remain unrated, they will be treated as if they were investment grade. Clearly, the highest risk weight should apply to any firms that elect to remain unrated.

- The Standardized Approach assigns too much capital—more than is required for economic protection—to investment-grade facilities (e.g., 1.6 percent for AA facilities) and not enough to non-investment-grade debt (e.g., 12 percent to B facilities).

For example, if we look at the period 1981–1999, there was not a single default on bonds rated AAA to AA- (corresponding to the first bucket of the Standardized Approach) within one year of an entity's holding that rating (though a few exceptions did occur in subsequent years). Yet the Standardized Approach requires 1.6 percent of capital on such assets held by a bank.

The New Internal Ratings-Based Approach

Under the Internal Ratings Based (IRB) approach to assessing risk capital requirements, banks will have to categorize banking-book exposures into at least five broad classes of assets with different underlying credit-risk characteristics; the classes are corporates, banks, sovereigns, retail, and equity. This classification is broadly consistent with established bank practices. Within the corporate and retail asset classes, subclasses are separately identified. The IRB proposes a specific treatment for securitization exposures.

The IRB approach provides for distinct analytical frameworks for different types of loan exposures, e.g., corporate and retail lending. Here, we'll focus on corporate loans and bonds.

Banks adopting the IRB approach will be allowed to use their own internal risk ratings methodology to assess credit risk, subject to the approval by the regulator of the bank's internal rating system and the validation of the way the bank produces the key risk parameters for calculating credit risk.

These key risk parameters include the probability of default (PD) for each rating category, the loss given default (LGD), and the exposure at default (EAD) for loan commitments.

Under the IRB, the calculation of the potential future loss amount, which forms the basis of the minimum capital requirement, encompasses unexpected losses. It is derived from a formula whose key inputs are the PD, LGD, EAD, and maturity (M) of the facility.

In the Foundation approach, banks estimate the PD associated with each borrower, and the supervisors will supply the other inputs, as follows:

- LGD = 45 percent for senior unsecured facilities and 75 percent for subordinated claims; the existence of collateral will lower the estimated LGD.
- EAD = 75 percent for irrevocable undrawn commitments.[2]
- M = 2.5 years except for repo-style transactions, where the effective maturity will be six months.

In the Advanced IRB approach, banks that meet rigorous standards in terms of their internal ratings system and capital allocation process will be permitted to set the values of all the necessary inputs. That is, they won't be restricted to estimating the PD of their assets, but can also estimate the LGD, EAD, and M risk parameters.

Still, the Basel Committee has stopped short of permitting banks to calculate their capital requirements on the basis of their own internal credit-risk portfolio models, which would have allowed each bank to capture unique portfolio effects that tend to reduce total bank risk exposure. Instead, the IRB approach allocates capital facility by facility (although some portfolio effects are indirectly captured in the formula through the average asset correlation embedded in the calculation of the risk weights). However, the Basel Committee does encourage banks to use more sophisticated approaches and models to assess credit risk under Pillar II of the new rules.

---

2. The credit conversion factor is zero percent only for unconditionally and immediately cancelable commitments.

PILLAR II: THE SUPERVISORY REVIEW PROCESS

The supervisory review process of capital adequacy is intended to ensure that a bank's capital position and strategy are consistent with its overall risk profile. Early supervisory intervention will be encouraged if the capital amount is thought not to provide a sufficient buffer against risk.

Supervisors will have the ability to require banks to hold capital in excess of minimum required regulatory ratios depending on a variety of factors such as the experience and quality of its management and control process, its track record in managing risks, the nature of the markets in which the bank operates, and the volatility of its earnings. In assessing capital adequacy, the regulators will have to consider the effects of business cycles and the overall macroeconomic environment, as well as the systemic impact on the banking system should the bank fail.

Before such a process can be implemented, regulators need to define a sound conceptual framework for the determination of bank capital adequacy. The key questions here are: How can "soundness" be defined and quantified? What is the minimum acceptable soundness level, and how can regulators be sure that a bank operates above this minimum soundness level? The danger of the Basel II supervisory approach is that determinations of capital adequacy on a bank-by-bank basis will prove to be arbitrary and inconsistent.

To be consistent with the risk-adjusted return on capital methodology that we describe in Chapter 15, soundness should be defined as the probability of insolvency over a one-year horizon. Minimum soundness then becomes the insolvency probability consistent with an investment-grade rating for the bank, i.e., BBB or better. Most banks currently target an insolvency probability of 4 to 5 basis points (i.e., 0.04 to 0.05 percent), which is consistent with an AA rating.

Under the new Accord, all internationally active banks will be expected to develop internal processes and techniques to carry out a self-assessment of their capital adequacy in relation to objective and quantifiable measures of risks. Banks should perform comprehensive and rigorous stress tests to identify possible events or changes in market conditions that could have an adverse effect on the bank.

PILLAR III: MARKET DISCIPLINE

The Basel Committee intends to foster market transparency so that market participants can better assess bank capital adequacy. Disclosure requirements have been introduced according to which banks will have to publish detailed qualitative and quantitative information about capital levels, including details of capital structure and reserves for credit and other potential losses, risk exposures, and capital adequacy. These requirements cover not only the way in which a bank calculates its capital adequacy, but also the techniques it employs in its risk assessment.

The combination of increased pressure from other global regulations intended to improve disclosure (such as the Sarbanes-Oxley Act in the United States) and the Basel third pillar of market discipline should substantially improve disclosure in the banking industry. The hope is that high-quality disclosure standards will allow market participants to better assess banks' risk profiles, risk management, and capital strength. The market will then be able to impose its own discipline on bank risk taking, for example, by reducing the share price of the bank or by making it more expensive for the bank to raise money.

The disclosure requirements build on the guidelines on "Enhancing Bank Transparency" published in September 1998 by the Basel Committee. The committee recommended that banks provide timely information across six broad areas: financial performance, financial position (including capital, solvency, and liquidity), risk management strategies and practices, risk exposures (including credit risk, market risk, liquidity risk, operational risk, legal risk, and other risks), accounting policies, and basic business, management, and corporate governance information. These disclosures should be made at least annually, and more frequently if necessary. These recommendations have also been adopted by the G-12.

The requirements of Pillar III of Basel II should be viewed against the backdrop of the substantial changes underway in the financial system. Banks' operations have increasingly become more complex and sophisticated. Today banks have considerable exposure to financial markets and are increasingly active in markets for complex financial products such as derivatives. These products can be used to hedge existing risks on banks' balance sheets or to take on new risks. For instance, the growth of credit derivatives and the increasing use of securitization have had a profound impact on the structure of banks' risk profiles. In addition, large banks tend to operate internationally, in some cases with a majority of their operations taking place outside their home country.

CONCLUSION

The Basel Committee had no desire to change the capital requirements for the banking system as a whole; it has calibrated its new capital adequacy regime to make sure that, overall, capital levels will remain unchanged. However, there will be a redistribution of capital among individual banks according to each bank's risk profiles and business activities.

The Basel Committee has studied the potential impact of the Basel II framework by means of several quantitative impact studies (QISs), carried out before and after the finalization of the broad framework. Overall, the results of these studies suggest the new rules will have an effect that is consistent with the original objectives set by the Basel Committee. QIS3 showed that there is an incentive for large banks operating internationally to adopt the advanced IRB approach. They should enjoy, on average, a slight reduction in total capital, even when we include the new charge for operational risk, compared with the current situation.

For smaller, domestically oriented banks, capital requirements could be substantially lower under the IRB approaches, due especially to the favorable capital treatment received by retail exposures (for which the capital charge will probably be reduced by 45 to 50 percent on average). Retail exposures, such as credit card receivables, do not require as much capital as corporate exposures because they are part of large, stable, diversified portfolios composed of many small transactions. It follows that the loss distribution for retail exposures shows little dispersion around the expected loss, and the activity therefore requires relatively little capital to be set against unexpected loss levels.

In addition, small and medium-sized enterprises (SMEs), which, under Basel II, are considered to be retail exposures, benefit from a size adjustment that can lead to a reduction in required capital of up to 20 percent compared to similar large corporate exposures that exhibit the same default rate. This favorable treatment was a response to the fear, voiced by a number of influential commentators, that the new capital regime would reduce the supply of credit to SMEs and make borrowing more expensive for them. SMEs are an important component of the economy. Therefore, an adverse Basel II treatment would have adversely affected economic growth, innovation, and employment.

CHAPTER 4

Corporate Governance and Risk Management

Following a series of high-profile corporate scandals in the early years of the millennium, the conduct and organization of risk management by senior executives and boards have received a great deal of attention. These scandals included, most notoriously, the failure of energy giant Enron in 2001, a wave of "new technology" and telecom industry accounting scandals at companies like WorldCom and Global Crossing, and, to prove that the problem wasn't confined to the United States, the collapse of the Italian dairy products giant Parmalat in late 2003.

In most of these instances, either boards were provided with misleading information or there was a breakdown in the process by which information was transmitted to the board and shareholders. In many cases, the breakdown involved financial engineering and the nondisclosure of economic risks—as well as outright fraud.

The dramatic collapse in public confidence caused by these scandals continues to put pressure on boards and management committees to carry out their corporate governance and risk management responsibilities in a more effective manner. The regulatory and rating agencies are themselves under significant pressure to upgrade their capabilities in order to protect all stakeholders.

The scandals have also led to a wave of legislation in the United States and elsewhere that is designed to mend perceived failures in corporate governance practices. A striking feature of these reforms is that they will penalize inattention and incompetence just as much as deliberate malfeasance.

In the short term, U.S. corporations need to make sure that they are complying with these key reforms, which include the Sarbanes-Oxley Act

(SOX) of 2002 and associated changes in stock exchange rules as described in Boxes 4-1 and 4-2.

B O X   4 - 1

SARBANES-OXLEY (SOX)

In response to the series of accounting and management scandals that sur-faced soon after the millennium, the U.S. Congress passed the Sarbanes-Oxley Act of 2002 (SOX). The act creates a more rigorous legal environment for the board, the management committee, internal and external auditors, and the CRO (chief risk officer).

SOX places primary responsibility on the chief executive officer and the chief financial officer of a publicly traded corporation for ensuring the ac-curacy of company reports filed with the Securities and Exchange Com-mission. SOX requires these senior corporate officers to report on the completeness and accuracy of the information contained in the reports, as well as on the effectiveness of the underlying controls.

Specifically, SOX calls for the CEO and CFO to certify quarterly and annually that the report filed with the Securities and Exchange Commission does not contain any untrue statements or omit any material facts. Senior officers must certify that the financial statements fairly present (in all ma-terial respects) the results of the corporation's operations and cash flows. They also must take responsibility for designing, establishing, and main-taining disclosure controls and procedures.

The CEO and CFO must also disclose to the audit committee and to the company's external auditors any deficiencies and material weaknesses in internal controls, as well as any fraud (material or not) involving anyone with a significant role in internal control. The act requires that senior man-agement annually assess the effectiveness of the corporation's internal con-trol structure and procedures for financial reporting.

The act also seeks to make sure that the board of the company includes some members who are experts in understanding financial reports. Comp-anies are now compelled to disclose the number and names of persons serv-ing on the critical audit committee whom the board has determined to be "financial experts." A financial expert is someone with an understanding of generally accepted accounting principles and financial statements, and should also have experience with internal accounting controls and an un-derstanding of the function of the audit committee.

BOX 4-2

U.S. EXCHANGES TIGHTEN UP THE RULES

In January 2003 the U.S. Securities and Exchange Commission issued a rule—as directed by the Sarbanes-Oxley Act—that requires U.S. national securities exchanges and national securities associations (i.e., the NYSE, Amex and Nasdaq) to make sure that their securities listing standards conform to the existing and evolving SEC rules.

These standards cover a number of areas that are critical to corporate governance and risk management, such as

- Composition of the board of directors, e.g., the board must have a majority of independent directors
- Establishment of a corporate governance committee with duties such as the development of broad corporate governance principles and oversight of the evaluation of the board and management
- Duties of the compensation committee, e.g., it should make sure that CEO compensation is aligned with corporate objectives
- Activities of the audit committee, e.g., to review external auditors' reports describing the quality of internal control procedures, and to adopt and disclose corporate governance guidelines and codes of business conduct

---

Together with the Basel II regulatory capital reform that we described in Chapter 3, these initiatives are shaping the overall corporate governance and risk management environment. For example, SOX strengthens the process of financial reporting and therefore sets the stage for better risk reporting and disclosure.

In the longer term, a key challenge for boards all around the world is to develop a new level of rigor in the risk-related questions they are able to ask of management (beyond any regulatory requirements). This is something that is still a work in progress at many boards, if industry surveys are to be believed (Box 4-3).

The new focus on board risk governance is a particular challenge for complex risk-taking organizations such as banks, securities firms, insurance companies, and energy companies. Risk analytic disciplines that have evolved over the past decade in risk management are likely to play an increasingly important role in the work of boards, risk management committees, and audit committees as they explore their responsibilities.

BOX 4-3

MCKINSEY'S CORPORATE GOVERNANCE SURVEY

In June 2002, the management consultants McKinsey undertook a survey of U.S. corporate directors, with the support of an industry publication, *Directorship*. It received a response from nearly 200 directors, who together sat on almost 500 boards. Almost two-thirds of the respondents were from companies with $1 billion or more in revenues or market capitalization. The survey's findings show that risk governance is still a "work in progress" for many boards:

- *Risk management.* More than 40 percent of those surveyed did not have effective processes for identifying, safeguarding against, and planning for key risks; amazingly, almost one-fifth had no process at all. The lack of an effective risk management process creates a key challenge for corporate governance. How can strategic decisions be made in the absence of a formal assessment of the risks associated with the various strategic options?
- *Oversight of chief risk officer.* More than a quarter of directors with a financial/risk perspective claim to have some concerns about the way the board conducts its oversight of the CRO, and 60 percent have not even observed the nature of this oversight.
- *Compensation.* Answers to the survey seemed to show an insufficient focus on how the corporation's chosen compensation policy might drive corporate strategy, and the effect this might have on achieving the corporation's preferred risk profile.
- *Understanding the business.* Over 40 percent of directors admitted that they did not have a full understanding of where the value of the business is created. When asked to rate their colleagues, directors believe that almost half are low or average performers.
- *Director independence.* Directors believed that more than a quarter of their nonexecutive director colleagues should not be considered truly independent (i.e., having no ties to the company or management except through being a director).

In this chapter we'll use the example of an archetypal bank to try to answer three critical questions:

- How does best-practice risk management relate to best-practice corporate governance?

- How do boards and senior executives organize the delegation of risk management authority through key committees and risk executives?
- How can agreed risk limits be transmitted down the line to business managers in a way that can be monitored and that makes sense in terms of day-to-day business decisions?

Our aim is to give an idea of how risk management should be articulated from the top of an organization to the bottom. We'll also touch on some contentious issues, like the appropriate relationship between audit and risk management functions in a corporation.

SETTING THE SCENE—CORPORATE GOVERNANCE AND RISK MANAGEMENT

From a corporate governance perspective, a primary responsibility of the board is to look after the interests of shareholders. For example, does it make sense for the corporation to assume a particular risk, given the projected returns of the business activity? The board also needs to be sensitive to the concerns of other stakeholders such as debt holders. Debt holders are most interested in the extreme downside of risk—how likely is it that a risk will damage a corporation so badly that it will become insolvent?

The board also needs to be on the alert for any conflict that may arise between the interests of management to assume risks and the interests of the company's stakeholders. (This kind of conflict of interest is often referred to in the academic literature as an "agency risk.") Conflicts of interest can easily happen if, for example, executives are rewarded with options that they can cash in if the share price of the company rises above a certain level for a short time.

Such an arrangement gives management an incentive to push the share price up, but not necessarily in a sustainable way. For example, management might encourage business lines to earn short-term rewards in exchange for assuming long-term risks. By the time the chickens come home to roost, managers may well have picked up their bonuses or even changed jobs.

This all explains why it is becoming difficult to draw a line between corporate governance and risk management, and we can see some clear effects of this at an organizational level. For example, over the last few years, many corporations have created the role of chief risk officer (CRO). A key duty of the new CRO is often to act as a senior member of the management committee and to attend board meetings regularly. The board and the management committee increasingly look to the CRO to integrate corporate governance responsibilities with the risk function's existing market, credit, operational, and business risk responsibilities.

TRUE RISK GOVERNANCE

The primary responsibility of the board is to ensure that it develops a clear understanding of the bank's business strategy and the fundamental risks and rewards that this implies. The board also needs to make sure that risks are made transparent to managers and to stakeholders through adequate internal and external disclosure.

Although the board is not there to manage the business, it is responsible for overseeing management and holding it accountable. It must also contribute to the development of the overall strategic plan for the firm, taking into consideration how any changes might affect business opportunities and the strategy of the firm. This necessarily includes the extent and types of risks that are acceptable for the firm; i.e., the board must characterize an appropriate "risk appetite" for the firm.

The board may be challenged by the complexity of the risk management process, but the principles at a strategic level are quite simple. There are only four basic choices in risk management:

- Avoid risk by choosing not to undertake some activities.
- Transfer risk to third parties through insurance, hedging, and outsourcing.
- Mitigate risk, such as operational risk, through preventive and detective control measures.
- Accept risk, recognizing that undertaking certain risky activities should generate shareholder value.

In particular, the board should ensure that business and risk management strategies are directed at economic rather than accounting performance, contrary to what happened at Enron and some of the other firms involved in highly publicized corporate governance scandals.

To fulfill its risk governance responsibilities, the board must ensure that the bank has put in place an effective risk management program that is consistent with these fundamental strategic and risk appetite choices. And it must make sure that there are effective procedures in place for identifying, assessing, and managing all types of risk, i.e. business risk, operational risk, market risk, liquidity risk, and credit risk.

This includes making sure that all the appropriate policies, methodologies, and infrastructure are in place. The infrastructure includes both operating elements (e.g., sophisticated software, hardware, data, and operational processes) and personnel.

This might sound like an onerous task, but there are various levers that the board can pull. For example, one way to gauge how seriously a company takes its risk management process is to look at the human capital that is employed:

- What kind of a career path does the risk management function offer?
- Whom do risk managers report to?
- What salaries are paid to risk managers in comparison to "reward-oriented" personnel such as traders?
- Is there a strong ethical culture in evidence?

An effective board will also establish strong ethical standards and work to ensure that it understands the degree to which management follows them. Some banks have recently set up ethics committees within their business divisions to try to make sure that "soft" risks such as unethical business practices don't slip through the mesh of their "hard" risk-reporting framework.

According to *BusinessWeek*, "Enron didn't just fail because of improper accounting or alleged corruption at the top. . . . The unrelenting emphasis on earnings growth and individual initiative, coupled with a shocking absence of checks and balances, tipped the culture from one that rewarded aggressive strategy to one that increasingly relied on unethical corner cutting."[1]

Another important lever available to the board is the firm's performance metrics and compensation strategy. The board has a critical responsibility to make sure that the way staff are rewarded and compensated is based on risk-adjusted performance (see Chapter 15) and is aligned with shareholders' interests.

The increase in misreporting after the millennial stock market boom paralleled the rise of equity-based compensation for CEOs, which arguably provided a perverse incentive to executives to manipulate financial results to boost the share price in the short term.

---

1. "At Enron, the Environment Was Ripe for Abuse," *BusinessWeek,* Feb. 25, 2002.

A related responsibility is to ensure that any major transactions the bank enters into are consistent with the risk authorized and the associated strategies of the bank.

The board should ensure that the information it obtains about risk management is accurate and reliable. Directors should demonstrate healthy skepticism and require information from a cross section of knowledgeable and reliable sources, such as the CEO, senior management, and internal and external auditors. Directors should be prepared to ask tough questions, and they should make themselves able to understand the answers.

The duty of the board is not, however, to undertake risk management on a day-to-day basis, but to make sure that all the mechanisms used to delegate risk management decisions are functioning properly.

COMMITTEES AND RISK LIMITS—OVERVIEW

We've set out some of the goals of best-practice risk governance. Now we'll take a look at some of the mechanisms that financial institutions and other nonfinancial risk-taking corporations use to translate these goals into reality.

In the following we'll focus on corporate governance in the banking industry, where practices are most advanced—except perhaps in the areas of business conduct and conflict of interest. However, many of the same principles and structures could be applied in other industries.

At most banks, the board charges its main committees, e.g., the audit and risk management committees, with ratifying the key policies and associated procedures of the bank's risk management activities. These committees also make sure that the implementation of these key policies is effective.

The committees help to translate the overall risk appetite of the bank, approved by the board, into a set of limits that flow down through the bank's executive officers and business divisions. All banks, for example, should have in place a credit-risk management committee to keep an eye on credit-risk reporting, as well as a system of credit-risk limits.

The exact name for each committee tends to vary quite a lot across the industry, as does the specific duties of each committee. For our purposes, we'll imagine an archetypal bank with a senior risk committee to oversee risk management practices and detailed reporting. Junior risk committees that look after specific types of risk, such as the credit-risk committee, often report to this senior risk committee.

Let's now look at two specific mechanisms for risk governance, before examining how risk committees use risk metrics and limit frameworks to delegate risk authority down through the bank.

A KEY TRADITIONAL MECHANISM—THE SPECIAL ROLE OF THE AUDIT COMMITTEE OF THE BOARD

The role of the audit committee of the board is critical to the board's oversight of the bank. The audit committee is responsible not only for the accuracy of the bank's financial and regulatory reporting, but also for ensuring that the bank complies with minimum or best-practice standards in other key activities, such as regulatory, legal, compliance, and risk management activities. Audit committee members are now required to be financially literate, so that they can carry out their duties.

We can think of auditing as providing independent verification for the board on whether the bank is actually doing what it says it is doing. Although some of the audit committee's functions can sound quite close to risk management, it is this key verification function that separates the audit committee's work from the work of other risk committees.

The audit committee's duties involve not just checking for infringements, but also overseeing the quality of the processes that underpin financial reporting, regulatory compliance, internal controls, and risk management.

In a later section, we look specifically at how the audit function, which often has a direct reporting relationship with the audit committee, acts as an independent check on the bank's risk management process.

To function properly, an audit committee needs members with the right mix of knowledge, judgment, independence, integrity, inquisitiveness, and commitment. In most banks, a nonexecutive director leads the audit committee, and most members are nonexecutives. The audit committee also needs to establish an appropriate interaction with management—independent, but productive, and with all the necessary lines of communication kept open.

The audit committee needs to ask itself several key questions with respect to each of its principal duties. For example, with respect to financial statements, the audit committee needs to be satisfied not only that the financial statements are correct, but also that the company adequately addresses the risk that the financial statements may be materially misstated (intentionally or unintentionally).

The audit committee also needs to be clear about the reporting and risk management elements of governance that it oversees on behalf of the board. For example, these might include financial reporting, operational effectiveness, and efficiency as well as compliance with laws and regulations.

A KEY NEW MECHANISM—THE EVOLVING ROLE OF A RISK ADVISORY DIRECTOR

It is not likely that all board members will have the skills that will allow them to determine the financial condition of a complex risk-taking corporation such as a bank (or an insurance company, or an energy company).

This is especially likely if the selection of nonexecutives on the board is designed to include nonexecutives who come from outside the firm's industry and are truly independent of the corporation. This is a problem because many of the recent corporate governance scandals have shown that it is easy for executives to bamboozle nonexecutives who lack the skills to ask probing questions, or to understand the answers to these questions in a rigorous manner.

There are various ways to square this circle, but they all come back to the board's establishing some kind of support for interpreting information about risk and risk processes that is independent of the senior executive team.

One approach is for the board to gain the support of a specialist risk advisory director, that is, a member of the board (not necessarily a voting member) who specializes in risk matters. An advisory director works to improve the overall efficiency and effectiveness of the senior risk committees and the audit committee, as well as the independence and quality of risk oversight by the main board. The concerns of such a director are listed in Box 4-4, which in effect is also a checklist of some of the key duties of the board with regard to risk management.

In terms of specific activities, the advisory director might

- Participate in audit committee meetings to support members.
- Participate periodically in key risk committee meetings to provide independent commentary on executive risk reporting.
- Meet regularly with key members of management.
- Observe the conduct of business.

BOX   4 - 4

WHAT MIGHT A RISK ADVISORY DIRECTOR DO?

In the main text, we describe a new mechanism of corporate governance, the risk advisory director. Such a director should review, analyze, and become familiar with

- Risk management policies, methodologies, and infrastructure
- Daily and weekly risk management reports
- The overall business portfolio and how it drives risk
- Business strategies and changes that shape risk
- Internal controls to mitigate key market, credit, operational, and business risks
- Financial statements, critical accounting principles, significant accounting judgments, material accounting estimates, and off-balance-sheet financings
- Financial information and disclosures that are provided in support of securities filings
- Internal audit and external audit reports and associated management letters
- Interplay between the company and its affiliates, including intercompany pricing issues, related-party transactions, and interrelationship of the external auditors selected for each of the enterprises
- Relevant regulatory, accounting profession, industry, rating agency, and stock exchange–based requirements and best practices
- Practices of external competition and industry trends in risk management
- Industry corporate governance and risk-related forums

- Share insights on best-practice corporate governance and risk management with respect to best-in-class policies, methodologies, and infrastructure.
- Provide a high-level educational perspective on the risk profiles of key business areas and on the risks associated with the business model.

A key goal of the advisory director would be an ongoing examination of the interface between corporate governance and risk management in terms of risk policies, methodologies, and infrastructure.

THE SPECIAL ROLE OF THE RISK MANAGEMENT COMMITTEE OF THE BOARD

At a bank, the risk management committee of the board is responsible for independently reviewing the identification, measurement, monitoring, and controlling of credit, market, and liquidity risks, including the adequacy of policy guidelines and systems. If the committee identifies any issues concerning operational risk, it typically refers these to the audit committee for review.

The board of directors also typically delegates to the risk management committee the responsibility for approving individual credits above a certain amount, as well as for reviewing individual credits within limits delegated to the chairman and chief executive officer by the board, but above certain reporting thresholds. These aspects are usually set out in a formal document—e.g., the "investment and lending delegation of authority resolution"—approved by the board.

The risk management committee reports back to the board on a variety of items, such as all loans and/or credits over a specified dollar limit that are special, or being made to related parties (e.g., bank officers). The risk management committee also monitors credit and securities portfolios, including major trends in credit, market, and liquidity risk levels, portfolio composition, and industry breakdowns.

The risk management committee also typically provides opportunities for separate, direct, and private communication with the chief inspector, the external auditors, and the management committee.

ROLES AND RESPONSIBILITIES IN PRACTICE

We've described the basic structures and mechanisms for risk governance at the board level. But how do these structures and mechanisms work together to make sure that the day-to-day activities of the bank conform to the board-agreed general risk appetite and the limits set by the board and management committees?

The senior risk committee of the bank recommends to the risk committee of the board an amount at risk that it is prudent for the risk committee of the board to approve. In particular, the senior risk committee of the bank determines the amount of financial risk (i.e., market risk and credit risk) and nonfinancial risk (i.e., operational risk and business risk) to be assumed by the bank as a whole, in line with the bank's business strategies. At the top of the tree, the risk committee of the board approves the bank's risk appetite each year, based on a well-defined and broad set of risk measures (such as the amount of overall interest rate risk). The risk committee of the board delegates authority to the senior risk committee of the bank, chaired by the CEO of the firm, whose membership includes, among others, the chief risk officer (CRO), the head of compliance, the heads of the business units, the CFO, and the treasurer.

The senior risk committee of the bank is also responsible for establishing, documenting, and enforcing all policies that involve risk, and for delegating specific business-level risk limits to the CRO of the bank. The CRO is typically a member of the management committee and is responsible, among other things, for designing the bank's risk management strategy. Specifically, the CRO is responsible for the risk policies, risk methodologies, and risk infrastructure as well as for corporate governance.

The senior risk committee of the bank delegates to the CRO the authority to make day-to-day decisions on its behalf, including the authority to approve risks in excess of the limits provided to the bank's various businesses as long as these limits do not breach the overall risk limits approved by the board.

At many banks, the CRO plays a pivotal role in informing the board, as well as the senior risk committee of the bank, about the appetite for risk across the bank. The CRO also communicates the views of the board and senior management down through the organization. Each business unit, for example, may be given a mandate to assume risk on behalf of the bank up to a specific risk limit. The senior risk committee of the bank must also satisfy itself that the bank's infrastructure can support the bank's risk management objectives. The senior risk committee of the bank provides a detailed review and approval (say, annually) of each business unit mandate in terms of the respective risk limits, and delegates the monitoring of these limits to the CRO.

In large banks, the process for developing and renewing this authority is explicit. For example, business unit risk authority typically expires one year after the senior risk committee of the bank approves it. The CRO may approve an extension of an authority beyond one year to accommodate the senior risk committee's schedule.

A balance needs to be struck between ensuring that a business can meet its business goals and the maintenance of overall risk standards (including ensuring that limits can be properly monitored). Key infrastructure and corporate governance groups are normally consulted when preparing a business unit's mandate.

The CRO is responsible for independently monitoring the limits throughout the year. The CRO may order business units to reduce their positions or close them out because of concerns about market, credit, or operational risks.

The CRO also delegates some responsibilities to the heads of the various business units. For example, at an investment bank, the head of global trading is likely to be made responsible for the risk management and performance of all trading activities, and he or she, in turn, delegates the management of limits to the business managers. The business managers are responsible for the risk management and performance of the business, and they, in turn, delegate limits to the bank's traders.

This delegation process is summarized in Figure 4-1 with reference to market-risk authorities.

At the level of each major business, there may also be a business risk committee. The business risk committee is typically made up of both business and risk personnel. The focus of the business risk committee is to make sure that business decisions are in line with the corporation's desired risk/reward trade-offs and that risks are managed appropriately at the business line level (see Box 4-5).

The business risk committee might be responsible for managing business-level design issues that set out exactly how a particular risk will be managed, reflecting the agreed-upon relationship between the business and the bank's risk management function. The business risk committee also approves policies that define the appropriate measurement and management of risk, and provides a detailed review of risk limits and risk authorities within the business unit.

Below the board committee level, executives and business managers are necessarily dependent upon each other when they try to manage and report on risk in a bank (Figure 4-2). Business managers also ensure timely, accurate, and complete deal capture and sign off on the official profit and loss (P&L) statement.

The bank's operations function is particularly critical to risk oversight. In the case of an investment bank, for example, it is this function that independently books trades, settles trades, and reconciles front- and back-office positions—which should provide the core record of all the bank's dealings. Operations staff also prepare the P&L report and independent valuations (e.g., mark to market of the bank's positions) and support the operational needs of the various businesses.

Meanwhile, the bank's finance function develops valuation and finance policy and ensures the integrity of the P&L, including reviews of

FIGURE 4-1

Delegation Process for Market Risk Authorities

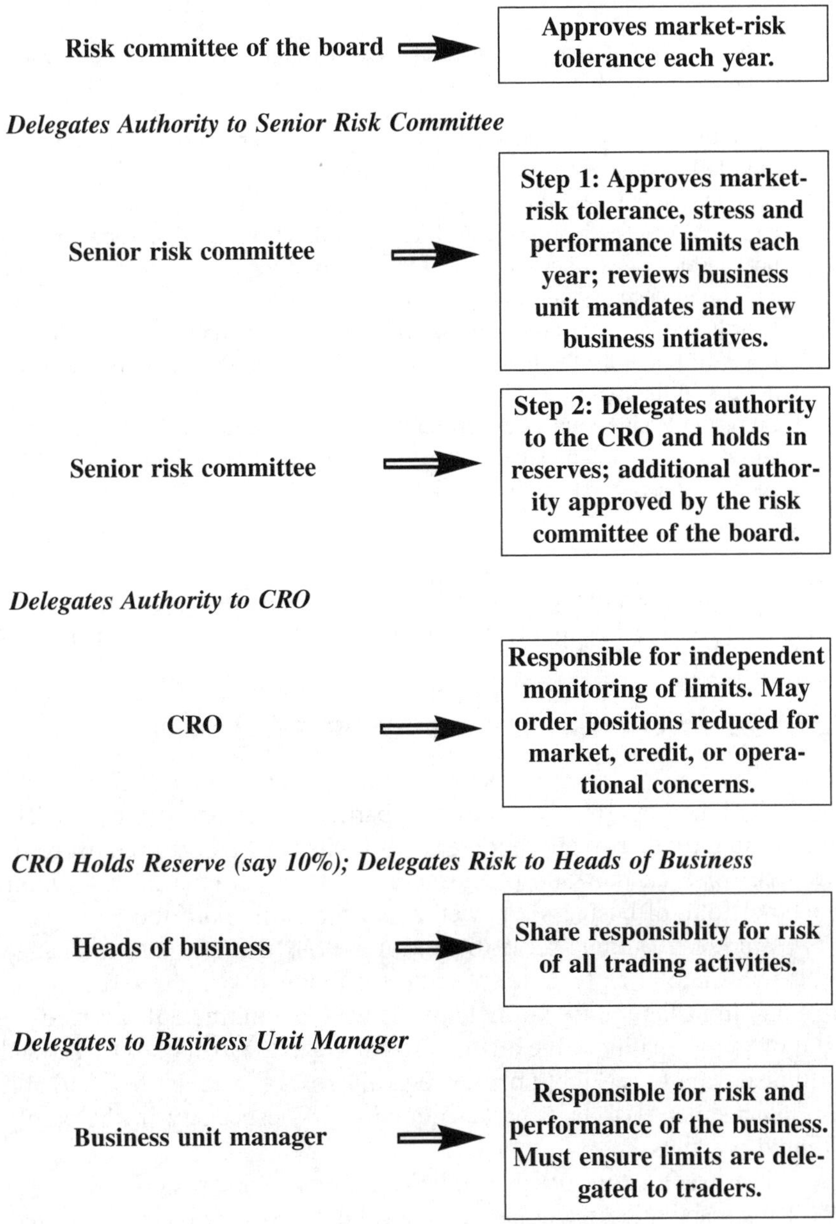

Risk committee of the board ➡ | Approves market-risk tolerance each year.

Delegates Authority to Senior Risk Committee

Senior risk committee ➡ | Step 1: Approves market-risk tolerance, stress and performance limits each year; reviews business unit mandates and new business intiatives.

Senior risk committee ➡ | Step 2: Delegates authority to the CRO and holds in reserves; additional authority approved by the risk committee of the board.

Delegates Authority to CRO

CRO ➡ | Responsible for independent monitoring of limits. May order positions reduced for market, credit, or operational concerns.

CRO Holds Reserve (say 10%); Delegates Risk to Heads of Business

Heads of business ➡ | Share responsiblity for risk of all trading activities.

Delegates to Business Unit Manager

Business unit manager ➡ | Responsible for risk and performance of the business. Must ensure limits are delegated to traders.

B O X   4 - 5

FORMAT FOR OBTAINING APPROVAL
OF A BUSINESS MANDATE

The format for obtaining approval of a business unit mandate can be quite standardized, as follows:

- First, the business unit seeking approval provides an overview and points out the key decisions that need to be taken.
- Second, the business unit brings everyone up to date about the business, e.g., key achievements, risk profile, and a description of any new products (or activities) that may affect the risk profile.
- Third, the business unit outlines future initiatives.
- Fourth, the business unit proposes financial (i.e., market and credit) risk limits in line with the business strategy and the limit standards that we discuss in the main text.
- Fifth, the business unit describes all the nonfinancial risks that it is exposed to. This might include the impact of any finance, legal, compliance, business conduct, and tax issues.

---

any independent valuation processes. Finance also manages the business planning process and supports the financial needs of the various businesses.

LIMITS AND LIMIT STANDARDS POLICIES

To achieve best-practice corporate governance, a corporation must be able to tie its board-approved tolerance to particular business strategies. This means, in turn, that an appropriate set of limits and authorities must be developed for each portfolio of business and for each type of risk (within each portfolio of business), as well as for the entire portfolio.

Market-risk limits serve to control the risk that arises from changes in the absolute price (or rate) of an asset. Credit-risk limits serve to control and limit the number of defaults as well as limiting a downward migration in the quality of the credit portfolio (e.g., the loan book). The bank will also want to set tight policies regarding exposure to both asset/liability management risk and market liquidity risk, especially in the case of illiquid products.

The exact nature of each limit varies quite widely, depending upon the bank's activities, size, and sophistication. It is best practice for insti-

FIGURE 4-2

Interdependence for Managing Risk

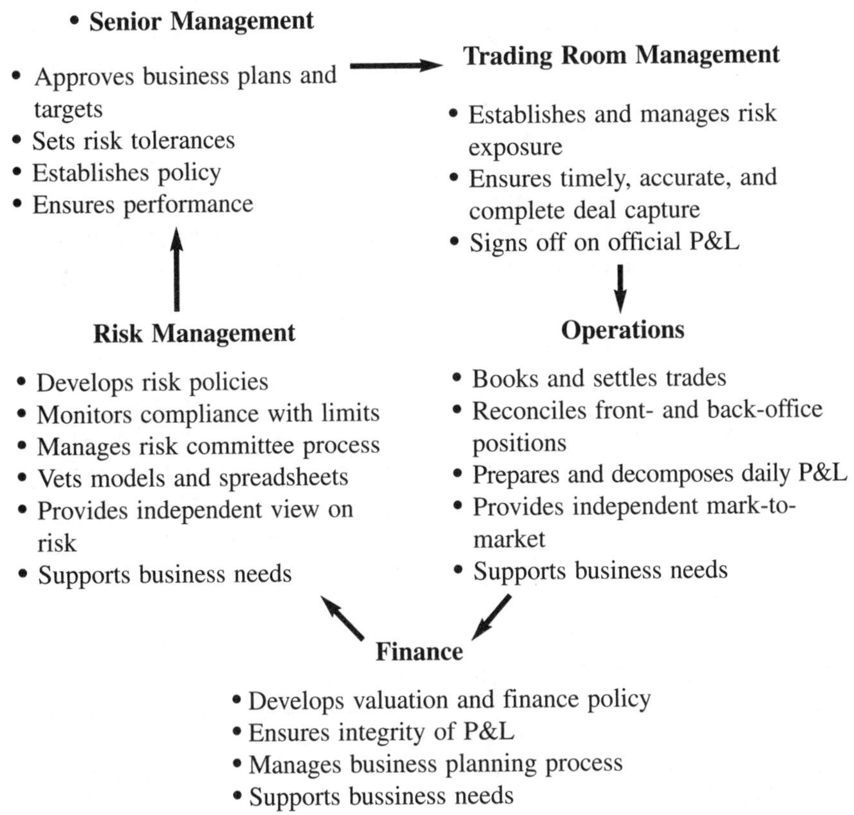

• **Senior Management**

Trading Room Management

• Approves business plans and ⟶
  targets
• Sets risk tolerances
• Establishes policy
• Ensures performance

• Establishes and manages risk
  exposure
• Ensures timely, accurate, and
  complete deal capture
• Signs off on official P&L

Risk Management   **Operations**

• Develops risk policies
• Monitors compliance with limits
• Manages risk committee process
• Vets models and spreadsheets
• Provides independent view on
  risk
• Supports business needs

• Books and settles trades
• Reconciles front- and back-office
  positions
• Prepares and decomposes daily P&L
• Provides independent mark-to-
  market
• Supports business needs

Finance

• Develops valuation and finance policy
• Ensures integrity of P&L
• Manages business planning process
• Supports bussiness needs

tutions to set down on paper the process by which they establish risk limits, review risk exposures, and approve limit exceptions, and to develop an analytic methodology used to calculate the bank's risk exposures.

At many banks, best-practice risk governance will call for the development and implementation of sophisticated risk metrics, such as value-at-risk (VaR) measures for market risk and credit risk or potential exposure limits by risk grade for credit risk.

As we discuss further in Chapter 7, risk-sensitive measures such as VaR are good at expressing risk in normal market conditions and for most kinds of portfolios, but less good in extreme circumstances or for specialized portfolios (e.g., certain kinds of option portfolios). So limits should also be related to scenario and stress-testing measures to make sure the bank can survive extreme volatility in the markets.

Most institutions employ two types of limits—let's call them limit type A and limit type B. Type A (often referred to as tier 1) limits might include a single overall limit for each asset class (e.g., a single limit for interest-rate products), as well as a single overall stress-test limit and a cumulative loss from peak limit. Type B (often referred to as tier 2) limits are more general and cover authorized business and concentration limits (e.g., by credit class, industry, maturity, region, and so on).

The setting of the risk limit level in terms of a particular metric should be consistent with certain underlying standards for risk limits (proposed by the risk management function and approved by the senior risk committee).

It's not realistic on practical grounds to set limits so that they are likely to be fully utilized in the normal course of events—that would be bound to lead to limit transgressions. Instead, limit setting needs to take into account an assessment of the business unit's historical usage of limits. For example, type A limits for market risk might be set at a level such that the business, in the normal course of its activities and in normal markets, has exposures of about 40 percent to 60 percent of its limit. Peak usage of limits, in normal markets, should generate exposures of perhaps 85 percent of the limit.

A consistent limit structure helps a bank to consolidate its approach to risk across many businesses and activities. Additionally, if the limits are expressed in a common language of risk, such as economic capital, then type B limits can be made fungible across business lines. Nevertheless, such transfers would require the joint approval of the head of a business and the CRO.

STANDARDS FOR MONITORING RISK

Once a bank has set out its risk limits in a way that is meaningful to its business lines, how should it monitor those limits to make sure they are followed? Let's take the example of market risk, which is perhaps the most time-sensitive of limits.

First, all market-risk positions should be valued daily. Units that are independent of traders should prepare daily profit and loss statements and provide them to (nontrading) senior management. All the assumptions used in models to price transactions and to value positions should be independently verified.

There should be timely and meaningful reports to measure the compliance of the trading team with risk policy and risk limits. There should be a timely escalation procedure for any limit exceptions or transgressions, i.e., it should be clear what a manager must do if his or her subordinates breach the limits.

The variance between the actual volatility of the value of a portfolio and that predicted by means of the bank's risk methodology should be evaluated. Stress simulations should be executed to determine the impact of major market- or credit-risk changes on the P&L.

The bank must distinguish between data used for monitoring type A limits (where data must be independent of risk takers) and data used to supply other kinds of management information. For other types of analysis, where timeliness is the key requirement, risk managers may be forced to use front-office systems as the most appropriate sources. For example, real-time risk measurement, such as that used to monitor intraday trading exposures, may simply have to be derived from front-office systems.

But data used in limit monitoring must be

- Independent of the front office
- Reconciled with the official books of the bank in order to ensure their integrity;
- Derived from consolidated data feeds
- In a data format that allows risk to be properly measured, e.g., it might employ the market-risk VaR or credit-risk VaR methodology

Business units should be under strict orders to advise the risk management function that they might exceed a limit well before the limit excess happens. For example, there might be an alert when an exposure is at, say, 85 percent of the type A or type B limit. The CRO, jointly with the head of the business line, might then petition the senior risk committee of the bank for a temporary increase in limits. The business risk committee should also approve the need for an increase in limits prior to the request's being passed to the senior risk committee of the bank.

If risk management is advised of a planned excess, then it should be more likely that the excess will be approved—this gives the business unit a necessary incentive to provide early warnings.

What happens if the limit is breached? The risk management function, as illustrated in Figure 4-3, should immediately put any excess on a daily "limit type A or limit type B exception report," with an appropriate

FIGURE 4-3

Limit Excess Escalation Procedure

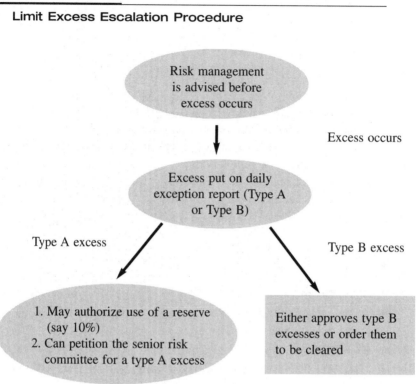

explanation and a plan of action to cope with the excess. The head of risk management may authorize the use of a reserve.

Limit type A excesses must be cleared or corrected immediately. Limit type B excesses should be cleared or approved within a relatively short time frame—say, a week. The risk managers should then report all limit excesses across the bank on an exception report, which may be discussed at a daily risk meeting and which should distinguish between limit type A and type B excesses. No manager should have the power to exclude excesses from the daily excess report.

It should be noted that when limits become effective, they impose a hidden cost: the bank cannot assume additional risk and thus may have to give up profitable opportunities. As a limit is approached, the opportunity cost of the limit should be evaluated, so that the bank can decide in good order whether or not the limit should be relaxed.

WHAT IS THE ROLE OF THE AUDIT FUNCTION?

We've set out, in general terms, a risk management process that should be able to support best-practice risk governance. But how does the board know that the executives and business managers are living up to the board's stated intentions (and to minimum legal and regulatory requirements)?

The answer lies in the bank's audit function and the periodic investigations it carries out across the bank. A key role of the audit function is to provide an independent assessment of the design and implementation of the bank's risk management.

For example, regulatory guidelines typically call for internal audit groups to review the overall risk management process. This means addressing the adequacy of documentation, the effectiveness of the process, the integrity of the risk management system, the organization of the risk control unit, the integration of risk measures into daily risk management, and so on.

Let's again take the example of market risk. Regulatory guidelines typically call for auditors to address the approval process for vetting derivatives pricing models and valuation systems used by front- and back-office personnel, the validation of any significant change in the risk measurement process, and the scope of risks captured by the risk measurement model.

Regulators also require that internal auditors examine the integrity of the management information system and the independence, accuracy, and completeness of position data.

Above and beyond any local regulatory requirements, a key audit objective should be to evaluate the design and conceptual soundness of the risk measures (including the methodologies associated with stress testing). Internal auditors should verify the accuracy of models through an examination of the back-testing process.

Audit should also evaluate the soundness of elements of the risk management information system (the "risk MIS"), such as the processes used for coding and implementation of internal models. This should include examining controls over market position data capture, as well as controls over the parameter estimation processes (e.g., volatility and correlation assumptions).

Audit responsibilities often include providing assurance as to the design and conceptual soundness of the financial rates database that is used to generate parameters entered into the market VaR and credit VaR analytic engines. Audit also reviews the adequacy and effectiveness of the procedures for monitoring risk, the progress of plans to upgrade risk management systems, the adequacy and effectiveness of application controls within the risk MIS, and the reliability of the vetting processes.

Audit should also examine the documentation relating to compliance with the qualitative/quantitative criteria outlined in any regulatory guidelines. Audit should comment on the reliability of any value-at-risk reporting framework.

Box 4-6 sets out in general terms what a statement of audit's findings on the risk management function might look like. It also helps to make clear the dangers that might arise from any confusion between the role of risk management and that of audit. Box 4-7, in contrast, looks at an approach to scoring the risk management function that might be adopted by third parties, such as rating agencies, that need to compare the risk management structures of many different organizations.

BOX 4-6

EXAMPLE: STATEMENT OF AUDIT FINDINGS

If all is well from a risk management perspective, then audit should state that adequate processes exist for providing reliable risk control and ensuring compliance with local regulatory criteria (e.g., the 1998 BIS Capital Accord).

For example, in short form, the audit group's conclusion regarding risk control in a bank trading business might be that:

1. The risk control unit is independent of the business units.
2. The internal risk models are utilized by business management.
3. The bank's risk measurement model captures all material risks.

Furthermore, if all is well, then the audit group should state that adequate and effective processes exist for:

1. Risk-pricing models and valuation systems used by front- and back-office personnel
2. Documenting the risk management systems and processes
3. Validation of any significant change in the risk measurement process
4. Ensuring the integrity of the risk management information system
5. Position data capture (and that any positions that are not captured do not materially affect risk reporting)

(continued on following page)

BOX 4-6 *(Continued)*

6. The verification of the consistency, timeliness, and reliability of data sources used to run internal models, and that the data sources are independent
7. Ensuring the accuracy and appropriateness of volatility and correlation assumptions
8. Ensuring the accuracy of the valuation and risk transformation calculations
9. The verification of the model's accuracy through frequent back testing

BOX 4-7

IS IT POSSIBLE TO SCORE THE QUALITY OF AN INSTITUTION'S RISK MANAGEMENT?

In much of this chapter, we talk about establishing the right structures for best-practice risk governance. But is there any way to score risk management practice across an institution so that both the institution itself and external observers can gain some objective idea of the institution's risk management culture and standards?

One of the authors has worked with a credit rating agency to construct such a score.

Under this approach, the risks underlying each aspect of the enterprise risk management function within institutions are assessed using a questionnaire tailored along three key dimensions:

- Policies, e.g., is the tolerance for risk consistent with the business strategy? Is risk properly communicated internally and externally?
- Methodologies, e.g., are the risk methodologies tied into performance measurement? Are the mathematical models properly vetted? Does senior management understand the risks in the models?
- Infrastructure, e.g., are the appropriate people and operational processes (such as data, software, systems, and quality of personnel) in place to control and report on the risks?

(continued on following page)

B O X   4 - 7 *(Continued)*

The basic PMI (policies, methodologies, infrastructure) framework can be used for most industries, while within each of the three key dimensions, more detailed questions can be developed that tackle aspects relevant to a particular industry.

For example, for trading financial institutions, we might require a description of the process around limits delegation for market risk and credit risk (as it pertains to the trading book).

Gathering this information involves supplying questionnaires and also scheduling the time of senior management at the trading institution for review sessions. The completed assessments would be presented to an internal committee at the rating agency, where the primary credit analyst will take them into consideration in the rating agency's overall review of the institution.

A negative assessment could affect the credit rating of the institution—a clear indicator of how important the nexus between risk management, corporate governance, and risk disclosure has become.

There has been some discussion in the banking industry about whether the audit function should control the operational risk management function at the bank—after all, audit has a natural interest in the quality of internal controls.

Unfortunately, allowing the audit function to develop a bank's operational risk management function is an error. Audit's independence from the risk management function is a prerequisite for the value of any assurances it gives to the board. Unless this independence is preserved, there is a danger that audit will end up trying to give an independent opinion about the quality of risk management activities that audit itself has designed or helped administer. This would imply a classic conflict of interest right at the heart of bank risk governance.

CONCLUSION: STEPS TO SUCCESS

In complex risk-taking organizations, it's not really possible to separate best-practice risk management from best-practice corporate governance.

Boards can't monitor and control the financial condition of a risk-taking institution without excellent risk management and risk metrics.

Meanwhile, the risk management function depends on sponsors at the senior executive and board level to gain the investment it requires—and the influence it needs to balance out powerful business leaders.

It's worth stressing an important lesson of business history: many fatal risks in a corporation are associated with business strategies that at first look like runaway successes. It's only later on that the overlooked or discounted risks come home to roost.

At a best-practice institution, everything flows from a clear and agreed-upon risk management policy at the top. For example, senior management must approve a clear notion of the institution's risk appetite and how this can be linked to a system of limits and risk metrics.

Without this kind of platform, it's very difficult for risk managers further down the management chain to make key decisions on how they approach and measure risk. For example, without a clearly communicated concept of an institution's risk appetite, how would risk managers define a "worst-case risk" in any extreme risk scenario analysis?

The risk committees of the institution also need to be involved, to some degree, in setting the basic risk measurement methodologies employed by the institution. Most banks know that they have to be able to define their risk in terms of market risk and credit risk, but banks are now extending their risk measurement framework to include operational risk. It's important that risk committees understand the strengths and weaknesses of any new operational-risk metrics if they are to make sense of risk reports.

There are also unavoidable strategic, political, and investment reasons why the board and top executive management must be closely involved in determining an institution's risk management strategy. Without their involvement, how can the managers of the institution agree on a credible organizational infrastructure that avoids both gaps and duplications in risk oversight? The key to designing an efficient organization is to ensure that the roles and responsibilities of each risk mechanism and unit are carefully spelled out and remain complementary to one another.

We should not think of board and top management time spent on risk management as time spent on purely on the defensive "risk control" aspects of the business. A best-practice risk system can be applied to gain offensive advantages. A board with a sound understanding of the risk profile of its key existing or anticipated business lines can support aggressive strategic decisions with much more confidence. Sophisticated risk measures such as VaR and economic capital offer a way of setting risk limits, but they are also vital in helping the institution decide which business lines are profitable (once risk is taken into account).

Ideally, businesses would use the risk infrastructure as a tactical management tool in deal analysis and pricing, to help make sure that risk management and business decisions are aligned.

A joined-up approach to corporate governance and risk management has become a critical component of a globally integrated best-practice institution—from board level to business line.

CHAPTER 5

A User-Friendly Guide to the Theory of Risk and Return

While risk management is a practical activity, it cannot be understood independently of a fast-developing body of academic research about risk and reward. For example, the problem of how investors perceive the riskiness of an individual firm cannot be separated from modern theories about the interaction of risky securities in a large investment portfolio. Likewise, a decision about whether to spend money on managing a market-risk position should be shaped by a working knowledge of the theoretical models that have been devised to price options and futures contracts. It's also difficult to work out the trade-off between retaining and avoiding risk without some reference to the theory of risk valuation: risk management does not mean the complete elimination of risk.

In this chapter, we review four key theoretical models and demonstrate how they relate to both one another and the practice of risk management. Using straightforward language, we'll look at modern portfolio theory, the capital asset pricing model (CAPM), the classic Black-Scholes approach to pricing an option, and the Modigliani-Miller theory of corporate finance.

Like all theories of risk management, these approaches are based on simplifying assumptions. Real life is complicated and includes many details that models cannot, and maybe should not, accommodate. The role of models is to highlight the most important factors and the relationships among these factors. A "good" financial model is one that helps the analyst separate the wheat from the chaff, that is, the major explanatory variables from a noisy background.

As Milton Friedman made clear in his 1953 seminal article "The Methodology of Positive Economics," a model should be evaluated only in terms of its predictive power.[1] It can be simple and yet be judged successful if it helps predict the future and improves the efficiency of the decision-making process.

HARRY MARKOWITZ AND PORTFOLIO SELECTION

The foundations of modern risk analysis are to be found in a seminal paper by Harry Markowitz written in 1952, based on his Ph.D. dissertation at the University of Chicago, concerning the principles of portfolio selection.[2] (Markowitz was awarded the Nobel Prize in Economics for this research in 1990.)

Markowitz showed that rational investors select their investment portfolio using two basic parameters: expected profit and risk. While "profit" is measured in terms of the average (mean) rate of return, "risk" is measured in terms of how much returns vary around this average rate of return. The greater the variance of the returns, the riskier the portfolio.

When building a portfolio, investors like to reduce variance as much as possible by diversifying their investments. To put it simply, they avoid putting all their eggs in one basket. Even better, by investing in assets that fluctuate in different directions, investors can actively offset the specific risks inherent in individual stocks. (We can see the same behavior in individual firms: following such a business strategy, for example, Head Corp., which focused initially on ski equipment, diversified into supplying tennis equipment. This strategic move helped to reduce the impact of weather and season on its periodic profits.)

As a result, according to Markowitz, investors select financial assets, such as stocks and bonds, for their portfolio based on each asset's contribution to the portfolio's *overall* mean and variance. It follows that we must think of the risk of a single investment not in terms of its own variance, but in terms of its interaction with other assets in the portfolio.

Through the power of portfolio diversification, investors can dilute (i.e., reduce) the risk that is specific to an individual stock at virtually no cost. While it is true that the mitigation of risk may also lead to the lowering of expected profits, if assets are selected carefully, then diversification can allow investors to achieve a higher rate of return for a given level of risk.

---

1. M. Friedman, "The Methodology of Positive Economics," in *Essays in Positive Economics* (Chicago: University of Chicago Press, 1953).

2. H. M. Markowitz, "Portfolio Selection," *Journal of Finance* 7, 1952, pp. 77–91.

FIGURE 5-1

The Efficient Frontier of Markowitz

Expected return

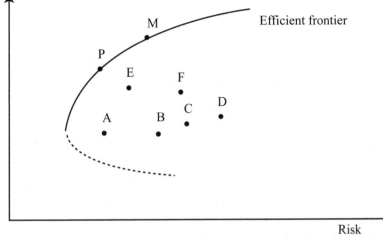

Risk
(standard deviation)

To the extent that investors succeed in achieving this state, they arrive at the *efficient frontier*, represented by the curved solid line in Figure 5-1. Put formally, this efficient frontier contains all portfolios of assets such that there are no other portfolios (or assets) that for a given amount of risk (in terms of standard deviation of rates of return) offer a higher expected rate of return.

For example, portfolio P in Figure 5-1 has the same amount of risk as portfolio A, but P has a higher expected rate of return. There is no portfolio in Figure 5-1 with the same amount of risk as P that also exhibits a higher expected rate of return than P.

Once a portfolio contains only assets that are on the efficient frontier, it can be seen that a higher expected rate of return can be achieved *only* by increasing the riskiness of the portfolio. Conversely, a less risky portfolio can be achieved *only* by reducing the expected return on the portfolio. The lower part of the frontier, which contains all the inefficient assets and portfolios, is represented by a dotted line. It indicates the most inefficient combinations of assets with the lowest possible expected return for a given level of risk.

We can extend this concept to consider the whole investment market. In this framework, if the market is in equilibrium, then portfolio M, the "market portfolio," will include all risky assets in the economy, each entering the portfolio in a proportion equal to its relative market value. For example, an imperfect but often useful proxy for all the risky equity assets in the economy of the United States is the S&P 500 index.

However, in this market portfolio, the power of diversification means that the specific, or idiosyncratic, risk of a security is not much taken into account by the market in its pricing of a security. So what kind of risk actually affects the risk/reward calculations of investors building an investment portfolio?

THE CAPITAL ASSET PRICING MODEL (CAPM)

In the mid-1960s, William Sharpe and John Lintner took the portfolio approach to risk management one step further by introducing a model based on overall capital market equilibrium.[3] For this breakthrough, Sharpe was awarded the Nobel Prize in 1990. (Lintner, a finance professor at Harvard Business School, had passed away many years earlier.) Building on Markowitz, the two professors showed that the risk of an individual asset can be decomposed into two portions:

1. Risk that can indeed be neutralized through diversification (called diversifiable or specific risk)
2. Risk that cannot be eliminated through diversification (called systematic risk)

To build their CAPM, Sharpe and Linter made the assumption that investors can choose to invest in any combination of a risk-free asset and a "market portfolio" that includes all the risky assets in an economy. Investors therefore weight their personal portfolios as a combination of these two investment vehicles, in various proportions based on their "risk appetite."

This conception allowed Sharpe and Lintner to define the premium that investors demand for taking on the risk of the market portfolio, as opposed to investing in the risk-free asset. This "market risk premium" is

---

3. W. F. Sharpe, "Capital Asset Prices: A Theory of Market Equilibrium under Conditions of Risk," *Journal of Finance* 19, 1964, pp. 425–442. J. Lintner, "Security Prices, Risk and Maximal Gains from Diversification," *Journal of Finance* 20, 1965, pp. 587–615.

simply the difference between the expected rate of return on the risky market portfolio and the risk-free rate.

For example, we might determine the market risk premium by subtracting the interest rate on an asset that is free of default risk, such as a certificate of deposit or U.S. Treasury bill, from the expected return on a market index such as the Dow Jones or S&P 500. (Agreeing upon the exact market risk premium evident in real-world data has proved to be a lively area of debate among financial economists, but we won't allow these technicalities to detain us here.)

Estimates of the market risk premium tell us how much investors have to be paid to take on some notional "average" amount of market risk generated by the complete market portfolio. But how can we estimate the risk, and the risk premium, for an individual asset?

Well, according to the CAPM, if the market is in equilibrium, the price (and, hence, the expected return) of a given asset will reflect the relative contribution of that asset to the total risk of the market portfolio. In the CAPM, this contribution is accounted for by means of a factor called beta (β). (Beta is often referred to as systematic risk in the wider literature.)

More formally, an asset's beta is a measure of the covariance between that asset's return and the return on the market, divided by the market's variance.

From an investor's perspective, beta represents that portion of an asset's total risk that cannot be neutralized by diversification in a portfolio of risky assets, and for which some compensation must be demanded. Put another way, the more beta risk a portfolio manager assumes, by investing in higher-beta securities, the higher the risk and also the higher the expected future rate of return of the portfolio.

Beta is the key to working out the expected return on an individual asset. We can think of this expected return as consisting of the interest on the riskless asset (invested over the same time period as the holding period of the asset), plus the market risk premium adjusted by beta. This can be represented more formally as

Expected rate of return on security = risk-free interest rate

+ beta risk × (expected rate of return on the market portfolio − risk-free interest rate)

Figure 5-2 is based on Sharpe's work. It shows the *market line*, which depicts the linear relationship between the expected rate of return on any

FIGURE 5-2

The Market Line Connecting the Beta Risk and Individual
Assets and their Expected Rates of Return

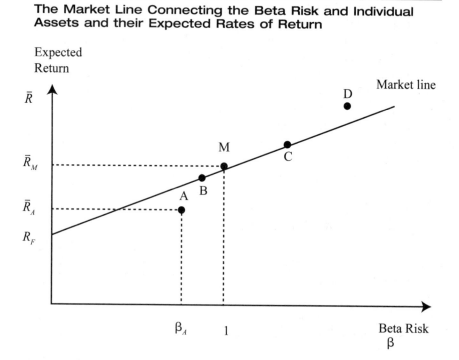

asset and its systematic risk as measured in relation to assets that are
beta-efficient.

In Figure 5-2, the intersection with the vertical axis yields the risk-
free interest rate, R_F. This rate of return reflects the yield on an asset with
zero beta. Assets B and C are beta-efficient, since they lie on the market
line; C is riskier than B, and therefore is expected to yield a higher return.
M, the market portfolio, is also beta-efficient, as its beta is 1, by definition. Asset A is inferior, since it lies under the line, meaning that another
asset (or a portfolio of assets) can be found with the same amount of beta
risk, but with a higher expected rate of return. Asset D is a "winner," since
it is expected to yield more in relation to its risk than assets on the market line. But if participants in the financial market realize that D is superior, they will increase the demand for D, putting pressure on its price. As
the price of this asset rises, its rate of return can be expected to fall until
D lies on the market line.

So how does beta vary across different kinds of securities? Well, as
a baseline, we can think of the beta factor for a risk-free asset as zero,

since the returns of that asset are indifferent to fluctuations in the capital market. Likewise, the beta of the complete market portfolio is 1, since by definition the market portfolio expresses the average beta risk for the whole market and thus requires no adjustment to take into account the specific risk of a stock. The beta of an individual stock (or other financial asset) can have any positive or negative value, depending upon its characteristics.

Let us illustrate this last point with a numerical example based on U.S. historical data. The average rate of return on the New York Stock Exchange CRSP (Center for Research in Security Prices) index over 70 years is approximately 15 percent. The average risk-free rate on risk-free U.S. government bonds is approximately 6 percent. Hence the market risk premium, on average, is 9 percent.

Now, if a given stock has a beta risk estimated at 0.8, its expected rate of return is 6 percent + 0.8(9 percent) = 13.2 percent. If the past is prologue (i.e., predicts the future), then we can expect the average rate of return on the market index to be 15 percent and the average rate of return on the specific stock to be 13.2 percent.

In this example, beta is positive but rather lower than the market average of 1. If the beta of a stock is higher than 1, the stock is considered "aggressive," or riskier than the market portfolio. Conversely, if the beta is lower than 1, the stock is considered "defensive," as it will have a mitigating effect on the total risk of the portfolio.

Figure 5-3, taken from Bloomberg L.P., shows the estimate of beta for IBM stock, based on weekly rates of return, for the period March 9, 2001, to February 28, 2003. The beta is estimated as the slope coefficient of a regression line of the rates of return for IBM on the rates of return for the market index. The regression line points to a raw, unadjusted beta of 1.17.

The most interesting class of assets is that defined as having a negative beta. Negative beta denotes an asset, such as gold, that consistently moves counter to market trends—when prices in the market tend to move up, this asset tends to lose value, and vice versa. Investment in such an asset serves to lower the risk of a portfolio without necessarily reducing its expected return.

When a market is in equilibrium, the chances of finding such a jewel are virtually nil. Market forces will naturally work to drive the price of this kind of asset up, bringing down its future expected rate of return. In other words, to reduce the riskiness of their portfolios, investors will have to sacrifice some reward.

FIGURE 5-3

Raw Beta Computation for IBM

<HELP> for explanation, <MENU> for similar functions.

DG25 **Equity BETA**

HISTORICAL BETA

IBM US Equity   **SPX**

INTL BUSINESS MACHINES CORP

Relative Index   S&P 500 INDEX

Period   **W** Weekly
Range   **3/02/01** To **2/28/03**
Market   **T** Trade

ADJ BETA	1.11
RAW BETA	1.17
Alpha (Intercept)	0.28
R2 (Correlation)	0.45
Std Dev of Error	3.86
Std Error of Beta	0.13
Number of Points	103

ADJ BETA = (0.67) * RAW BETA
  + (0.33) * 1.0

Source: Bloomberg.

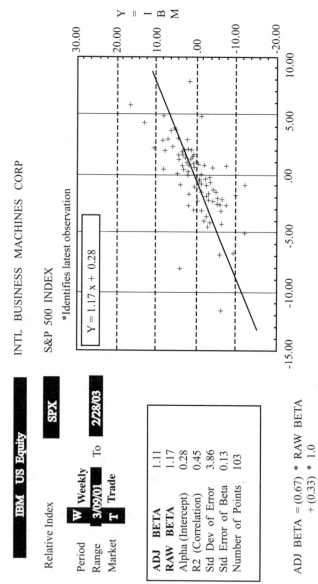

*Identifies latest observation

$Y = 1.17 x + 0.28$

The CAPM has become a key tool of financial economists in understanding the behavior that can be seen in the capital markets every day. But the beta of a stock is not simply a concern of investors; it's important to the managers of any company who are concerned about share price and the creation of shareholder value. Beta has numerous day-to-day implications for managers. For example, many firms employ a hurdle rate of return to assess whether a new investment is worthwhile in terms of building shareholder value. This hurdle rate is based upon the unique rate of return that the firm thinks investors demand; that is, it is based more or less explicitly upon assumptions the firm makes about its beta factor (or about the beta factor of any new project it is considering for an investment). If the firm misunderstands the demands of investors, it is likely to set the wrong hurdle rate. If it sets its target rate of return too high, it will turn down worthwhile investments; if it sets the target too low, it will make investments that offer too low a return. Either way, it will drive down its beta-adjusted returns and make its stock less attractive to investors on a risk-adjusted basis.

As we discuss in Chapter 15, corporations use a range of related new risk-adjusted measures to better understand the real rate of return they offer to investors. Banks increasingly use a measure called risk-adjusted return on capital (RAROC), and nonfinancial corporations often use a related measure called economic value added (EVA). The implementation of these performance measures necessitates the estimation of the beta factor for a given activity or division of the corporation.

HOW TO PRICE AN OPTION

The next important development in the analysis of risk arrived in 1973 with the publication of two papers on the pricing of options by Fischer Black and Myron Scholes and by Robert Merton.[4] At the time of the publication of their seminal paper, Black and Scholes were professors at the University of Chicago, while Merton was a professor at MIT. In 1998, Merton and Scholes received the Nobel Prize. (Black had passed away in 1995.)

Options are financial assets that entitle their holders to purchase or sell another asset by or on a predetermined day, at a predetermined price

---

4. F. Black and M. Scholes, "The Pricing of Options and Corporate Liabilities," *Journal of Political Economy* 81, 1973, pp. 637–654; R. C. Merton, "Theory of Rational Option Pricing," *Bell Journal of Economics and Management Science* 4(1), 1973, pp. 141–183.

called the striking price. An option to buy the asset is referred to as a *call*, while an option to sell the asset is called a *put*. (See also Chapter 6.)

The price paid up front for the call option is generally a fraction of the current price of the underlying asset on which the option (contract) is written. The remainder is paid at the time of execution or exercise, at some point in the future. Hence, one advantage of purchasing a call option is the ability to buy an asset on credit.

At the time of exercise, the purchaser retains the right to renege on his or her intention to complete the contract. So if the asset price at the time of exercise is lower than the price set in the option contract, the purchaser of the call can opt to let the contract expire. In effect, the call option offers a form of price insurance.

Figure 5-4 describes the cash flow from a call option at maturity (i.e., when it expires). The option has zero cash flow at maturity so long as the price of the underlying instrument is below the striking price (exercise price) *K*. For prices above the striking price, the owner of the call is entitled to the difference between the price of the underlying instrument and the striking price. This latter cash flow is described by the sloping line, increasing from point *K* to the right as the price of the underlying asset rises.

FIGURE 5-4

The Payoff for a Call Option at Maturity

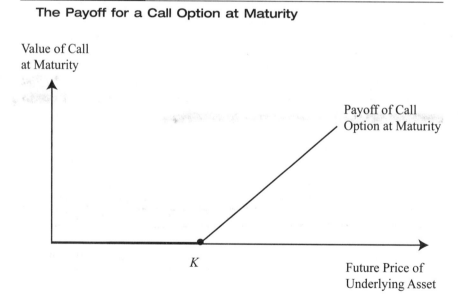

For a put option, the reverse is true. The buyer pays for the right to sell a stock in the future at a preset price. That exercise price constitutes a guaranteed minimum price. On the other hand, if the market price of the asset is higher than the price the put purchaser would receive from exercising the put, he or she can choose to ignore the option contract and opt instead to sell the asset on the open market for its full price. So a put option, held with the underlying asset, provides insurance against a reduction in value of the underlying asset to below the exercise price.

In their publications in 1973, Black and Scholes (frequently referred to as B&S in the literature) developed a classic model for pricing options. Merton, who collaborated with B&S, also published his important paper in 1973, offering an alternative way to prove the valuation model and many additional extensions. Moreover, in addition to calculating equilibrium market prices for publicly traded options, this model specified the various components of an option and their interrelationships.

For example, as we've discussed already, a call option can be characterized as a "package deal" that includes

- Buying a stock (or other asset)
- Taking out a loan
- Buying insurance

It can be shown that over a very short time interval, a call option can be decomposed into buying a certain ratio of the underlying instrument (this ratio is referred to as the "delta" of the option) and taking out a loan (with the amount of the loan being proportional to the probability that the option will be exercised). Options theory has proved invaluable to portfolio and risk management. Using these ideas, portfolio managers can dynamically tailor investment positions to reflect changing expectations, market conditions, and client needs. Purchasing puts against the assets held in a portfolio is synonymous with taking out insurance on those assets. Purchasing and selling combinations of calls and puts can help investors maneuver in volatile or uncertain markets. (See a discussion of options as risk mitigators in Chapter 6.)

The detailed mathematics that lie behind the B&S model is somewhat complex and is not readily calculated without the aid of computer technology. But the functions that govern an option's price are quite intuitive. Simply stated, the price of an option is a function of

- The price of the underlying asset
- The exercise (or striking) price set in the contract

- The prevailing risk-free rate of interest
- The volatility of the underlying asset
- The time remaining until the predetermined exercise date

If the stock price increases and we hold all the other parameters constant, then the value of the call option increases. Similarly, if the exercise price declines or the maturity increases, then the value of the call option increases. As the underlying asset becomes more volatile, the value of the call increases. This is because a call option has no downside risk, that is, no matter how far the call is out-of-the-money at expiration, its value is still zero, while increasing volatility increases the probability that the option will end up in-the-money at maturity, i.e., the stock price is more likely to reach a higher value. Furthermore, as the interest rate increases, the value of the call increases (because the present value of the exercise payment in the event of exercise declines as interest rates increase). Similar arguments hold for put options, although the sensitivity of the put options to some of the factors is reversed.

Of all these factors, the most crucial to the valuation and risk management of an option is the volatility of the underlying asset. It's often said that options are "risk-friendly": an increase in the volatility (i.e., an increase in the risk) of the underlying asset, assuming that all other parameters remain constant, leads to an increase in the price of the option, both for calls and for puts. As you may recall, volatility is measured in terms of the standard deviation (the square root of the variance) of the rate of return for the underlying asset during some selected historical period.

In applying historical data to the calculation of future volatilities, we are making a problematic assumption: that volatility remains constant over time. Where there are liquid options markets, however, the B&S model offers one way of working around this problem. Remember that the B&S model offers a way to price options provided that we have access to the inputs, listed earlier. On the other hand, if we already have the price of an option from a liquid options market, then we can use this "output" as one of the inputs. The formula can then be used to calculate a missing input, such as volatility. In effect, using the B&S formula in this way is computing the volatilities *implied* by the prices of options in the market. That's why this number is often simply called "implied volatility."

Implied volatilities are of tremendous practical importance to those who regularly trade options in the market, and they are often re-input into the B&S model to calculate the price of a slightly different option series with different exercise prices or maturities. But because implied volatility cannot be directly observed and is dependent on the model, it has in the past been a weak link in the operational risk management of option desks. A trader who prices option positions for risk management purposes using an implied volatility number that he or she computes from the market can be faced with some severe temptations. In the past, traders at certain investment banks have deliberately input wrong implied volatility numbers to transform the apparent value of their under-the-water options portfolio. Implied volatility is a particular worry, because it's the one input into the B&S model that cannot be checked by an auditor without some degree of specialized knowledge. This is one example of how issues surrounding the principles of risk modeling affect the operational practice of risk management, a theme we'll return to in Chapter 14.

The B&S model also provides insights into how options introduced into a portfolio of financial assets interact with those assets and affect the overall risk of the portfolio. The systematic risk (beta) of a call or put option is a function of the beta of the underlying asset, multiplied by the *elasticity* of the call or put. By elasticity, we mean the percentage change in the value of the option for a 1 percent change in the price of the underlying security. The model determines that the elasticity of a call is positive and greater or equal to 1, while the elasticity of a put is less than or equal to 0. Hence, adding call options to a portfolio will tend to increase the overall risk of the portfolio (assuming a positive beta), while adding puts will have a mitigating effect on a portfolio's risk. Shorting calls, i.e., writing call options, can also have a mitigating effect on the portfolio risk, since such a position has a negative beta.

The B&S model can also be used to compute the *hedge ratio* of an option position, also known as the *delta*. This ratio describes the change in value of an option resulting from a small change in the price of the underlying asset. The hedge ratio indicates how the risk of a financial asset can be hedged with options. The price of both the underlying asset and the options changes over time, so the hedge ratio is in fact dynamic, requiring that adjustments to the portfolio be made in order to maintain a target level of hedging. The hedge ratio of a call is between 0 and 1, and the delta of a put option is between -1 and 0.

For example, imagine that the delta of a call option that is slightly out-of-the-money is 0.5, meaning that if the price of the underlying stock increases (decreases) by \$1, the value of the call increases (decreases) by \$0.50. This implies that if we want to neutralize, over a short time horizon, the risk of a long position in a call contract on 100 shares, we should sell short 50 shares.

The insights of the model introduced by Black and Scholes in the 1970s have led to further applied research in finance, particularly in relation to volatility. For example, in the last two decades, in reaction to evidence that volatility in financial markets may undergo major shifts in its behavior over time (more technically, that it is "nonstationary"), researchers have begun to make use of a more dynamic approach to financial asset valuation. In particular, Robert Engle, a statistics professor (previously at San Diego and currently at New York University) and a leading researcher in this area, introduced the ARCH (autoregressive conditional heteroskedasticity) volatility model during the 1980s in an attempt to estimate volatility as an "auto-regressive" process. The key feature of the model is that it treats today's volatility as a function of the previous day's volatility and also introduces a correction factor for deviations from an expected volatility. (Robert Engle was the recipient of the Nobel Prize in Economics in 2003 for his work on volatility modeling.)

MODIGLIANI AND MILLER (M&M)

In order to complete this brief introduction to the theoretical basis of modern risk management, we must turn to the work published by Franco Modigliani and Merton Miller in 1958 (for which they were both awarded the Nobel Prize in Economics in 1985).[5] Their work does not directly involve financial markets, but rather focuses on corporate finance. Modigliani and Miller showed that in a perfect capital market, with no corporate or income taxes, the capital structure of a firm (i.e., the relative balance between equity and debt capital) has no effect on the value of the firm.

The implication of their work is that a corporation cannot increase its value by assuming greater debt, despite the fact that the expected cost of debt is lower than the expected cost of equity. Increasing the leverage of a firm (i.e., taking on more debt relative to equity) means increasing the financial risk of that firm. Hence, equity holders (whose claims on the firm's assets are subordinate to those of lenders and bond holders) will demand compensation for this risk and expect higher rates of return. It's a variation on the theme that has run through this chapter: investors look not for higher returns, but for higher risk-adjusted returns.

---

5. F. Modigliani and M. H. Miller, "The Cost of Capital, Corporation Finance, and the Theory of Investment," *American Economic Review* 4, 1958, pp. 261–297.

CONCLUSION

Many of the contributors to the academic framework that we have just outlined will accompany us throughout this book, providing an essential platform for risk analysis and evaluation.

Risk has many facets and definitions. The theoretical models help us to define risks in a consistent way and indicate which measures of risk are relevant to specific situations. They also point up the importance of

- Eliminating arbitrage opportunities when valuing financial instruments and positions
- The critical difference between idiosyncratic (specific) risk and systematic risk
- The dependence of financial modeling on key parameters and inputs

Above all, perhaps, they help us forge a rational link between the risk management perspective of the corporation and the desires of its shareholders—something that's difficult to do in any rigorous way without reference to the CAPM and related theories.

Later chapters will also underline the day-to-day advantages of promoting a basic understanding of risk modeling in a firm. Whenever firms are using models to assess risk or value assets, they will find themselves in need of statistical tools and procedures, and of up-to-date data on both the bank's transaction positions and the rates available in the wider markets. Banks must compile data from many internal sources and systems, as well as use external and historical market data for interest rates, foreign exchange rates, commodities, securities, and derivatives. The results drawn from these data—e.g., estimates of volatility and the correlation between major risk factors—are key inputs into the empirical assessment of risk. But the results depend absolutely on the completeness and accuracy of the underlying data. This is the reason why data are vital as an input into measuring and managing risk, and why it is essential that valuation models are widely disseminated and understood across the staff. In many modern banking business lines, widespread basic risk literacy—from the back office to the boardroom—has become a vital part of the "risk culture" of the corporation. In Chapter 14 we discuss model risk and many of the issues concerning the use of models, as well as using data to achieve reliable estimators of critical parameters.

CHAPTER 6

Interest-Rate Risk and Hedging with Derivative Instruments

In this chapter we look at a specific kind of market risk, namely, interest-rate risk, and at how institutions can manage the risk arising from particular interest-rate positions.

Interest-rate risk substantially affects the values of the assets and liabilities of most corporations and is often a dominant factor affecting the values of pension funds, banks, and many other financial intermediaries. For example, in 2004, according to the Office of the Comptroller of the Currency (OCC), mortgage-related assets, which include mortgages and mortgage-backed securities (MBSs), made up 28 percent of U.S. commercial banks' assets. Like fixed-interest government bonds, these assets fall in value when interest rates rise. Worse, MBSs suffer from "extension risk" because consumers have the option to extend the duration of the loan when interest rates go up (making the value of the instruments much more sensitive to rising rates); borrowers also have the option to prepay their mortgage when interest rates decline. This need not matter if banks have carefully hedged their exposure, but it can otherwise lead to huge losses.

We'll first look at measures of interest-rate risk for fixed-income instruments, and then we'll describe the key derivative instruments used to manage interest-rate risk. This chapter helps set the scene for Chapter 8, which describes how the asset-liability management (ALM) function of a financial institution manages whole portfolios of instruments to control the effect of changes, or expected changes, in interest rates.

HOW DOES INTEREST-RATE RISK ARISE?

The simplest form of interest-rate risk is the risk that the value of a fixed-income security held by an institution will change, as a result of a change in market interest rates.

As rates go up in the wider market, the value of owning an instrument offering a fixed rate of interest naturally falls (compared to the value of owning newly issued fixed-income securities that pay a higher coupon). To the extent that the security represents an open position—that is, to the extent that the position is not perfectly offset by changes in the value of other instruments in the institution's portfolio—the firm will suffer an economic loss. Open positions arise most often from differences in the maturities, nominal values, and rate reset dates between instruments and cash flows that are *asset*-like (i.e., longs) and those that are *liability*-like (i.e., shorts). A major mismatch between the maturities of assets and liabilities can lead to liquidity risk (Chapter 8). The degree to which such exposures threaten a firm depends not only on the amount held and each position's sensitivity to interest-rate changes, but also on the degree to which these sensitivities are correlated within portfolios and, more broadly, across trading desks and business lines.

Even when instruments seem at first sight to largely offset each other's economic exposure, an imperfect correlation between offsetting instruments, both within the same maturity for different issuers and across the yield curve, can generate significant risks. The yield curve, often called the *term structure of interest rates*, measures the relationship between the discount rates and the time to maturity of bonds.

Risk managers often refer to something that they call "curve risk." Curve risk arises in portfolios when long and short positions of different maturities are effectively hedged against a *parallel shift* in yields, but are not hedged against a change in the *shape of the yield curve*. Parallel shifts occur when a shock in the market has an equal effect on yields of instruments with different maturity dates; conversely, the yield curve is said to "change shape" when a shock in the market has a stronger effect on, say, the returns of shorter-dated instruments than it has on the returns of longer-dated instruments. This may affect the slope of the yield curve and its curvature.

Figure 6-1a–c shows different shapes that the yield curve can assume: flat, upward-sloping, and downward-sloping. Most of the time, as at the end of January 2005 in the United States, the yield curve was upward-sloping, with short-term rates being lower than long-term rates (Figure 6-2).

FIGURE 6-1

Yield Curves

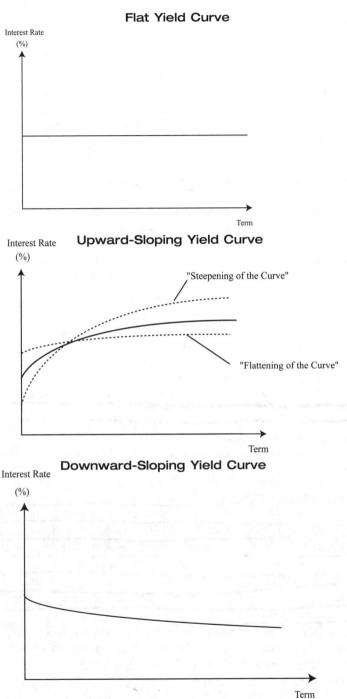

Curve risk is not the only worry. Even if offsetting positions have the same maturity, "basis" risk can arise if the rates of the positions are imperfectly correlated. For example, three-month Eurodollar instruments and three-month Treasury bills both naturally pay three-month interest rates. However, these rates are not perfectly correlated with each other, and spreads between their yields may vary over time. As a result, a three-month Treasury bill funded by three-month Eurodollar deposits represents an imperfectly hedged position.

BOND PRICE AND YIELD TO MATURITY

Bond portfolio managers and fixed-income derivatives traders keep a close eye on their screens for moves in the yield curve that affect the value of bonds and other fixed-income securities. They pay close attention to financial announcements, such as comments from the U.S. Federal Reserve, that may signal a change in the fed funds rate, which, in turn, will change the shape of the yield curve and drive bond prices up or down.

In fact, the price of a bond, as discussed in this section, can be derived directly from the term structure of interest rates for any given class of credit risk: government bonds, corporate bonds rated AAA, those rated AA, and so on. (Conversely, the yield curve can be implied from the term structure of bond prices, where this is known.)

The pricing of bonds is based on the present value concept. That is, we need to work out the value that the future cash flows associated with a security might have today. This clearly involves discounting the future cash flows to reveal their present values—but what discount rates should we use? The problem is complicated because different discount rates may apply to different kinds of bonds with different maturities. We've already covered one reason for this in our discussion of the yield curve: interest rates vary, and usually are an increasing function of time to maturity (i.e. upward sloping). Another factor that affects the relevant discount rates is the risk of the bond and, especially, its credit risk, i.e., the probability of default and the extent of the loss that is expected in such an event. A further factor that affects bond prices is liquidity risk—the risk that the market for the bond might not be liquid enough for the seller to receive a "fair" price at the time of sale.

Let us start with the valuation of, say, a 10-year U.S. government bond. This helps to clarify the problem, because government bonds can essentially be regarded as being free of credit risk. The bondholder is promised an annual fixed coupon and the payment of the principal amount at the maturity of the bond. So, if the notional amount (or principal) is $1,000 and the coupon rate is 5 percent, the bondholder will receive $50 per year for the first nine years and at the end of the 10-year period the sum of the last coupon and the principal, i.e., $1,050.

The problem we face in assessing the present value of the bond is that $50 received after, say, eight years is necessarily worth less than $50 received at the end of the first year, if only because of the opportunity cost associated with obtaining cash later rather than earlier. We can begin by discounting one dollar to be received a year from now to express the price today of one future dollar. For example, if the relevant discount rate is 10 percent per annum, then a dollar next year is worth $1/(1 + 0.1) = \$0.909$ today; that is, the price today of one dollar a year from now is 90.9 cents.

If the discount rate is also 10 percent between year 1 and year 2, then the price today of one dollar to be received after two years is $1/(1 + 0.1)^2 = \$0.826$, or 82.6 cents. It is worth 90.9 cents in terms of year 1 dollars, and $90.9/1.01 = 82.6$ cents in terms of present dollars. In Box 6-1 we give the formula for the bond price and a numerical example.

The value of the bond can therefore be found by discounting all the expected future payments by the relevant discount factors. (These discount factors are also referred to as "zero-coupon rates," referring to zero-coupon bonds, which have only a single bullet payment at maturity.) If all yearly discount rates are known, then our job is rather simple. In practice, however, we can't observe interest rates directly; dealers report only bond prices. The yield curves that traders and fund managers observe on their screens are calculated, i.e., derived implicitly, from these bond prices so that the discounted value of the scheduled coupons and redemption value of the bonds is equal to the actual observed bond prices.

Now we can ask the following question: for a given current bond price and cash-flow stream from the bond, what is the single discount yield across all coupon dates that, if applied to the cash-flow stream, will result exactly in the price of the bond? This yield is the *yield to maturity* (YTM) of a bond, and it measures the average annual yield of the bond over its lifetime, given its present price. There is a one-to-one relationship between the YTM of a bond and its price: given the stream of coupon payments, together with the redemption value and the bond price, one can derive the bond yield; conversely, given the stream of coupon payments, the redemption value, and the bond yield, one can calculate the price of the bond. In fact, many bonds are quoted not in dollars but in terms of yield (YTM). In Box 6-1 we show how to calculate the yield to maturity.

When reading the financial press or observing a quotation screen, one needs to be careful, as the loose term *yield curve* can refer in practice

BOX 6-1

VALUATION OF A BOND AND YIELD TO MATURITY

The present value of a bond is determined by

- Its stream of future cash flows, which consist of the n annual coupon payments cF during the life of the bond and the repayment of principal F at the maturity date n, with c being the coupon rate.
- Its discount curve, or zero-coupon curve, which specifies the annualized spot rates $R_1, R_2, \ldots, R_n$ at which each cash flow should be discounted to produce its present value.

The first coupon, payable in one year, has a present value of $\dfrac{cF}{1 + R_1}$.

Similarly, the coupon payable in two years has a present value of $\dfrac{cF}{(1 + R_2)^2}$. The bond has a present value that is the sum of the present values of its future cash flows:

$$P = \frac{cF}{1 + R_1} + \frac{cF}{(1 + R_2)^2} + \ldots + \frac{cF}{(1 + R_{n-1})^{n-1}} + \frac{cF + F}{(1 + R_n)^n} \qquad (6\text{-}1)$$

By definition, the yield to maturity y satisfies the relation

$$P = \frac{cF}{1 + y} + \frac{cF}{(1 + y)^2} + \ldots + \frac{cF}{(1 + y)^{n-1}} + \frac{cF + F}{(1 + y)^n} \qquad (6\text{-}2)$$

The yield to maturity of a bond, y, is the single rate of interest that makes the present value of the future cash flows equal to the price of the bond. This single rate is used to discount all the cash flows. It is only when the spot zero-coupon curve is flat (i.e., when all the spot zero-coupon rates are the same across all maturities and equal to R) that the yield to maturity y is equal to the interest rate R.

NUMERICAL EXAMPLE

The following term structure of interest rates applies to a three-year bond that pays an annual coupon of 4 percent and has a nominal value of $100:

t	1	2	3
R_t (%)	3	3.75	4.25

Then, according to Equation (6–1), the price of the bond is

$$P = \frac{4}{1.03} + \frac{4}{1.0375^2} + \frac{104}{1.0425^3} = 99.39 \qquad (6\text{-}3)$$

The yield to maturity y is the solution of Equation (6–2), i.e.,

$$P = \frac{4}{1 + y} + \frac{4}{(1 + y)^2} + \frac{104}{(1 + y)^3} = 99.39 \qquad (6\text{-}4)$$

which gives $y = 4.22$ percent.

to either the term structure of zero-coupon discount rates or the term structure of yields to maturity.

There are many theories and empirical studies concerning the structure and behavior of the yield curve for government bonds. We mentioned before that yield usually increases with time to maturity, a shape known as the *normal yield curve*, as shown in Figure 6-2. At the end of January 2005, the one-year Treasury bill rate was 3 percent, while the five-year T-note had a yield to maturity of 3.7 percent, the 10-year bond yielded 4.1 percent, and a 30-year government bond yielded 5 percent per annum.

Different yield curves, or, equivalently, different spread curves (the spread curve is the difference between the corporate yield curve and the risk-free government yield curve), can be estimated for corporate bonds with different credit ratings. The rating agencies—Standard & Poor's, Moody's, and others—periodically publish the yield curves for corporate

F I G U R E   6 - 2

U.S. Treasury Yield Curve—January 28, 2005

<HELP> for explanation.   N248 **Govt**   **IYC**

Hit <PAGE> for more info or <MENU> for list of curves.

YIELD CURVE – US TREASURY ACTIVES   Page   1/2

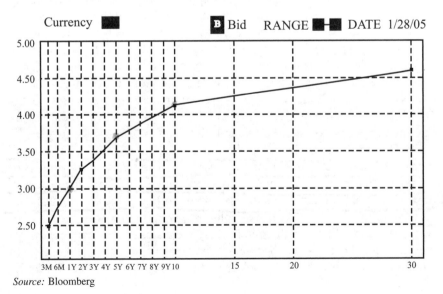

Source: Bloomberg

bonds based on their ratings. These curves represent the average yields of the bonds belonging to a given credit-rating category.

Traders and fund managers often base their decisions on the "forward curve," or the term structure of forward rates, that is, what is the expected interest rates for a three-month bond, six months from now, for a given risk category of bonds. The forward rates can be derived directly from the spot (current) term structure of interest rates. When the spot yield curve is upward-sloping, the forward curve is above the spot curve, and, conversely, when the spot curve is downward-sloping, the forward curve is below the spot curve.

For example, we can estimate the one-year forward interest rate for government bonds between one and two years from now from the yields to maturity of one- and two-year government T-notes. If the one- and two-year T-notes have a yield to maturity of 2 percent and 2.5 percent, respectively, then the expected future interest rate between the end of year 1 and the end of year 2 is estimated as $(1 + 0.025)^2/(1 + 0.020) - 1 = 0.030$ or 3.0 percent. The forward rate of 3 percent, in this case, is the rate of interest that, when compounded with the one-year rate of 2 percent, will generate a yield to maturity of 2.5 percent for a two-year bond.

The forward rate is a key building block of interest-rate risk management and of the interest-rate derivatives used by investors, financial institutions, and corporations to hedge interest-rate risk. The forward rate can be locked in by arbitrage. For example, the 3 percent forward rate between year 1 and year 2 can be achieved with certainty by buying a two-year T-note and shorting a one-year note (or, equivalently, borrowing the price of the two-year T-note for one year at the one-year rate of 2 percent). For this trade, there is no initial cash outflow. At the end of year 1, closing out the short position will necessitate cashing out $100(1.02) = $102. At the end of year 2, the two-year T-note will mature and pay $100(1.025)^2 = 105.06, generating a return of $(1.025)^2/1.02 - 1 = 3$ percent during the investment period between year 1 and year 2.

This practice of financing the purchase of long-dated securities by borrowing short term is commonly known as a *repurchase agreement* or "repo." When an investor enters into a repo agreement, he sells a security to another party and simultaneously agrees to buy it back at a later date at a prearranged price. In the example just given, the investor buys a two-year T-note and finances the purchase by means of a repo. That is, the investor sells the two-year T-note to the dealer for $100 and makes a commitment to buy the note back from the dealer one year later for $102.

In practice, dealers require a protective cushion against credit risk because the value of the bond will fluctuate over time, and it may depreciate in value if interest rates increase. For example, if interest rates increase such that the T-note is worth $98 and the investor defaults, then the dealer has lost $2 (since the dealer provided $100 at the inception of the repo and now holds a T-note worth only $98). So dealers demand a haircut, i.e., they lend less than the full amount of the bond (say, $98). The difference ($2) can be thought of as collateral against the loan.

Repos allow investors to finance a significant portion of their investment with borrowed money. But these borrowings, or *leverage* mean that the profit or loss on any position is multiplied; even a small change in market prices can have a significant financial effect on the investor.

Leverage through the use of repos was part of the undoing of California's Orange County in December 1994 after the Federal Reserve had boosted the Fed funds rate six times during the previous year for a total of 250 basis points. Mr. Citron, the Orange County treasurer, had managed to borrow $12.9 billion through the repo market. This enabled him to accumulate around $20 billion of securities even though the fund he managed had only $7.7 billion invested in it. In the favorable upward-sloping-curve environment in the years before 1994, Mr. Citron was able to increase the return of the fund by 2 percent compared to similar pools of assets. When interest rates started to rise, however, the market value of his positions dropped substantially, generating a loss of $1.5 billion by December 1994 (7 percent of the total investment in the fund). At the same time, some of the lenders to the fund stopped rolling over their repo agreements. Ultimately, Orange County filed for bankruptcy.

THE RISK FACTOR SENSITIVITY APPROACH

At the trading desk level and for specific financial markets, traders long ago developed specialized measures of the sensitivity of an instrument to changes in the value of primary risk factors. Depending on the market, such primary risk factors might take the form of interest rates, yield to maturity, volatility, stock price, and so on. In the case of fixed-income products, a popular risk measure among traders is "DV01," also known as "value of an 01." DV01 is a trader's abbreviation for the change (delta) in the value of a security after a change in yield or a change in interest rate of 1 basis point, that is, 1 percent of a percentage point, or 0.0001.

The DV01 measure is consistent with the conventional "duration" analysis of a bond, which is often thought of as the average life of a bond.

More formally, it is the weighted average of the dates (expressed in years) of each cash flow, where the weights are the present value of the cash payments divided by the sum of the weights, i.e., the price of the bond itself.

The "modified duration" of a bond, a measure often used in bond calculations, is the duration divided by 1 plus the yield to maturity of the bond. Box 6-2 offers a more technical explanation of the relationship between bond price, bond duration, and modified duration.

BOX 6-2

DURATION OF A BOND

Given the pricing equation for a bond, i.e., Equation (6–2) in Box 6–1, the duration of the bond can be defined as the weighted average of the dates (expressed in years) of each cash flow, where the weights are the present value of the cash payment divided by the sum of the weights, i.e., the price of the bond itself:

$$D = \frac{\dfrac{1 \cdot cF}{1 + y} + \dfrac{2 \cdot cF}{(1 + y)^2} + \ldots + \dfrac{(n - 1)\cdot cF}{(1 + y)^{n-1}} + \dfrac{n \cdot (cF + F)}{(1 + y)^n}}{P} \qquad (6\text{--}5)$$

Note that the sum of the weights in Equation (6–5) is equal to 1, i.e.,

$$\frac{\dfrac{cF}{1 + y}}{P} + \frac{\dfrac{cF}{(1 + y)^2}}{P} + \ldots + \frac{\dfrac{cF}{(1 + y)^{n-1}}}{P} + \frac{\dfrac{(cF + F)}{(1 + y)^n}}{P} = 1 \ (6\text{--}6)$$

since the numerator of Equation (6–6) is, according to Equation (6–2), the price of the bond.

NUMERICAL EXAMPLE (CONTINUATION OF BOX 6-1 EXAMPLE)

Consider the three-year bond presented in Equation (6–3) in Box 6–1. Its duration is

$$D = \frac{\dfrac{1 \cdot 4}{1.0422} + \dfrac{2 \cdot 4}{1.0422^2} + \dfrac{3 \cdot 104}{1.0422^3}}{99.39} = 2.89$$

(continued on following page)

BOX 6-2 *(Continued)*

Note that the duration of this three-year bond is less than three years, its maturity. The duration would be exactly three years only for a three-year zero-coupon bond.

DURATION AS A MEASURE OF INTEREST-RATE SENSITIVITY

The differentiation of Equation (6–2), which relates the bond price P to its yield to maturity y, offers

$$\Delta P \cong -P\frac{D}{1 + y}\,\Delta y = -PD^*\,\Delta y \qquad (6\text{–}7)$$

where ΔP is the change in price corresponding to a change in yield ΔY and

$$D^* = \frac{D}{1 + y} \qquad (6\text{–}8)$$

D^* as defined in Equation (6–8) is called *modified duration*.

There is a linear relationship between the change in price of a bond and the change in yield. The higher the duration, the higher the price volatility. However, as the price-yield relationship for a bond is nonlinear, duration is only a first-order approximation of the impact of a change in yield on the price of a bond. This means that it only offers a good approximation for small variations in yield (see Figure 6B–1).

FIGURE 6B-1

Duration as a Measure of Interest Rate Sensitivity

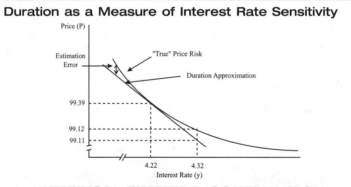

NUMERICAL EXAMPLE (CONTINUATION)

Assume a change of 10 basis points in the yield of the three-year bond defined by Equations (6–3) and (6–4) in Box 6-1, with a price $P = 99.39$, a duration $D = 2.89$, and a yield $y = 4.22$ percent. Then, according to Equation (6–7),

$$\Delta y = 0.001$$

$$\Delta P \cong -99.39\,\frac{2.89}{1.0422}\,0.001 = -0.28$$

For small parallel shifts of the yield curve, the price sensitivity of a fixed-income product can be approximated by a simple (linear) function of the change in yield. That is, the percentage change in the price of a bond is the negative of the product of the change in yield to maturity and the modified duration of the bond.

Consider, for example, a bond trading at $90 with a yield to maturity of 5 percent and a modified duration of eight years. According to this approximation, a 5-basis-point increase in yield results in a price decline of 0.05% × 8 = 0.4% or $0.36.

Figure 6-3 offers an example of the price sensitivity of par bonds of different maturities, expressed in dollars per million of notional value, for a change in yield of 1 basis point. This example illustrates that the longer the maturity of the bond, the higher its duration and the more sensitive the price of the bond to a change in yield.

But duration and related measures offer only a first-order approximation of the impact of a change in yield on the price of a bond. A more accurate approximation of the price change requires a second-order adjustment known as the convexity adjustment (Figure 6-4). The straight line in Figure 6-4 represents the value of the bond around its current value when the changes in value are adjusted for duration. The dotted curve represents the value of the bond around its current value after it has been adjusted for both duration and convexity. The value of the bond adjusted for convexity follows very closely the exact price of the bond, represented by

FIGURE 6-3

Interest-Rate Sensitivity Measures: Value of an "01"

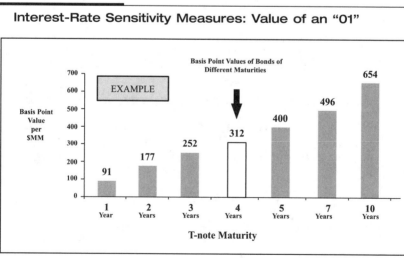

FIGURE   6-4

"Convexity" Adjustment to Interest Rate Sensitivity

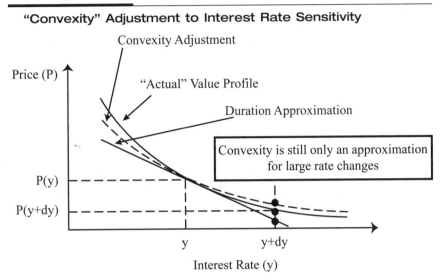

the continuous black curved line, although it is not perfect and still is only an approximation when there are large variations in yields.

PORTFOLIOS OF INSTRUMENTS

For a portfolio of instruments priced from the same yield curve, price sensitivities can be easily aggregated by calculating the weighted-average duration of the instruments held in the portfolio.

Alternatively, price sensitivities can be expressed in terms of a benchmark representative instrument, for example, the four-year Treasury note (T-note) in Figure 6-3. In this case, each position is converted into the duration equivalent of the reference instrument, that is, the four-year T-note. For instance, the 10-year T-note has a duration that is 2.1 times greater than the duration of a four-year T-note, so a $1 million 10-year T-note is said to be equivalent to $2.1 million of the reference four-year T-note (Figure 6-5). The risk of the portfolio is then evaluated as if it were a single position in the reference asset.

In the next chapter, we propose a more encompassing risk measure for fixed-income portfolios, value-at-risk, or VaR. This measure allows risk managers to aggregate both the duration effect and the convexity adjustment into a single number (as well as to compare and aggregate financial risks arising from many other sources).

FIGURE 6-5

Interest-Rate Sensitivity Measures: Relative Value of an "01"

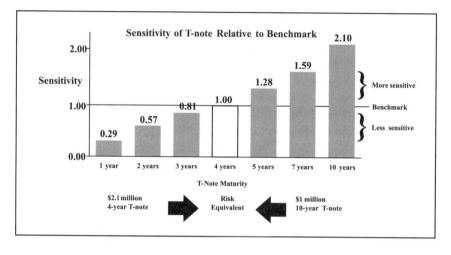

INSTRUMENTS FOR HEDGING
INTEREST-RATE RISK

We've discussed how interest-rate risk arises and some specific ways of measuring this risk. But what kind of instruments and strategies can be used to manage the risks that we have measured (beyond simply selling the instruments or assets that give rise to the exposure)?

The answer, of course, lies in the world of derivatives contracts, such as swaps, forwards, futures, and options, whose values are derived from various underlying assets or rates. In this section, we describe how derivatives can be used to manage interest-rate risk. But the same basic principles apply to derivatives based on other asset types, such as equities, stock indices, currencies, and commodities.

Over the years, and especially since the 1970s, many different kinds of derivative instruments with varying levels of complexity and customization have been invented to hedge (or assume) financial risk. Some instruments are traded on formal exchanges around the world, such as the Treasury bond futures traded on the Chicago Board of Trade (CBOT) or the Eurodollar futures traded on the Chicago Mercantile Exchange (CME). These exchange-traded derivatives are fairly simple and standardized contracts, backed by a clearinghouse to ensure contract integrity.

But most derivatives are not traded on exchanges, but instead are private bilateral contracts between a dealer and a customer known as over-the-counter or OTC derivatives. Such OTC derivative contracts can be highly customized to the needs of a customer; the drawback is that they are less liquid than exchange-traded futures, and their execution is backed only by the capital of the provider or dealer. This is why the key players in the OTC derivatives market are all financial institutions with a good credit standing. Interest-rate swaps, swaptions, forward-rate agreements, caps, floors, and collars—the key derivative instruments used by investors, corporations, and financial institutions to manage interest-rate risk—are all traded over-the-counter.

The size of government debt, on a worldwide basis, is enormous. Coupled with corporate bonds and bank loan portfolios, it gives rise to a huge pool of assets and liabilities that are sensitive to changes in interest rates. So it is not surprising to find that the OTC market for interest-rate derivatives is also very sizable, having reached $164.4 trillion ($164,400,000,000,000) in notional value at mid-2004. While press headlines tend to concentrate on risk management failures and speculation in the derivative markets, there's no doubt that interest-rate derivatives are an essential tool for managing risk. In late 2004, Alan Greenspan, chairman of the U.S. Federal Reserve, praised the greater use of derivatives by banks to shift their interest-rate risks, and said that they have added significantly to the banking sector's strength.[1] Let's now look at some particular types of instrument.

Forward and Futures Contracts

A forward contract allows its buyer to lock in today the future price of an asset such as an interest-rate-linked security, a currency, a stock, or a commodity. The buyer has to pay the agreed-upon price on the settlement date, whether or not the rate or the price of the underlying asset has moved in his or her favor. The seller is also required to deliver the asset on the settlement date, whatever the asset's price on the spot market. There is no upfront fee to pay in a forward transaction, and no cash changes hands before the settlement date. Forward contracts are essentially OTC instruments, and therefore can be highly customized. Some contracts are settled through the delivery of the underlying asset against payment of the agreed-upon price (forward price). Other contracts, such as interest-rate forwards, are "cash settled," i.e., one party has to pay the other the difference between the contract value of the forward and its spot value at the maturity date.

---

1. Federal Reserve Chairman Alan Greenspan at the American Bankers Association annual meeting on October 5, 2004.

A futures contract is simply a forward contract that is traded on an exchange. Unlike forwards, futures have standardized terms, such as the underlying cash instrument or rate, the notional amount, and maturities. (This standardization is essential if the exchange market in the contract is to be liquid.) At its initiation, a futures contract has zero value. But anyone buying a futures contract must deposit an initial payment, called *margin*, with the clearinghouse of the exchange. Then, every day, the contract is "marked to market" and daily installments, positive or negative, that correspond to the change in the daily value of the futures price (determined in the marketplace) are paid. The total of the daily installments and the payment at maturity equal the futures price set when the contract was initiated.

Both forwards and futures allow investors to protect open positions from adverse price movements: any losses and gains on the open positions are offset by the payoff of the derivatives contracts. In the case of interest-rate forwards or futures, if the actual interest rate at the maturity of the contract is different from the predetermined rate, money is paid or received, depending on whether the difference is positive or negative.

In practice, there's a slight wrinkle in the definition of contracts on short-term interest rates. For example, a futures contract on a one-year T-bill rate is defined as 100 minus the promised interest rate. Thus, if the predetermined futures rate is 2.5 percent, then the contract is on a predetermined price of 97.5 (= 100 − 2.5). If, at the end of the year, the actual rate on a one-year T-bill is 3.2 percent, the realized value is then 100 − 3.2 = 96.8. In such a case, the holder of the long position will be paid by the seller of the contract the sum of 97.5 − 96.8 = 0.7 per unit of the contract.

Such a contract allows a company to hedge a "one-period" rate change and is similar to the forward rate agreement (FRA) contracts that are traded on the OTC markets. FRA contracts are very popular with short-term borrowers who are trying to fix today the effective interest rate they will have to pay at a future date.

The contracts just described are all "cash settled" at maturity, meaning that cash is paid by the losing party to the gaining party. In the case of some futures contracts on long-term rates, however, settlement is made by delivering specific long-term bonds (usually from a list of government bonds).

Futures, forwards, and FRA contracts offer the investor many opportunities to hedge future rate changes, and to fix future rates at the present time. They are traded in very competitive markets, and the bid/offer spread for these OTC contracts is usually very narrow.

Swaps

Another simple instrument for hedging interest-rate risk, and possibly the most frequently used, is the interest-rate swap. A swap is an OTC agreement between two parties to exchange the cash flows of two different securities throughout the life of the contract. It can be viewed as a series of forwards and, as with forwards, the contract is binding on both sides of the transaction (whether or not the contract has evolved in one party's favor).

Interest-rate swaps are very flexible hedging instruments. They are used by treasurers in asset and liability management and by bond portfolio managers to reduce or extend the duration of an open position.

The most common form of interest-rate swap is the fixed-floating interest-rate swap, where the "fixed" side pays a fixed interest rate on a notional amount, e.g., $1 million, quarterly or semiannually, and the "floating" side pays a floating rate on the same notional amount. The reference rate on the floating side might be LIBOR, the rate in the commercial paper markets, or any other reference agreed upon by the parties to the contract. There is no exchange of principal, as the principal on both sides of the swap cancels out both at the inception and at the maturity of the contract.

In a currency swap, on the contrary, both sides of the transaction exchange the principal amounts, denominated in different currencies, both at the start and at the maturity of the transaction. The exchange rate for the two currencies is decided when the swap is initiated, so that both sides are locked into the future exchange rate. At intervals (monthly, quarterly, semiannually, and so on) throughout the life of the currency swap, both sides exchange interest-rate payments, either fixed or floating, denominated in the relevant currencies.

As is the case with forwards and futures, no up-front fee is payable when a swap is initiated, as all swap transactions are priced initially so that the net present value (NPV) of both legs of the swap is the same. As time goes on and interest rates vary, the NPV of both legs of the swap varies and the difference between the NPVs can become negative or positive. If interest rates rise, the cash flows on the floating leg increase, as does the contract's NPV. Conversely, the NPV of the fixed leg declines.

Interest-rate swaps are used by corporations or financial institutions to change the nature of their payments on loans either from fixed to variable rates or from variable to fixed rates, depending on the nature of the corporation's income stream. Swaps are a convenient tool for managing the interest-rate risks implied by the company's forecasts of interest-rate behavior: if interest rates are expected to rise sharply, the company will try to fix interest payments; in a declining interest-rate environment, the company will tend to convert fixed rates into variable rates.

For example, imagine that parties A and B enter into a five-year interest-rate swap with a notional value of $100 million. Party A will pay party B each year, at year-end, a sum equal to $100 million times a fixed interest rate, say 4 percent, and will receive from party B a sum equal to $100 million times the one-year T-bill rate plus a spread of, say, 1 percent. So, each year party A pays a fixed amount of $4 million to party B, while party B pays an amount determined by the variable rate (the T-bill rate at the beginning of the period plus 1 percent).

In practice, there is a netting procedure, and only the difference is paid. So, if the T-bill rate at the beginning of the year is less than 3 percent, party A pays party B the difference between 4 percent and the T-bill rate plus 1 percent times $100 million. For example, if the one-year T-bill rate is 2.5 percent, party A will pay party B [0.04 −(0.025 + 0.01)] × $100,000,000 = $500,000. If the one-year T-bill rate is 3.8 percent, then party B will pay party A the sum of [(0.038 + 0.010) − 0.040] × $100,000,000 = $800,000.

Swap transactions are often used by corporate treasurers as a way of bridging the gap that tends to exist between the particular needs of a company and the needs of the market. For example, a treasurer may for practical reasons issue a five-year bond denominated in Swiss francs, paying a fixed coupon, also in Swiss francs, although his preferred exposure might be in U.S. dollars floating with a LIBOR reference. His preferred exposure can be achieved by means of a currency swap: on one side of the transaction, the treasurer receives the cash flows of the bond issued in Swiss francs; on the other side of the transaction, he pays floating LIBOR.

Interest-rate and currency swaps are the major components of the OTC derivatives market. But the basic principle of swapping has been applied to all asset classes, such as equities and commodities. Asset swaps have become very popular, as they allow investors to transfer the cash flows and the risk associated with various kinds of assets to other market players in exchange for floating interest payments, usually based on LIBOR.

Options: Calls, Puts, and Exotics

Call options are contracts that allow the buyer to purchase the underlying instrument (say, a particular bond) at a predetermined price (the striking or exercise price) during a given period or at the maturity date. An option that can be exercised only at the maturity of the contract is termed a "European" option, while one that can be exercised at any time, up to and including the maturity date, is termed an "American" option. Call options give the buyer the right to exercise the option when the future price movement of the underlying bond or rate is favorable to the buyer, i.e., when the price of the underlying instrument at the exercise time is above the predetermined exercise price. But the purchaser of an option, unlike the counterparty to a forward, future, or swap, may allow the contract to expire without exercise. For this one-sided right, the buyer must pay a premium.

It is important to emphasize the difference between purchasing a call option and purchasing a futures or forward contract. The futures must be executed at maturity at the agreed-upon terms, whereas the call may end unexercised if the price goes against the buyer. Another important difference is that while the buyer of a call pays the seller of the contract a price that reflects the value of the right, futures and forward contracts have zero value at initiation; the futures price for the futures transaction is set at such a level that the contract has a zero present value.

A put option is the opposite of a call option; it gives the holder the right to *sell* the underlying bond at a predetermined price, at any time up to (American put) or exactly and only at (European put) the maturity date. A stand-alone put option on a bond is therefore a bet on the decline in the value of the bond (or, equivalently, a bet on an increase in interest rates). Put options also allow the holder of an open position to insure against a loss of value: the open position and the option "hedge" offset each other. In this case, we can view the exercise price of the option contract, relative to the current value of the bond, as the insurance "deductible," that is, the amount of value that the bond must lose before the option insurance takes effect.

It can be shown that buying a futures contract is similar to simultaneously buying a call option and selling a put option on the same underlying bond, where the exercise price of the call and the put are equal to the forward price of the bond. In the same way, one can create a synthetic call option by buying a forward contract and a put option on the same underlying instrument.

A huge number of strategies for hedging interest-rate risks can be put in place by buying and selling call and put options at different exercise prices for different maturities. In effect, "slices" of the future probability distributions of the prices of the underlying instruments can be priced via options and can be traded. The different strategies are characterized by various risk-return trade-offs, hopefully in line with the risk appetite of the investor.

Buying a put and a call with the same exercise price is called a *straddle* and represents a bet on increased volatility, that is, sharp moves up or down in the price of the underlying asset. An investor can therefore "sell volatility" in interest rates by selling a straddle, i.e., by selling a put and a call contract simultaneously that have the same exercise price and maturity. Traders often use straddles when an announcement about a change in interest rates is expected and when the outcome of the announcement is uncertain, or before some other major macroeconomic decision by a government or central bank. On the other side of the deal, an investor who purchases a straddle is really insuring against a major increase or a major decrease in the price of the underlying asset during the life of the option.

Volatility can be purchased more cheaply by buying a put and a call option at different exercise prices, with both options out-of-the-money. For example, if the bond price is 100, one might buy a put option with an exercise price of 95 and a call with an exercise price of 105. Such a "strangle" will be much cheaper than an at-the-money straddle with an exercise price of 100.

Caps, Floors, and Collars

Let's use the huge market in the United States for adjustable-rate mortgages (ARMs) as an intuitive way to explore caps, floors, and collars. About half of all new mortgage loans have adjustable rates, rather than a rate that is fixed over the life of the mortgage.

The adjustable interest rate on an ARM might be based on the rate of the six-month Treasury bill; over the next six months, the borrower will pay that rate plus a spread of, say, 2 percent per annum. Often, adjustable-rate borrowers are offered a "cap" on the interest rate of their long-term loans, so that when short-term interest rates rise above a predetermined rate, say 5 percent, the borrower does not pay more than the 5 percent cap plus the add-on (for a total of 7 percent, in our example).

This cap is clearly an attractive feature for the borrower, and it costs money to put it in place. In order to reduce the cost of the cap, the borrower might also be offered a "floor." A floor sets a minimum interest payment per period: even when short-term interest rates decline substantially, the borrower won't benefit from the reduction in rates below this floor. In our numerical example, if the floor is set at a T-bill rate of 2 percent, the borrower will pay a minimum of 4 percent (i.e., the 2 percent floor plus the 2 percent add-on).

Now, the floor and the cap can be set at such levels that their premiums exactly offset each other. Such an arrangement is often termed a "zero-cost collar" or "zero-cost cylinder."

We can see caps and floors and their combinations used in many different risk management markets. For example, the collar, or cylinder, as a combination of a ceiling and floor agreement on periodic payments, is a very popular way to hedge foreign currency positions.

Swaptions

Options on a swap are referred to as "swaptions" and represent the right to enter into a swap on or before a specified date at currently determined terms. Such options may be either European or American in style. If the buyer of the swaption has the right to pay a fixed rate in the swap upon exercise, it is called a payer's swaption. If the buyer of the swaption has the right to receive a fixed rate, it is called a receiver's swaption. Such options may be structured with fixed and floating legs in different currencies. A swaption clearly offers more flexibility than a straight swap, but the purchaser must pay an option premium for that added benefit.

Exotic Options

So far, we've considered straightforward or "plain vanilla" options. Options with more complicated terms are known as *exotic options*. One of the most popular is an option that has as its reference the *average* price of the underlying instrument over some agreed-upon period of time. For example, one might purchase a call contract from a major bank that entitles the owner to receive the difference, if positive, between the average price of a 30-year bond, say one month before its maturity date, and an exercise price agreed upon in advance (say, 100). The volatility of an average rate option is smaller than the volatility of the corresponding vanilla option.

Knock-in and knock-out options are also quite common. These options may be exercised or expire during an agreed-upon time period before the formal maturity date of the option contract if the price of the underlying instruments "hits" a certain, predetermined price level. These options, like most exotic options, are "path dependent": their value is dependent on certain paths that the price of the underlying instrument may take. There is an endless list of exotic options (more are invented every year) with names such as Himalayan, octopus, ratchet, chooser, lookback, and barrier options.

Pricing and hedging exotic options rely on complex mathematical models that are prone to model risk (see Chapter 14). In addition, some of these exotic structures, such as barrier options, can expose the seller of the option to significant risks, as there is no perfect hedge for them.

FINANCIAL ENGINEERING

Forwards, swaps, and options are the main building blocks of financial engineering. They can be used separately to hedge specific risks, or combined to form complex structures that meet the needs of customers.

In particular, derivatives allow investors and institutions to break apart or "segment" risks (or, conversely, to handle them together). Take, for example, a U.S. fund manager who holds a bond denominated in euros. The fund manager is exposed to interest-rate risk in the euro fixed-income market and to changes in the dollar/euro exchange rate. The manager can hedge both risks by means of a currency swap. Alternatively, she can hedge the foreign exchange exposure through a currency forward or currency option. The fund manager could also avoid the trouble of hedging only the currency exposure by entering into a so-called quanto swap. Under this structure, she would receive the coupon of the bond in dollars at a prearranged exchange rate and pay U.S. LIBOR floating.

There is almost no limit to the imagination of the structurers in banks who are responsible for devising complex instruments intended to match the risk/return appetite of their clients. But financial engineering is not by itself risk management, and in the world of derivatives, often there is a fine line between hedging and speculation. Firms can be tempted to enter into complex transactions that enhance portfolio returns. Enhancing returns always means taking on more risk, in some form or other. Often, it means marginally increasing returns in the present in exchange for assuming an unlikely but potentially very severe loss in the future, as we discussed in Chapter 1. Too often, the risk embedded in complex structures is not fully understood by corporations entering into complex derivative transactions (Box 6-3), or is not fully communicated to senior managers or other stakeholders.

Earlier we mentioned the story of Orange County and its collapse, due in part to excessive leverage. The other reason for the failure of Orange County was that the fund purchased complex inverse floating-rate notes

BOX 6-3

THE RISKS OF COMPLEX DERIVATIVES

Back in the 1990s, before the bond market crash of 1994, Bankers Trust (BT) proposed to clients such as Procter & Gamble (P&G) and Gibson Greetings that they enter into complex leveraged swaps to achieve a lower funding cost. In the swap with P&G, BT would pay a fixed rate to P&G for five years, and P&G would pay a floating rate, which was the commercial paper rate minus 75 basis points if rates remained stable. But, through a complex formula, the floating rate would increase considerably if rates rose during the period—for example, an increase of 100 basis points in rates produced a spread over the commercial paper rate of 1,035 basis points! Each basis-point move in the yield curve was magnified around 30 times.

The Fed increased the Fed funds rate by 250 basis points in 1994, causing colossal losses for both P&G and Gibson Greetings. Both companies sued BT for misrepresenting the risk embedded in these complex swap transactions. BT never quite recovered from the damaging impact of these events on its reputation and, much later, was acquired by Deutsche Bank.

---

whose coupon payments decline when interest rates rise (as opposed to conventional floaters, whose payments increase in such a circumstance). It was the combination of excessive leverage and a risky, and eventually wrong, interest-rate bet embedded in the securities bought by the fund that led to the Orange County debacle.

The board as well as the senior management of corporations need to understand the natural risks the corporation is running. Senior management needs to deploy robust policies and risk measures that tie the firm's use of derivatives to its risk appetite and to the business strategy it has communicated to stakeholders. Our next chapter explores the VaR framework that is now widely used by financial institutions and major corporations to measure and communicate risk across their various activities.

CHAPTER 7

From Value-at-Risk to Stress Testing

The measurement of market risk has evolved from simple naïve indicators that distort the measurement of risk, such as the face value or "notional" amount of an individual security, through more complex measures of price sensitivities such as the basis point value or duration approach of a bond (Chapter 6), to sophisticated risk measures such as the latest value-at-risk (VaR) methodology (Figure 7-1) for whole portfolios of securities.

FIGURE 7-1

Traditional Measures of Market Risk

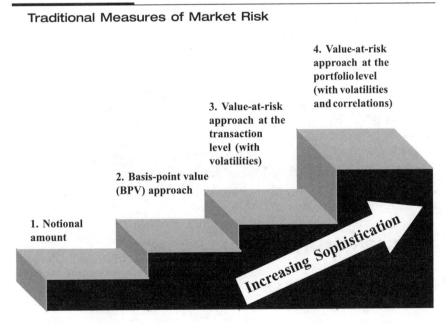

4. Value-at-risk
approach at the
portfolio level
(with volatilities
and correlations)

3. Value-at-risk
approach at the
transaction
level (with
volatilities)

2. Basis-point value
(BPV) approach

1. Notional
amount

Increasing Sophistication

In this chapter we'll explain the principles that lie behind VaR and make clear the strengths and weaknesses of the approach in nonmathematical language. We'll also look at some specialist measures of risk for derivatives (the "Greeks") and at a key supplement to any VaR approach: stress testing and worst-case scenarios.

VaR has proved to be a very powerful way of assessing the overall market risk of trading positions over a short horizon, such as a 10-day period, and under "normal" market conditions. In effect, the methodology allows us to capture in a single number the multiple components of market risk, such as curve risk, basis risk, and volatility risk.

However, each time there is turmoil in the world's markets, the limitations of even the most sophisticated measures of market risk are revealed. VaR has proved unreliable as a measure of risk over long time periods or under abnormal market conditions. The danger posed by exceptional market shocks such as the crisis in the world markets in 1998 that capsized the giant U.S. hedge fund Long-Term Capital Management (LTCM)—shocks that are often accompanied by a drying up of market liquidity—can be captured only by means of supplemental methodologies.

Worries that VaR and other industry-standard risk measures might even exacerbate market volatility have also surfaced. Some influential commentators argue that the herd mentality that is so typical of the financial industry means that market-sensitive risk management systems, such as VaR, actually make markets less stable and more prone to crisis. This is because financial institutions may have to sell assets in the affected classes when markets become volatile in order to keep within the VaR limits set by senior management; this depresses market prices even further and increases the volatility and correlation of the risk factors for these assets. This, in turn, might cause another set of financial institutions to exceed their VaR limits, forcing them to reduce their exposure by selling still more of the same assets—perpetuating a vicious circle.

It's a controversial argument, but then VaR is controversial in so many ways. Let's first take a quick look at the evolution of measures of market risk in the derivative markets before we explore how VaR is calculated, and its resulting strengths and weaknesses.

THE NOTIONAL AMOUNT APPROACH

Until relatively recently, major banks often assessed the amount of market risk generated by their trading desks in terms of the notional or nominal amounts of the portfolio held by the desk. For example, the risk of a portfolio might be assessed with reference to the fact that it contained $30 million of government debt or $30 million of options on the equity of, say, a telecom company. These flawed nominal measures were often routinely presented to senior management and the board as measures of market risk. This is an appealingly simple approach, but it is fatally flawed, since it does not

- Reflect the fact that different assets have vastly different price volatilities (e.g., government bonds are much less likely to fluctuate violently in price than are telecom stocks)
- Take into account the tendency for the value of different assets in the portfolio to rise and fall at the same time (i.e., the "correlation" of the assets in the portfolio)
- Differentiate between short and long positions that might cancel one another out or partially hedge one another (e.g., a long position in a forward contract on the euro with notional value of $100 million maturing in June, and a short position in a forward contract on the euro with a notional value of $50 million maturing in July)

In the case of derivative positions, there are often very large discrepancies between the notional amount, which may be huge, and the true amount of market exposure, which is often small. For example, two call options on the same underlying instrument with the same notional value and the same time to expiration may have very different market values if their strike prices are different—the first option may be deep in-the-money, and the other one may be deep out-of-the money. The first option might be very valuable, while the second might be almost worthless, meaning that they represent very different risk exposures.

As another example, imagine a situation in which interest-rate swaps are written with many different counterparties, and some of these swaps are being used to hedge the market risk exposure created by the other swaps. In this instance, the deals are designed to cancel each other out in terms of their effect on the aggregate market risk in the portfolio. Adding up the notional amounts of the deals will generate an entirely misleading picture of the market risk of the portfolio (although it will offer some indication of overall credit risk exposure).

PRICE SENSITIVITY MEASURES FOR DERIVATIVES

In Chapter 6 we looked at some of the specific measures of market risk in the interest-rate and bond markets. But bond-market traders are not the only practitioners who depend on market-specific risk measures. More recently, practitioners in the derivative markets have developed their own specialized risk measures to describe the sensitivities of derivative instruments to various risk factors. The risk measures are named after letters in the Greek alphabet, and are therefore known collectively as the "Greeks." How do these measures relate to the risk measures that we discussed in Chapter 6?

First, consider a European call option on an individual stock that does not pay any dividend. According to the classic Black-Scholes formula for option pricing, the price of this option is a function of the stock price, the risk-free rate of interest, the instantaneous volatility of the stock return, the strike price, and the option's maturity.

In the option price equation, the stock price plays the same role as the yield in the bond-price relationship that we described in Chapter 6. The sensitivities of the call option price with respect to the stock price are known as the delta and gamma, so we can think of the delta and gamma price risks of a derivative as analogous to the duration and convexity of a bond, respectively. Table 7-1 gives the definitions of the Greeks in more detail.

The list of sensitivities for derivatives in Table 7-1 is longer than a similar list for a standard bond. This is because the value of a derivative is affected by additional risk factors, such as volatility, the discount rate, the passage of time, and, when several risk factors are involved, the correlation between the risk factors.

Weaknesses of the Greek Measures

Traders on options desks use the Greeks to monitor the sensitivities of their market positions and to discuss risk with trading desk risk managers. But each of the sensitivities measured by the Greeks provides only a partial measure of financial risk. The measurements of delta, gamma, and vega complement one another, but they cannot be aggregated to produce an overall measure of the risk generated by a position or a portfolio. In particular,

- Sensitivities cannot be added up across risk types, e.g., the delta and gamma risk of the same position cannot be summed.

TABLE 7-1

The Greek Alphabet for a European Equity Call Option

Delta, or price risk	Delta measures the degree to which an option's value is affected by a small change in the price of the underlying instrument.
Gamma, or convexity risk	Gamma measures the degree to which the option's delta changes as the reference price underlying the option changes. The higher the gamma, the more valuable the option is to its holder. For a high-gamma option, when the underlying price increases, the delta also increases, so that the option appreciates more in value than a gamma-neutral position. Conversely, when the underlying price falls, the delta also falls, and the option loses less in value than if the position were gamma neutral. The reverse is true for short positions in options: high-gamma positions expose their holders to more risk than gamma-neutral positions.
Vega, or volatility risk	Vega measures the sensitivity of the option value to changes in the volatility of the underlying instrument. A higher vega typically increases the value of the option to its holder.
Theta, or time decay risk	Theta measures the time decay of an option. That is, it reflects how much the value of the option changes as the option moves closer to its expiration date. Positive gamma is usually associated with negative time decay, i.e., a natural price attrition of the option as its maturity declines.
Rho, or discount rate risk	Rho measures the change in value of an option in response to a change in interest rate, more specifically, a change in the zero-coupon rate of the same maturity as the option. Typically, the higher the value of rho, the lower the value of the option to its holder.

- Sensitivities cannot be added up across markets, e.g., one cannot sum the delta of a euro/U.S. dollar call and the delta of a call on a stock index.

Since the sensitivities cannot be aggregated, they cannot be used to assess the magnitude of the overall loss that might arise from a change in the risk factors. As a consequence,

- Sensitivities cannot be used directly to measure the amount of capital that the bank is putting at risk.

- Sensitivities do not facilitate financial risk control. Position limits expressed in terms of delta, gamma, and vega are often ineffective, since they do not translate easily into a "maximum dollar loss acceptable" for the position.

This explains the desire for a comprehensive measure of market risk for individual securities and for portfolios. Value-at-risk is one answer to this quest for a consistent measure of market risk.

DEFINING VALUE-AT-RISK

Value-at-risk (VaR) can be defined as the worst loss that might be expected from holding a security or portfolio over a given period of time (say a single day, or 10 days for the purpose of regulatory capital reporting), given a specified level of probability (known as the *confidence level*).

For example, if we say that a position has a daily VaR of $10 million at the 99 percent confidence level, we mean that the realized daily losses from the position will on average be higher than $10 million on only one day in every 100 trading days (i.e., two to three days each year).

This means that VaR is *not* the answer to the simple question: How much can I lose on my portfolio over a given period of time? The answer to this question is "everything," or almost the entire value of the portfolio! Such an answer is not very helpful in practice: it is the correct answer to the wrong question. If all markets collapse at the same time, then naturally prices may plunge and, at least in theory, the value of the portfolio may drop near to zero.

Instead, VaR offers a probability statement about the potential change in the value of a portfolio resulting from a change in market factors over a specified period of time. Crucially, the VaR measure also does not state by *how much* actual losses are likely to exceed the VaR figure; it simply states how likely (or unlikely) it is that the VaR measure will be exceeded.

Most VaR models are designed to measure risk over a short period of time, such as one day, or 10 days in the case of the market-risk measurements required by the regulators for regulatory capital. The confidence level for the calculation of market risk introduced by the Basel Committee in 1998 (BIS 1998) is set at 99 percent. However, for the purposes of allocating internal capital, VaR may be derived at a higher confidence level, say 99.96 percent; this level of confidence is consistent with the level of confidence inherent in an AA credit rating awarded by a public ratings agency.

There are two key steps in calculating VaR. First, derive the forward distribution of the portfolio, or the returns on the portfolio, at the chosen horizon (in this case, one day). We describe later on how this distribution can be derived using three different approaches: historical price distributions (nonparametric VaR); assumptions about normal distributions (parametric VaR); and Monte Carlo analysis.

This distribution is then plotted out as the curve shown in Figure 7-2. This figure shows us how likely it is (vertical axis) that losses of a particular dollar value (horizontal axis) will occur.

Second, identify the required percentile of this distribution so that a particular loss number can be read off. We've selected the first percentile of the distribution in Figure 7-2 because, in this example, we assumed that management has asked for a VaR number measured at the 99 percent confidence level. In Figure 7-2, we also assume that the distribution is a normal bell-shaped curve, rather than a distribution that is skewed toward particularly light or heavy losses. Thus, a confidence level of 99 percent corresponds to a VaR of 2.33 standard deviations.

FIGURE 7-2

Defining Value-at-Risk

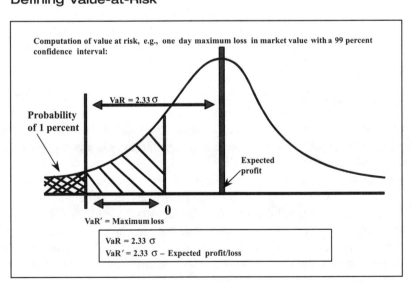

If the confidence level had been set at 99.96 percent, then we would have calculated the 4-basis-point (bp) quantile, and we would have ended up with a larger number for the VaR. (Note that the extent to which the VaR number rises as confidence levels are set more stringently depends upon the shape of the distribution.)

The VaR of the position or portfolio is simply the maximum loss at this 99 percent confidence level, measured relative to the expected value of the portfolio at the target horizon. That is, VaR is the distance of the first percentile from the mean of the distribution.

VaR = expected profit/loss − worst-case loss at the 99 percent confidence level

An alternative and even simpler definition of VaR is that it represents the worst-case loss at the 99 percent confidence level, i.e.,

VaR' = worst-case loss at the 99 percent confidence level

VaR' is also known as *absolute VaR*. However, only our first definition of VaR is consistent with economic capital attribution and the kind of risk-adjusted return on capital (RAROC) calculations we describe in Chapter 15. (Essentially, this is because capital needs to be provided only as a cushion against unexpected losses; in VaR the expected profit or loss is already priced in, and accounted for, in the return calculation.)

So, how exactly does the VaR number relate to economic capital and to regulatory capital? VaR represents the economic capital that shareholders should invest in the firm (or set aside against a particular position or portfolio) to limit the probability of default to a given predetermined level of confidence. Regulatory capital, on the other hand, is the minimum amount of capital imposed by the regulator, as described in Chapter 3. Even when regulatory capital measures are based on a VaR calculation rather than on much simpler rules, economic capital differs from regulatory capital because the confidence level and the time horizon chosen are usually different. For example, when banks are determining their economic capital for market risk, they may choose a higher confidence level than the 99 percent set by the regulator. They may also vary the time horizon when making economic capital calculations, perhaps using one day for very liquid positions, such as a government bond, and as much as several weeks for illiquid positions, such as long-dated over-the-counter equity derivatives. By contrast, the regulator arbitrarily sets the time horizon at 10 days for any position in the trading book.

From 1-Day VaR to 10-Day VaR

VaR is often used to manage market risk over a 1-day time horizon. For this purpose, it's necessary to derive VaR from the daily distribution of the portfolio values. However, we mentioned earlier that the regulators have set a time horizon of 10 days for the purpose of VaR calculations that are used to report regulatory capital requirements. Ideally, this "10-day VaR" would be derived from a corresponding distribution of results over a 10-day horizon. This is problematic, however, as it implies that the time series of data used for the analysis must be much longer—indeed, 10 times longer—than that employed in any one-day VaR analysis. As a result, many banks employ a work-around that allows them to derive an approximation of 10-day VaR from daily VaR data by multiplying the daily VaR by the square root of time (here, 10 days). The "square root of time" rule is endorsed by the regulators; it should be noted, however, that it is not a sound practical approach and remains something of a rule of thumb.

HOW IS VaR USED TO LIMIT RISK IN PRACTICE?

VaR is an aggregate measure of risk across all risk factors. A special attraction is that it can be calculated at each level of activity in the business hierarchy of a company. For example, it can be calculated for each activity (e.g., trading desk) at both the business unit level (e.g., equity trading) and the level of the firm as a whole.

At the level of the firm, VaR offers a good way of representing the (short-term) "risk appetite" of the firm, since it measures the maximum loss that the firm might incur, under normal market conditions, over a short period of time (in effect, 1 to 10 days). The risk appetite of the firm over a longer period of time, say a quarter, is usually set in terms of a worst-case scenario analysis. For example, the board of the bank can set a limit on the maximum loss that it is prepared to tolerate over a quarter if the worst-case crisis that the bank's risk managers think plausible in that period should, in fact, occur.

At many financial institutions, the board of directors sets an overall VaR limit whose control is delegated to the chief executive officer (CEO). In practice, this control is often delegated, in turn, to a risk management committee chaired by the CEO. In many banks, the risk management committee appoints a chief risk officer (CRO) or similar risk executive to report on firmwide risk and therefore help maintain effective control of this limit. We discuss this cascade of accountability in more detail in Chapter 4. Box 7-1 reviews the strengths of VaR, not only as a measurement tool, but also as a managerial instrument.

BOX 7-1

VaR IS FOR MANAGING, AS WELL AS MEASURING, RISK

In the main text, we highlight the problems inherent in the simplifying assumptions that must be made whenever a VaR number is calculated. In this box, let's remind ourselves of the great strengths of VaR and its wide range of uses:

- *VaR provides a common, consistent, and integrated measure of risk across risk factors, instruments, and asset classes.* For example, it allows managers to measure the risk of a fixed-income position in a way that is comparable and consistent with their risk assessment of an equity derivative position. VaR also takes into account the correlations between the various risk factors, somewhat in the spirit of portfolio theory.

- *VaR can provide an aggregate measure of risk and risk-adjusted performance.* This single number can then be easily translated into a capital requirement. VaR can also be used to reward employees on the basis of the risk-adjusted return on capital generated by their activities. In other words, it can be used to measure risk-adjusted performance (see Chapter 15).

- *Business-line risk limits can be set in terms of VaR.* These limits can be used to ensure that individuals do not take more risk than they are allowed to take. Risk limits expressed in VaR units can easily be aggregated up through the firm, from the business line at trading desk level to the very top of the corporation. The drill-down capability of a VaR system allows risk managers to detect which unit is taking the most risk, and also to identify the type of risk to which the whole bank is most exposed, e.g., equity, interest-rate, currency, or equity vega.

- *VaR provides senior management, the board of directors, and regulators with a risk measure that they can understand.* Managers and shareholders, as well as regulators, can decide whether they feel comfortable with the level of risk taken on by the bank in terms of VaR units. VaR also provides a framework for assessing, *ex ante*, investments and projects on the basis of their expected risk-adjusted return on capital.

(continued on following page)

BOX 7-1 *(Continued)*

- *A VaR system allows a firm to assess the benefits from portfolio diversification within a line of activity and across businesses.* VaR allows managers to assess the daily revenue volatility they might expect from any given trading area, but it also allows them to compare the volatilities of different business areas, such as equity and fixed-income businesses, so that they can understand better how each business line offsets, or contributes to, the revenue volatility of the whole firm.

- *VaR has become an industry-standard internal and external reporting tool.* VaR reports are produced daily for managers of business lines, and are then aggregated for senior management. VaR is also communicated to the regulators and has become the basis for calculating regulatory capital in some areas of risk measurement. The rating agencies take VaR calculations into account in establishing their ratings of banks. Increasingly, VaR and the results of the back testing of VaR are published in banks' annual reports as a key indicator of risk.

Figures 7-3*A* and *B* helps us to visualize what VaR measures mean in practice, and how they are used to manage risk on a trading desk. (For this example, we'll stick with the nonparametric, or historical VaR, approach to calculating VaR, one of a set of calculation approaches that we explain in more detail later on.) In this illustrative example, the average daily revenue for our example bank's trading portfolio during 1998 was C$0.451 million. But what we are really interested in is the distribution of the bank's gains and losses, represented in Figure 7-3*B*, which tells us how frequently the bank incurred each loss amount. The first percentile of the historical distribution represented in Figure 7-3*B*, i.e., the cutoff point on this distribution such that only 1 percent of the daily revenues lies on the distribution's left-hand side, is C$25.919 million. This represents VAR', or the absolute VaR to a 99 percent level of confidence. From our earlier discussion, we know that to work out the true one-day historical VaR for the portfolio, we need to take the expected profit or loss into account. So our VaR number to a 99 percent level of confidence based on this 12-month set of data is 0.451 − (−25.919) = C$26.37 million.

Now let's turn again to Figure 7-3*A* to discuss how VaR limits are used as a practical tool for managing market risk. Retrospectively, 1998 is an interesting year for the purpose of analyzing risk management decisions. Market participants were surprised by the severe market disruptions in August 1998 after the Russian government defaulted on its debt.

Liquidity suddenly evaporated from many financial markets, causing asset prices to plunge and producing large losses for many financial institutions (and the near-collapse of the U.S. hedge fund LTCM). Figure 7-3*A*
shows the aggregate VaR creeping up slowly during the first part of the
year, then increasing substantially during May and June as market volatility edged higher. During that period, the Senior Risk Committee limit for
the bank remained at $58 million, well above the daily VaR (Figure 7-3*A*).
As risk kept increasing during the summer, the Senior Risk Committee
limit was lowered to $38 million in July before the August market crisis.
At the peak of the market disruption during the month of August, the new
VaR limit became binding, putting pressure on the bank's trading businesses to lower their risks. We can see from the figure that the bank experienced substantial trading losses during the month of August, and after
this the VaR limit was further reduced in order to oblige the trading businesses to reduce their risk exposure still further.

As a general point, VaR limits for individual business lines such as
trading desks must be set at a level consistent with the firm's overall VaR
limit. Otherwise the risk exposures of all the business units might remain

FIGURE 7-3A

Net Daily Trading Revenues during 1998 versus
One-Day VaR at the 99 Percent Confidence Level.

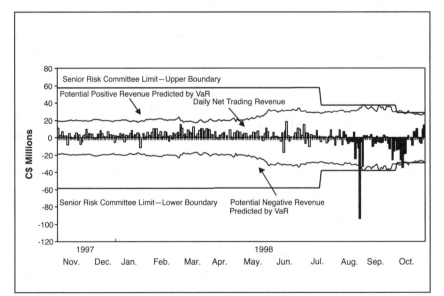

FIGURE 7-3B

Net Daily Trading Revenues for 1998 (C$ Millions)

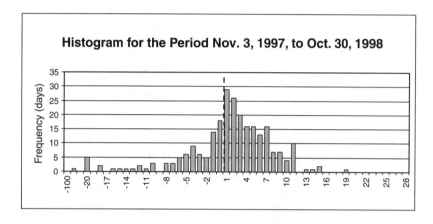

within their own limits, while the firm's aggregate risk breached the over-all VaR limit set at the top of the firm.

HOW DO WE GENERATE DISTRIBUTIONS FOR CALCULATING VAR?

To calculate VaR, we first need to select the factors that drive the volatil-ity of returns in the trading or investment portfolio. We can then use these risk factors to generate the forward distribution of the portfolio values at the risk horizon (or, equivalently, the distribution of the changes in the value of the portfolio). Only after generating the distribution can we cal-culate the mean and the quantiles of this distribution to arrive at the port-folio VaR.

1. Selection of the Risk Factors

The change in the value of the portfolio is driven by changes in the mar-ket factors that influence the price of each instrument. The relevant risk factors depend on the composition of the portfolio. The selection of risk factors is straightforward for a simple security, but it requires judgment for more complex products.

In the case of a simple security, such as a U.S. $/euro forward, the value of the position is affected only by the U.S. $/euro forward rate. In the case of a U.S. $/euro call option, the value of the position depends not

TABLE 7-2

Example of a Selection of Risk Factors

U.S.$/euro forward	U.S.$/euro option
▪ U.S.$/euro forward rate	▪ US$/euro exchange rate
	▪ US$ interest rates
	▪ Euro interest rates
	▪ US$/euro volatility

only on the U.S. $/euro exchange rate, but also on the dollar and euro interest rates over the maturity of the option and on the U.S. $/euro volatility (Table 7-2).

In the case of a stock portfolio, the risk factors are the prices of the individual stocks that make up the portfolio. For a bond portfolio, the choice of the risk factors depends on the degree of "granularity" that one needs in order to understand the risk in hand. For example, the risk factor for each bond might simply be its yield to maturity, as described in Chapter 6. Alternatively, it might be a selection of zero-coupon rates on the risk-free term structure of interest rates for each currency. The selection might comprise the overnight, 1-month, 3-month, 6-month, 1-year, 3-year, 5-year, 10-year, and 30-year zero-coupon rates, as well as the spread in prices between different issuers for the same terms (so that the calculation captures issuer risk).

2. Choice of a Methodology for Modeling Changes in Market Risk Factors

Having identified the risk factors that generate the volatility in the portfolio's returns, the risk analyst must choose an appropriate methodology for deriving the distribution. There are three alternatives:

- ▪ The analytic variance-covariance approach
- ▪ The historical simulation approach
- ▪ The Monte Carlo simulation approach

Analytic Variance-Covariance Approach: Case of a Portfolio Linear in Risks

To simplify the derivation of VaR, we can choose to make certain assumptions. Under the analytic variance-covariance approach or "delta normal" approach, we assume that the risk factors and the portfolio values are log-normally distributed or, equivalently, that their log returns (the log of the returns) are normally distributed. This makes the calculation much simpler, since the normal distribution is completely characterized by its first two moments, and the analyst can derive the mean and the variance of the portfolio return distribution from

- The multivariate distribution of the risk factors
- The composition of the portfolio

A simple example should help make the process clear. Suppose our example portfolio is composed of two stocks, Microsoft and Exxon. In this example, the risk factors that generate the returns in the portfolio are straightforward to identify: the stock prices for each of the companies, the volatility of both stocks, and the correlation coefficient that describes the extent to which the stock prices of Microsoft and Exxon go up and down together.

From historical data on the behavior of the two stocks, we can estimate the simple historical mean and standard deviation of the daily returns for each of the two stocks for each day over a one-year trading period. We could obtain this stock price information from any of the major market information providers, such as Reuters or Bloomberg.

The historical data also allow us to estimate a correlation risk factor for the price relationship between the two stocks. The correlation risk factor is quite important: when the stocks are perfectly correlated, the VaR will be the sum of the VaRs of the individual stocks. Most stocks are not strongly correlated, however, so the VaR tends to be considerably less than the sum of the VaRs of the individual stocks.

Under this approach, remember that we assume that the rates of return on the stocks follow a multivariate normal distribution. This assumption means that we can apply our risk-factor analysis to the present portfolio to generate a distribution of returns of the portfolio into the future. Of course, we must take into account the present price of the portfolio and the percentage of each stock that the portfolio contains.

Having generated the distribution using our five risk factors, we can plot the distribution so that it looks rather like the curve in Figure 7-2, referred to earlier in our discussion. It is now a simple enough matter to read off the VaR number that is relevant to our selected confidence level (e.g., 99 percent), as we described earlier for Figure 7-2.

Our discussion of this approach to calculating VaR begs a major question: how dangerous is our simplifying assumption that returns are normally distributed? In fact, there is a large amount of evidence that many individual return distributions are not normally distributed, but rather exhibit what are known as "fat tails." The term *fat tails* arises out of the shape of certain distributions when plotted on a graph. In these distributions, there are more observations far away from the mean than is the case in a normal or bell-shaped distribution. So whereas a normal distribution tails off quickly (to reflect the rarity of unlikely events), the tail of a fat-tailed distribution remains relatively thick. We can see the difference in Figure 7-4, where the dotted line represents a normal distribution and the continuous line a fatter-tailed distribution.

Fat tails in distributions should worry risk managers because they imply that extraordinary losses occur more frequently than a normal distribution would lead us to believe.

We would expect the VaR derived from a fat-tailed distribution to be higher than that derived from a normal distribution—perhaps much higher. It follows that if we assume that a distribution is normal in our VaR calculation, when in fact it has a fat tail, we are likely to underestimate the VaR number associated with the financial portfolio.

FIGURE 7-4

Comparison of the Normal and a Fat-Tailed Distribution

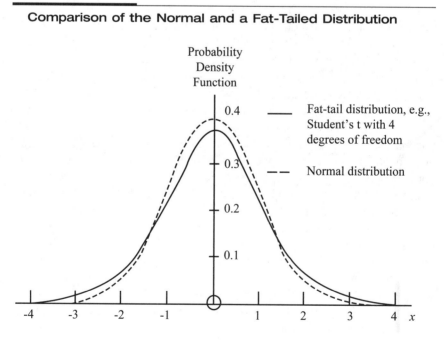

Luckily, even if the returns of an individual risk factor do not follow a normal distribution, we can reasonably expect that the returns of a well-diversified portfolio (i.e., a portfolio subject to many different risk factors) will still exhibit a normal distribution. This effect is explained by the central limit theorem, which tells us that the independent random variables of a well-behaved distribution will have a mean that converges, in large samples, to a normal distribution.

In practice, this result implies that a risk manager can assume that a portfolio has a normal distribution of returns, provided that the portfolio is fairly well diversified and the risk-factor returns are sufficiently independent from one another (even when they are not, themselves, normally distributed).

However, the potential effect on VaR calculations of fat tails, lumpy portfolios, and correlated risk-factor returns should send a warning signal to support staff and senior managers who use VaR numbers to gain comfort about risk levels.

Historical Simulation Approach

The historical simulation approach to VaR calculation is conceptually simple and does not oblige the user to make any analytic assumptions about the distributions. However, at least two or three years of historical data are necessary to produce meaningful results. We've already applied the principles of this approach in our earlier example of the VaR number associated with trading revenues in 1998. In this special case, there was only one risk factor: the daily trading revenue of the firm. In the following, we consider the more usual case: analyzing the VaR of a whole portfolio of securities.

First, the changes in relevant market prices and rates (the risk factors) that have been seen are analyzed over a specified historical period, say, two years. The portfolio under examination is then revalued, using changes in the risk factors derived from the historical data, to create the distribution of the portfolio returns from which the VaR of the portfolio can be derived. Each daily simulated change in the value of the portfolio is considered as an observation in the distribution.

Three steps are involved:

- Select a sample of actual daily risk factor changes over a given period of time, say 500 days (i.e., two years' worth of trading days), using the same period of time for all the factors.

- Apply those daily changes to the current value of the risk factors, revaluing the current portfolio as many times as the number of days in the historical sample. Sum these changes across all positions, keeping the days synchronized.

- Construct the histogram of portfolio values and identify the VaR that isolates the first percentile of the distribution in the left-hand tail (assuming VaR is derived at the 99 percent confidence level).

Let's illustrate the approach using an example. Assume that the current portfolio is composed of a three-month U.S. \$/DM call option. The market risk factors for this position are

- U.S. \$/DM exchange rate
- U.S. \$ three-month interest rate
- DM three-month interest rate
- Three-month implied volatility of the U.S. \$/DM exchange rate

In the following, we neglect the impact of interest-rate risk factors and consider only the level of the exchange rate and its volatility. The first step is to report daily observations of the risk factors we've selected over the past 100 days, as shown in abbreviated form in columns 2 and 3 of Table 7-3.

Historical simulation, like Monte Carlo simulation, requires the repricing of the position in question using the historical distribution of the risk factors. In this example, we use the Black-Scholes model adapted by

TABLE 7-3

Historical Market Values for the Risk Factors Over the Last 100 Days

Day (t)	U.S.\$/DM (FX_t)	FX Volatility (σ_t)
−100	1.3970	0.149
−99	1.3960	0.149
−98	1.3973	0.151
...	...	...
−2	1.4015	0.163
−1	1.4024	0.164

TABLE 7-4

Simulating Portfolio Values Using Historical Data
(Current Value of the Portfolio: $1.80)

	Change from Current Value ($1.80)
Alternative price 100 = C(FX$_{100}$; σ_{100}) = $1.75	−$0.05
Alternative price 99 = C(FX$_{99}$; σ_{99}) = $1.73	−$0.07
Alternative price 98 = C(FX$_{98}$; σ_{98}) = $1.69	−$0.11
. . . .	
Alternative price 2 = C(FX$_{2}$; σ_{2}) = $1.87	+$0.07
Alternative price 1 = C(FX$_{1}$; σ_{1}) = $1.88	+$0.08

TABLE 7-5

Identifying the First Percentile of
the Historical Distribution of the
Portfolio Return

Rank	Change from Current Value
100	−$0.05
99	−$0.07
98	−$0.11
. . .	. . .
2	+$0.07
1	+$0.08

Garman-Kholhagen (1983) to currency options. The results of this step are reported in Table 7-4.[1]

The last step consists of constructing the histogram of the portfolio returns based on the last 100 days of history or, equivalently, sorting the changes in portfolio values to identify the first percentile of the distribution. Table 7-5 shows the ranking of the changes in the value of the portfolio. Using this, we identify the first percentile as -$0.07.

---

1. F. Black, and M. Scholes, "The Pricing of Options and Corporate Liabilities," *Journal of Political Economy* 81, 1973, pp. 637-654; M. B. Garman and S. Kolhagen, "Foreign Currency Option Values," *Journal of International Money and Finance* 2, December 1983, pp. 231-237.

FIGURE 7-5

VaR from Historical Simulations

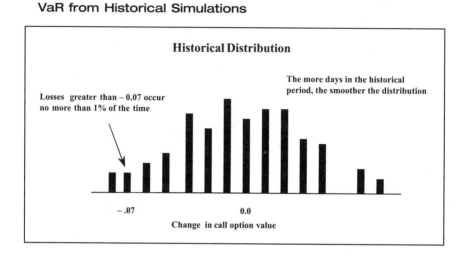

Figure 7-5 shows the histogram of these values. VaR (1; 99) at the 99 percent confidence level is simply the distance to the mean ($0.01) of the first percentile, i.e., VaR (1; 99) = $0.08, while absolute VaR is the first percentile itself, i.e., VaR' (1; 99) = $0.07. Note that this histogram is similar to the histogram that we derived for daily trading revenues in Figure 7-3*b*.

This three-step procedure can easily be generalized to any portfolio of securities.

The major attraction of historical simulation is that the method is completely nonparametric (i.e., we don't need to worry about setting parameters) and does not depend on any assumptions about the distribution of the risk factors. In particular, we do not need to assume that the returns of the risk factors are normally distributed and independent over time.

The nonparametric nature of historical simulation also obviates the need to estimate volatilities and correlations. Historical volatilities and correlations are already reflected in the data set, so all we need to calculate are the synchronous risk-factor returns over a given historical period. Historical simulation has also no problem accommodating fat tails in distributions, since the historical returns already reflect actual synchronous moves in the market across all risk factors. Another advantage of historical simulation over the variance-covariance approach is that it allows the analyst to calculate confidence intervals for VaR.

The main drawback of historical simulation is its complete dependence on a particular set of historical data, and thus on the idiosyncrasies of this data set. The underlying assumption is that the past, as captured in this historical data set, is a reliable representation of the future (i.e., the past is prologue). This implicitly presumes that the market events embedded in the historical data set will be reproduced in the months to come. However, the historical period may cover events, such as a market crash or, conversely, a period of exceptionally low price volatility, that are unlikely to be repeated in the future. Historical simulation may also lead to a distorted assessment of the risk if we employ the technique regardless of any structural changes anticipated in the market, such as the introduction of the euro in the foreign exchange markets at the beginning of 1999.

Another practical limitation of historical simulation is data availability. One year of data corresponds to only 250 data points (trading days) on average, i.e., 250 scenarios. By contrast, Monte Carlo simulations usually involve at least 10,000 simulations (i.e., scenarios). Employing small samples of historical data inevitably leaves gaps in the distributions of the risk factors and tends to underrepresent the tails of the distributions, i.e., the occurrence of unlikely but extreme events.

Monte Carlo Approach

Monte Carlo simulation consists of repeatedly simulating the random processes that govern market prices and rates. Each simulation (scenario) generates a possible value for the portfolio at the target horizon (e.g., 10 days). If we generate enough of these scenarios, the simulated distribution of the portfolio's values will converge toward the true, although unknown, distribution. The VaR can be easily inferred from the distribution, as we described earlier.

Monte Carlo simulation involves three steps:

1. *Specify all the relevant risk factors.* As in the other approaches, we need to select all the relevant risk factors. In addition, we have to specify the dynamics of these factors, i.e., their stochastic processes, and we need to estimate their parameters (volatilities, correlations, mean reversion factors for interest-rate processes, and so on).

2. *Construct price paths.* Price paths are constructed using random numbers produced by a random-number generator. For a simple portfolio without complex exotic options, the forward distribu-

tion of portfolio returns at a 10-day horizon can be generated in one step. Alternatively, if the simulation is performed on a daily basis, a random distribution is drawn for each day to calculate the 10-day cumulative impact.

When several correlated risk factors are involved, we need to simulate multivariate distributions. Only in the case where the distributions are independent can the randomization be performed independently for each variable.

3. *Value the portfolio for each path (scenario).* Each path generates a set of values for the risk factors for each security in the portfolio that are used as inputs into the pricing models. The process is repeated a large number of times, say 10,000 times, to generate the distribution, at the risk horizon, of the portfolio return. This step is equivalent to the corresponding procedure for historical simulation, except that Monte Carlo simulation can generate many more scenarios than historical simulation.

VaR at the 99 percent confidence level is then simply derived as the distance to the mean of the first percentile of the distribution, as for our other calculation methods.

Monte Carlo simulation is a powerful and flexible approach to VaR. It can accommodate any distribution of risk factors to allow for fat-tailed distributions, where extreme events are expected to occur more commonly than in normal distributions, and "jumps" or discontinuities in price processes. For example, a process can be described as a mixture of two normal distributions or as a jump-diffusion process where the number of jumps in any time interval is governed by, say, a Poisson process (both processes are consistent with fat tails).

Monte Carlo simulation, like historical simulation, allows the analyst to calculate the confidence interval of VaR, i.e., the range of likely values that VaR might take if we repeated the simulation many times. The narrower this confidence interval, the more precise the estimate of VaR. Monte Carlo simulation has a particular advantage here: it is easy to carry out sensitivity analyses by changing the market parameters used in the analysis, such as the term structure of interest rates.

One disadvantage of the Monte Carlo approach is that the analyst must be able to estimate the parameters of the distributions, such as the means, the variances, and the covariances. The major limitation of the approach, however, is more pragmatic: the amount of computer resources it consumes. Variance-reduction techniques can be used to reduce the computational time, but Monte Carlo simulation remains very computer intensive and cannot be used to calculate the VaR of very large and complex portfolios.

Pros and Cons of the Different Approaches

Each of the approaches we have described has advantages and limitations; no single technique is "perfect," and no technique dominates the others.

For this reason, it is important that financial professionals and managers who rely on VaR numbers to measure risk—or to gain comfort about the risks that an institution is taking—be familiar with the basic principles of the VaR calculation. Increasingly, equity analysts and investors also need to understand these numbers if they are to assess the information that a bank makes public about its risk profile.

Table 7-6A through C summarizes the pros and cons of the different approaches. Together with the information contained in this chapter, it can be used to frame questions about how any particular VaR number has been produced.

Above all, people using VaR numbers must remember that they are not a "magic bullet" for measuring and managing risk. In the right hands, VaR techniques help to offer risk analysts a rational and comparable snapshot of the risk of a particular position or portfolio. But like every financial measure, VaR numbers in the wrong hands can be used to mislead and obfuscate. Their reliability as a decision-making tool depends upon the skill and experience of the analyst, the nature of the problem that is being explored, and the ability of decision makers to ask intelligent questions about meaning and provenance.

TABLE 7-6A

Pros and Cons of the Variance-Covariance Approach

Pros	Cons
Computationally efficient; it takes only a few minutes to run the position of the entire bank.	Assumes normality of the return portfolio.
Because of central limit theorem, the methodology can be applied even if the risk factors are not normal, provided the factors are numerous and relatively independent.	Assumes that the risk factors follow a multivariate log-normal distribution, and thus does not cope very well with "fat-tailed" distributions.

(continued on following page)

TABLE 7-6A *(Continued)*

Pros and Cons of the Variance-Covariance Approach

Pros	Cons
No pricing model is required; only the Greeks are necessary, and these can be provided directly by most of the systems that already exist within banks (i.e., the legacy systems).	Requires the estimation of the volatilities of the risk factors as well as the correlations of their returns.
It is easy to handle incremental VaR.	Security returns can be approximated by means of a Taylor expansion. In some instances, however, a second-order expansion may not be sufficient to capture option risk (especially in the case of exotic options).
	Cannot be used to conduct sensitivity analysis.
	Cannot be used to derive the confidence interval for VaR.

TABLE 7-6B

Pros and Cons of the Historical Simulation Approach

Pros	Cons
No need to make any assumption about the distribution of the risk factors.	Complete dependence on a particular historical data set and its idiosyncrasies. That is, extreme events such as market crashes either lie outside the data set and are ignored, or lie within the data set and (for some purposes) act to distort it.
No need to estimate volatilities and correlations; they are implicitly captured by the actual (synchronous) daily realizations of the market factors.	Cannot accommodate changes in the market structure, such as the introduction of the euro in January 1999.
Fat tails of distributions, and other extreme events, are captured so long as they are contained in the data set.	Short data set may lead to biased and imprecise estimation of VaR.
Aggregation across markets is straightforward.	Cannot be used to conduct sensitivity analyses.
Allows the calculation of confidence intervals for VaR.	Not always computationally efficient when the portfolio contains complex securities.

TABLE 7-6C

Pros and Cons of the Monte Carlo Simulation Approach

Pros	Cons
Can accommodate any distribution of risk factors.	Outliers are not incorporated into the distribution.
Can be used to model any complex portfolio.	Computer intensive.
Allows the calculation of confidence intervals for VaR.	
Allows the user to perform sensitivity analyses and stress testing.	

Perhaps the key "lesson learned" about VaR numbers, however, is that they must be supplemented by the methodologies we turn to in the next section: stress testing and worst-case scenarios.

STRESS TESTING AND SCENARIO ANALYSIS

As we discussed earlier, VaR is far from being a perfect measure of risk. Its use and reliability are often dictated by the availability of data; for instance, reliable data for implied volatilities can be obtained only for short maturities. And to facilitate the implementation of a VaR model, especially in the case of the analytic variance-covariance and Monte Carlo approaches, it is common to assume that market conditions will remain normal. Prices and values are assumed to have a "smooth" behavior that excludes the possibility of jumps and other extreme events.

We don't yet know how to construct a VaR model that would combine, in a meaningful way, periods of normal market conditions with periods of market crises characterized by large price changes, high volatility, and a breakdown in the correlations among the risk factors.

Another problem is that VaR is usually calculated within a static framework and is therefore appropriate only for relatively short time horizons, which in turn means that we can't include dynamic liquidity risks in the VaR analysis.

All this means that stress testing and scenario analysis must be used as supplementary methodologies to help us analyze the possible effects of extreme events that lie outside normal market conditions. Regulators view stress testing and scenario analysis as a necessary complement to the use of internal VaR models.

The purpose of stress testing and scenario analysis is to determine the size (though not the frequency) of potential losses related to specific scenarios. The selection of an appropriate scenario is largely based on expert judgment. The scenario may consist of extreme changes in the value of a risk factor (interest rate, exchange rate, equity price, or commodity price), such as a shift of 100 bp in the level of interest rates over the period of a month; replication scenarios that attempt to reproduce the multi-risk-factor effects of extreme historical events; and hypothetical one-time events that depend on imagined future developments.

Risk-Factor Stress Testing

Back in 1995, the Derivative Policy Group recommended some specific guidelines for risk-factor stress testing that help give us a flavor of the range of stresses banks now use to test out their derivative exposures:[2]

- Parallel yield-curve shift of plus or minus 100 bp
- Yield-curve twist of plus or minus 25 bp
- Equity index values change of plus or minus 10 percent
- Currency changes of plus or minus 6 percent
- Volatility changes of plus or minus 20 percent

These extreme price and rate variations may dramatically affect the value of a portfolio with strong nonlinearity and large negative gammas. Portfolios of this kind incur losses whether prices fall or rise, and the magnitude of the losses accelerates as the change in price increases. (Recall that gamma is the nickname for the second derivative of the instrument's value with respect to the value of the underlying asset.)

The regulators also now require that financial institutions run scenarios that capture the specific characteristics of their portfolios, i.e., scenarios that involve the risk factors to which their portfolios are most sensitive. Following the market crisis of the summer of 1998, when the disappearance of liquidity in some financial markets led to several well-publicized losses (we recount the story of the near-collapse of LTCM in Chapter 14), regulators required financial institutions to include liquidity

---

2. Derivatives Policy Group. A framework for voluntary Oversight, 1995.

risk in their scenario analyses. Many institutions now also apply stress-testing approaches to their credit and operational risk exposures.

Stress-Testing Envelopes

Stress testing is becoming more and more sophisticated, and one of the challenges is to work out a rigorous way of applying different kinds of stress to portfolios in a consistent manner.

Here we'll consider a "stress-envelope" methodology, which combines stress categories with the worst possible "stress shocks" across all possible markets for every business. For example, the methodology might designate seven stress categories corresponding to the various risk categories: interest rates, foreign exchange rates, equity prices, commodity prices, credit spreads, swap spreads, and vega (volatility). For each stress category, the worst possible stress shocks that might realistically occur in the market are defined. In the case of interest rates, for example, the methodology defines six stress shocks to accommodate both changes in the *level* of rates and changes in the *shape* of the yield curve. In the case of credit spreads and equities, there is only one stress shock, i.e., the widening of credit spreads and the fall of equity prices, respectively. All other stress categories make use of one or two stress shocks (increases or decreases in spreads or prices), as shown in Table 7-7.

The number of markets, currencies, and businesses must be determined empirically for each institution.

We can think of the stress envelope itself as the change in the market value of a business position in a particular currency or market in

TABLE 7-7

Stress Categories and the Number of Stress Shocks

	Stress Category	Stress Shocks
1	Interest rates	6
2	Foreign exchange	2
3	Equity	1
4	Commodity	2
5	Credit spreads	1
6	Swap spreads	2
7	Vega (volatility)	2

FIGURE 7-6

The Seven Major Components of the
Stress-Envelope Approach

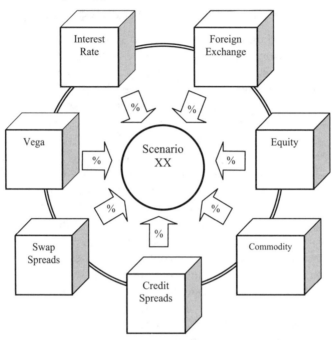

response to a particular stress shock. A scenario can then be created using a combination of several stress shocks (Figure 7-6).

As well as testing hypothetical extreme changes in risk factors, a scenario might also correspond to extreme historical events, such as the stock
market crash of October 1987. On the October 19, 1987, stock prices in
the United States fell by 23 percent, or approximately 22 times their daily
standard deviation. Other historical scenarios might include the failure of
the European exchange-rate mechanism in September 1992 or the tightening of monetary policy by the Federal Reserve in the United States in
May 1994 (and the subsequent fall in bond prices).

Boxes 7-2 and 7-3 present examples of historical replication scenarios. We might also build hypothetical extreme scenarios to explore the risks
of plausible structural changes in the market that are likely to damage a
portfolio. For example, we might set values around an event in which the
Chinese devalue their currency, causing a crisis in Asia.

REPLICATION SCENARIO 1: STOCK MARKET CRASH

As an example of a historical replication scenario, consider a stock market crash reminiscent of the crisis in the global financial markets in October 1987, characterized by a combination of the following events:

- Equity markets around the globe fall by 20 percent on average, with Asian markets, such as Hong Kong, declining by 30 percent, and there is an upward shift in implied volatilities from 20 to 50 percent.
- The U.S. dollar rallies against other currencies as a consequence of a flight to quality. Asian currencies lose up to 10 percent against the dollar.
- Interest rates fall in Western markets. Hong Kong interest rates rise by 40 bp at the long end of the term structure and by 100 bp at the short end.
- Commodity prices drop as a result of fears of a recession; copper and oil prices decline by 5 percent.

REPLICATION SCENARIO 2: U.S. MONETARY TIGHTENING

In this example of a historical replication scenario, consider a U.S. inflation scare and a tightening of monetary policy by the U.S. Federal Reserve along the lines of that seen in May 1994, characterized by

- A 100-bp increase in the overnight interest rate and a 50-bp upward shift in the long end of the curve.
- Interest rates also increase in other G-7 countries and Switzerland, but not as much as in the United States.
- G-7 currencies depreciate against the U.S. dollar as investors chase higher rates.
- Credit spreads widen.
- Equity markets decline from 3 to 6 percent, with an upward shift in implied volatilities.

Advantages of Stress Testing
and Scenario Analysis

The major benefit of stress testing and scenario analysis is that they show us how vulnerable a portfolio might be to a variety of extreme events. During a market crisis, historical correlations change as volatilities increase. Correlations may suddenly increase dramatically and become +1 as many markets collapse at the same time and liquidity dries up. Alternatively, correlations may approach −1 as markets or instruments move in opposite directions. For example, a market event may trigger a flight to quality, with liquid and illiquid markets exhibiting almost perfect negative correlation.

Each portfolio has specific characteristics that make it vulnerable to a particular scenario and/or stress tests. Obviously, a high-yield bond portfolio is vulnerable to a widening of credit spreads. An equity portfolio that is diversified across many countries and sectors of activities is sensitive to a change in the correlation structure of the world's equity markets. An equity derivative book that is short gamma is vulnerable to a sharp increase in volatility. Stress testing and scenario analyses are very useful in highlighting these unique vulnerabilities for senior management.

Limitations of Stress Testing
and Scenario Analysis

Stress testing and scenario analysis are important building blocks in any risk management methodology, but they can't tell us how likely it is that a particular event will come to pass. They also have many other limitations that we must bear in mind:

- Scenarios are based on an arbitrary combination of stress shocks. Yet many such combinations are inconsistent with the basic laws of economics. They may violate, for example, no-arbitrage conditions such as interest-rate parity. When constructing a scenario, it is important to examine the chain of events to make sure that it makes economic sense. The chain of events that may logically follow an initial major shock depends on the context, and may be quite different from one crisis to another. For example, the Asian crisis of the summer of 1997 was quite different from the Asian crisis of the summer of 1998 (triggered by the partial default of Russia).

- The potential number of combinations of basic stress shocks is overwhelming. In practice, only a relatively small number of scenarios can be routinely analyzed. This means that the scenarios have to be selected according to the vulnerabilities of the particular portfolio. Again, the choice is necessarily somewhat arbitrary. The usefulness and accuracy of the diagnosis that emerges from the scenario analysis depends on the judgment and experience of the analysts who design and run these scenarios. Even the best analysts rely on the past as a guide to the future. Yet history is unlikely to repeat itself exactly.

- Market crises unfold over a period of time, during which liquidity may dry up. Yet most scenario analyses are static in nature; i.e., they are one-period models and do not allow for the trading of positions in an environment in which liquidity varies from one period to the next. Stretching the period from one day to one week, or to six months, does not make the model more dynamic, as it continues to assume that events occur simultaneously and that the portfolio remains constant during the period. The modeling framework usually does not allow for dynamic hedging or the unwinding of positions.

SUMMARY OF KEY RISKS—
VaR AND STRESS TESTING

The stress-testing and scenarios methodologies presented in the previous section can be combined with the VaR approach to produce a summary of significant risks.

Such a report ranks the risk exposure of the firm's positions. For each position, it shows the VaR and the loss corresponding to the stress scenario that would affect the position the most. For example, a high-yield portfolio might well be most exposed to a widening of credit spreads, so the relevant scenario is based on stress-envelope values for a widening of credit spreads.

As stress testing becomes more sophisticated, it's important that institutions devote some thought to how risk analysts report the results of stress tests and present these results to decision makers. There's no point in uncovering the unique vulnerability of an institution to a particular set of events, if that information does not prompt an appropriate response from management.

CHAPTER 8

Asset-Liability Management

Asset-liability management (ALM) is the structured decision-making process for matching (and deliberately mismatching) the mix of assets and liabilities on a firm's balance sheet. In the banking industry, where ALM is a critical discipline, the key objectives are to

- Stabilize net interest income (NII), that is, the difference between the amount the bank pays out in interest for funding and the amount it receives from holding assets such as loans (as measured by accounting earnings).
- Maximize shareholder wealth or net worth (NW), as reflected by long-term economic earnings.
- Make sure the bank doesn't assume too much risk from the mismatching of maturities and amounts between assets and liabilities and from funding liquidity risk (the danger that the bank won't be able to raise funds quickly and cheaply enough to fulfill its obligations and remain solvent).

These objectives give ALM a very wide scope, which can include managing market risk (i.e., interest-rate risk, foreign exchange risk, commodity price risk, and equity price risk), liquidity risk, trading risk, funding and capital planning, taxation, and regulatory constraints, as well as profitability and growth. ALM also involves off-balance-sheet activity, such as the use of hedges designed to offset interest-rate exposures.

While value-at-risk (VaR) is the technique adopted by most financial institutions to control market and credit risk in the trading book, ALM involves a distinct set of techniques used to control risk in the banking book, such as gap analysis, duration gap analysis, and long-term VaR. (The difference in techniques is driven by the fact that most of the assets and liabilities in the banking book have long maturities and are much less liquid than are traded financial instruments.)

ALM strategy is the responsibility of the treasurer of the company, but the control of the *risk* in the balance sheet is typically a part of the mandate of the risk management function—and should remain independent of the risk takers. ALM management typically operates under the assumption that there is no credit risk (e.g., loans do not default), leaving credit risk under the purview of the groups within risk management who are responsible for managing corporate and retail credit risk.

ALM is particularly critical for financial institutions, such as commercial banks, savings and loans, insurance companies, and pension funds. Banks, for example, are involved in collecting deposits and extending loans to retail and corporate clients. This financial intermediation activity generates two types of imbalances: first, an imbalance between the amount of funds collected and lent, and second, an imbalance between the maturities as well as the interest rate sensitivities of the sources of funding and the loans extended to clients.

These imbalances drive the net worth of the bank—and its risk profile. For example, deposits generally have a shorter maturity than loans, so the net worth of many banks benefits from a fall in interest rates: the bank pays less interest to its depositors but continues for a period to receive the higher rate from its borrowers. Conversely, the net worth of the same banks will tend to deteriorate if interest rates go up. If this downside risk is not managed, it can lead to insolvency in individual institutions or even in whole banking industries (Box 8-1).

Banks' earnings are particularly sensitive to changes in interest rates and in the cost of funds. But many ALM principles apply equally to corporations outside the financial sector whose assets and liabilities are sensitive to market risk factors. Like banks, these firms face many funding and capital planning issues.

In this chapter, we first define interest-rate risk and liquidity risk in the context of ALM, and we explain the roles of the ALCO (asset-liability management committee) responsible for coordinating the management of the firm's balance sheet. Then we present techniques for assessing interest-rate risk in the balance sheet, i.e., gap analysis, duration gap/duration of equity, and long-term VaR. We also discuss funding liquidity risk management and, finally, funds transfer pricing.

B O X   8 - 1

THE SAVINGS AND LOAN CRISIS

The savings and loan (S&L) industry in the United States prospered through most of the twentieth century thanks to the upward-sloping shape of the yield curve. The upward-sloping curve meant that the interest rate on a 10-year residential mortgage (a typical product offered by S&Ls) exceeded rates on the short-maturity savings and time deposits that were the S&L's main source of funding. In the banking industry's vocabulary, S&Ls simply had to "ride the curve" to make money.

However, during the period October 1979 to October 1982, the Fed's restrictive monetary policy led to a sudden and dramatic surge in interest rates, with the yield from Treasury bills rising as high as 16 percent. The increase in short-term rates pushed up the cost of funds for S&Ls, sweeping away the interest-rate margin they depended on. Indeed, in this period, the spike in their cost of funding meant that S&Ls generated *negative* net interest margins on many of their long-term residential mortgage portfolios.

The failure of the S&Ls to manage their interest-rate risk helped to spark the long-running S&L crisis in the United States, which gathered force through the 1980s as S&Ls desperately sought to repair their balance sheets with new business activities and risky lending—only to find themselves losing even more money through poorly controlled credit and business risk. Ultimately, a large number of S&Ls failed or were taken over, especially in 1988 and 1989. The number of S&Ls fell from 4,000 to 2,600 between 1980 and 1989, and the crisis necessitated one of the world's most expensive banking system bailouts—courtesy of the American taxpayer.

INTEREST-RATE RISK AND LIQUIDITY RISK

Interest-rate risk and liquidity risk are the two major risks affecting balance sheet management.

Interest-rate risk has an impact on

- *Net interest income (NII)*, i.e., interest earned, less interest paid on interest-bearing assets and liabilities. NII, traditionally a key indicator of bank profitability, is affected by the pricing mismatches of assets and liabilities (on- and off-balance-sheet). The impact of interest-rate volatility on NII is usually analyzed over a short time horizon, such as one quarter or one year, and is

referred to as earnings-at-risk (EaR). It relies essentially on accounting data.

- *Net worth (NW),* i.e., the net present value of assets minus the
net present value of liabilities, plus or minus the net present
value of off-balance-sheet items. Net worth analysis is meant to
provide an economic measure of shareholders' wealth, and it
should also provide an institution with early warning of potential
solvency problems. The impact of interest rates on NW is considered over a relatively long time horizon.

- *Noninterest income.* The income from servicing loans and other
fee-based income is known in the financial industries as "noninterest income," but it, too, can be affected by interest rate fluctuations. For example, a change in interest rates might affect
mutual fund sales fees, fees from securities lending, mortgage
and loan application fees, refinancing fees, securitization fees,
and so on.

Interest-rate risk also has an effect on a firm's capital-to-asset ratio,
business volume, and product mix as well as on the pricing of assets and
liabilities, liquidity risk, and credit risk.

To mitigate interest-rate risk, the structure of the balance sheet has
to be managed in such a way that the effect on assets of any movement of
interest rates remains highly correlated with its effect on liabilities, even
in a volatile interest-rate environment. The amount of earnings volatility
that is acceptable will depend on the risk appetite of the institution;
the board may well approve risk limits to constrain earnings volatility resulting from interest-rate volatility. These limits are generally based on
worst-case scenarios, such as a 200-basis-point (bp) parallel shift in interest rates across all maturities (up and down); each scenario can be considered in relation to its impact on accounting profit, net worth, and
capital-to-asset ratio. To take a rather simple and static example, the board
might approve a limit for a plausible worst-case scenario at a maximum
negative impact of $1 billion on the NW of the institution and $200 million on NII.

As we'll see later on in this chapter, some banks use sophisticated
computer simulations that determine the impact on NII and NW of numerous interest-rate scenarios, balance sheet trends, and strategies over
various time horizons. These more complex simulations may specify
strategies for originating funds through retail products (e.g., through at-
tracting more deposits) and for the refinancing of maturing liabilities.

Foreign exchange risk and commodity risk can also be important components of balance sheet risk management, depending on the institution's activities.

Funding liquidity risks can stem from both external market conditions and structural problems within the bank's balance sheet. The near collapse of the giant hedge fund Long-Term Capital Management (LTCM) in 1998 offers an example of a funding liquidity crisis that was largely prompted by unexpected external conditions (see Chapter 14). The case of Continental Illinois Bank (Box 8-2), which had to be rescued in 1984 after investors began to worry about the condition of the bank's credit portfolio and cut off short-term funding, is an example of how internal credit portfolio problems can precipitate a funding liquidity crisis that is then exacerbated by weaknesses in the institution's funding strategy.

Like most complicated decisions, asset-liability management decisions are driven by trade-offs. For example, there is a trade-off between liquidity and interest-rate risk: short-term liabilities (assets) offer less interest rate risk and higher funding liquidity risk than longer-term liabilities (assets).

There is also a trade-off between cost and risk. For example, in order to mitigate liquidity risk in a positively sloped yield-curve environment, institutions can increase the maturity of their funding liabilities, but this will clearly cost them more than will cheaper shorter-term funding. They might achieve the same effect by reducing the maturity of their assets (such as their commercial loans), but this is not always possible, since asset maturity is often driven by the nature of the bank's business and its competitive environment.

The challenge of managing liquidity risk lies in optimizing the borrowing capacity of the firm, and in coordinating contractual maturities of assets and liabilities (either directly or synthetically through the use of derivatives, primarily interest-rate swaps).

It follows from our discussion that all the components of an ALM policy are linked together—interest-rate risk management, funding liquidity risk management, profit planning, product pricing, and capital management—and must be part of a holistic approach to balance sheet management.

ALCO

The asset-liability management committee is the traditional name in the banking industry for what is often known today as the senior risk committee.

BOX 8-2

LIQUIDITY CRISIS AT CONTINENTAL ILLINOIS

Continental Illinois was the largest bank in Chicago, and one of the largest in the United States, before it had to be rescued by regulatory agencies in May 1984 after a massive liquidity crisis.

The bank had been pursuing a growth strategy since the late 1970s and in the five years prior to 1981, its commercial and industrial lending jumped from approximately $5 billion to more than $14 billion (and total assets grew from $21.5 billion to $45 billion).

The first signs of Continental's problems surfaced with the closing of Penn Square Bank in Oklahoma. This smaller bank had been issuing loans to oil and natural gas companies in Oklahoma during the oil and natural gas boom of the late 1970s. It passed large loans that it could not service through to substantial institutions such as Continental Illinois. But as prices for oil and gas dropped from 1981 onwards, some of the oil and natural gas companies began to default on their debt, and in 1982, U.S. regulators stepped in to close Penn Square.

Continental was the largest participant in Penn Square's oil and gas loans (more than $1 billion) and suffered heavy losses on those loans, and also on loans in its own loan portfolio. Many other banks also suffered credit losses in this period, but Continental was unusual in that it had only a small retail banking operation and a relatively small amount of core deposits. It relied primarily on federal funds and on issuing large certificates of deposit to fund its lending business.

When Penn Square failed, Continental found itself increasingly unable to fund its operations from the U.S. markets and turned to raising money in foreign wholesale money markets, such as Japan, at much higher rates.

But when rumors about Continental's still-worsening financial condition spooked the international markets in May 1984, the bank's foreign investors quickly began to withdraw the funds deposited in the bank ($6 billion in 10 days). In a matter of a few days, Continental Illinois was confronted with a full-blown liquidity crisis, obliging the U.S. regulatory authorities to step in to avoid the danger of a domino effect on other banks—which they feared might put the entire U.S. banking system at risk.

ALCO is typically chaired by the CEO and composed of the senior executive team of the bank along with key executives in the risk management and treasury groups. This key corporate governance committee might meet once a week to review the risk positions of the bank, discuss specific risk-related issues, and endorse policy decisions proposed by the chief risk officer, such as trading and lending limits. (Chapter 4 discusses risk committee organization in more detail.)

While the senior risk committee is the structure through which coordination of the institution's risk management takes place, ALCO, in its more restrictive definition, is a subcommittee, co-chaired by the chief risk officer and the treasurer, that gives a strategic direction in terms of product mix, pricing, and risk profile.

Each operating entity in the bank assesses the structural interest-rate risks that arise in its business and transfers such risks to its local treasury unit for management, or transfers the risks to separate books managed by the local ALCO. The risks can then be managed through

- On-balance-sheet business strategies that involve changes in the product mix and pricing of loans, deposits, and other borrowings. These are *core* business decisions.
- On-balance-sheet investment or funding strategies that involve changes in the maturity mix and rate characteristics of investment securities and of wholesale funding. These are *discretionary* business decisions.
- Off-balance-sheet strategies that involve the use of off-balance-sheet items, such as derivatives, to manage balance-sheet risks.

As an example, let us suppose that a bank has a balance sheet composed of floating-rate deposits and fixed-rate loans. This exposes the bank to interest-rate risk, namely, if rates increase, it will have to pay out more to attract depositors, and its profitability will decline.

To achieve the right product mix, it may be necessary for the institution to restructure its assets or liabilities (or possibly both). It may also have to reprice its retail products to make them more or less attractive to customers:

- Asset restructuring involves reducing the proportion of fixed-rate assets and increasing the proportion of floating-rate assets. This can be achieved by increasing the interest rate the bank charges on fixed-rate assets and reducing the rate the bank charges on floating-rate assets.
- Liability restructuring involves increasing the proportion of fixed-rate liabilities and reducing the proportion of floating-rate liabilities. This can be achieved by offering a higher rate on fixed-rate liabilities and a reduced rate on floating-rate liabilities.

- The institution can also enter into an interest-rate swap that pays fixed rates and receives floating rates; this swap has the effect of converting a portion of the bank's floating-rate debt to a fixed-rate resource to reduce the potential impact of an increase in interest rates.

It's easier to implement a hedging strategy than it is to change the firm's business strategy, but a number of factors affect the decision on how to manage a bank's interest-rate risk profile.

Entering into derivatives transactions such as swaps, options, or futures is simple, easy, and fast. However, it requires the proper back- and front-office infrastructures to monitor those transactions and assess their risks.

Likewise, some firms have policies that limit the use of derivatives, or operate in countries where derivatives markets are not yet developed. These firms have to manage their interest-rate risk by changing the product mix and pricing in their business strategy, in a way that is consistent with customer needs.

We can see from our discussion so far that ALM involves answering three critical risk-related questions:

- *How much risk do you want to take?* Answering this question is a function of the risk appetite of the firm.
- *How much risk do we have now?* Answering this question means developing tools to measure the risks of the firm's assets and liabilities.
- *How do we move from where we are now to where we want to be?* Answering this question involves the execution of cost-effective risk management strategies of the kind we outlined earlier.

In the next sections we describe some tools used by financial institutions to measure their balance-sheet sensitivity to interest-rate changes. The first tools we'll look at are simple approaches; they provide partial, though useful, answers to complicated questions.

GAP ANALYSIS

Gap analysis is the approach used by most banks to measure interest-rate risk in their balance sheets. The *gap* is defined as the difference between the amounts of rate-sensitive assets and rate-sensitive liabilities maturing or repricing within a specific time period. In other words,

Gap = rate-sensitive assets (RSA) − rate-sensitive liabilities (RSL)

A firm is said to have a *positive gap* within a specific time period when its rate-sensitive assets exceed its rate-sensitive liabilities, i.e., "assets reprice before liabilities," in the professional jargon. It describes the case in which an institution's short-term assets are funded by long-term liabilities. An increase (decrease) in interest rates leads to an increase (decrease) in NII.

When the gap is negative, we refer to it as "liabilities reprice before assets." It describes the case in which the institution's long-term assets are funded with short-term liabilities. An increase (decrease) in interest rates leads to a decrease (increase) in NII. This is typically the case for financial intermediaries operating in an interest-rate environment where the yield curve has a positive slope. Financial institutions are then said to "ride the yield curve" by borrowing on short maturities and lending long-term: the positive spread between short-term and long-term rates generates a profit margin as long as rates remain stable. This profit margin is, however, at risk when rates start to move up (Box 8-1). In Table 8-1 and Figure 8-1 we show the values at maturity, or at repricing time, of assets and liabilities for each time period, and the gap between them.

Traditionally, banks put numbers around their positive and negative gap risk by means of a detailed gap analysis. Table 8-1 illustrates the concept of gap and "cumulative gap" in such an analysis.

The bar chart in Figure 8-1 depicts assets in terms of positive bars and liabilities in terms of negative bars, and also tracks the cumulative gap. The positive cumulative gap bars in Figure 8-1 indicate that the institution

TABLE 8-1

Gap Analysis

Maturity Period	1	2	3	4	5	6	7	8	Total
Assets	100	120	150	200	50	60	70	50	800
Liabilities	20	30	40	50	100	200	150	210	800
Gap	80	90	110	150	−50	−140	−80	−160	
Cumulative gap	80	170	280	430	380	240	160	0	

FIGURE 8-1

Gap Analysis: Asset/Liability Position

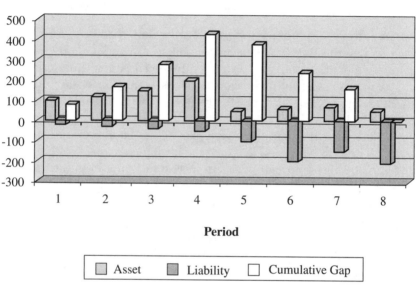

Period

| ☐ Asset | ■ Liability | ☐ Cumulative Gap |

has borrowed long-term and lent short-term. Negative cumulative gap bars would indicate the reverse, i.e., that the institution has funded long-term assets with short-term liabilities.

Putting this kind of gap analysis into practice involves

- *Slotting on- and off-balance-sheet items into different time buckets.* The length of the time buckets depends on the composition of the balance sheet and the maturity mix of assets and liabilities. Generally, narrow buckets are used for short-term items and wide buckets are used for long-term items. The length of the buckets varies according to the type of institution. For example, a commercial bank typically uses the following gap structure: up to one month, over one month and up to three months, over three months and up to six months, over six months and up to one year, over one year and up to three years, and beyond three years. More granularity can be introduced in both the short-term and the long-term end of the maturity spectrum in order to achieve a smoother distribution of assets and liabilities across buckets. Box 8-3 discusses how different instruments are slotted into the right buckets.

BOX 8-3

SLOTTING INSTRUMENTS INTO THE RIGHT GAP-ANALYSIS TIME BUCKETS

In general, an instrument must be slotted into a time bucket that corresponds to the shorter of the repricing maturity and the remaining contractual maturity. Floating-rate instruments should be slotted into the time bucket corresponding to their repricing maturity. For example a five-year floating-rate bond with a coupon of six-month LIBOR should be slotted into the six-month bucket, because the bond reprices according to movements of the six-month LIBOR interest rate. A three-year floating-rate bond with six-month repricing maturity and only two months remaining maturity will be slotted into the two-month bucket.

Only the principal amount is placed into the bucket. All future cash flows should be ignored so that the total amount on the balance sheet matches the total in the gap report. However, the accrued interest should be slotted into the bucket corresponding to the period in which it will be received (if it is shown on the balance sheet). For example, in the case of an amortizing loan, where the borrower makes equal annual payments over the loan period, only the principal amount repaid in each period should be slotted into the corresponding time bucket. In the case of a zero-coupon bond, the carrying value, i.e., the purchase price plus accrued interest, is slotted into the bucket corresponding to the remaining maturity. (The balance sheet will also reflect the carrying value.)

Liabilities with contractual maturity are straightforward: they can be slotted into the bucket corresponding to their maturity. In the case of liabilities with noncontractual maturities, such as deposits in checking accounts, it is necessary to perform a statistical analysis based on the bank's past experience. For example, 40 percent of the items might be slotted into the first bucket because they are viewed as short-term or subject to flight; the balance might be viewed as long-term core deposits, and would therefore be slotted into the last bucket.

Home mortgages, mortgage-backed securities, and asset-backed securities are subject to prepayment. To work out how to slot these into time buckets, the bank may have to perform a statistical analysis of the amount that's likely to be prepaid in the future, based on the institution's experience (the problem becomes more complex when prepayment depends on the level of interest rates, as for home mortgages). The same applies to deposit redemption: historical data can provide information on the speed and the extent of depositors' response to higher-yielding deposit accounts.

See Box 8-4 for a discussion of off-balance-sheet items.

- *Producing a cumulative gap report.* The cumulative gap in one period is the cumulative gap in the previous period plus the gap in the current period (Figure 8-1).
- *Setting gap limits.* Gap limits are defined as the maximum permitted difference between assets and liabilities within a specific time bucket. Gap limits can be defined in terms of dollar value or as a percentage of interest-rate-sensitive assets. For long maturities, gap limits can be formulated in terms of a percentage of shareholders' equity (NW).
- *Formulating gap management strategies.*

In order to use the gap report to control the volatility of the NII, it is necessary to define the relationship between NII and the gap position. In other words, it is necessary to estimate the impact of the gap position on the income statement (Table 8-2).

Table 8-2 assumes that there will be a straightforward "parallel shift" in the yield curves for all the firm's interest-rate-sensitive assets and liabilities, rather than a more complex shift in yield-curve relationships. It omits other risks, such as

- *Basis risk.* Consider, for example, a situation in which rates have gone up and the gap is positive. Assume, however, that the rate increase on the asset side is smaller than the rate increase on the liability side. As a result, the increase in the cash inflows might

TABLE 8-2

Example Relationship between NII and the Gap Position

	Interest Rate	Gap	Impact on NII
Scenario 1:	Up	+	+
Net assets will benefit from an increase in rates			
Scenario 2	Up	−	−
Net liabilities will cost more if rates go up			
Scenario 3	Down	+	−
Net assets will earn less from a decline in rates			
Scenario 4	Down	−	+
Net liabilities will cost less as a result of a decrease in rates			

be less than the increase in the cash outflows, resulting in a fall in the NII.

- *Mismatches within each bucket.* Within a bucket, assets may reprice toward the end of the time zone and liabilities may reprice towards the beginning. For example, assets may have a five-month maturity and liabilities may have only a three-month maturity. Therefore, for an increase in rates, the increase in cash outflows starts earlier than the increase in cash inflows. Despite a positive gap and rising rates, the impact on NII might be negative.

- *Timing of rate changes.* The timing of interest-rate changes may be different for the asset side and the liability side. The increase in rates on the liability side may be immediate, whereas the timing of the rate change on the asset side may come later. This may be due to lags in the repricing of assets: such a repricing decision needs the agreement of the ALCO, and competitive pressures may not allow the bank to pass on to the customer any increase in funding cost. Here again, the impact on NII of an increase in rates might be negative even when the gap analysis suggests that the impact should be positive.

- *Embedded options risk.* Retail products offer customers different types of "free" options, such as a prepayment option on mortgages and personal loans, and mortgage commitment options (i.e., the bank is committed to the best rate for a period of time before the customer signs the mortgage contract). In a sense, deposit withdrawal is another option risk, as depositors have, at any instant, the option to walk away and invest their funds in higher-yield short-term instruments, such as money market funds, if interest rates move up. These options are interest-rate-dependent, and they are hard to incorporate into the gap framework.

- *Maturing of items with off-market interest rates.* As maturity shrinks, all items on the balance sheet will eventually end up in the first bucket of any gap analysis. It is likely that several of these items have off-market coupons. For example, a 10-year bond with a 10 percent coupon that matures in less than three months will fall into the first bucket. The current interest rate may be 5 percent, low compared with the coupon on the asset when it was purchased 10 years ago. Even if rates go up by 1 percent, an item with a 10 percent coupon will be replaced by an item with, say, a 6 percent coupon. This will have a negative impact on NII, even though the gap was positive and rates went up.

- *Average versus beginning-of-the-period balances.* The balances during the period differ from the balances at the beginning of the period. After all, financial institutions are dynamically managed; thus, their positions change all the time. This issue can be addressed by reducing the length of the time buckets.

Pros and Cons of Gap Analysis

Gap analysis is attractive because it is simple. It relies on accounting data and does not involve complex mathematics (such as duration and convexity) and statistics (such as volatilities and correlations). It is a very effective tool for balance sheets that are dominated by instruments that do not have options embedded in them.

However, the approach is prone to inaccuracies for several reasons:

- Gap reports identify only repricing risks. As we outlined earlier, various kinds of risk are not captured in the gap-analysis framework. In particular, gap analyses do not consider basis risk and yield-curve risk, such as a steepening of the yield curve. It is also not possible to capture foreign exchange risk in gap reports, or the correlation risk between interest-rate changes in two currencies.
- Gap analysis does not consider the impact of offsetting positions in different buckets. For example, mismatches in the 1–3-month bucket may offset the mismatches in the 6–12-month bucket. It may be necessary to hedge only the net mismatch.
- Gap analysis ignores interest flows and the associated reinvestment risk of coupons and interest payments.
- Gap analysis uses only accounting data, i.e., book values, which may differ significantly from market value and therefore may bias the measurement of risk.
- Gap analysis may result in large discontinuities in reported positions when positions switch buckets. For example a 194-day asset, which is in the 7–12-month bucket today, will move to the 3–6-month bucket after two weeks. This may cause a huge reported mismatch in both buckets.

Gap analysis is static in nature; it cannot take into account the impact of new volumes on gap positions. However, *dynamic gap* reporting addresses this issue. Dynamic gap reporting accounts for the rollover strategy of the institution, i.e., its origination strategy and its funding policy. It deals with how maturing assets are replaced by new products, such as the incentives a bank might offer to new customers to take variable-rate mortgages in a declining-interest-rate environment (while maturing mortgages are mostly fixed-rate).

EARNINGS AT RISK

On a periodic basis, the potential impact of the firm's various gap positions (and current gap limit policies) on the income statement for the current quarter and the full year must be calculated. These calculations offer the bank an earnings-at-risk (EAR) measure.

Consider the gap table shown in Box 8-4. Here we suppose that all the bank's assets and liabilities are linear instruments without embedded options, such as loans, bonds, forward rate agreements (FRAs), and swaps. For simplicity, we'll also assume that all these items are evenly spread across the gap-analysis time buckets, and that the rate changes are the same across all maturities (i.e., there is a parallel shift of the yield curve). Let us next consider the impact of a 100-bp increase in rates for the quarter and the full year.

Impact for the Quarter

The gap report in Box 8-4 (before hedging) shows negative gaps for both the first (0–1 month) and the second (1–3 months) buckets, i.e., -$50,000 and -$250,000, respectively. As assets and liabilities are spread evenly across each bucket, the change in interest rates will affect the first-quarter NII for 2.5 months for the first bucket and for 1 month for the second bucket (Figure 8-2). Since the average maturity of the gap for the first bucket is 0.5 month, there is an excess of liabilities over assets of $50,000; hence, an increase in interest rate of 1 percent will cost the institution an additional 1 percent for the remaining 2.5 months until the end of the quarter, or $50,000 \times 2.5/12 \times 1/100 = \$104.17$.

For each bucket, the impact of the interest-rate shock on NII is equal to the gap, times the repricing gap (in terms of years), times the size of the interest-rate change. Similarly, we can derive the impact of an interest-rate shock of 100 bp on the NII for the year.

BOX 8-4

HOW DO WE SLOT DERIVATIVE INSTRUMENTS INTO TIME BUCKETS?

Off-balance-sheet items such as interest-rate swaps, futures, forwards, options, caps, and floors represent both assets and liabilities to the bank, so how they are slotted into time buckets depends on the structure of each instrument.

Consider a five-year, $10 million interest-rate swap paying a fixed 10 percent and receiving a floating six-month LIBOR. This swap can be viewed as the sum of a five-year fixed-rate asset, which can be slotted into the corresponding maturity bucket, and a five-year floating-rate liability repricing every six months, which can be slotted into the bucket containing the six-month term. The cumulative gap for the swap is zero.

Consider now a long position in a three-month futures contract, six months from now. This futures position is equivalent to borrowing for three months and then investing for nine months, so we can treat it like a nine-month asset and a three-month liability. As for the swap, the cumulative gap for the futures position is zero. Forward instruments, such as forward rate agreements, are treated in a similar fashion.

The table shows how a gap report for Bank XYZ treats a five-year $200 million swap hedge. The swap means that the bank pays a five-year fixed rate of 5 percent and receives a floating rate of three-month LIBOR.

Gap Report for Bank XYZ

	0–1 Month	1–3 Months	3–6 Months	6–12 Months	1–3 Years	Beyond 3 Years	Total
Assets	50	60	130	180	150	320	890
Liabilities	100	310	100	150	130	100	890
Gap before hedging	−50	−250	30	30	20	220	
Swap (hedge)	0	200	0	0	0	−200	
Net gap after hedging	−50	−50	30	30	20	20	

Numbers are in $000.

FIGURE 8-2

Impact of Gap on NII for the Quarter

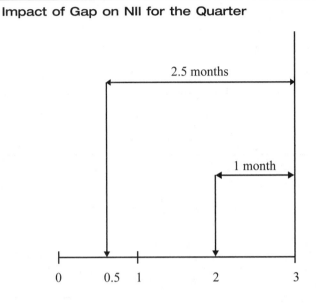

Time (Months)

0–1-month bucket: $-\$50,000 \times 2.5/12 \times 1/100 = -\$104.17$
1–3-month bucket: $-\$250,000 \times 1/12 \times 1/100 = \underline{-\$208.33}$
Total $-\$312.50$

Impact for the Year

With a one-year horizon, the average repricing gap for the 0–1-month bucket is 11.5(=12-.5) months; it is 10 months for the 1–3-month bucket, 7.5 months for the 3–6-month bucket and 3 months for the 6–12-month bucket (Figure 8-3). Then, again with reference to the gap table in Box 8-4, the full impact for the year, before hedging with the swap, is

0–1-month bucket: $-\$50,000 \times 11.5/12 \times 1/100 =$ $-\$479.17$
1–3-month bucket: $-\$250,000 \times 10/12 \times 1/100 = -\$2,083.33$
3–6-month bucket: $\$30,000 \times 7.5/12 \times 1/100 =$ $\$187.50$
6–12-month bucket: $\$30,000 \times 3/12 \times 1/100 =$ $\underline{\$75.00}$
Total $-\$2,300.00$

FIGURE 8-3

Impact of Gap on NII for the Year

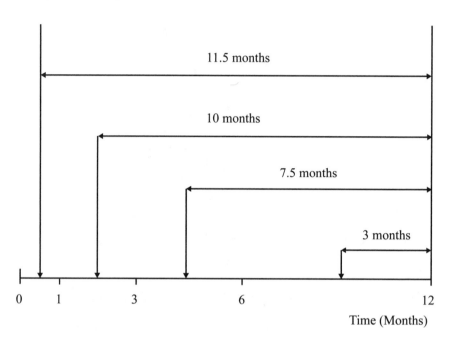

Now, what is the impact of the hedge described in the gap table in Box 8-4? If we assume that the repricing of the floating-rate leg of the swap hedge is exactly three months from now, the hedge reduces the impact on NII by

$$\$200,000 \times 9/12 \times 1/100 = \$1,500$$

Thus, the net impact on NII after hedging is –\$800 (= –\$2,300 + \$1,500).

The Multicurrency Balance-Sheet Issue

Firms with multicurrency balance sheets are exposed to mismatches in the currency position of assets and liabilities, in addition to interest-rate risk. There are two approaches to dealing with multicurrency balance sheets:

- Consolidated gap reporting, which consists of converting all foreign currency positions into the home currency; this approach implicitly assumes that all foreign exchange risks have been hedged. Moreover, consolidated gap analysis is likely to over-state interest-rate risk, as rates in different currencies are not perfectly correlated, i.e., they are unlikely to all move in the same direction at the same time.

- Separate currency gap reporting, which consists of preparing a gap report for each currency. This approach can be confusing if too many reports are produced, as it becomes difficult to figure out the aggregate interest-rate risk in the firm's balance sheet.

DURATION GAP APPROACH

The approaches we've looked at so far should be viewed as "back of the envelope" calculations. The gaps measured by gap analysis offer some sense of the interest-rate exposure of the balance sheet, but they are not a very precise measure of interest-rate exposure for reasons that we've al-ready mentioned.

Duration, as introduced in Chapter 6, is a measure of the interest-rate sensitivity of any cash flow series. The duration concept is useful as a complement to gap and EaR analysis because it summarizes cash flow characteristics, taking into account both the size and timing of these cash flows. It does not hide cash flow timing mismatches within the maturity buckets, as gap analysis can.

So how do we use the duration concept to improve our estimate of changes in NII? Box 8-5 offers a more technical explanation, but basically we need to calculate the duration gap for NII. This calculation depends on the duration of the rate-sensitive assets, the market value of the rate-sensitive liabilities, and the duration of the rate-sensitive liabilities. The calculation is quite straightforward because durations are additive.

If an asset (or liability) does not generate any cash flow during the accounting period, then it influences NII only in an accrual sense and should be excluded from the calculation.

The duration gap approach is very easy to implement as long as the accounting information is available. However, the same limitations that ap-ply to the duration concept as a measure of interest-rate risk also apply here.

- The term structure of interest rates is assumed to be flat, only parallel shifts in the yield curves are considered, and the rate change is assumed to be small. That is, the calculation assumes

BOX 8-5

DURATION AND NET INTEREST INCOME

In this box, we supply some of the mathematical notation for our main text discussion of duration and net interest income. The dollar change in NII (ΔNII) approximately equals the duration gap for NII (DG_{NII}) multiplied by the change in interest rates (Δi):

$$\Delta NII = DG_{NII} \times \Delta i$$

where the duration gap DG_{NII} is the difference between the market value of the rate-sensitive assets MV_{RSA} times 1 minus the duration of the rate-sensitive assets D_{RSA}, and the market value of the rate-sensitive liabilities MV_{RSL} times 1 minus the duration of the rate-sensitive liabilities D_{RSL}:

$$DG_{NII} = MV_{RSA} \times (1 - D_{RSA}) - MV_{RSL} \times (1 - D_{RSL})$$

To be precise, here NII is the book value amount expected at the end of the accounting period, say, one quarter or one year. If an asset (or liability) does not generate any cash flow during the accounting period, then it influences NII only in an accrual sense and should be excluded from the calculation.

that there is no risk from changes in the shape of the yield curve and that there is no convexity risk (though this last can be corrected by a convexity adjustment, as explained in Chapter 6).

- The same rate change affects both the assets and the liabilities (there is no basis risk, no correlation risk, and no volatility risk.)
- Deposit withdrawals and loan prepayments are not interest-rate-sensitive (there is no embedded options risk).

Duration of Equity

EaR is an accounting concept. It cannot fully convey the impact of a rate change on net wealth from a shareholder's perspective. To capture this impact, we need the *duration of equity* measure, described in technical terms in Box 8-6. As we note in the box, the duration of equity is quite long, much longer than the duration of the assets or the liabilities. Equity can be viewed as a highly leveraged purchase of an asset with high price volatility, funded by a less price-volatile liability.

One cannot hedge both NII and NW simultaneously, as the hedge position that would reduce the duration of NII to zero differs from the

BOX 8-6

DURATION OF EQUITY

How do we calculate the duration of equity? The market value of equity, net worth or NW, is simply the difference between the market value of assets MV_A and the market value of liabilities MV_L:

$$NW = MV_A - MV_L$$

From this economic identity and the definition of the duration of a fixed-income position (Chapter 6), it follows that the duration of equity D_{NW} is

$$D_{NW} = \frac{(MV_A \times D_A - MV_L \times D_L)}{NW}$$

where D_A and D_L denote the duration of the assets and liabilities, respectively. For example, suppose we have \$100 in assets with a duration of 7.5 years and \$90 in liabilities with a duration of 2.3 years; then the duration of equity is

$$D_{NW} = \frac{(100 \times 7.5 - 90 \times 2.3)}{10} = 54.3$$

The duration of equity is quite long, much longer than the duration of the assets or the liabilities. Equity can be viewed as a highly levered purchase of an asset with high price volatility, funded by a less price-volatile liability. In the previous example, assuming a yield of 5 percent on both assets and liabilities, a 10 bp (= 0.1 percent = 1/1000) increase in rates would lead to a change in NW of

$$\Delta NW = - NW \times D_{NW} \times \frac{\Delta i}{1 + i} = - 10 \times 54.3 \times \frac{1/1000}{1.05} = - \$0.52$$

hedge position that would reduce the duration of equity to zero. It is therefore critical to articulate clearly the objectives of any hedging program.

LONG-TERM VaR

Duration gap analysis allows a more accurate assessment of interest-rate risk in the balance sheet than simple gap analysis. However, both frameworks are static in nature and do not capture the fact that the balance sheet evolves over time. New retail products are originated, and maturing assets and liabilities are rolled over as they mature—not necessarily into instruments with similar characteristics.

Long-term VaR (LT-VaR) is an extension of the classic VaR framework presented in Chapter 7 in the context of the trading book. The time horizon in a classic VaR framework is very short: one day for market-risk management purposes, and ten days for regulatory capital reporting. For the banking book, the risk horizon is much longer, at least one year. The objective of LT-VaR is to generate the statistical distributions of EaR and NW at different horizons, say next quarter and end of year for EaR and one and two years for NW, in order to produce the worst-case EaR and NW at a given confidence level, say 99 percent.

This ambitious procedure can be achieved only by means of powerful Monte Carlo simulations of the

- Correlated term structure of interest rates, such as swap rates, cost-of funds rates, and mortgage rates, over very long horizons
- Implied volatilities for various types of instruments
- Interest-rate-sensitive prepayment of mortgages and other loans, as well as changes in deposits and savings balances, including seasonal variations in demand for loans and deposits
- Loan defaults
- Renewals (retention rates) and new volume (new origination) for retail products such as mortgages and other consumer loans on the asset side of the balance sheet, and funding products on the liability side

At each step of the simulation, pricing models must be used to assess the value of assets and liabilities at that point in time. The simulation should also trigger hedges, when required along a simulation path, in order to comply with any ALCO policy regarding maximum risk exposures (e.g., gap limits).

Pros and Cons of LT-VaR

LT-VaR is a dynamic and forward-looking VaR framework that helps firms manage risk over a long-term horizon. However, it is complex, and modelers must have access to the firm's detailed balance-sheet positions.

Bank businesses that focus on lending to corporate clients are characterized by a limited number of relatively large loans, but retail banks authorize thousands and thousands of small loans, credit cards, mortgages, and so on. Retail products must be aggregated into homogeneous pools so that LT-VaR simulation can be conducted at the pool level.

The quality of any simulation depends on the assumptions that drive the dynamics of interest rates and the changes in the balance-sheet structure. Inconsistent assumptions can distort the results, potentially misleading the ALCO in some very important decisions.

LIQUIDITY-RISK MEASUREMENT

One should not confuse interest-rate sensitivity with funding liquidity risk. Interest-rate sensitivity is determined by the frequency of the repricing of assets and liabilities. In contrast, the contractual maturity of an item determines whether it contributes to a funding liquidity gap.

For example, a three-year fixed-rate loan has an interest-rate sensitivity of three years and a liquidity maturity of three years. A variable-rate, three-year loan priced off six-month LIBOR has an interest-rate sensitivity of six months and a liquidity maturity of three years.

A business unit's impact on institutional liquidity can be characterized by means of a liquidity measurement system. This must at least be directionally correct; a liability-gathering unit should be credited for supplying liquidity, and an asset-generating unit should be charged for using liquidity.

Table 8-3 illustrates a spectrum of funding sources and indicates that a bank might assign a higher liquidity credit for stable funds than for hot funds. *Hot funds* are funds supplied by depositors that could be quickly

TABLE 8-3

Funds Source Spectrum

Open Market	Direct	Unconventional	Core Funds	Capital Market Funds

HOT ◄───► STABLE

| Brokers/Dealers (e.g., Negotiable CDs) | Wholesale Placements (e.g., Large CDs, BAs, Repos, Fed Funds) | Customized Term Placements (e.g., Special 5-Year CDs) | • DDAs
• MMAs
• Savings
• CDs | • Common Equity
• Preferred Equity
• Term Notes/ Bonds |

removed from the bank in the event of a crisis (e.g., funds from dealers). Table 8-3 ranks the sources of funds in terms of their liquidity.

One can illustrate the key features of a best-practice liquidity quantification scheme through a simplified version of this liquidity ranking process. The liquidity ranking process should enable the bank to quantify credits and charges depending on the degree to which a business unit is a net supplier or net user of liquidity.

Liquidity can be quantified using a symmetrical scale. Such scales help managers to compute a business unit's liquidity score more objectively, through a ranking and weighting process. A quantification scheme such as this also helps the bank to determine the amount of liquidity in the system and to set targets in terms of a desirable and quantifiable level of liquidity.

The liquidity rank (LR) attributed to a product is determined by multiplying the dollar amount of the product by its rank. For example, if business unit XYZ is both a supplier and a user of liquidity, then a net liquidity calculation needs to be made. Looking at Table 8-4, if we assume that business unit XYZ supplied $10 million of the most stable liquidity, $3 million of the next most stable, and so on, then a total credit of 94 (5 × 10 + 4 × 3 + 3 × 6 + 2 × 5 + 1 × 4 = 94) would be assigned.

TABLE 8-4

Liquidity Rank Measurement Units

Business Unit XYZ's Net Liquidity Rank Measurement Units			
Liquidity Suppliers		Liquidity Users	
Rank Score	Amount ($MM)	Rank Score	Amount ($MM)
+5	$10	−1	$4
+4	$3	−2	$8
+3	$6	−3	$6
+2	$5	−4	$3
+1	$4	−5	$10
Total	94	Total	−100
Net		−6 (= 94 − 100)	

Similarly, if we assume in our example that business unit XYZ used $10 million of the most expensive liquidity, $3 million of the next most expensive, and so on, then a total charge of 100 (4 × 1 + 8 × 2 + 6 × 3 + 3 × 4 + 10 × 5 = 100) would be assigned. The net result of the two calculations is a liquidity rank of minus $6 million.

The LR approach is simply a heuristic tool that helps managers to control the liquidity profile of their institution. The next step is to charge each business unit for the liquidity risk that it generates.

FUNDS TRANSFER PRICING

Funds transfer pricing is always a controversial issue in organizations, as it affects the measured profitability of the various business lines.

The rationale for funds transfer pricing is that there are economies of scale and scope in centralizing the management of interest-rate risk. Business units have no control over the dynamics of yield curves and other market indices such as the prime rate. So the objective of funds transfer pricing is to remove the noncontrollable interest-rate risk from business results, and to charge each business for the cost of funding its activity and hedging its interest-rate risk.

Each business unit will then be able to secure its profit margin at the time of origination of its products (say, mortgages), and can focus on developing and managing the business side of its activity as well as the credit quality of its portfolio. (Credit risk and other risks such as basis risk, e.g., the spread between the prime rate and LIBOR for variable-rate loans indexed on the prime rate, and options risk, e.g., commitment risk for mortgages, usually remain with the business unit.)

The issue remains: what is the appropriate cost of funds to charge to the business units? We recommend matched-maturity funds transfer pricing, an approach illustrated by the following example. Consider a financial institution with the following balance sheet:

	Unit	Balance	Maturity (years)	Rate	Interest Income (Expense)
Assets					
Corporate loan	Corporate	$100	1	8%	$8.00
Liabilities					
Savings account	Retail	$100	0.25	3%	($3.00)
			Net	5%	$5.00

At first glance, one might consider charging the corporate unit only 3 percent as its cost of funds, leading to a healthy profit margin of 5 percent for the unit. But this would be unfair. The corporate unit would be benefiting from the bank's retail franchise, which allows the retail unit to raise funds at a cost that is well below the market funding rate otherwise applied to the institution. Charging the corporate unit only 3 percent also fails to account for gap risk—after all, the bank is funding a one-year asset by means of a three-month liability.

The correct approach consists of charging both business units, i.e., the corporate and retail units, the firm's cost of funds, say LIBOR if the firm has a credit rating of AA, so that both business units are rewarded (penalized) for their ability to lend (raise funds) above (below) the funding cost.

Assume that the three-month and one-year LIBOR rates are 4 percent and 6 percent, respectively; then the matched-maturity transfer pricing is

Assets	Liabilities
Corporate banking:	
$100 1-year loan @ 8%	$100 1-year transfer liability @ 6%
Retail banking:	
$100 3-month transfer asset @ 4%	$100 3-month savings account @3%
Treasury:	
$100 1-year transfer asset @ 6%	$100 3-month transfer liability @ 4%

It follows that the profit margins are

- 2 percent for the corporate banking unit (not 5 percent)
- 1 percent for the retail banking unit (not 0 percent)
- 2 percent for the treasury unit as a compensation for the cost of rolling over the three-month liability over one year and for hedging the gap risk.

The total corresponds to the net margin of 5 percent in the previous table.

CHAPTER 9

Credit Scoring and Retail Credit Risk Management[1]

This chapter introduces the problem of credit risk in relation to retail banking, an industry that is familiar to almost everyone at some level. Once seen as unglamorous compared to the big-ticket lending of corporate banking and trading, retail banking has been transformed over the last few years by innovations in products, marketing—and risk management. It typically contributes the most stable streams of profit in the global banking industry.

Retail banking serves both small businesses and consumers and includes the business of accepting consumer deposits as well as that of providing consumer credit. Retail lending encompasses

- *Home mortgages.* Fixed-rate mortgages and adjustable-rate mortgages (ARMs) are secured by the residential properties financed by the loan. The loan-to-value ratio (LTV) represents the proportion of the property value financed by the loan and is a key risk variable.

- *Home equity loans.* Sometimes called home equity line of credit (HELOC) loans, these can be considered a hybrid between a consumer loan and a mortgage loan. They are secured by residential properties.

- *Installment loans.* These include revolving loans, such as personal lines of credit that may be used repeatedly up to a specified limit. They also include credit cards, automobile and similar loans, and all other loans not included in automobile loans and revolving credit. Ordinary installment loans are usually secured

---

1. We acknowledge the coauthorship of Rob Jameson for sections of this chapter.

by such things as automobiles, residential property, personal property, or financial assets.

- *Credit card revolving loans.* These are unsecured loans.
- *Small business loans (SBL).* These are secured by the assets of the business or by the personal guarantees of the owners. Business loans of up to $100,000 to $200,000 are usually considered as part of the retail portfolio.

In the United States and Canada, retail banking and consumer lending exceeds corporate lending by about 75 percent, with household debt in the United States exceeding $8.4 trillion in the year 2002 (more than double the amount owed in 1992). This number compares with corporate bond debt of about $2.5 trillion in the same period. Home mortgages and home equity loans in the United States account for 70 percent of the total, with the next-largest categories being credit cards and nonrevolving credits.

Retail banking businesses, as defined in Box 9-1, have proved particularly important to the financial industry in the postmillennium years. A dramatic fall in equity markets and a record rise in corporate defaults in the postmillennium period placed financial companies such as insurance companies, investment banks, and broker-dealers under financial pressure.

BOX 9-1

BASEL'S DEFINITION OF RETAIL EXPOSURES

The Basel Committee, the banking industry's international regulatory body, defines retail exposures as homogeneous portfolios that consist of

- A large number of small, low-value loans
- With either a consumer or business focus
- Where the incremental risk of any single exposure is small

Examples are

- Credit cards
- Installment loans (e.g., personal finance, educational loans, auto loans, leasing)
- Revolving credits (e.g., overdrafts, home equity lines of credit)
- Residential mortgages

Small business loans can be managed as retail exposures, provided that the total exposure to a small business borrower is less than 1 million euro.

By contrast, retail business remained remarkably healthy, producing stable earnings that helped to keep many universal banks from reporting major losses.

We'll first take a look at one of the main reasons for this benign performance: the different nature of retail credit risk and commercial credit risk. Then we'll take a more detailed look at credit scoring, which will include the "darker side" of risk in the retail credit businesses. Credit scoring is now a widespread technique, not only in banking, but also in many other sectors where there is a need to check the credit standing of a customer (e.g., a telephone company) or the likelihood that a client will file a claim (e.g., an insurance company).

THE NATURE OF RETAIL CREDIT RISK

The credit risks generated by retail banking are significant, but they have a very different dynamic from the credit risk of commercial and investment banking businesses. The defining feature of retail credit exposures is that they arrive in bite-sized pieces, so that default by a single customer is never expensive enough to threaten a bank.

Another key feature is that retail customers tend to be financially independent of one another. Corporate and commercial credit portfolios, by contrast, often contain concentrations of exposures to corporations that are economically intertwined in particular geographical areas or industry sectors.

Of course, a retail bank with a retail portfolio that is diversified across regions and products has significantly less credit concentration risk than a retail portfolio that is concentrated in a particular region or product. But the general rule is that most retail credit portfolios behave much more like large and well-diversified portfolios than do "lumpy" corporate lending portfolios. Retail banks can therefore make better estimates of the percentage of the portfolio that they "expect" to default in the future and the losses that this might cause. This robust expected loss number can then be treated much like other costs of doing business, such as the cost of maintaining branches or processing checks (rather than being treated as a threat to the bank's solvency).

The high predictability of retail credit losses mean that the expected loss rate dominates retail credit risk and can be built into the price charged to the customer. By contrast, the risk of loss from many commercial credit portfolios is dominated by the risk that credit losses will rise to some unexpected level.

Another key feature of many retail portfolios is that a rise in defaults is often signaled in advance by a change in customers' behavior, e.g., customers who are under financial pressure might fail to make a minimum payback on a credit card account. Warning signals like this are carefully monitored by well-run retail banks (and their regulators) because they allow the bank to take preemptive action to reduce credit risk. The bank can

- Alter the rules governing the amount of money it lends out to existing customers to reduce its exposures.
- Alter its marketing strategies and customer acceptance rules to attract less risky customers.
- Price in the risk by raising interest rates for certain kinds of customers to take into account the higher likelihood of default.

By contrast, a commercial credit portfolio is something of a supertanker. By the time it is obvious that something is going wrong, it's often too late to do much about it.

Regulators accept the idea that retail credit risk is relatively predictable (although Box 9-2 explains some important exceptions to this rule). As a result, retail banks will be asked to set aside a relatively small amount of risk capital under the new Basel Capital Accord compared with the current Basel rules. But banks will have to provide regulators with probability of default (PD), loss given default (LGD), and exposure at de-

---

BOX 9-2

DOES RETAIL CREDIT RISK HAVE A DARK SIDE?

In the main text, we deal mainly with how credit scoring helps put a number to the expected level of credit risk in a retail transaction. But there is a dark side to retail credit, too. This is the danger that losses will suddenly rise to unexpected levels because of some unforeseen but systematic risk factor that influences the behavior of many of the credits in a bank's retail portfolio.

The dark side of retail risk management has four prime causes:

- Not all innovative retail credit products can be associated with enough historical loss data to make their risk assessments reliable.

(continued on following page)

BOX 9 - 2 *(Continued)*

- Even well-understood retail credit products might begin to behave in an unexpected fashion under the influence of a sharp change in the economic environment, particularly if risk factors all get worse at the same time (the so-called perfect storm scenario). For example, in the mortgage industry, one ever-present worry is that a deep recession combined with higher interest rates might lead to a rise in mortgage defaults at the same time that house prices, and therefore collateral values, fall very sharply.
- The tendency of consumers to default (or not) is a product of a complex social and legal system that continually changes. For example, the social and legal acceptability of personal bankruptcy, especially in the United States, is one factor that seemed to influence a rising trend in personal default during the 1990s.
- Any operational issue that affects the credit assessment of customers can have a systematic effect on the whole consumer portfolio. Because consumer credit is run as a semiautomated decision-making process rather than as a series of tailored decisions, it's vital that the credit process be designed and operated correctly.

Almost by definition, it's difficult to put a risk number to these kinds of wild-card risk. Instead, banks have to try to make sure that only a limited number of their retail credit portfolios are especially vulnerable to new kinds of risk, such as subprime lending. A *little* exposure to uncertainty might open up a lucrative business line and allow the bank to gather enough information to measure the risk better in the future; a *lot* makes the bank a hostage to fortune.

Where large conventional portfolios such as mortgage portfolios are vulnerable to sharp changes in multiple risk factors, banks must use stress tests to gauge how devastating each plausible worst-case scenario might be (see Chapter 7).

fault (EAD) statistics for clearly differentiated segments of their portfolios. The regulators say that segmentation should be based on credit scores or some equivalent measure, and on vintage of exposures, that is, the time the transaction has been on the bank's books.

Credit risk is not the only risk faced by retail banking, as Box 9-3 makes clear, but it is the major financial risk across most lines of retail business. We'll now take a close look at the principal tool for measuring retail credit risk: credit scoring.

BOX 9-3

THE OTHER RISKS OF RETAIL BANKING

In the main text, we focus on credit risk as the principal risk of retail credit businesses. But just like commercial banking, retail banking is subject to a whole range of market, operational, business and reputation risks:

- *Interest-rate risk* is generated on both the asset and liability side whenever the bank offers specific rates to both borrowers and depositors. This risk is generally transferred from the retail business line to the treasury of a retail bank, where it is managed as part of the bank's asset-liability and liquidity risk management (see Chapter 8).
- *Asset valuation risks* are really a special form of market risk, where the profitability of a retail business line depends on the accurate valuation of a particular asset, liability, or class of collateral. Perhaps the most important is prepayment risk in mortgage banking, which describes the risk that a portfolio of mortgages might lose its value when interest rates fall because consumers intent on remortgaging pay down their existing mortgage unexpectedly quickly, removing its value. The valuation and the hedging of retail assets that are subject to prepayment risk is complex because it relies on assumptions about customer behavior that are hard to validate. Another example of a valuation risk is the estimation of the residual value of automobiles in auto-leasing business lines. Where this kind of risk is explicitly recognized, it tends to be managed centrally by the treasury unit of the retail bank.
- *Operational risks* in retail banking are generally managed as part of the business in which they arise. For example, fraud by customers is closely monitored and new processes, such as fraud detection mechanisms, are put in place when they are economically justified. Under the new Basel Capital Accord, banks will allocate regulatory capital against operational risk in both retail and wholesale banking. A subdiscipline of retail operational risk management is emerging that makes use of many of the same concepts as bank operational risk at a firmwide level (see Chapter 13).
- *Business risks* are one of the primary concerns of senior management. These include business volume risks (e.g., the rise and fall of mortgage business volumes when interest rates go up and down), strategic risks (such as the growth of Internet banking or new payments systems), and decisions about mergers and acquisitions.

(continued on following page)

B O X   9 - 3   *(Continued)*

- *Reputation risks* are particularly important in retail banking. The bank has to preserve a reputation for delivering on its promises to customers. But it also has to preserve its reputation with regulators, who can remove its business franchise if it is seen to act unfairly or unlawfully.

CREDIT SCORING—COST, CONSISTENCY, AND BETTER CREDIT DECISIONS

Every time you apply for a credit card, open an account with a telephone company, submit a medical claim, or apply for auto insurance, it is almost certain that a *credit scoring* model, or, more precisely, a *credit-risk scoring* model, is ticking away behind the scenes.[2]

The model uses a statistical procedure to convert information about a credit applicant or an existing account holder into numbers that are then combined (usually added) to form a score. This score is then regarded as a measure of the credit risk of the individual concerned, that is, the probability of repayment. The higher the score, the lower the risk.

Credit scoring is important because it allows banks to avoid the most risky customers and helps them to assess whether certain kinds of businesses are likely to be profitable by comparing the profit margin that remains once operating and default expenses are subtracted from gross revenues.

But credit scoring is also important for reasons of cost and consistency. Major banks typically have millions of customers and carry out billions of transactions each year. By using a credit-scoring model, banks can automate as much as possible the adjudication process for small credits and credit cards. Before credit scoring was widely adopted, a credit officer would have to review a credit application and use a combination of experience, industry knowledge, and personal know-how to reach a credit decision based on the large amount of information in a typical credit application. Each application might typically contain about 50 bits of infor-

---

2. Good general references to credit scoring include Edward M. Lewis, *An Introduction to Credit Scoring* (San Raphael, Calif.: Fair Isaac Corporation, 1992); L. C. Thomas, J. N. Crook and D. B. Edelman, eds., *Credit Scoring and Credit Control* (Oxford: Oxford University Press, 1992); and V. Srinivasan and Y. H. Kim," Credit Granting: A Comparative Analysis of Classification Procedures," *Journal of Finance* 42, 1987, pp. 665–683.

mation, although some applications may call for as many as 150 items. The number of possible combinations of information is staggering, and, as a result, it is almost impossible for a human analyst to treat credit decisions in identical ways over time.

By contrast, credit-risk scorecards consistently weight and treat the information items that they extract from applications and/or credit bureau reports. The credit industry calls these items *characteristics*, and they correspond to the questions on a credit application or the entries in a credit bureau report. The answers given to the questions in an application or the entries of a credit bureau report are known as *attributes*. For example, "four years" is an attribute of the characteristic "time at address." Similarly, "rents" is an attribute of the characteristic "residential status."

Credit-scoring models assess not only whether an attribute is positive or negative, but also by how much. The weighting of the values associated with each answer (or attribute) is derived using statistical techniques that look at the odds of repayment based on past performance. ("Odds" is just the term the retail banking industry uses to mean "probability.") Population odds are defined as the ratio of the probability of a good event to the probability of a bad event in the population. For example, an applicant with 15:1 odds has a probability of 1 in 16, i.e., 6.25 percent, of being a bad customer (by which we mean delinquent or the subject of a charge-off).

The statistical techniques employed to weight the information in a credit report include linear or logistic regression, mathematical programming or classification trees, neural nets, and genetic algorithms (with logistic regression being the most common).

Figure 9-1 shows what a credit-scoring table might look like, in this case one used to differentiate between credit applications.

WHAT KIND OF CREDIT-SCORING MODELS ARE THERE?

For the purpose of scoring consumer credit applications, there are really three types of models:

- *Credit bureau scores.* These are often known as FICO scores, because the methodology for producing them was developed by Fair Isaac Corporation (the leader in credit-risk analytics for retail businesses). In the United States and Canada, bureau scores are maintained and supplied by companies such as Equifax and

FIGURE 9-1

Example of Application Scoring Table

	Less than 6 months	6 months to 1 year	1 year 7 months to 6 years 8 months	6 years 9 months to 10 years 5 months	10 years 6 months or more	
Years on Job	5	14	20	27	39	
Own or Rent	Own or buying 40	Rent 19	All others 26			
Banking	Checking account 22	Saving account 17	Checking and savings account 31	None 0		
Major Credit Cards	Yes 27	No 11				
Occupation	Retired 41	Professional 36	Clerical 27	Sales 18	Service 12	All others 27
Age of Applicant	18–25 19	26–31 14	32–34 22	35–51 26	52–61 34	62 and over 40
Worst Credit Reference	Major derogatory -15	Minor derogatory -4	No record -2	One satisfactory 9	Two or more satisfactory 18	No investigation 0

Source: Lewis, 1992, p. xv.

TransUnion. From the bank's point of view, this kind of generic credit score has a low cost, is quickly installed, and offers a broad overview of an applicant's overall creditworthiness (regardless of the type of credit for which the applicant is applying). For example, Fair Isaac credit bureau risk scores can be tailored to the preferences of a financial institution (they usually range from 300 to 850; subprime lending, discussed in Box 9-4, typically targets customers with scores below 660).

BOX 9-4

THE PROBLEM OF SUBPRIME LENDING

Subprime lending—the extension of credit to customers with poor or impaired credit histories and credit scores—is proving to be one of the most promising and problematic of retail bank businesses.

It's a potentially lucrative area because subprime customers will pay much higher rates of interest and fees than customers with a reliable track record. But it's clearly also a risky business for the unwary bank. If subprime customers turn out to be much more prone to default than the bank has calculated, or if their behavior changes as part of a social trend, then the associated costs can cut through even the fat interest margins and fees associated with the sector.

Subprime lending is a new sector for most retail banks. That means that banks lack the historical data to predict the default rate of their subprime customers reliably. In particular, because subprime lending hardly existed in its present form in the last economic recession, it is quite unclear what might happen to subprime default statistics if there is a sharp rise in unemployment.

Worse still, there are many legal, ethical, and reputation challenges associated with subprime lending. Is the bank extracting unfairly large insurance fees or transaction charges? Is it ethical to charge relatively poor customers high rates of interest, or to encourage them to borrow money when they are likely to struggle to pay it back? Over the last few years, consumer groups and some local U.S. regulators have accused some subprime specialists and also some major U.S. banks of "predatory lending." Where such accusations can be proven, they damage a bank's reputation and regulatory relationships as well as leading to expensive legal settlements.

- *Pooled models.* These models are built by outside vendors, such as Fair Isaac, using data collected from a wide range of lenders with similar credit portfolios. For example, a revolving credit pooled model might be developed from credit card data collected from several banks. Pooled models cost more than generic scores, but not as much as custom models. They can be tailored to an industry, but they are not company specific.
- *Custom models.* These models are usually developed in-house using data collected from the lender's own unique population of credit applications. They are tailored to screen for a specific applicant profile for a specific lender's product. Custom models have allowed some banks to become expert in particular credit segments, such as credit cards and mortgages. They can give a bank a strong competitive edge in selecting the best customers and offering the best risk-adjusted pricing.

Let's take a closer look at the generic information offered by credit bureaus. Credit bureau data consist of numerous "credit files" for each individual who has a credit history. Each credit file contains five major types of information:

- *Identifying information.* This is personal information; it is not considered credit information as such and is not used in scoring models. The rules governing the nature of the identifying information that can be collected are set by local jurisdictions. In the United States, for example, the U.S. Equal Opportunity Acts prohibits the use of information such as gender, race, or religion in credit-scoring models.
- *Public records (legal items).* This information comes from civil court records and includes bankruptcies, judgments, and tax liens.
- *Collection information.* This is reported by debt collection agencies or by entities that grant credit.
- *Trade line/account information.* This is compiled from the monthly "receivables" tapes that credit grantors send to the credit bureaus. The tapes contain reports of new accounts as well as updates to existing account information.
- *Inquiries.* Every time a credit file is accessed, an inquiry must be placed on the file. Only inquiries that are placed for the extension of new credit are seen by other credit grantors.

Some credit bureaus, such as Equifax, allow individuals to obtain their own score, together with an explanation of how to improve their current score (and what-if analyses, such as the impact on the score of reducing the balance on the customer's credit cards).

FROM CUTOFF SCORES TO DEFAULT RATES AND LOSS RATES

In the early stages of the industry development of credit-scoring models, the actual probability of default assigned to a credit applicant did not much matter. The models were designed to put applicants *in ranked order* in relation to their *relative* risk. This was because lenders used the models not to generate an absolute measure of default probability, as such, but to choose an appropriate cutoff score, i.e., the point at which applicants were accepted, based on subjective criteria.

We can see more clearly how cutoff scores work if we look at Figure 9-2, which shows the distribution of "good" and "bad" accounts by credit score. Suppose we set the minimum acceptable score at 300 points. If only

FIGURE 9-2

Distributions of "Good" and "Bad" Accounts

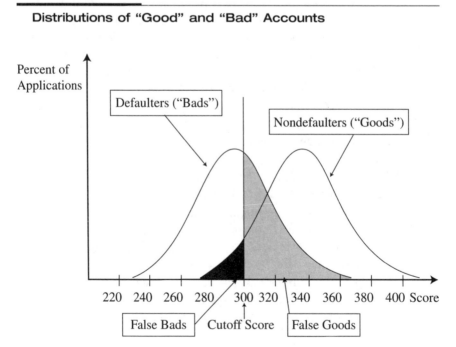

applications scoring that value or higher were accepted, the firm using the scoring system would avoid lending money to the body of bad customers to the left of the vertical line, but would forgo the smaller body of good accounts to the left of the line. Moving the minimum score line to the right will cut off an even higher fraction of bad accounts but forgo a larger fraction of good accounts, and so on. The score at which the minimum score line is set—the cutoff score—is clearly an important decision for the business in terms of both its likely profitability and the risk that the bank is taking on.

Given the cutoff score, the bank can determine, based on its actual experience, the loss rate and profitability for the retail product. Over time, the bank can adjust the cutoff score in order to optimize the profit margin product by product. In retail banking, unlike wholesale banking, banks have lots of customers, and it doesn't take much time to accumulate enough data to assess the performance of a scorecard. Usually, the statistics on loss rates and profitability are updated on a quarterly basis.

The new Basel Capital Accord requires that banks segment their retail portfolios into subportfolios with similar loss characteristics, especially similar prepayment risk. Banks will have to estimate both the PD and the LGD for these portfolios. This can be achieved by segmenting each retail portfolio by score band, with each score band corresponding to a risk level. For each score band, the bank can estimate the loss rate using historical data, then, given an estimate of the LGD, the bank can infer the implied PD. For example, for a loss rate of 2 percent and a 50 percent LGD, the implied PD is 4 percent.

The bank should adopt similar risk management policies with respect to all borrowers and transactions in a particular segment. These policies should include underwriting and structuring of the loans, economic capital allocations, pricing and other terms of the lending agreement, monitoring, and internal reporting.

MEASURING AND MONITORING THE PERFORMANCE OF A SCORECARD

The purpose of credit scoring is to predict which applications will be good or bad in the future. To do this, the scorecard must be able to differentiate between the two by assigning high scores to good credits and low scores to poor ones. The goal of the scorecard, therefore, is to minimize the overlapping area of the distribution of the good and bad credits, as we saw in Figure 9-2.

This leads to a number of practical problems that are of interest to risk managers. How can we measure a scorecard's performance? How do we know when to adjust and rebuild scorecards, or to change the operating policy?

The most popular validation technique currently employed is the cumulative accuracy profile (CAP) and its summary statistic, the accuracy ratio (AR), illustrated in Figure 9-3. On the horizontal axis are the percentiles of the predicted default scores in the data set. On the vertical axis are the actual defaults in percentage terms taken from the bank's records. For example, assume that the scoring model predicts that 10 percent of the accounts will default in the next 12 months. If our model were perfect, the actual number of accounts that defaulted over that time period would correspond to the first decile of the score distribution—the perfect model line

Cumulative Accuracy Profile (CAP) and Accuracy Ratio (AR)

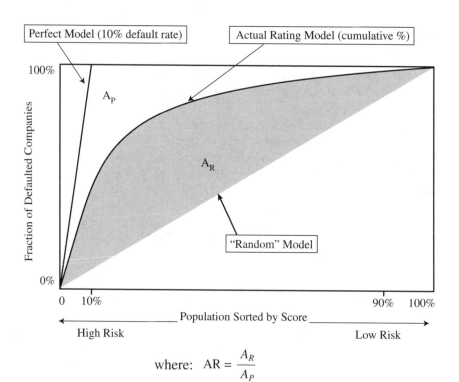

$$\text{where: } AR = \frac{A_R}{A_P}$$

in the figure. Conversely, the 45-degree line corresponds to a random model that cannot differentiate between good and bad customers.

Clearly, the bank hopes that its scoring model results are relatively close to the perfect model line. The area under the perfect model is denoted A_P, while the area under the actual rating model is denoted A_R. The accuracy ratio is AR $= A_R/A_P$, and the closer this ratio is to 1, the more accurate is the model.

The performance of a scoring model can be monitored, say, every quarter, by means of a CAP curve, and the model replaced when its performance deteriorates. The performance of scoring systems tends not to change abruptly, but it can deteriorate for several reasons: the characteristics of the underlying population might change over time, and/or the behavior of the population might evolve so as to change the variables associated with a high likelihood of default.

Another reason for replacing a scoring model is that the bank has changed the nature of the products that it is offering to customers. If a financial institution that offers auto loans decides to sell this business and issue credit cards instead, it is highly probable that the target customer population will be different enough to justify the development of a new custom scorecard.

FROM DEFAULT RISK TO CUSTOMER VALUE

As the technology of scorecards has developed, banks have progressed from scoring applications at one point in time to periodic "behavior scoring." Here, the bank uses information on the behavior of a current customer, such as usage of the credit line and social demographic information, to determine the risk of default over a fixed period of time. The approach is similar to application scoring, but it uses many more variables that describe the past performance of customers.

This kind of risk modeling is no longer restricted to the estimation of the probability of a customer's defaulting. Over the last few years, lenders have begun to shift from simply assessing default risk to making more subtle assessments that are directly linked to the value of the customers to the bank. Credit-scoring techniques have been applied to new areas, such as response scorecards that predict whether the consumer is likely to respond to a direct marketing offer, usage scorecards that predict how likely it is that the customer will make use of the credit product, and attrition scorecards that estimate how long the customer will remain loyal to the lender. Each customer may now be described by a number of different scores (Table 9-1).

TABLE 9-1

Some Different Kinds of Scorecards

Credit bureau scores are the classic FICO credit scores available from the main credit bureaus in the United States and Canada.

Application scores support the initial decision as to whether to accept a new applicant for credit.

Behavior scores are risk estimators similar to application scores, but they use information on the behavior of existing credit account holders, e.g., usage of credit and delinquency history.

Revenue scores aim at predicting the profitability of existing customers.

Response scores predict the likelihood that a customer will respond to an offer.

Attrition scores estimate the likelihood that existing customers will close their accounts, won't renew a credit such as a mortgage, or will reduce their balance on existing credits.

Insurance scores predict the likelihood of claims from insured parties.

Tax authority scores predict whom the tax inspector should audit in order to collect additional revenues.

At the same time, lenders are concentrating more on the profitability of the consumer rather than simply the customer's default probability. After all, there's not much point in issuing costly credit cards to creditworthy customers who never use them. Conversely, customers who are relatively more likely to default might be more profitable than more creditworthy customers if they tend to borrow money more often or are prepared to pay a higher rate of interest.

Leading banks are therefore experimenting with ways to take into account the complex interplay of risk and reward. They are moving away from traditional credit default scoring toward product profit scoring (which seeks to estimate the profit the lender makes on a specific product from the customer) and to customer profit scoring (which tries to estimate the total profitability of the customer to the lender). Using this kind of advanced information, lenders can select credit limits, interest margins, and other product features to maximize the profitability of the customer. And they can adjust these risk, operating, and marketing parameters during their relationship with the customer.

In particular, the market is becoming accustomed to "risk-based pricing" for credit products: the idea that customers with different risk profiles should pay different amounts for the same product. Increasingly, banks understand that a "one price fits all" policy in a very competitive market leads to what the industry calls *adverse selection*, i.e., the bank will primarily attract high-risk customers, to whom the product is attractive, and discourage low-risk customers (for the opposite reason). The problem of adverse selection is clearly important from a risk management perspective, to a degree that is likely to become apparent only when the economic climate deteriorates.

Figure 9-4 summarizes the customer relationship cycle that best-practice banks are developing. *Marketing initiatives* include targeting new and existing customers for a new product or tailoring an existing product and/or offer to the specific needs of a customer; these initiatives are the result of detailed marketing studies that analyze the most likely response of various client segments. *Screening applicants* consists of deciding which applications to accept or reject on the basis of scorecards, in terms of both granting the initial credit line and setting the appropriate pricing for the risk level of the client. *Managing the account* is a dynamic process that involves a series of decisions based on observed past behavior and activity. These include modifying a credit line and/or the pricing of a product, authorizing a temporary excess in the use of a credit line, renewing a credit line, and collecting past due interest and/or principal on a delinquent account. *Cross-selling* initiatives close the loop on the customer relationship cycle. Based on a detailed knowledge of existing customers, the bank can

FIGURE 9-4

The Customer Relationship Cycle

Marketing Initiatives	Screening Applicants	Managing Accounts
Target prospect/existing customer?	Accept/reject?	Increase/decrease credit line?
	Tier pricing?	Tier pricing?
Tailor product offering/ message?	Initial credit line?	Collect?
Mail/don't mail?		Authorize?
How frequently?		Reissue?
		Customer service level?

Cross-Sell

initiate actions to induce existing customers to buy additional retail products. For example, for a certain category of customers who already have checking and savings accounts, the bank can offer a mortgage, a credit card, insurance products, and so on. In this retail relationship cycle, risk management has become an integral part of the broader business decision-making process.

THE NEW REGULATORY APPROACH

Traditionally, consumer credit evaluation has modeled each loan or customer in isolation—a natural outcome of the development of application scoring. But lenders are really interested in the characteristics of whole *portfolios* of retail loans. This interest has been reinforced by the emphasis on internal ratings–based modeling in the new Basel Capital Accord. As we discussed in Chapter 3, the new regulations will allow banks to insert their own estimated parameters for probability of default and loss given default into a credit risk model (similar in principal to that applied to commercial loans) to estimate the distribution of default loss for segments of their consumer loan portfolio.

The new Accord considers three retail subsectors—residential mortgages, revolving credit, and other retail exposures such as installment loans—with three different formulas for the risk-weighted assets. It's an approach that has highlighted the need for banks to develop accurate estimates of default probability (rather than simply rely on relative credit scores), and to be able to segment their loan portfolios. Provided banks can convince regulators that their risk estimates are accurate, they will be able to minimize the amount of capital required to cover expected and unexpected retail default losses. Results from the third quantitative impact study (QIS3) conducted by the Basel Committee show that the capital reduction resulting from the adoption of the advanced IRB approach is close to 50 percent for retail portfolios.[3]

SECURITIZATION AND THE TRANSFER OF CONSUMER RISK

Another motivation for improving consumer credit risk modeling arises from the increase in the volume of securitization of such loans.

---

3. Basel Committee on Banking Supervision, *Supplementary Information on QIS3*, Bank for International Settlements, May 27, 2003.

Securitization is the process by which a set of cash flows from a retail portfolio, such as mortgage payments on a mortgage portfolio, is transformed into the payouts of securities through various legal and financial engineering procedures. First, the bank originates credit market assets, for instance home mortgages, credit card receivables, or auto loans. Then it creates a security by pooling together many similar assets whose aggregate income will provide the returns on the security. Finally, the security is sold to outside investors, and the corresponding assets and liabilities are taken off the bank's books.

The phenomenon of securitization initially took hold in the U.S. home mortgage markets. By the late 1970s, a substantial proportion of home mortgages was being securitized, and the trend intensified in the 1980s. Today, around 50 percent of all home mortgages are securitized in the United States. A catalyst for the development of mortgage securitization in the United States was the federal government's sponsorship of some key financial agencies, namely, the Federal National Mortgage Association (FNMA, or Fannie Mae), the Federal Home Loan Mortgage Corporation (FHLMC, or Freddie Mac), and the Government National Mortgage Association (GNMA, or Ginnie Mae). These agencies issue securities whose income is derived from pools of home mortgages originated by banks and other financial intermediaries. In order to qualify for inclusion in these pools, mortgages must meet various requirements in terms of structure and amount. Overall, residential mortgage-backed securities (MBS) constitute 30 percent of the securitized sector.

Many variants of the original MBSs have appeared over the years. Commercial mortgage-backed securities (CMBSs) are frequently considered a different type of instrument altogether, because the risk characteristics and the degree of conformity are different from those associated with home mortgages.

Collateralized mortgage obligations (CMOs) are a variation on the MBS approach that differs not in the nature of the underlying instruments, but in the temporal structure of expected payments. CMO payments are divided into tranches, with the first tranche receiving the first set of payments and other tranches taking their turn. This structure makes the duration of the securities different, and potentially easier to use for asset-liability management purposes.

Asset-backed securities (ABSs) is a term that applies to instruments based on a much broader array of assets than MBSs, including, for example, credit card receivables, auto loans, home equity loans, and leasing receivables.

Selling the cash flows from these loans to investors through some kind of securitization means that the bank gains a principal payment up front, rather than having the money trickle in over the life of the retail product. The securities might be sold to third parties or issued as tranched bonds in the public marketplace, i.e., classes of senior and subordinated bonds awarded ratings by an independent rating agency. The structure of the tranches, their rating, and the spread paid over LIBOR depend on the credit quality of the assets securitized, i.e., the average credit score of the assets in the pool.

Securitizations can take many forms in terms of their legal structure, the reliability of the underlying cash flows, and the degree to which the bank sells off or retains the riskier tranches of cash flows. In some instances, the bank substantially shifts the risk of the portfolio to the investors and through this process reduces the economic risk (and the economic capital) associated with the portfolio. The bank gives up part of its income from the borrowers, and is left with a profit margin that should compensate it for the initiation of the loans and for servicing them.

In other instances, the securitization is structured with regulatory rules in mind to reduce the amount of risk capital that regulators will require the bank to set aside for the particular consumer portfolio in question. Sometimes, this means that only a much smaller amount of the economic risk of the portfolio is transferred to investors—a practice known as *regulatory arbitrage.*

Regulators have become concerned about this practice in recent years, particularly when banks *seem* to transfer risk to investors through the structure of the securitization, but then step back in to support the cash flows underpinning the securitization following a period of weak collateral pool performance. Banks have an interest in doing this because it helps them preserve their reputation with investors for consistent credit quality over repeated sales. Losing a good reputation, and the ability to sell loans economically, may increase the bank's liquidity and interest-rate risk and expose it to burdensome regulatory supervision. But the practice has made regulators wonder whether any economic risk is being transferred, or whether securitizations are simply a funding mechanism. (Unlike the present 1988 Basel Accord, the new Basel Accord to be implemented beginning in 2007 has been designed to take into account the degree to which banks shed or retain risk through securitizations.)

Even when banks are knowingly indulging in regulatory arbitrage, this does not necessarily mean that the bank is behaving in a risky fashion—it might be that the bank as a whole is obliged by regulatory rules to set aside too much regulatory capital from a strictly economic perspective, so that securitization offers one way to redress the balance. Of course, it is up to the senior managers and the board of the bank to make sure that this is the case (and regulators may anyway be annoyed by the idea that the bank is "gaming" their rules).

There's another risk management issue wrapped up in securitization strategies: it is vital that the bank recognizes the true economic value of any credit-risky cash flows that it retains from the securitization (rather than their inflated nominal value). In the recent past, a number of smaller U.S. banks have massively misvalued such risky residual assets to the extent of becoming insolvent, and worried regulators have had to tighten up the rules on how banks account for residuals.

Quite apart from regulatory arbitrage, banks have an incentive to securitize assets, since securitization provides an effective means for banks to deal with their funding problems. Generating mortgages and then securitizing them immediately obviates the need for ongoing funding for those assets. The money that investors pay up front for securities can be immediately lent out again to other customers; it's a way of putting the banks' assets to work more efficiently. But banks need to watch out for the effect this strategy can have on liquidity. Can the bank be certain that the option of funding through securitization will remain open if circumstances change (such as deterioration in the institution's credit rating)?

RISK-BASED PRICING

As discussed earlier, risk-based pricing (RBP) is an increasingly popular activity in retail financial services, encouraged by both competitive and regulatory trends. By risk-based pricing for financial services we mean explicitly incorporating risk-driven account economics into the annualized interest rate that is charged to the customer at the account level. The key economic factors here include operating expenses, the probability of take-up (i.e., the probability that the customer will accept a product offering), the probability of default, the loss given default, the exposure at default, the amount of capital allocated to the transaction, and the cost of equity capital to the institution. Many leading financial institutions have already adopted some form of RBP for acquisitions in their auto loan, credit card, and home mortgage business lines.

Still, RBP in the financial retail area remains in its infancy. A bank's key business objectives are seldom adequately reflected in its pricing strategy. For example, the ability to properly price low-balance accounts versus high-balance revolvers is often inadequate. Further, setting cutoff scores in concert with *tiered pricing*[4] is often based on ad hoc heuristics rather than deep pragmatic analytics. The weaknesses in RBP are due in large part to a lack of automation in most banks' pricing process as well as a lack of good analytical tools for evaluating risk-based pricing strategies.

A tiered pricing policy that sets price as an increasing function of riskier score bands can make risk-based pricing easier and more effective. A well-designed RBP strategy allows the bank to map alternative pricing strategies at the credit score level to key corporate metrics (e.g., revenue, profit, loss, risk-adjusted return, market share, and portfolio value) and is a critical component of best-practice retail management. RBP incorporates key factors from both the external market data (such as the probability of take-up, which in turn is a function of price and credit limit) and internal data (such as the cost of capital).

RBP enables retail bank managers to raise shareholder value by achieving management objectives while taking multiple constraints into consideration, including trade-offs among profit, market share, and risk. Mathematical programming algorithms (such as integer programming solutions) have been developed in order to efficiently achieve these management objectives, subject to the aforementioned constraints. Pricing is a key tool for retail bankers as they balance the goal of increasing market share against the goal of reducing the rate of bad accounts.

Another key objective may be to increase expected net profit while simultaneously constraining expected losses. RBP helps banks to set cutoff scores and to set the score at which the financial institution switches prices. The presumption underlying credit-scoring models is that there exists a metric that can divide good credits and bad credits into distinct distributions (e.g., the probability distribution of scores given that an account is good versus the probability distribution of scores given that an account is bad). As we saw in Figure 9-2, a relatively higher cutoff implies less loss but also a reduced market share, while a low cutoff implies higher expected losses.

To increase market share in a risk-adjusted manner, a retail bank might examine the rate of bad accounts as a function of the percentage of the overall population acceptance rate (strategy curve). Traditional retail pricing leaves a considerable amount of money on the table; better pricing can improve key corporate performance metrics by 10 to 20 percent or more.

---

4. By tiered pricing, we mean pricing differentiated by score bands above the cutoff score—the higher the score, the lower the price.

TACTICAL AND STRATEGIC RETAIL CUSTOMER CONSIDERATIONS

There are various tactical applications for the new scoring technologies, such as determining which customers are more likely to stay (or to leave) and finding approaches to reduce attrition (or increase loyalty) among the right customers. The new technologies might also help banks decide on the best product to offer a particular customer, help them work out how to interest customers in new types of services, such as retirement planning, and help them determine how aggressively they should be approaching customers.

There are also many strategic considerations. For example, is the bank extracting enough "lifetime value" from an individual account? How much future value can the bank expect from its customer portfolio, and what are the real sources of this value? Ideally, the bank should be able to compare its performance relative to its peers (e.g., in terms of market share) as it strives to win and keep the right kind of customer portfolios.

CONCLUSION

In this chapter, we've seen that many quantitative advances have emerged in the retail credit risk area to help shape business strategies throughout the customer life cycle.

At credit origination, analytical models can now help to identify customers who are likely to be profitable, predict their propensity to respond to an offering, align consumer preferences with products, assess borrowers' creditworthiness, determine line/loan authorization, apply risk-based pricing, and evaluate the relationship value of the customer.

Throughout loan servicing, analytical methods are used to anticipate consumer behavior or payment patterns, determine opportunities for cross selling, assess prepayment risk, identify any fraudulent transactions, optimize customer relationship management, and prioritize the collection effort (to maximize recoveries in the event of delinquency). Increasingly, risk-based pricing can be used to analyze trade-offs among corporate metrics and to determine the "optimal" multitier, risk-based pricing strategy.

CHAPTER 10

Commercial Credit Risk and the Rating of Individual Credits

Commercial credit risk is the largest and most elementary risk faced by many banks, and it is a major risk for many other kinds of financial institutions and corporations as well. Assessing commercial credit risk is a complicated task, since many uncertain elements are involved in determining both how likely it is that an event of default will happen and how costly default will turn out to be if it does occur. It's therefore no surprise to find that there are many different approaches to the problem.

Some of the newest approaches employ equity market data to track the likelihood of default by public companies, while other approaches have been developed to assess credit risk at the portfolio level using mathematical and statistical modeling; we'll take a look at these modern quantitative approaches to the problem in the next chapter. Other approaches to the credit-risk conundrum are more traditional and are based on credit-risk assessments within an overall framework known as a *credit rating system*—the subject of the present chapter.

To make a credit assessment, analysts must take into consideration many complex attributes of a firm—financial and managerial, quantitative and qualitative. They must ascertain the financial health of the firm, determine whether earnings and cash flows are sufficient to cover any debt obligations, analyze the quality of the firm's assets, and examine its liquidity position. In addition, analysts must take into account the nature of the industry to which the potential client belongs, the status of their new client within that industry, and the potential effect of macroeconomic events on the firm (including any country risks, such as a political upheaval or currency crisis).

A credit rating system is simply a way of organizing and systematizing all these procedures so that credit analysts—across a firm and through time—arrive at ratings that are rational, coherent, and comparable.

We'll look first at how credit rating agencies (key players in the development of modern ratings) arrive at their public credit ratings of large corporations.

Then we'll take a look at how banks arrive at their own private internal ratings of firms, large and small, that lack a public credit rating. Internal risk rating systems are one of the banking industry's oldest and most widely used credit-risk measurement tools, but practices are changing fast as a result of both regulatory and competitive pressures. Internal rating systems allow the analysis of thousands of borrowers within a consistent framework and permit comparisons across the entire loan portfolio. Large banks use these internal ratings in several critical aspects of credit-risk management, such as loan origination, loan pricing, loan trading, credit portfolio monitoring, capital allocation and reserve determination, profitability analysis, and management reporting (Box 10-1).

Since these internal risk rating systems are such a key element of the credit risk management systems of financial institutions, it is not surprising that they are at the center of the new Basel II regulatory capital attribution process. A bank's internal risk rating system and the associated probability of default (PD) and loss given default (LGD) statistics will be key inputs into the new regulatory capital calculations. However, banks will be able to use their own internal risk rating systems to set credit risk capital requirements only if they meet certain criteria (Box 10-2).

BOX 10-1

PURPOSE OF INTERNAL RISK RATING SYSTEMS (IRRS)

Traditionally IRRS are used by financial institutions for a variety of purposes:

- *Setting limits and acceptance or rejection of new transactions.* The strength of the rating awarded to an entity or transaction is likely to play a key role in the decision to accept or reject a particular transaction. Credit-risk limits are often set in terms of rating categories. Also, concentration limits by name, industry, and country are established and revised annually by the senior risk committee of the bank.

(continued on following page)

BOX 10-1 *(Continued)*

- *Monitoring of credit quality.* Ratings should be reviewed periodically—at least once a year or if a specific event justifies the revision of the credit assessment of a borrower. Credit migration is a critical component in monitoring the credit quality of the loan portfolios of banks.
- *Attribution of economic capital.* Best-practice institutions will have a risk-adjusted return on capital (RAROC) system in place to assess the contribution to shareholder value of the firm's activities and portfolios (see Chapter 15). Internal ratings are key input in the economic capital allocation process to credit portfolios.
- *Adequacy of loan loss reserves.* Both regulators and management use the distribution of portfolio quality, as measured by internal ratings, to judge the adequacy of the financial accounting-based reserve for loan losses and the provision for losses in the current accounting period.
- *Adequacy of capital.* Again, both regulators and management, and also rating agencies, use the portfolio risk profile, as measured by internal ratings, to judge the fundamental creditworthiness of the institution as a whole.
- *Pricing and trading of loans.* Internal ratings are key inputs for credit portfolio models (see Chapter 11), from which the risk contribution of each facility in a credit portfolio can be derived. In turn, these risk contributions help determine the minimum spread that an institution should charge on a credit facility in order to factor in the cost of credit risk. Failing to take account of the relative cost of extending credit destroys shareholder value (see Chapter 15).

BOX 10-2

CRITERIA TO BE MET BY IRRS TO BE ELIGIBLE FOR BASEL II

To be eligible for the internal ratings–based (IRB) approach proposed in the new Basel Capital Accord (described in Chapter 3), a bank must demonstrate that it meets certain minimum criteria both at its adoption of the IRB approach and on an ongoing basis. Most of these criteria focus on the ability of the internal risk rating system to rank-order and quantify risk in a consistent, reliable, and verifiable fashion. The main criteria are

(continued on following page)

BOX 10-2 *(Continued)*

- *Meaningful differentiation of risk.* The Basel II rules suggest a minimum of six to nine rating categories for nondefaulted borrowers as well one category for defaulted borrowers. A borrower's grade must be defined as an assessment of borrower risk on the basis of a specified and distinct set of rating criteria. The grade definition should include an estimated probability of default range and the criteria used to distinguish that level of credit risk. If a bank has a loan concentration within a particular range of default risk, it must offer a minimum grade differentiation within this range.
- *Reliable estimation of risk components.* A bank's rating definitions must be sufficiently detailed to allow those charged with assigning ratings to consistently assign the same grade to borrowers or facilities posing similar risks. Rating consistency must be satisfied across business lines and geographical locations. The rating process should also be independent of the staff in the bank who originate the deals (to prevent any conflict of interest).
- *Clarity of the documentation of rating systems and decisions.* To maintain consistency and integrity in the rating process, banks must ensure that the process is applied uniformly across the institution. Therefore, the risk rating assignment process must be well documented. Organizational controls to ensure the independence of the grade assignment and its validation must be in place.
- *Risk quantification and back testing.* The IRB approach requires banks to translate internal borrower and facility ratings into firm probability of default (PD) and loss given default (LGD) estimates, respectively. Banks will be allowed to use a range of data sources (internal, external, and pooled) and quantification methodologies to make these estimates. But the estimates must be back-tested using historical data to verify that they are accurate estimates of actual default rates and credit losses going forward. The relative scarcity of credit and default data compared to, say, market-risk data makes back testing a daunting task. Banks are required to collect data on borrower and facility ratings histories, including key data that are used to derive ratings. Banks must also collect default histories, including cause, timing, and components of loss. In addition, banks must capture predicted and realized default rates, LGDs, and exposures at default by rating category.

RATING AGENCIES

The External Agency Rating Process

The issuance of bonds by corporations is a twentieth-century phenomenon. Soon after bonds began to be issued, companies such as Moody's (1909), Standard & Poor's (1916), and other agencies started to offer independent assessments of how likely it was that particular bonds would repay investors in the way they were intended to do. Over the last 30 years, the introduction of new financial products has led to the development of new methodologies and criteria for credit rating: Standard & Poor's (S&P) was the first rating company to rate mortgage-backed bonds (1975), mutual funds (1983), and asset-backed securities (1985).

A credit rating is not, in general, an investment recommendation for a given security. In the words of S&P, "A credit rating is S&P's opinion of the general creditworthiness of an obligor, or the creditworthiness of an obligor with respect to a particular debt security or other financial obligation, based on relevant risk factors."[1] When rating a security, a rating agency focuses more on the potential downside loss than on the potential upside gain. In Moody's words, a rating is, "an opinion on the future ability and legal obligation of an issuer to make timely payments of principal and interest on a specific fixed income security."[2] S&P and Moody's have access to a corporation's internal information, and since they are considered to have expertise in credit rating and are generally regarded as unbiased evaluators (but see Box 10-3), their ratings are widely accepted by market participants and regulatory agencies. Financial institutions, when required by their regulators to hold investment-grade bonds, use the ratings of credit agencies such as S&P and Moody's to determine which bonds are of investment grade.

There are two main classes of ratings. With *issuer credit ratings*, the rating is an opinion on the obligor's overall capacity to meet its financial obligations. In the issuer credit rating category are counterparty ratings, corporate credit ratings, and sovereign credit ratings. Another class of rating is *issue-specific credit ratings*. In this case, the rating agency makes a distinction, in its rating system and symbols, between long-term and short-term credits. The short-term ratings apply to commercial paper (CP), certificates of deposit (CD), and put bonds.[3] In rating a specific issue, the

---

1. *S&P Corporate Ratings Criteria*, 1998, p. 3.
2. *Moody's Credit Ratings and Research*, 1998, p. 4.
3. A put bond is a bond stipulation that allows the holder to redeem the bond at face value at a specific, predetermined time, so that if interest rates go up, the holder can avoid losing money (so long as the stipulation remains in operation).

BOX 10-3

ARE THE RATING AGENCIES UP TO THE JOB?

In the main text, we say that rating agencies are regarded as unbiased evaluators of credit risk. This is a simplification: over the last few years, there has been mounting criticism of the *role* and *performance* of rating agencies.

The criticism of the role that agencies play is based on their dominance of the credit rating market and their source of income. For example, the demand for ratings is artificially encouraged by a growing reliance on ratings as a tool of regulation. Since 1975, U.S. Securities and Exchange Commission regulations have relied on ratings from what it calls "nationally recognized statistical rating organizations" (NRSROs) to distinguish among the risk of various credit-risky securities.

The importance of complying with SEC and other government regulations that refer to officially recognized credit ratings has put NRSROs in a quasi-monopolistic position. At the time of writing, only four NRSROs were recognized: Moody's, Standard & Poor's, Fitch (a third relatively large agency), and a much smaller agency called the Dominion Bond Rating Service.

Critics also point to a long-standing conflict of interest in the way that ratings are funded. Ideally, users of the ratings, such as investors, would pay agencies to rate companies: the company under the microscope would not make any payments at all to the rating agency. In reality, the largest rating agencies rely on issuer fees for the majority of their income, leading to fears that in certain circumstances they might lose their objectivity. The potential for conflicts of interest might become worse in the future if the main agencies further develop risk consultancy and advisory services that take additional fees from the corporations that they rate.

The agencies respond by saying that they have put many processes in place to prevent any conflict of interest affecting a rating, and that they have a good track record of making accurate ratings.

Rating agencies have also been criticized for their performance. Some commentators said that the rating industry performed poorly in "calling" the 1997 crisis in the Asian markets. Many companies in the region were downgraded only after the crisis was well under way.

They also seemed to perform poorly in spotting very highly leveraged or poorly managed companies (such as the failed energy giant Enron) at the tail end of the millennial stock boom. The agencies themselves admit that there were an unusually high number of "fallen angels"—that is, sudden downgrades from investment-grade status—at the end of the last economic

(continued on following page)

BOX 10-3 *(Continued)*

---

cycle. But they point to their long-term record and say that many of the investors who use credit ratings in their investment decisions want relatively stable credit ratings, not ratings that jump up and down along with market perceptions.

As a result of the criticism, regulatory authorities such as the U.S. Securities and Exchange Commission are conducting a series of long-running investigations into the way the rating industry works.[1] The rating industry might not yet face revolutionary change, but it will certainly have to put up with a lot more criticism and informal oversight than in the past.

---

1. See, for example, *Report on the Role and Function of Credit Rating Agencies in the Operation of the Securities Markets*, U.S. Securities and Exchange Commission, January 2003, available at http://www.sec.gov/news/studies/ credratingreport0103.pdf.

---

attributes of the issuer, as well as the specific terms of the issue, the quality of the collateral, and the creditworthiness of the guarantors, are taken into account.

The rating process includes quantitative, qualitative, and legal analyses. The quantitative analysis is mainly financial analysis and is based on the firm's financial reports. The qualitative analysis is concerned with the quality of management; it includes a thorough review of the firm's competitiveness within its industry as well as the expected growth of the industry and its vulnerability to business cycles, technological changes, regulatory changes, and labor relations.

Figure 10-1 illustrates the process of rating an industrial company. The process allows the analyst to work through sovereign and macroeconomic issues, industry outlook, and regulatory trends, to specific attributes (including quality of management, operating position, and financial position), and eventually to the issue-specific structure of the financial instrument.

The assessment of management, which is subjective in nature, investigates how likely it is that management will achieve operational success and takes the temperature of its tolerance for risk. The rating process includes meetings with the management of the issuer to review operating and financial plans, policies, and strategies. All the information is reviewed and discussed by a rating committee with appropriate expertise in the relevant industry, which then votes on the recommendation. The issuer can appeal the rating before it is made public by supplying new information. The rating decision is usually issued four to six weeks after the agency is asked to rate a debt issue.

FIGURE 10-1

Moody's Rating Analysis of an Industrial Company

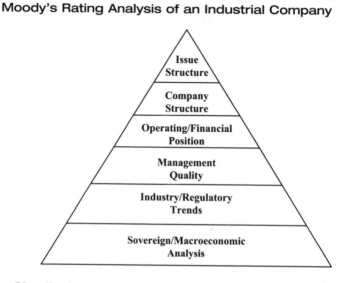

Usually the ratings are reviewed once a year based on new financial reports, new business information, and review meetings with management. A "credit watch" or "rating review" notice is issued if there is reason to believe that the review may lead to a credit rating change. A change of rating has to be approved by the rating committee.

Credit Ratings by S&P and Moody's

Standard & Poor's (S&P) is one of the world's major rating agencies, operating in more than 50 countries. Moody's operates mainly in the United States but has many branches internationally. Tables 10-1 and 10-2 pro-

TABLE 10-1

S&P Ratings Category Definitions

AAA	An obligation rated AAA has the highest rating assigned by Standard & Poor's. The obligor's capacity to meet its financial commitment on the obligation is extremely strong.
AA	An obligation rated AA differs from the highest rated obligations only in small degree. The obligor's capacity to meet its financial commitment on the obligation is very strong.

(continued on following page)

TABLE 10-1 *(Continued)*

A	An obligation rated A is somewhat more susceptible to the adverse effects of changes in circumstances and economic conditions than obligations in higher rated categories. However, the obligor's capacity to meet its financial commitment on the obligation is still strong.
BBB	An obligation rated BBB exhibits adequate protection parameters. However, adverse economic conditions or changing circumstances are more likely to lead to a weakened capacity of the obligor to meet its financial commitment on the obligation.
BB	An obligation rated BB is less vulnerable to nonpayment than other speculative issues. However, it faces major ongoing uncertainties or exposure to adverse business, financial, or economic conditions which could lead to the obligor's inadequate capacity to meet its financial commitment on the obligation.
B	An obligation rated B is more vulnerable to nonpayment than obligations rated BB but the obligor currently has the capacity to meet its financial commitment on the obligation. Adverse business, financial, or economic conditions will likely impair the obligor's capacity or willingness to meet its financial commitment on the obligation.
CCC	An obligation rated CCC is currently vulnerable to nonpayment, and is dependent upon favorable business, financial, and economic conditions for the obligor to meet its financial commitment on the obligation. In the event of adverse business, financial, or economic conditions, the obligor is not likely to have the capacity to meet its financial commitment on the obligation.
CC	An obligation rated CC is currently highly vulnerable to nonpayment.
C	The C rating may be used to cover a situation where a bankruptcy petition has been filed or similar action has been taken, but payments on this obligation are being continued.
D	The D rating, unlike other ratings, is not prospective; rather, it is used only where a default has actually occurred—and not where a default is only expected. Standard & Poor's changes ratings to D either: ■ On the day an interest and/or principal payment is due and is not paid. An exception is made if there is a grace period and S&P believes that a payment will be made, in which case the rating can be maintained; or ■ Upon voluntary bankruptcy filing or similar action. An exception is made if S&P expects that debt service payments will continue to be made on a specific issue. In the absence of a payment default or bankruptcy filing, a technical default (i.e., covenant violation) is not sufficient for assigning a D rating.
+ or −	The ratings from AA to CCC may be modified by the addition of a plus or minus sign to show relative standing within the major rating categories.
R	The symbol is attached to the ratings of instruments with significant non-credit risks. It highlights risks to principal or volatility of expected returns which are not addressed in the credit rating. Examples include: obligations linked or indexed to equities, currencies, or commodities; obligations exposed to severe prepayment risk—such as interest-only or principal-only mortgage securities; and obligations with unusually risky interest terms, such as inverse floaters.

Source: Reproduced from *Corporate Ratings Criteria* of S&P for 1998.

TABLE 10-2

Moody's Rating Category Definition

Aaa	Bonds which are rated Aaa are judged to be of the best quality. They carry the smallest degree of investment risk and are generally referred to as "gilt edged." Interest payments are protected by a large or by an exceptionally stable margin and principal is secure. While the various protective elements are likely to change, such changes as can be visualized are most unlikely to impair the fundamentally strong position of such issues.
Aa	Bonds which are rated Aa are judged to be of high quality by all standards. Together with the Aaa group they comprise what are generally known as high-grade bonds. They are rated lower than the best bonds because margins of protection may not be as large as in Aaa securities or fluctuation of protective elements may be of greater amplitude or there may be other elements present which make the long-term risk appear somewhat larger than the Aaa securities.
A	Bonds which are rated A possess many favorable investment attributes and are to be considered as upper medium-grade obligations. Factors giving security to principal and interest are considered adequate, but elements may be present which suggest a susceptibility to impairment some time in the future.
Baa	Bonds which are rated Baa are considered as medium-grade obligations (i.e., they are neither highly protected nor poorly secured). Interest payments and principal security appear adequate for the present but certain protective elements may be lacking or may be characteristically unreliable over any great length of time. Such bonds lack outstanding investment characteristics and in fact have speculative characteristics as well.
Ba	Bonds which are rated Ba are judged to have speculative elements; their future cannot be considered as well-assured. Often the protection of interest and principal payments may be very moderate, and thereby not well safeguarded during both good and bad times over the future. Uncertainty of position characterizes bonds in this class.
B	Bonds which are rated B generally lack characteristics of the desirable investment. Assurance of interest and principal payments or of maintenance of other terms of the contract over any long period of time may be small.
Caa	Bonds which are rated Caa are of poor standing. Such issues may be in default or there may be present elements of danger with respect to principal or interest.
Ca	Bonds which are rated Ca represent obligations which are speculative in a high degree. Such issues are often in default or have other marked shortcomings.
C	Bonds which are rated C are the lowest rated class of bonds, and issues so rated can be regarded as having extremely poor prospects of ever attaining any real investment standing.

Source: Moody's *Credit Ratings and Research,* 1995.

vide the definitions of the ratings categories used by S&P and Moody's for long-term credit. Issues rated in the four highest categories (i.e., AAA, AA, A, and BBB for S&P and Aaa, Aa, A, and Baa for Moody's) are generally considered to be of investment grade. Some financial institutions, for special or approved investment programs, are required to invest only in bonds or debt instruments that are of investment grade. Obligations rated BB, B, CCC, CC, and C by S&P (Ba, B, Caa, Ca, and C by Moody's) are regarded as having significant speculative characteristics. BB (Ba in Moody's) is the least risky, and C is the most risky.

S&P uses plus or minus signs to modify its AA to CCC ratings in order to indicate the relative standing of a credit within the major rating categories. Similarly, Moody's applies numerical modifiers 1, 2, and 3 in each generic rating classification from Aa through Caa. The modifier 1, for example, indicates that the obligation ranks at the higher end of its generic rating category; thus B1 in Moody's rating system is a ranking equivalent to B+ in S&P's rating system.

How accurate are agency ratings? The answer is provided in Figure 10-2, which shows the average cumulative default rates for corporate bond issuers for each rating category over bond holding periods of 1 year up to 15 years after bond issuance. The figure is based on data from the period 1981 to 2004. It can be seen that the lower the rating, the higher the cumulative default rates. The Aaa and Aa bonds experienced very low default rates; after 10 years, less than 1 percent of the issues had defaulted. Approximately 35 percent of the B-rated issues, however, had defaulted after 10 years.

Historical data seem to offer a general validation of agency ratings. But they are useful for another reason: they allows risk analysts to attach an objective likelihood of default to any company that has been rated by an agency or that has been rated by banks in a manner thought to be equivalent to an agency rating.

While the major rating agencies use similar methods and approaches to rate debt, they sometimes come up with different ratings for the same debt investment. Academic studies of the credit rating industry have shown that only just over half of the firms rated AA or Aa and AAA or Aaa in a large sample were rated the same by the two top agencies. The same study found that smaller agencies tend to rate debt issues higher than or the same as S&P and Moody's; only rarely do they award a lower rating.[4]

---

4. R. Cantor and F. Packer, "Sovereign Credit Ratings," Federal Reserve Bank of New York, *Current Issues in Economics and Finance* 1(3), 1995.

FIGURE 10-2

(a) Cumulative Average Default Rates for Bonds with
Different Ratings, 1981–2004

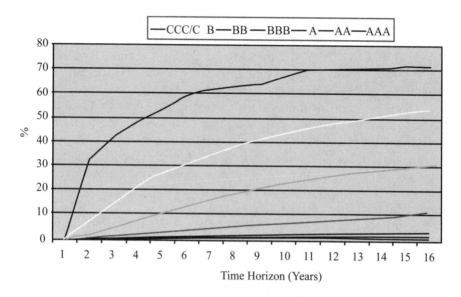

Time Horizon (Years)

(b) Cumulative AverageDefault Rates for Speculative-Grade
and Investment-Grade Debt, 1981–2004

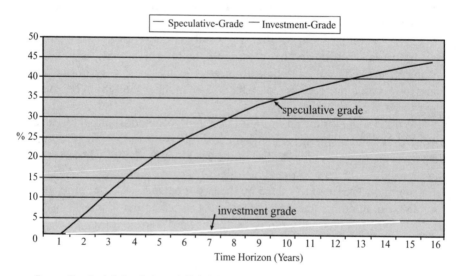

Time Horizon (Years)

Source: Standard & Poor's Annual Global Corporate Default Study, January 26, 2005.

DEBT RATING AND MIGRATION

Bankruptcy, whether defined as a legal or an economic event, usually marks the end of a corporation in its current form. It is a discrete event, yet it is also the final point in a continuous process—the moment when it is finally recognized that a firm cannot meet its financial obligations. Analysts who focus solely on the event of bankruptcy disregard a lot of useful information about the status of a firm, its total value, and the value of its liabilities.

Of course, credit agencies do not focus simply on default. At discrete points in time, they revise their credit ratings of corporate bonds. This evolution of credit quality is very important for an investor holding a portfolio of corporate bonds.

Using transition matrices, we can see how different rating categories have changed over time. Table 10-3 is based on S&P's experience from 1981 to 2004; it contains the empirical results for the migration from one credit-risk category to all other credit-risk categories within one year. The values on the diagonals of the transition matrix show the percentage of bonds that remained in the same risk category at the end of the specified time period as at the beginning.

For example, we see that 91.67 percent of the bonds rated AAA remained in the same rating category a year later. Observe that 7.69 percent were downgraded to AA, 0.48 percent downgraded to A, and so on. Similar multiyear transition matrices can also be produced (for reasons of space, these are not shown in this chapter). For example, on average, a firm rated BBB remained in the same risk category after two years in 70.36 percent of the cases, while there was a 7 percent chance of the firm's being upgraded to a rating of A. Bonds rated BBB had a 0.84 percent chance of defaulting within two years.

Such transition matrices highlight the differences between the higher and the lower ratings grades. For example, bonds with an initial rating of CCC defaulted in 32.35 percent of cases within one year, in 42.35 percent of cases within two years; and in 59.49 percent of cases within five years. For bonds rated AAA, the percentages were 0 percent for one year, 0 percent for two years, and 0.12 percent for five years, respectively. After five years, however, only 54 percent of the AAA-rated bonds had maintained their initial rating, while about 19 percent had had their ratings withdrawn (these data are not shown in Table 10-3).

Clearly, issuers that are rated AAA can't be upgraded; they either maintain their rating or are downgraded. CCC-rated bonds can maintain their rating, be upgraded, or go into default. But what of BBB-rated bonds?

TABLE 10-3

Average Transition Rates, 1981–2004 (%)

From/To	AAA	AA	A	BBB	BB	B	CCC/C	D
AAA	91.67	7.69	0.48	0.09	0.06	0	0	0
AA	0.62	90.49	8.1	0.6	0.05	0.11	0.02	0.01
A	0.05	2.16	91.34	5.77	0.44	0.17	0.03	0.04
BBB	0.02	0.22	4.07	89.71	4.68	0.08	0.2	0.29
BB	0.04	0.08	0.36	5.78	83.37	8.05	1.03	1.28
B	0	0.07	0.22	0.32	5.84	82.52	4.78	6.24
CCC/C	0.09	0	0.36	0.45	1.52	11.17	54.07	32.35

Source: Standard & Poor's, *Annual Global Corporate Default Study,* Jan. 26, 2004.

Based on their history, they seem to have an equal chance of being up-graded or downgraded within a period of one and two years. However, over periods of five and ten years, they seem more likely to be upgraded than downgraded.

The transition matrices play a major role in the credit evaluation system of JP Morgan's CreditMetrics, an approach to portfolio credit-risk measurement that we'll take a closer look at in the next chapter. Transition matrices are important to CreditMetrics because the approach uses the past (i.e., historical data) as the basis for estimating probabilities for future migration among risk categories.

INTRODUCTION TO INTERNAL RISK RATING

The ratings from agencies offer a useful credit-risk assessment to many audiences, from investors to corporations to banks. But banks are in the business of lending money to a very wide spectrum of companies, not just those that issue public debt (and that therefore find it useful to invest in gaining a credit rating). Many smaller and private companies are not even listed on a public stock exchange, so that much of the financial data that can be gathered about them are of unproven quality.

In this section we look at the internal risk rating system (IRRS) of a typical bank. A robust IRRS should offer a carefully designed, structured, and documented series of steps for the assessment of each rating. The goal is to generate accurate and consistent risk ratings for many different types of company, yet also to allow professional judgment to significantly influence a rating where this is appropriate.

In order to be reliable, any such classification method must be consistent over time and must be based on sound economic principles. The IRRS we describe here is based on the authors' extensive experience as, in one case, a bank chief risk officer, and also as money managers at major commercial banks dealing with counterparty credit risk. The approach presented here is also consistent with the directives in the new Basel Capital Accord, which obliges banks to put in place a systematic procedure for credit-risk assessment.

Typically, a bank IRRS assigns two kinds of ratings. First, it assigns an obligor default rating (ODR) to each borrower (or group of borrowers) that identifies the borrower's probability of default. Second, it assigns a loss given default rating (LGDR) to each available facility, independently of the ODR, that identifies the risk of loss from that facility in the event of default on the obligation.

To understand the fundamental difference between these two kinds of rating, let's consider the key concept of *expected loss*. The expected loss of a particular transaction or portfolio is the product of the amount of credit *exposure at default* (say, $100) multiplied by the *probability of default* (say, 2 percent) for an obligor (or borrower) and the *loss rate given default* (say, 50 percent) in any specific credit facility. In this example, the expected loss is $100 \times 0.02 \times 0.50 = \$1$.

The ODR represents simply the probability of default by a borrower in repaying its obligation in the normal course of business. The LGDR, on the other hand, assesses the conditional severity of the loss, should default occur. The severity of the loss on any facility is considerably influenced by whether the bank has put in place risk mitigation tools such as guarantees, collateral, and so on.

As well as identifying the risks associated with a borrower and a credit facility, an IRRS also provides a key input for the capital charges used in various pricing models and for risk-adjusted return on capital (RAROC) systems of the kind we describe in Chapter 15. It can also assist in establishing loan loss reserves, the accounting provisions that the bank sets aside to cover the expected cost of default. The IRRS can be used to rate credit risks in most of the major corporate and commercial sectors, but it is unlikely to cover all business sectors. Typically, a bank's principal IRRS excludes real estate credits, banks, agriculture, public finance, and other groups of credits identified as having special factors that need to be considered in their credit assessments.

A typical IRRS, as shown in Table 10-4, includes a category 0 to capture the government debt of developed economies (say, Canadian or U.S. federal government debt), as this is regarded as being without risk.

TABLE 10-4

Risk Rating Continuum (Prototype Risk
Rating System)

Risk	RR	Corresponding Probable S&P or Moody's Ratings	
Sovereign	0	Not applicable	
Low	1	AAA	
	2	AA	Investment
	3	A	Grade
	4	BBB+/BBB	
Average	5	BBB−	
	6	BB+/BB	
	7	BB−	Below
	8	B+/B	Investment
	9	B−	Grade
High	10	CCC+/CCC	
	11	CC−	
	12	In default	

Category 1 is reserved for corporate debt with the highest credit quality. The average risk grades (e.g., BBB and BB) are often split to obtain greater differentiation in risk assessment, as they often correspond to the range of risk where most of the credits are concentrated.

The steps in the IRRS (eight in our illustrative system: seven for the ODR and one for the LGDR) typically start with a financial assessment of the borrower (initial obligor rating) that sets a floor on the obligor rating. A series of further steps (six) arrive at a final obligor rating. Each one of Steps 2 to 7 may result in a downgrade of the initial rating attributed at Step 1. These steps include analyzing the managerial capability of the borrower (Step 2), examining the borrower's absolute and relative position within the industry (Step 3), reviewing the quality of the financial information (Step 4), analyzing country risk (Step 5), comparing the preliminary ODR reached in Step 5 to default ratings provided by external rating agencies and by consulting and software firms such as KMV Corporation (Step 6; see Chapter 11), and considering the impact of the loan structure on the default probability (Step 7). The process ensures that all credits are objectively rated using a consistent process to arrive at accurate ratings.

The LGDR is derived in a final phase (Step 8) independent from the ODR.

Our eight steps are really the "factory floor" of any credit rating system. The usefulness of any internal rating, and the integrity of the bank's risk management system as a whole, relies upon each step being executed in a robust fashion. So let's take a closer look at each of the steps.

FINANCIAL ASSESSMENT (STEP 1)

Introduction

This step formalizes the thinking process of a good credit analyst (or good equity analyst), whose goal is to ascertain the financial health of an institution. The credit analyst might begin by studying the institution's financial reports to determine whether the earnings and cash flows are sufficient to cover the debt repayments. The credit analyst will study the degree to which the trends associated with these "financials" are stable and positive. The credit analyst will also want to analyze the company's assets to determine whether they are of high quality, and to make sure that the obligor has substantial cash reserves (e.g., substantial working capital[5]). The analyst will also want to examine the firm's leverage. Similarly, the credit analyst will want to analyze the extent to which the firm has access to the capital markets, and whether it is able to borrow the money that it will need to carry out its business plans. The rating should reflect the company's financial position and performance and its ability to withstand any financial setbacks.

Procedure

A prototype financial assessment table encompassing the risk rating 4 is shown in Table 10-5. The three main assessment areas, as illustrated in the column heads of Table 10-5, are (1) earnings and cash flow; (2) asset values, liquidity, and leverage; and (3) financial size, flexibility, and debt capacity.

A measure for earnings and cash flow in column 1 would take into account interest coverage expressed in terms of key accounting ratios—for example, the ratio of earnings before interest and taxes (EBIT) to interest expense and the ratio of earnings before interest, taxes, depreciation, and amortization (EBITDA) to interest expense.[6] The analysis would

---

5. Working capital is defined as the difference between current assets and current liabilities.

6. For definitions of key accounting ratios, see the appendix to this chapter.

emphasize the current year's performance, with some recognition of the previous few years as appropriate. When assessing companies in cyclical industries, the analyst should adjust the financial results and key ratios so that the cyclical effect is incorporated.

A measure for leverage in column 2 might be ratios of debt to net worth such as total liabilities to equity or (total liabilities minus debt) to equity.

When assessing the financial size, flexibility, and debt capacity category, the size of the market capitalization will be an important factor. The "access to capital markets" bullet point in this third assessment area refers to the demonstrated ability (or potential in the near term) to issue public securities (equities or medium- to long-term debt instruments).

The analyst would calculate a risk rating for each of the three assessment areas and then arrive at an assessment of the best overall risk rating.[7] This is the initial obligor rating.

TABLE 10-5

Step 1—Financial Assessment

RR	• Earnings (E) • Cash Flow (CF)	• Asset Values (AV) • Liquidity (LIQ) • Leverage (LEV)	• Financial Size (FS) • Flexibility (F) • Debt Capacity (DC)
4	• Very satisfactory earnings and cash flow with substantial extra coverage • Positive and quite consistent/stable trends	• Assets of above average quality • Good liquidity/working capital • Better than average leverage • Appropriate matching of tenor of liabilities to assets	• General access (rated BBB+/BBB) to capital markets; may experience some barriers because of difficult market or economic conditions • Ready access to alternative financing through banks or other financial institutions, if sought • Bank debt modest with large unused capacity

7. As an appropriate control, the average might first be compared to the worst of the three risk levels. The rating should not be more than 1.0 better than the worst rating. In other words, if it exceeds this control, then it must be adjusted downward. For example, if the three assessment areas were respectively rated 2, 2, and 5 then the average is 3, but the rating should be adjusted to 4 (which is 1.0 better than the 5 risk level). If the worst of the three risk levels is not an integer (say 4.5), then reducing it by 1 would leave a rating of 3.5. One typically uses judgment and sets the rating at either 3 or 4.

T A B L E   1 0 - 6

Some Key Financial Ratios

1.	EBIT interest coverage ($\times$)
2.	EBITDA interest coverage ($\times$)
3.	Funds from operations/total debt (%)
4.	Free operating cash flow/total debt (%)
5.	Pretax return on capital (%)
6.	Operating income/sales (%)
7.	Long-term debt/capital (%)
8.	Total debt/capitalization (%)

Industry Benchmarks

The analysis of a firm's competitive position and operating environment helps in assessing the firm's general business risk profile. This profile can be used to calibrate quantitative information drawn from the financial ratios for the firm, shown in Table 10-6. For example, the credit quality of a counterparty rises as an increasing function of the ratio of EBITDA to the amount of interest owed (i.e., EBITDA interest coverage).

A company with an excellent business in a growing or stable sector can assume more debt than a company with less glowing prospects.[8]

ADJUSTMENT FACTORS FOR OBLIGOR DEFAULT RATING (ODR)

Management and Other Qualitative Factors (Step 2)

This second step considers the impact on an obligor rating of a variety of qualitative factors, such as discovering unfavorable aspects of a borrower's management. Step 2 analysis may bring about a downgrade if standards are not acceptable.

A typical Step 2 approach would require such activities as examining day-to-day account operations, assessing management, performing an environmental assessment, and examining contingent liabilities.

---

8. Business risk is defined as the risk associated with the level and stability of operating cash flows over time.

For example, in the case of day-to-day account operations, is the firm's financial reporting on a timely basis and of good quality? Does the firm satisfactorily explain any significant variations from projections? Are credit limits and terms respected? Does the company honor its obligations to creditors?

In the case of a management assessment, the analyst might check that management skills are sufficient for the size and scope of the business. Does management have a record of success and appropriate industry experience? Does management have adequate depth (for example, are succession plans in place)? Is there an informed approach to identifying, accepting, and managing risks? Does management address problems promptly, exhibiting the will to take hard decisions as necessary, with an appropriate balance of short- to long-term concerns? Is management remuneration prudent and appropriate to the size, financial strength, and progress of the company?

Industry Ratings Summary (Step 3a)

This portion of the third step explicitly recognizes the importance of the interaction between an industry rating and the relative position of the borrower within its industry. Experience has shown that poorer-tier performers in weak, vulnerable industries are major contributors to credit losses.

To take this into account, the analyst needs to rate each type of industry on, say, a scale of 1 to 5 using an industry assessment (IA) ratings scheme for each industry. To calculate the industry assessment, the analyst first assigns a score of 1 (minimal risk) to 5 (very high risk) for each of a set of, say, eight criteria established by the bank. For example, each industry might be described in terms of its competitiveness, trade environment, regulatory framework, restructuring, technological change, financial performance, long-term trends affecting demand, and vulnerability to macroeconomic environment.

Tier Assessment (Step 3b)

The criteria and process used to assess industry risk can often be reapplied to determine a company's relative position (say, on a scale of tiers 1 to 4) within an industry. A business should be ranked against its appropriate competition. That is, if the company supplies a product or service that is subject to global competition, then it should be ranked on a global basis. If the company's competitors are by nature local or regional, as is the case for many retail businesses, then it should be ranked on that basis (while recognizing that competition may increase).

In a four-tier system, tier 1 players are major players with a dominant share of the relevant market (local, regional, domestic, international, or niche). They have a diversified and growing customer base and have low production costs that are based on sustainable factors (such as a diversified supplier base, economies of scale, location and resource availability, continuous upgrading of technology, and so on). Such companies respond quickly and effectively to changes in the regulatory framework, trading environment, technology, demand patterns, and macroeconomic environment.

Tier 2 players are important or above-average industry players with a meaningful share of the relevant market (local, regional, domestic, international, or niche).

Tier 3 players are average (or modestly below average) industry players, with a moderate share of the relevant market (local, regional, domestic, international, or niche).

Tier 4 players are weak industry players with a declining customer base. They have a high cost of production as a result of factors such as low leverage with suppliers, obsolete technologies, and so on.

Industry/Tier Position (Step 3c)

This final part of the third step (Step 3c) combines the assessments of the health of the industry (i.e., the industry rating) and the position of a business within its industry (i.e., the tier rating). While the tier rating can be lowered if the industry/tier assessment is weak, it will not be raised if this position is strong. The process reveals the vulnerability of a company, particularly during recessions. Low-quartile competitors within an industry class almost always have higher risk (modified by the relative health of the industry).

Financial Statement Quality (Step 4)

This fourth step recognizes the importance of the quality of the financial information provided to the analyst. This includes consideration of the size and capabilities of the accounting firm compared to the size and complexities of the borrower and its financial statements. Again, the rating should not be raised even if the result is good; the point of this step is to define the highest *possible* rating that can be obtained.

Country Risk (Step 5)

This fifth step adjusts for the effect of any country risk. Country risk is the risk that a counterparty or obligor will not be able to pay its obligations because of cross-border restrictions on the convertibility or availability of a given currency. It is also an assessment of the political and economic risk of a country. Country risk exists when more than a prescribed percentage (say 25 percent) of the obligor's (gross) cash flow (or assets) is located outside of the local market. Country risk may be mitigated by hard currency cash flow received or earned by the counterparty. Hard currency cash flow refers to revenue in a major (i.e., readily exchanged) international currency (primarily U.S. and Canadian dollars, sterling, euro, and Japanese yen).

Again, Step 5 limits the best possible rating. For example, if the client's operation has a country rating in the "fair" category, then the best possible obligor rating might be limited to 5.

Comparison to External Ratings (Step 6)

When the obligor is rated by an external rating agency or when it is included in the database of an external service providing default probability estimates, such as KMV, the preliminary ODR produced in Step 5 is compared to these external ratings. The intent is not to align the internal rating with that of an external agency but to ensure that all appropriate risk issues have been factored into the final ODR.

When the ODR differs substantially from the external rating, then the rater should review the assessment on which the rating process is based (Steps 1 to 5). If the comparison suggests that important risk factors were overlooked or underestimated in the preliminary analysis, then these factors should be incorporated in the final ODR by revising Steps 1 through 5.

This step can be viewed as a sanity check to validate the internally derived ODR and ensure the completeness of the analysis followed in Steps 1 through 5.

Loan Structure (Step 7)

The risk rating process (Steps 1 through 6) assumes that most credits have an appropriate loan structure in place. If so, Step 7 has no impact on the ODR. However, if the loan structure is not sufficiently strong and is viewed as having a negative impact on the risk of default of the obligor, then a downgrade is required. As a general rule, the weaker the preliminary ODR concluded in Step 6, the more stringent the loan structure should be to be regarded as appropriate.

The components of the loan structure that may affect default risk are the financial covenants, the term of the debt, its amortization scheme, and change-of-control restrictions. For example, in the case of high-risk companies, financial ratio requirements should be progressive and should fit tightly with the company's own forecasts. In addition, significant amortization of debt over the tenure of the facilities should be imposed, and non-merger restrictions should be put in place.

LOSS GIVEN DEFAULT RATING (LGDR)

Step 8 assigns a loss given default rating to each facility. This rating is determined independently of default probabilities. The probability of default and the loss experienced in the event of default are separate risk issues and therefore should be looked at independently. Typically, each LGDR is mapped to an LGD factor, i.e., a number between 0 and 100 percent, with 0 percent corresponding to the case of total recovery and 100 percent to the situation where the creditor loses all the amount due. The LGD should be calculated net of the recovery cost.

Different evaluation methods are used depending on whether the credit is unsecured or is secured by third-party support or collateral.

The presence of security should mitigate the severity of the loss given default for any facility. The quality and depth of security varies widely and will determine the extent of the benefit in reducing any loss.

When the credit is secured by a guarantor, the analyst must be convinced that the third party/owner is committed to ongoing support of the obligor.

When a facility is protected by collateral, the collateral category should reflect only the security held for the facility that is being rated. (Exceptions are where all security is held for all facilities, and where all facilities are being rated as one total.) Documentation risk (the proper completion of security) is always a concern and should be considered when assessing the level of protection.

Collateral can have a major effect on the final LGDR, but the value of collateral is often far from straightforward. The value of securities used as collateral is often a function of movements in market rates. In the most worrying situation, collateral values tend to move down as the risk of obligor default rises. For example, real estate used as collateral for a loan to a property developer has a strong tendency to lose its value during a property downturn—the moment in the sector cycle when a property developer is most likely to default.

CONCLUSION

We've seen how credit analysts can systematically employ a series of quantitative and judgmental tools to arrive at an ODR and LGDR.

As we discuss in Chapter 3, the new Basel Capital Accord (Basel II) puts a special emphasis on the internal rating–based approach for credit-risk attribution. In the future, many banks will be able to use their internal ratings to calculate the amount of regulatory risk capital they must put aside for key credit risks. But to do so, banks will have to prove that their internal rating system meets certain standards.

We can expect that over time, most of the world's larger banks will adopt a system of rigorous internal ratings that live up to the quality standards outlined in the Accord, in pursuit of compliance or to protect their reputation in the face of raised industry standards.

In doing so, they will also improve their ability to differentiate and price risk in pursuit of some key business goals. These include improved risk selection, risk-adjusted pricing, risk-adjusted profitability analysis, improved investor communication, and more efficient risk transfer.

The credit rating system we've described can also be used by nonfinancial corporations to assess any credit granted to major customers. Also, financial institutions such as insurance companies can use similar systems to evaluate loans to corporations and the credit risk associated with any private bond issues that they purchase for their portfolios.

Definitions of Key Financial Ratios

1. EBIT interest coverage =
(times interest earned)

$$\frac{\text{Earnings from continuing operations before interest and taxes}}{\text{Gross interest incurred before subtracting (1) capitalized interest and (2) interest income}}$$

2. EBITDA interest coverage =
(cash interest coverage)

$$\frac{\text{Earnings from continuing operations before interest, taxes, depreciation, and amortization}}{\text{Gross interest incurred before subtracting (1) capitalized interest and (2) interest income}}$$

3. Funds from operations/total debt =

$$\frac{\text{Net income from continuing operations plus depreciation, amortization, deferred income taxes, and other noncash items}}{\text{Long-term debt plus current maturities, commercial paper, and other short-term borrowings}}$$

4. Free operating cash flow/total debt =

$$\frac{\text{Funds from operations minus capital expenditures, minus (plus) the increase (decrease) in working capital (excluding changes in cash, marketable securities, and short-term debt)}}{\text{Long-term debt plus current maturities, commercial paper, and other short-term borrowings}}$$

5. Pretax return on capital =

$$\frac{\text{Pretax income from continuing operations plus interest expense}}{\text{Sum of (1) average of beginning of year and end of year current maturities, long-term debt, noncurrent deferred taxes, and equity and (2) average short-term borrowings during year as disclosed in footnotes}}$$

6. Operating income/sales =

$$\frac{\text{Sales minus cost of goods manufactured (before depreciation and amortization), selling, general and administrative, and research and development costs}}{\text{Sales}}$$

7. Long-term debt/capitalization =

$$\frac{\text{Long-term debt}}{\text{Long-term debt plus shareholders' equity (including preferred stock) plus minority interest}}$$

8. Total debt/capitalization =

$$\frac{\text{Long-term debt plus current maturities, commercial paper, and other short-term borrowings}}{\text{Long-term debt plus current maturities, commercial paper, and other short-term borrowings plus shareholders' equity (including preferred stock) plus minority interest}}$$

Source: S&P's Corporate Ratings Criteria, 1998.

CHAPTER 11

New Approaches to Measuring Credit Risk

In Chapter 10 we described the traditional way in which rating agencies and large banks rate the credit risk of bonds and corporate loans, using a judgmental approach supported by certain key financial numbers. In this chapter we look at new ways to put objective and absolute numbers on the risk of default, and we describe efforts to model and measure credit risk in whole bank portfolios using statistical and economic tools, including the Merton model, the actuarial approach, reduced-form models, and recent hybrid models.

We can think of these new approaches as an attempt by banks to apply to credit risk the kind of "rocket science" quantification that has made such a difference to their management of market risk and derivative trading.

It's an exciting industry project, but one with some potential pitfalls. As the financial industry develops better ways to estimate credit risk, it will come to depend more and more heavily on these new techniques. It's important that a wide range of support staff and senior managers understand in principle the strengths and the limitations of the new approaches to credit modeling.

WHY IS CREDIT MODELING SO IMPORTANT—AND SO DIFFICULT?

There are many management reasons why banks want to attach absolute and objective numbers to the credit risks that they run. One of the most fundamental reasons is so that they can accurately attribute credit risk (regulatory or economic) capital either to a transaction or a whole portfolio, as described in Box 11-1. This is important for risk management purposes, but it also allows the bank to price the transaction accurately, for example,

BOX 11-1

CREDIT VaR AND CALCULATION OF
AN ECONOMIC CAPITAL CHARGE

Economic capital is the financial cushion that a bank employs to absorb un-expected losses, e.g., those related to credit events such as default and/or credit migration. It's clearly important that a bank reserve the right amount of economic capital if it is to remain solvent to any degree of confidence (see Chapter 15). But economic capital is also increasingly important for helping banks to price risk and to set sophisticated risk limits for individual businesses.

The modeling approaches we describe in the main text potentially allow a bank to model the distribution of values of its portfolio of obligors and derive an economic capital number, or VaR number, in the same way that we described for market risk in Chapter 7.

Figure 11B-1 illustrates how a capital charge related to credit risk can be derived from the distribution of values of a credit portfolio. In this figure,

$P(c)$ = value of the portfolio in the worst-case scenario at the $(1 - c)$ percent confidence level, say 99 percent if c is equal to 1 percent

FV = forward value of the portfolio = $V_0(1 + PR)$

V_0 = current marked-to-market value of the portfolio

Credit VaR and Calculation of Economic Capital

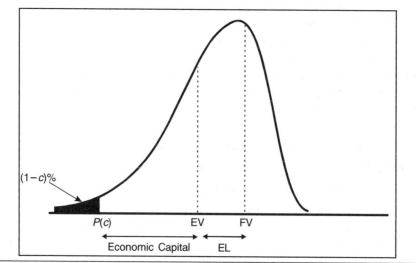

(continued on following page)

BOX 11-1 *(Continued)*

PR = promised return on the portfolio

EV = expected value of the portfolio = $V_0(1 + ER)$

ER = expected return on the portfolio

EL = expected loss = FV − EV

The expected loss is not part of required economic capital, precisely because it is expected and is therefore priced into the interest charge that the customer pays on each loan. The capital charge is instead a function of the portfolio's unexpected losses. That is,

$$\text{Capital} = EV - P(c)$$

As with market risk, the confidence level is set in line with the bank's risk appetite or solvency standard—often its target credit rating. For example, if the confidence level is 1 percent, then the bank would be able to reassure itself that 99 times out of 100, it would not incur losses above the economic capital level over the period corresponding to the credit-risk horizon (say, one year).

by adjusting the interest rate charged to the customer to be in line with the customer's risk of default. Objective estimates of default also offer an independent check on traditional "judgmental" ratings.

A bank also needs to assess the credit quality of its loan portfolio as a whole, since the stability of the bank depends to a large extent on the number and extent of credit-related losses across its entire credit portfolio in any given period. But accurately estimating the risk of loans or bonds and modeling portfolio-wide credit risk is a complicated task that must take into account multiple factors. Some factors are economy-wide, such as the level of interest rates or the growth rate of the economy. Other factors are specific to the individual credit, such as the business risk of the firm or its capital structure.

Regulation is also helping to promote the formal quantification of credit risk and the use of credit portfolio models in the banking industry. We've already discussed in this book how future bank regulation will encourage better differentiation among individual obligors based on their credit ratings. Analytical approaches to estimating credit risk will increasingly drive the amount of regulatory capital a bank has to set aside. Bank capital aside, regulators will also tell bank examiners to look at the quality of the loan portfolio and the level of concentration by industry and region (Pillar II of the new Basel II regulations described in Chapter 3).

There are many decisions to be made when selecting the appropriate approach to credit modeling. For example, should the credit modeler evaluate credit risk as a discrete event and concentrate only on a potential default event, or should the modeler analyze the dynamics of the debt value and the associated credit spread over the whole time interval to maturity? Another important issue is the data sources that are available to help assess credit risk. To what extent are relevant market data available, and to what extent are the available data of sufficiently high quality? Are markets sufficiently efficient to convey reliable information?

An even more fundamental problem is the determination of what we mean by default and how this might relate to notions of credit risk, bankruptcy, and loss from default. In practice, default is distinct from bankruptcy. Bankruptcy describes the situation in which the firm is liquidated, and the proceeds from the asset sale are distributed to the various claim holders according to prespecified priority rules. Default, on the other hand, is usually defined as the event when a firm misses a payment on a coupon and/or the reimbursement of principal at debt maturity. Cross-default clauses on debt contracts are such that when the firm misses a single payment on a debt, it is declared in default on all its obligations.

The relationship between default and bankruptcy is far from constant over time. Since the early 1980s, "Chapter 11" regulation in the United States has protected firms in default and helped to maintain them as going concerns during a period in which they attempt to restructure their activities and their financial structure. Figure 11-1 compares the number of bankruptcies to the number of defaults during the period 1973 to 2004 for North American public companies.

WHAT DRIVES CREDIT RISK
AT THE PORTFOLIO LEVEL?

The first factor affecting the amount of credit risk in a portfolio is clearly the credit standing of specific obligors. One bank might concentrate on prime or investment-grade obligors, so that there is a very low probability of default for any individual obligor in its portfolio. Another bank might choose to concentrate on more risky, speculative-grade obligors who pay a much higher coupon rate on their debt. The critical issues for both types of institutions are to charge the appropriate interest rate, or spread, to each borrower so that the lender is compensated for the risk it undertakes, and to set the right amount of risk capital aside. Only by setting the right

FIGURE 11-1

Quarterly Defaults/Bankruptcies, North American Public Companies, 1973–2004 (through Q1)

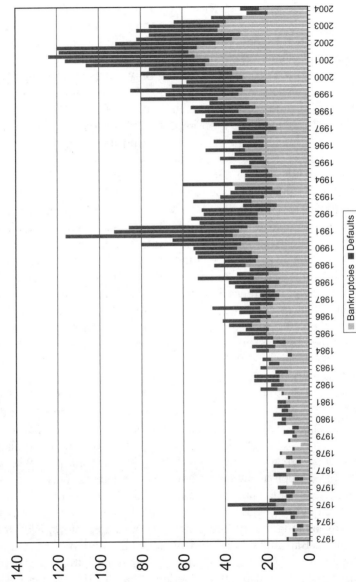

■ Bankruptcies ■ Defaults

Source: KMV Corporation.

261

amount of capital aside can the bank limit the chance of defaulting itself to the level of confidence approved by its board.

The second factor is *concentration risk*, or the extent to which the obligors are diversified in terms of number, geography, and industry. A bank with only a few big-ticket corporate clients, most of which are in commercial real estate, is rightly considered to be more risky than a bank that has made many corporate loans to borrowers that are distributed over many industries. Also, a bank serving only a narrow geographical area is likely to be hit hard by a slowdown in the economic activity of that particular region (and see a subsequent rise in defaults).

This leads us to the third important factor that affects the risk of the portfolio: the state of the economy. During the good times of economic growth, the frequency of default falls sharply compared to periods of recession. Conversely, the default rate rises again as the economy enters a downturn. To make things worse, periods of high default rates, such as 2001–2002, are characterized by a low rate of recovery on defaulted loans, that is, banks tend to find that the various assurances and collateral that they use to secure the loans are less valuable during a recession.

In Figure 11-2 we present the record of defaults from 1981 to 2004. In 1990 and 1991, and more recently in 2001–2002, when the world economies were in recession, the frequency of defaults increased substantially. But recessions are not created equal in terms of the number of defaults they precipitate. In 2002, the total amount of debt that defaulted reached the unprecedented level of $190 billion compared with the earlier peak of $24 billion in 1991.

Downturns in the credit cycle often uncover the hidden tendency of customers to default together, with banks being affected to the degree that they have allowed their portfolios to become concentrated in various ways (e.g., customer, region, and industry concentrations). The CreditMetrics and KMV models we discuss later in this chapter are an attempt to discover the degree of correlation and concentration risk in a bank portfolio, while the CreditRisk+ approach attempts much the same thing, only with an emphasis on uncovering the macroeconomic factors that cause default correlations.

The quality of the portfolio can also be affected by the maturities of the loans, as longer loans are generally considered more risky than short-term loans. Banks that build portfolios that are not concentrated in particular maturities—*time diversification*—can reduce this kind of portfolio maturity risk. This also helps to reduce liquidity risk, or the risk that the bank will run into difficulties when it tries to refinance large amounts of its assets at the same time (see Chapter 8).

FIGURE 11-2

Corporate Defaults Worldwide (Number of Firms and the Amount Defaulted)

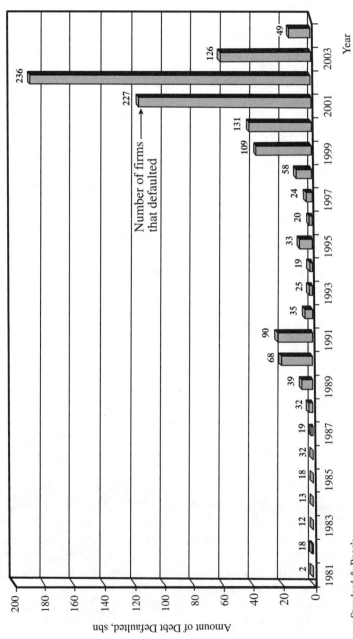

Source: Standard & Poor's.

ESTIMATING PORTFOLIO
CREDIT RISK—OVERVIEW

We can make a *qualitative* assessment of the risk in a bank portfolio by examining the portfolio in relation to the risk factors we have just discussed. For example, do the risk policies and risk limits used by the bank put an appropriate upper limit on the amount lent to any one borrower or any one industry? But in order to put an *objective number* on the credit risk in a portfolio that can support the kind of calculation we see in Box 11-1, we must do something much more challenging: we must estimate the future distribution of the values of the loan portfolio after taking credit risk into account.

Estimating the future value of a credit portfolio is much more complicated than estimating the value of a portfolio of market-traded instruments such as stocks and bonds, and the main reason for this is that only small amounts of data about defaults are available. Whereas market prices move every day to help banks make their market value-at-risk estimations, large companies fall into default only very rarely. The relative rarity of default events also makes it difficult to estimate potential correlations among potential default events. While there is a lot of data available on market prices of market-traded debt instruments (bonds and so on) and their cross correlations, many debt instruments are traded only rarely, and the majority of bank loans are never traded at all.

To overcome some of the estimation problems, most approaches to portfolio credit risk derive default correlations (which are not directly observable) from equity correlations. That is, they assume that correlations in company share price movements that are visible on the equity markets can be used to infer default correlations. Still, the estimation problem remains huge, since many pairs of cross correlations must be estimated for any portfolio of obligors.

For example, even a small portfolio of 1,000 obligors requires the estimation of 499,500 correlations (1,000 multiplied by 999 and divided by 2). The problem can really be circumvented only by using a multifactor approach. Under a multifactor approach, we make the assumption that the rate of return for each firm, or stock, can be generated by a linear combination of a few country- or industry-based indexes. This approach reduces the calculation requirement to that of estimating the correlations among pairs of indexes—a much simpler exercise. But it also introduces a simplifying assumption that is a potential source of error.

CREDITMETRICS AND THE CREDIT MIGRATION APPROACH

Over the last decade, a number of new systematic approaches to portfolio credit-risk modeling have been made public. The CreditMetrics approach—initiated by JP Morgan, the leading U.S. bank, and subsequently spun off to RiskMetrics Inc.—is based on the analysis of credit migration. That is, the approach is underpinned by estimates of how likely it is that a borrower will move from one credit quality to another, including default, within a given time horizon (usually one year).

This approach allows a bank using CreditMetrics to estimate the full one-year forward distribution of the values of any bond or loan portfolio, where the changes in values are related to credit migration only. (The forward values and exposures of the debt instruments in the portfolio are derived from deterministic forward curves of interest rates.) A key assumption of the approach is that the past migration history of thousands of rated bonds accurately describes the probability of migration in the next period.

The CreditMetrics risk measurement framework can be thought of in terms of two main building blocks:

1. Credit value-at-risk due to credit for a single financial instrument
2. Credit value-at-risk at the portfolio level, which accounts for portfolio diversification effects

These building blocks are implemented by means of a four-step process. The first step of this approach is to specify a rating system, with rating grades, together with the probabilities of migrating from one credit quality to another over the credit risk horizon.

The second step is to specify a risk horizon, usually taken to be one year.

The third step is to specify the forward discount curve at the risk horizon for each credit category. This will allow us to value the bond using the zero curve corresponding to the potential future credit ratings of the issuer. In the case of default, the value of the instrument should be estimated in terms of the recovery rate, which is given as a percentage of face value or par.

In the fourth and final step, the information from the first three steps is combined to calculate the forward distribution of the changes in the portfolio value consequent on credit migration.

The key problem in all this is the estimation of the rating transition probabilities, or rating transition matrix, using historical default data from either an external or an internal rating system (Table 11-1). Let's take the case of an approach based upon the Standard & Poor's rating system and data. S&P employs seven principal rating categories. The highest credit rating is AAA; the lowest, CCC. (The rating agencies also supply more finely graded statistics, with each rating category from AA to CC being split into three subcategories, for example, S&P's rating category A is split into A+, A, and A-.) Default is defined as a situation in which the obligor cannot make a payment related to a bond or a loan obligation, whether the payment is a coupon payment or the redemption of principal.

We'll take as an example a bond issuer that currently has a BBB rating. The shaded line in Table 11-1 shows the probability, as estimated by Standard & Poor's, that the credit rating of this BBB issuer will migrate, over a period of one year, to any one of eight possible states, including default. The most probable situation is that the obligor will remain in the same rating category, BBB; this has a probability of 86.93 percent. The probability of the issuer's defaulting within one year is only 0.18 percent, while the probability of the issuer's being upgraded to AAA is also very small, i.e., 0.02 percent.

A transition matrix like this is produced by rating agencies for all their initial ratings, based on the history of credit events that have occurred

TABLE 11-1

Transition Matrix: Probabilities of Credit Rating Migrating From One Rating Quality to Another, Within One Year

Initial Rating	Rating at Year-End (%)							
	AAA	AA	A	BBB	BB	B	CCC	Default
AAA	90.81	8.33	0.68	0.06	0.12	0	0	0
AA	0.70	90.65	7.79	0.64	0.06	0.14	0.02	0
A	0.09	2.27	91.05	5.52	0.74	0.26	0.01	0.06
BBB	0.02	0.33	5.95	86.93	5.30	1.17	0.12	0.18
BB	0.03	0.14	0.67	7.73	80.53	8.84	1.00	1.06
B	0	0.11	0.24	0.43	6.48	83.46	4.07	5.20
CCC	0.22	0	0.22	1.30	2.38	11.24	64.86	19.79

Source: Standard & Poor's *CreditWeek,* April. 15, 1996.

in the firms rated by those agencies (Moody's publishes similar information). The probabilities published by the agencies are based on more than 20 years of data across all industries. Obviously, these data should be interpreted with care, since they represent average statistics across a heterogeneous sample of firms and over several business cycles. For this reason, many banks prefer to rely on their own statistics, which are more closely related to the composition of their loan and bond portfolios.

The rating agencies typically rate the obligor from a "through-the-cycle" perspective. In other words, the rating agencies discount the normal effects of the business cycle on an obligor as long as they believe that the structural estimation of the obligor's credit risk over the cycle hasn't changed. Conversely, analytic modelers (such as the KMV approach described later) typically rate the obligor from a "point-in-time" perspective, and therefore their ratings more appropriately reflect the probability of default in the short term. A bank that sets up an internal risk rating system needs to decide whether it wants the rating and any associated probability of default statistic to be based on a through-the-cycle or a point-in-time approach. If the bank decides to use a point-in-time approach, then the volatility of ratings, and therefore of credit VaR and economic capital, will clearly be larger than if it uses a through-the-cycle approach.

The realized transition and default probabilities vary quite substantially over the years, depending upon whether the economy is in recession or is expanding, as we saw in Figure 11-2. When implementing a model that relies on transition probabilities, the bank may have to adjust the average historical values—those shown in Table 11-1—to make them consistent with its assessment of the current economic environment. The probabilities on the diagonal of the transition matrix for a point-in-time approach are smaller than those for the through-the-cycle approach, since with a point-in-time approach there is less likelihood that the rating will remain the same in the subsequent periods.

The next step in creating our distribution of values for a single bond is to value the bond in each of its possible seven credit qualities. This requires us to specify seven possible one-year forward zero curves so that the bond can be priced in all of its possible states. These curves can be generated from market data, using bond prices, as depicted in Table 11-2. (Forward zero curves depict the implied discount rates for future cash flows, as reflected in current bond prices for given credit ratings and different maturities; see Chapter 6.) We cannot assume that the bond is worth nothing if the issuer defaults at the end of the year. Depending on the seniority of the instrument, a recovery rate of a percentage of par value is

TABLE 11-2

One-Year Forward Zero Curves for Each Credit Rating (%)

Category	Year 1	Year 2	Year 3	Year 4
AAA	3.60	4.17	4.73	5.12
AA	3.65	4.22	4.78	5.17
A	3.72	4.32	4.93	5.32
BBB	4.10	4.67	5.25	5.63
BB	5.55	6.02	6.78	7.27
B	6.05	7.02	8.03	8.52
CCC	15.05	15.02	14.03	13.52

Source: CreditMetrics, JP Morgan.

realized by the investor. These recovery rates are again estimated from historical data provided by the rating agencies. Table 11-3 shows the expected recovery rates for bonds of different seniority classes as estimated by Moody's. Therefore, in simulations performed to assess the portfolio distribution, the recovery rates are not taken as fixed, but rather as being drawn from a distribution of possible recovery rates. (As a rule, bank loan recovery rates tend to be much higher than bond recovery rates.)

We are now in a position to calculate the distribution of the changes in the bond value, at the one-year horizon, resulting from an eventual change in credit quality. Table 11-4 and Figure 11-3 show these changes for our example BBB bond.

TABLE 11-3

Recovery Rates by Seniority Class (Percent of Face Value, i.e., "Par")

Seniority Class	Mean (%)	Standard Deviation (%)
Senior secured	53.80	26.86
Senior unsecured	51.13	25.45
Senior subordinated	38.52	23.81
Subordinated	32.74	20.18
Junior subordinated	17.09	10.90

Source: Carty and Lieberman (1996).

TABLE 11-4

Distribution of the Bond Values, and Changes in Value of a
BBB Bond, in One Year

Year-End Rating	Probability of State p (%)	Forward Price V ($)	Change in Value ΔV ($)
AAA	0.02	109.35	1.82
AA	0.33	109.17	1.64
A	5.95	108.64	1.11
BBB	86.93	107.53	0
BB	5.30	102.00	−5.53
B	1.17	98.08	−9.45
CCC	0.12	83.62	−23.91
Default	0.18	51.11	−56.42

Source: CreditMetrics, JP Morgan.

The first percentile of the distribution, which corresponds to the credit value-at-risk or credit VaR of the credit instrument at a confidence level of 99 percent, is 23.91. That is, we can say that, if we have a portfolio of 100 independent obligors, all rated BBB, then, in a year we can expect one obligor to suffer a loss greater than 23.91.

However, we should also note the small but significant chance of a very large loss in the event of default. Any distribution curve fitted around the bars on this figure would exhibit what risk modelers call a long "downside tail," often referred to as a "fat tail"—a common feature of credit distributions.

Credit VaR for a Loan or Bond Portfolio

So far we have shown how to derive the future distribution of values for a given bond (or loan). In what follows, we focus on how to estimate potential changes in the value of a whole portfolio of creditors. We assume that the changes are due to credit risk only (i.e., there is no market risk), and that credit risk is expressed as potential rating changes during the year.

An important complicating factor in the portfolio assessment is the degree of correlation between any two obligors in terms of changes in credit ratings or default. The overall credit VaR is quite sensitive to these correlations, and their accurate estimation is therefore one of the key determinants of portfolio optimization.

FIGURE 11-3

Histogram of the One-Year Forward Prices and Changes in Value of a BBB Bond

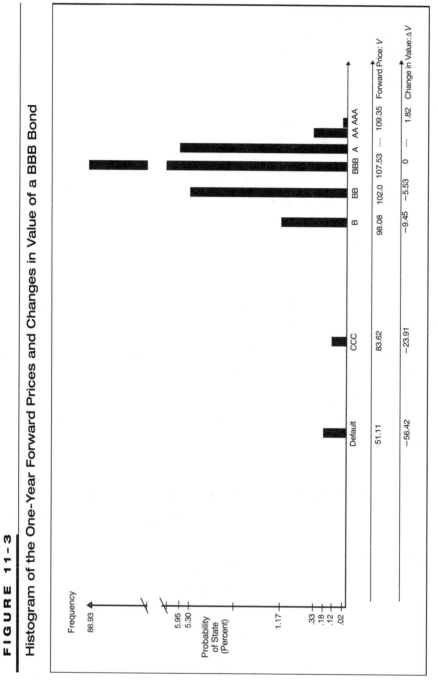

As we explained in our general discussion, default correlations might be expected to be higher for firms within the same industry or in the same region, and to vary with the relative state of the economy throughout the business cycle. If there is a slowdown in the economy or a recession, most of the assets of the obligors will decline in value and quality, and the likelihood of multiple defaults increases substantially. Thus, we cannot expect default and migration probabilities to stay stationary (i.e., stable) over time, and we need some kind of model that relates changes in default probabilities to fundamental variables.

CreditMetrics derives the default and migration probabilities from a correlation model of the firm's asset value. As the firm's true asset value is not directly observable, CreditMetrics makes use of a firm's stock price as a proxy for its asset value. (This is another simplifying assumption made by CreditMetrics that may affect the accuracy of the approach.) CreditMetrics estimates the correlations between the equity returns of various obligors. Then it infers the correlations between changes in credit quality directly from the joint distribution of these equity returns.

We can illustrate how these correlation estimates affect the joint probability of default of two creditors in the portfolio with a very simple numerical example. If the probabilities of default for obligors rated A and BB are p_A = 0.06 percent and p_{BB} = 1.06 percent, respectively, and the correlation coefficient between the rates of return on the two assets is taken from stock price analysis to be ρ = 20 percent, it can be shown that the joint probability of default is only 0.0054 percent, and that the correlation coefficient between the two default events is 1.9 percent. (If the default events were independent, then the joint probability of default would be simply the product of the two default probabilities, i.e., 0.06 $\times$ 1.06 = 0.0064 percent.). Asset return correlations are approximately 10 times larger than default correlations for asset correlations in the range from 20 percent to 60 percent (i.e., in our example, for an asset return correlation of 20 percent, the estimated default correlation is 1.9 percent). This shows that the joint probability of default is in fact quite sensitive to pairwise asset return correlations, and it illustrates how important it is to estimate these data correctly if one is to assess the diversification effect within a portfolio.

It can be shown that the impact of correlations on credit VaR is quite large. And it is larger for portfolios with relatively low-grade credit quality than it is for high-grade portfolios. Indeed, as the credit quality of the portfolio deteriorates and the expected number of defaults increases, this rise in defaults is magnified by an increase in default correlations.

The analytic approach to assessing a portfolio is not practicable for large portfolios. The number of paired correlations can become excessive. Instead, CreditMetrics makes use of numerical approximations by applying a MonteCarlo simulation approach to generate the full distribution of the portfolio values at the credit horizon of one year.

Estimation of Asset Correlations

As we discussed earlier, default correlations are derived from asset return correlations, for which, in turn, equity return correlations are a proxy. For a large portfolio of bonds and loans, with thousands of obligors, this still requires the computation of a huge correlation matrix to include the correlation for each pair of obligors.

To reduce the dimensionality of this estimation problem, Credit Metrics uses multifactor analysis. This approach maps each obligor to the countries and industries that are most likely to determine the obligor's performance. Equity returns are correlated to the extent that firms are exposed to the same industries and countries. To implement CreditMetrics, the user specifies the industry and country weights for each obligor, as well as the firm-specific risk, which is not correlated with any other obligor or to any index.

Applications of CreditMetrics

One of the keys to controlling the kind of "model risk" that we discuss in Chapter 14 is to make sure that models are applied only to the appropriate kind of problem. The CreditMetrics approach is primarily designed for bonds and loans, which are both treated in the same manner. It can also be easily extended to financial claims (such as receivables or financial letters of credit) for which we can derive the forward value at the risk horizon for all credit ratings. However, for derivatives such as swaps or forwards, the model needs to be somewhat adjusted or "twisted," because there is no satisfactory way to derive the exposure, and the loss distribution, within the proposed framework (since it assumes deterministic interest rates). This is why we must turn to structural or reduced-form modeling approaches for a more reliable way to price credit derivatives.

THE CONTINGENT CLAIM OR STRUCTURAL APPROACH TO MEASURING CREDIT RISK

The CreditMetrics approach to measuring credit risk, as described in the previous section, is rather appealing as a methodology. Unfortunately it has a major weakness: it relies on rating transition probabilities based on average historical frequencies of defaults and credit migration. The approach therefore implies that all firms within the same rating class have the same default rate and the same spread curve, even when recovery rates differ among obligors, and that the actual default rate is equal to the historical average default rate. Credit ratings and default rates are taken to be synonymous, that is, the rating changes when the default rate is adjusted, and vice versa.

This view was strongly challenged during the 1990s by researchers working for the consulting and software corporation KMV, a firm that specialized in credit-risk analysis. (The name KMV comes from the first letter of the last name of Stephen Kealhofer, John McQuown, and Oldrich Vasicek, the academics who founded KMV Corporation in 1989; KMV has since become a division of rating agency Moody's, but for clarity we continue to refer to the "KMV approach.") Indeed, the CreditMetrics assumption cannot be true because we know that default rates evolve continuously, whereas ratings are adjusted only periodically. This lag occurs because rating agencies necessarily take time to upgrade or downgrade companies whose default risk has changed.

Instead, the KMV researchers proposed a "structural" approach, based on an option-pricing model approach first introduced in 1974 by Nobel Prize winner Robert Merton. Let's look first at the underlying logic of the Merton model and then, in the next section, at KMV's adaptation of it into an analytical credit tool.

The Merton model is based on the limited liability rule, which allows shareholders to default on their obligations while surrendering the firm's assets to its various stakeholders—such as bondholders and banks—according to prespecified priority rules. The firm's liabilities are thus viewed as contingent claims issued against the firm's assets, with the payoffs to the various debtholders being completely specified by seniority and safety covenants. According to this logic, the firm will default at debt maturity whenever its asset value falls short of its debt value (at that time). Under this model, the default likelihood and the loss at default depend on the firm's asset value, the firm's liabilities, the asset volatility, and the default-free interest rate for the debt maturity.

To determine the value of the credit risk arising from a bank loan using this theoretical approach, we must first make two assumptions: that the loan is the only debt instrument of the firm, and that the only other source of financing is equity. In this case, the present value of credit risk is equal to the value of a put option on the value of the assets of the firm at a strike price that is equal to the face value of the debt (including accrued interest), and at a time to expiration corresponding to the maturity of the debt. If the bank purchased such a put option, it would completely eliminate the credit risk associated with the loan.

This implies that by purchasing the put on the assets of the firm for the term of the debt, with a strike price equal to the face value of the loan, a bank could, in theory, convert any risky corporate loan into a riskless loan. Thus, the value of the put option is the cost of eliminating the credit risk associated with providing a loan to the firm, that is, the cost of providing credit insurance.

It follows that if we make the various assumptions that are needed to apply the Black-Scholes (1973) (BS) model to equity and debt instruments, we can express the value of the credit risk of a firm in an option-like formula.

The Merton model illustrates that one can quantify the cost of credit risk, and hence also credit spreads, as a function of the riskiness of the assets of the firm and the time interval until debt is paid back. The cost is an increasing function of the leverage or debt burden of the firm. The cost is also affected by the risk-free interest rate: the higher the risk-free interest rate, the less costly it is to reduce credit risk. The numerical examples in Table 11-5 show the default spread for various levels of asset volatility and different leverage ratios.

The structural approach offered by the Merton model seems to offer a way of assessing the likelihood of default of an individual firm, and also

TABLE 11-5

Default Spread for Corporate Debt (for V_0 = 100, T = 1, and r = 10%[1])

Leverage Ratio LR	Volatility of Underlying Asset σ			
	0.05	0.10	0.20	0.40
0.5	0	0	0	1.0%
0.6	0	0	0.1%	2.7%
0.7	0	0	0.4%	5.6%
0.8	0	0.1%	1.7%	9.6%
0.9	0.1%	0.9%	4.6%	14.6%
1.0	2.2%	4.6%	9.5%	20.7%

[1] 10% is the annualized interest rate discretely compounded, which is equivalent to 9.5% continuously compounded.

an alternative to the credit migration approach to the estimation of portfo-lio credit risk. The merit of this approach is that each firm can be analyzed individually, based on its unique features, to arrive at an estimated likeli-hood of default. But this is also the principal drawback of the approach, since the information required for such an analysis is often not available to the bank or the investor.

KMV APPROACH

During the 1990s, KMV used the Merton model to develop a radically new approach to calculating default probabilities. KMV's methodology differs from CreditMetrics' in that it derives an objective "expected default frequency," or EDF, for each issuer using equity market information, rather than relying on judgmental credit ratings and the average historical tran-sition frequencies produced by the rating agencies for each credit class.

EDFs can be viewed as a "cardinal ranking" of obligors in term of their default risk, instead of the more conventional "ordinal ranking" pro-posed by rating agencies (which relies on letters such as AAA, AA, and so on). An EDF can easily be mapped onto any rating system to derive the equivalent rating of the obligor. Thus, with some careful interpretation, it can be used as independent check on traditional internal bank rating sys-tems and as an indication of the appropriate price for the credit risk of an individual firm.

KMV also expanded its methodology from calculating EDFs for in-dividual firms to measuring portfolio credit risk.

Because it relies on the insights of the Merton model, the EDF for each firm is a function of the firm's capital structure, the current asset value, and—importantly—the volatility of the asset returns. The value of the firm's assets is inferred from the market value of equity, meaning that the KMV approach is best applied to publicly traded companies, where the value of the equity is determined and made transparent by the stock market.

The KMV approach translates the information contained in the firm's stock price and balance sheet into an implied risk of default by means of a three-stage process:

- Estimation of the market value and volatility of the firm's assets as revealed in the stock markets
- Calculation of the "distance to default," which is an index meas-ure of default risk

- The scaling of the distance to default to actual probabilities of default, using a default database

Let's take a look at the two latter stages in more detail.

Calculation of the Distance to Default and the Probabilities of Default from the Distance to Default

In order to make the model tractable, the KMV approach assumes that the capital structure of a corporation is composed solely of equity, short-term debt (considered equivalent to cash), long-term debt (in perpetuity), and convertible preferred shares. In Merton's option-pricing framework for credit risk, default occurs when the firm's asset value falls below the value of the firm's liabilities. In practice, however, for most public firms, only the price of equity is directly observable (in some cases, part of the debt is also actively traded). Using a sample of several hundred companies, KMV observed that, in the real world, firms default when their asset value reaches a level that is somewhere *between* the value of total liabilities and the value of short-term debt. Therefore, the tail of the distribution of asset values below total debt value may not be an accurate measure of the actual probability of default.

The model may also suffer a loss of accuracy from factors such as the nonnormality of the asset return distribution, and from practical assumptions made during the model's implementation, such as the simplifying assumptions that the KMV analysts made about the capital structure of the firm. This may be further aggravated if a company is able to draw on (otherwise unobservable) lines of credit. If the company is in distress, using these lines might (unexpectedly) increase its liabilities while providing the necessary cash to honor promised payments.

For all these reasons, before computing the probabilities of default, the KMV approach implements an intermediate phase involving the computation of an index called the *distance to default* (DD). DD is the number of standard deviations between the mean of the distribution of the asset value and a critical threshold, the *default point* (DPT), set at the par value of current liabilities, including short-term debt, to be serviced over the time horizon plus half the long-term debt (Figure 11-4).

The calculation of DD allowed KMV's modelers to map the DD to the actual probabilities of default for a given time horizon (see Figure 11-5). KMV calls these probabilities expected default frequencies, or EDFs.

FIGURE 11-4

Distance to Default (DD)

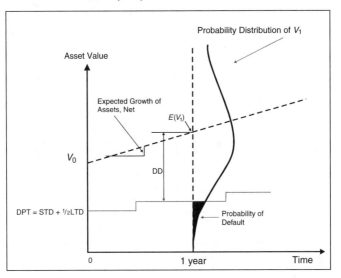

STD = short-term debt
LTD = long-term debt
DPT = default point = STD + $\frac{1}{2}$ LTD

DPT = distance to defaul, which is the distance between the expected asset value in one year, $E(V_1)$, and the default point, DPT. It is often expressed in terms of standard deviation of asset returns:

$$DD = \frac{E(V_1) - DPT}{\sigma}$$

Using historical information about a large sample of firms, including firms that have defaulted, one can track, for each time horizon, the proportion of firms of a given ranking, say DD = 4, that actually defaulted after one year. This proportion, say 40 basis points (bp), or 0.4 percent, is the EDF, as shown in Figure 11-5.

The Federal Express example offered in Box 11-2 illustrates the main causes of change in an EDF, i.e., variations in the stock price, the debt level (leverage ratio), and asset volatility.

How Useful Are EDFs?

KMV began providing a "Credit Monitor" service that publishes estimated EDFs in 1993. Many banks have found EDFs to be a useful leading indicator of default, or at least of the degradation of the creditworthiness of

FIGURE 11-5

Mapping of the Distance to Default into the EDFs for
a Given Time Horizon

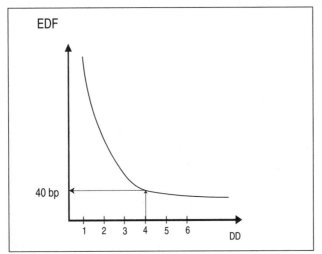

BOX 11-2

NUMERICAL EXAMPLE FOR CALCULATING THE DISTANCE TO DEFAULT AND ITS IMPLEMENTATION

This example is provided by KMV and relates to Federal Express on two
different dates: November 1997 and February 1998.

Federal Express ($ figures are in billions of $US)

	November 1997	February 1998
Market capitalization (price × shares outstanding)	$ 7.7	$ 7.3
Book liabilities	$ 4.7	$ 4.9
Market value of assets	$ 12.6	$ 12.2
Asset volatility	15%	17%
Default point	$ 3.4	$ 3.5
Distance to default (DD)	$\dfrac{12.6 - 3.4}{0.15 \cdot 12.6} = 4.9$	$\dfrac{12.2 - 3.5}{0.17 \cdot 12.2} = 4.2$
EDF	0.06% (6bp) ≡ AA⁻	0.11% (11bp) ≡ A⁻

issuers. Also, KMV analyzed more than 2,000 U.S. companies that have defaulted or entered into bankruptcy over the last 20 years; in all cases, KMV was able to show a sharp increase in the slope of the EDF a year or two prior to default.

When the financial situation of a company starts to deteriorate, EDFs tend to rise quickly until default occurs, as shown in Figure 11-6. On the vertical axis of Figure 11-7, the EDF is shown as a percentage, together with the corresponding Standard & Poor's rating. Changes in EDFs tend to anticipate—by at least one year—the downgrading of the issuer in traditional rating schemes run by agencies such as Moody's and Standard & Poor's (Figure 11-7).

Unlike Moody's and Standard & Poor's historical default statistics, EDFs are not biased by periods of high or low defaults. The distance to

FIGURE 11-6

EDF of a Firm That Defaulted versus EDFs of Firms in Various Quartiles and the Lower Decile

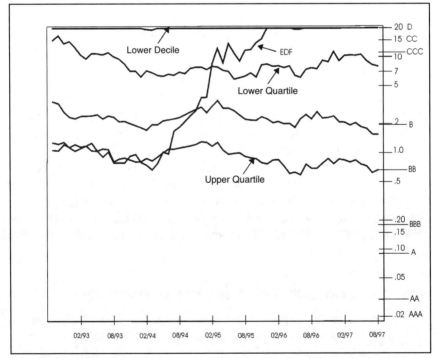

Note: The quartiles and decile represent a range of EDFs for a specific credit class (B-rated firms).
Source: KMV Corporation.

FIGURE 11-7

EDF of a Firm That Defaulted versus Standard
& Poor's Rating

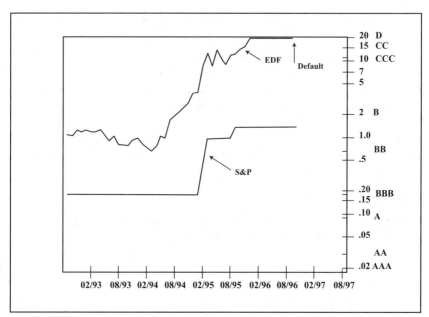

Source: KMV Corporation.

default can be observed to shorten during periods of recession, when default rates are high, and to increase during periods of prosperity, characterized by low default rates.

At the same time, we should not think of EDFs as replacing conventional credit ratings. Each approach has its own strengths and weaknesses, and each is most suitable for particular credit-risk management purposes. It should be emphasized again that in calculating the EDFs, qualitative considerations, such as the quality of management or the quality of control systems, are ignored.

THE EVALUATION OF CREDIT PORTFOLIOS

As we discussed earlier, the key risk measurement concern when individual obligors are combined into a portfolio is the estimation of the relevant credit-risk correlations. How likely is it that companies will default together? Both CreditMetrics and the KMV approach derive asset return correlations by means of an economic model that links correlations to fundamental factors. By imposing a structure on the return correlations, a better accuracy in forecasting correlations is achieved—and, as we mentioned earlier, such multifactor models reduce dramatically the number of correlations that need to be calculated.

It is assumed that the firm's asset returns are generated by a set of common, or systematic, risk factors and specific factors. To derive the asset return correlation between any number of firms, we therefore need to estimate the systematic factors and the covariance matrix for the common factors. How do we specify the structure of the factors?

CreditMetrics and KMV proposed relatively similar models, so here we will present only the KMV model (which is more comprehensive and elaborate). The KMV approach constructs a three-layer factor structure model, as shown in Figure 11-8.

FIGURE 11-8

Factor Model for Asset Return Correlations

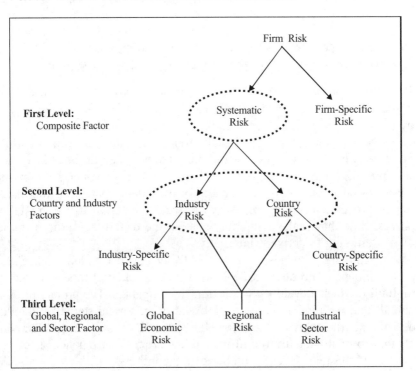

Source: KMV Corporation

- First level: a composite company-specific factor, which is constructed individually for each firm based on the firm's exposure to each country and industry
- Second level: country and industry factors
- Third level: global, regional, and industrial-sector factors

The process for determining country and industry returns can be illustrated as follows:

$$
\begin{bmatrix} Country \\ return \end{bmatrix} = \begin{bmatrix} Global \\ economic \\ effect \end{bmatrix} + \begin{bmatrix} Regional \\ factor \\ effect \end{bmatrix} + \begin{bmatrix} Sector \\ factor \\ effect \end{bmatrix} + \begin{bmatrix} Country \\ specific \\ risk \end{bmatrix}
$$

$$
\begin{bmatrix} Industry \\ return \end{bmatrix} = \begin{bmatrix} Global \\ economic \\ effect \end{bmatrix} + \begin{bmatrix} Regional \\ factor \\ effect \end{bmatrix} + \begin{bmatrix} Sector \\ factor \\ effect \end{bmatrix} + \begin{bmatrix} Industry- \\ specific \\ risk \end{bmatrix}
$$

THE ACTUARIAL AND REDUCED-FORM APPROACHES TO MEASURING CREDIT RISK

Two other approaches to estimating portfolio credit risk have been proposed. These are the actuarial approach, based on statistical models used by the insurance industry, and the reduced-form approach.

The structural model of default attempts to model the way in which firms default when their asset value falls below a certain boundary, such as a promised payment (e.g., the Merton 1974 framework). By contrast, the actuarial model and the reduced-form models treat the firm's bankruptcy process, including recovery, as factors external to the modeling process, i.e., they make assumptions about the bankruptcy process rather than attempting to derive it internally.

CreditRisk+, released in late 1997 by the investment bank Credit Suisse Financial Products (CSFP), is a purely actuarial model, based on mortality models developed by insurance companies. The probabilities of default that the model employs are based on historical statistical data on default experience by credit class. Unlike the KMV approach, there is no attempt to relate default to a firm's capital structure or balance sheet.

CreditRisk+ makes a number of assumptions:

- For a loan, the probability of default in a given period, say one month, is the same as in any other period of the same length, say another month.

- For a large number of obligors, the probability of default by any particular obligor is small, and the number of defaults that occur in any given period is independent of the number of defaults that occur in any other period.

Under these assumptions, and based on empirical observation, the probability distribution for the number of defaults during a given period of time (say, one year) is well represented by a certain shape of statistical distribution known as a Poisson distribution. We expect the mean default rate to change over time depending on the business cycle. This suggests that the distribution can be used to represent the default process only if, as CreditRisk+ suggests, we make the additional assumption that the mean default rate is itself changing, following a certain distribution.

In CreditRisk+, obligors are divided into bands, or subportfolios, and all obligors in a band are characterized by approximately the same loss given default (LGD). If we know the distribution of defaults in each band, then we can find the distribution of defaults over all bands for the whole portfolio. CreditRisk+ derives a closed-form solution for the loss distribution of the loan portfolio.

CreditRisk+ has the advantage that it is relatively easy to implement. First, as we just mentioned, closed-form expressions can be derived for the probability of portfolio bond or loan losses, and this makes CreditRisk+ very attractive from a computational point of view. In addition, marginal risk contributions by obligor can be computed. Second, CreditRisk+ focuses on default, and therefore it requires relatively few estimates and inputs. For each instrument, only the probability of default and the loss given default statistics are required.

One disadvantage of CreditRisk+ is that it ignores migration risk; the exposure for each obligor is fixed and is not sensitive to possible future changes in the credit quality of the issuer, or to the variability of future interest rates. (Indeed, this is the major difference between the approaches of CreditRisk+ and CreditMetrics.) Even in its most general form, where the probability of default depends upon several stochastic background factors, the credit exposures are taken to be constant and are not related to changes in these factors. In reality, credit exposure is often linked quite closely to risk factors such as the probability of default. For example, in the case of a loan commitment, a corporate borrower has the option of drawing on its credit line—and is more likely to exercise this option when its credit standing is deteriorating.

Finally, like the CreditMetrics and KMV approaches, CreditRisk+ is not able to cope satisfactorily with nonlinear products such as options and foreign currency swaps.

Reduced-Form Approaches

Over the last few years, researchers have developed reduced-form models based on a simplified interpretation of the mechanisms that drive credit spreads. These models treat spreads as if they were driven by only two factors: the likelihood of default and the expectations of market participants about recovery rates. Reduced-form models have developed into very important tools for traders in the credit markets, and they currently form the foundation of pricing models for credit derivatives.

The inputs to a reduced-form model are

- The term structure of default-free interest rates
- The term structure of credit spreads for each credit category
- The loss rate for each credit category

Meanwhile, the major assumptions are

- Zero correlations between credit events and interest rates
- Deterministic credit spreads, for as long as there are no credit events
- Constant recovery rates

Unlike structural model approaches, such as that of KMV, these reduced-form models don't attempt to predict default by looking at its underlying causes; they are essentially statistical (like CreditRisk+) and are based upon empirical market data. The reduced-form approach is therefore less intuitive than the structural models from an economic point of view, but it is calibrated using credit spreads that are observable in the world's financial markets and that do not require any balance-sheet information. The data used to feed the models are largely credit instrument prices derived from markets such as the corporate bond, corporate loan, and credit derivatives markets (as opposed to the equity price data from stock markets employed by the KMV approach).

In theory, by looking at the price of credit-risky securities over time and subtracting the price of similar securities that do not incur credit risk (such as U.S. government bonds), the "price of credit" can be made transparent. Unfortunately, there are many complications and other real-world problems. The reduced-form modelers' task is to overcome these problems and derive the term structure of risk-adjusted implied default probabilities from the term structure of credit spreads apparent in the market—and then to find the most valid way to reapply this information to a particular bank loan or portfolio in the pursuit of better risk analysis.

One complication is that the comparison between corporate bond yields and the yield to maturity of government bonds should be for the same duration (see the discussion of duration in Chapter 6).

Another more intractable problem is that the world's credit markets are very imperfect as sources of data. Unfortunately, credit risk is not the only determinant of prices for credit-risky securities—various other risk factors and market inefficiencies interfere with the credit price signals. In particular, although the corporate bond markets are large, the market for each individual bond tends to be quite illiquid and much less transparent than the share prices in an equity market (not least because many bond transactions are conducted over-the-counter rather than on a formal exchange). The heterogeneous nature of bonds as financial instruments is also tricky: many are structured with embedded options (e.g., convertible bonds), and bond prices may be affected by various regulations and taxes in local markets.

These are empirical challenges, but there are also more fundamental analytical challenges. For example, how do the various credit-risk factors interact over a period of time to produce the credit spread visible in bond market data? The relative contribution of default probability and loss given default (or recovery rate) is not at all clear in the market data, yet distinguishing between the effect of these factors in the historical data is important if the modeling results are to be applied to predict the future risk of loan portfolios.

The problem is important because intuition tells us that the default probability and the loss given default statistics associated with an instrument are likely to vary over time, and that the relationship between these two risk factors may also vary dramatically, depending on the nature of the credit portfolio. At the top of their business cycle, for example, airlines tend not to default, and if they do, any collateral to a bank loan can be sold for a top price. Five years later, the story on both counts will be very different.

Reduced-form models take various different shapes, depending upon their approach to these problems. For example, models may make certain assumptions about how the default rate increases over time—an attempt to replicate credit migration using what is often termed a "default intensity function."

Likewise, models may make the simplifying assumption that loss given default will stay constant for each credit over the time period, or they may try to replicate the real-world observation that recovery rates differ for various kinds of firms depending upon the economic cycle.

The latest models make sophisticated attempts to address all these weaknesses. For example, they may incorporate empirical loss given default data, attempt to compensate for liquidity effects in the bond market, or determine the key model parameters by means of a combination of bond-market data and equity-market data.

Over the 10 years since the earliest reduced-form models were developed in 1995, the industry has experimented with at least two generations of reduced-form models and has seen huge advances in reduced-form credit modeling. But the effort to specify models that will explain credit-market data and reveal absolute values for various kinds of credit risk remains a work in progress. The success of a reduced-form model is very dependent upon the quality of market data, and its application to a particular risk management problem is dependent upon a whole range of assumptions.

HYBRID STRUCTURAL MODELS

While the structural model approach is theoretically appealing, the predicted default probabilities and credit spreads calculated from the Merton model and some of its later extensions are too low compared to those observed empirically. The KMV proprietary model represented one attempt to circumvent this limitation. More recently, researchers have proposed hybrid structural models that combine the structural model approach with additional accounting and credit information.

The underlying reason for this effort is that default is a complex process and cannot be described simply in terms of an asset value crossing a particular default point. Instead, we must try to take into account the firm's behavior as it approaches the default point. For example, firms that are solvent according to the Merton model can still default on their obligations as a result of severe liquidity problems. Also, as the credit quality of a firm deteriorates, its capacity to borrow and to refinance its debt can determine whether or not it actually defaults.

The firm's borrowing capacity is the result of the borrower's ability to generate revenues for servicing its debt and the value of any assets it can employ as collateral. Both are clearly related to accounting information, such as the borrower's profitability, liquidity, and capital structure, as well as information about the business environment and the borrower's competitiveness (see Chapter 10).

For this reason, proponents of a hybrid approach are attempting to bring together various accounting and market variables to describe the value of the firm's assets and its borrowing capacity. In one such recent approach, for example, the variables are the firm's market equity, stock volatility, stock return, book value of total assets, current liabilities, long-term debt, and net income.[1]

CONCLUSION

There is no single solution to the problem of how we measure credit risk—no Holy Grail of credit modeling. Instead, there are a variety of approaches, all of which must be regarded as works in progress. The industry is still trying to understand the pros and cons of the various assumptions underlying the various proposed approaches.

So far, risk modelers have not found any easy way to integrate market risk and credit risk. Market-risk models disregard credit risk, and credit-risk models assume that market risk does not drive credit exposures. The next generation of credit models should remedy this important weakness.

Table 11-6 summarizes the key features of the principal existing credit models as we've discussed them in this chapter. The table may look complicated, but it makes clear again the great diversity of approaches in this field. Each approach is based on a somewhat different set of assumptions; even the definition of credit risk may not be the same. The input parameters common to all are credit exposures, recovery rates (or, equivalently, the loss given default), and default correlations.

As we've explained in this chapter, default correlations are captured in a variety of ways. The KMV approach derives default correlations from asset return correlations; CreditMetrics relies on a similar model but employs equity return correlations as a proxy for asset returns. In the other models, the default probabilities are conditional on common systemic or

---

1. Jorge Sobehart and Sean Keenan, "Hybrid Probability of Default Models-A Practical Approach to Modeling Default Risk," working paper, Citigroup Global Markets, October 2003.

TABLE 11-6

Key Features of Credit Models

	Credit Migration Approach		Contingent Claim Approach	Actuarial Approach	Reduced-Form Approach
Software	CreditMetrics	CreditPortfolio-View	KMV	Credit Risk+	Kamakura
Definition of risk	Δ Market value	Δ Market value	Δ Market value	Default losses	Default losses
Credit events	Downgrade/default	Downgrade/default	Δ Continuous default probabilities (EDFs)	Δ Actuarial default rate	Δ Default intensity
Risk drivers	Correlated asset values	Macro factors	Correlated asset values	Expected default rates	Hazard rate
Transition probabilities	Constant	Driven by macro factors	Driven by ■ Individual tern structure of EDF ■ Assest value process	N/A	N/A
Correlation of credit events	Standard multivariate normal distribution (equity-factor model)	Conditional default probabilities function of macro factors	Standard multivariate normal asset returns (asset-factor model)	Conditional default probabilities function of common risk factors	Conditional default probabilities function of macro factors
Recovery rates	Random (beta distribution)	Random (empirical distribution)	Random (beta distribution)	Loss given default deterministic	Loss given default deterministic
Interest rates	Constant	Constant	Constant	Constant	Stochastic
Numerical approach	Simulation/analytic Econometric	Simulation Econometric	Analytic/simulation Econometric	Analytic	Tree-based/simulation Econometric

macro factors. Any change in these factors affects all the probabilities of default, but to a different degree, depending on the sensitivity of each obligor to each risk factor.

How do the different approaches perform against each other? We ran a simulation on a large diversified benchmark portfolio of obligors and compared the various credit-risk models; the assumptions for each application were kept consistent. The results showed that the models produce similar estimates of credit value at risk.

The asset returns correlation model appears to be a critical factor in CreditMetrics and in the KMV approach. When correlations are forced to 1, the values at risk are approximately 10 times greater than when correlations are assumed to be 0. For models based on the principle of credit migration, the results are shown to be quite sensitive to the initial rating of the obligors. The credit VaR for speculative portfolios is five or six times greater than it is for investment-grade portfolios.

We concluded from our study that all of the models are reasonable frameworks in which to capture credit risk for " plain vanilla" bond and loan portfolios. For derivative instruments, such as swaps or loan commitments, which have contingent exposures, the models need to be extended to allow for stochastic interest rates. The incorporation of credit derivatives into portfolio models is another major challenge and will create a new level of complexity, since the portfolio distribution is based on actual probabilities of default, while the pricing of the derivatives relies on risk-neutral probabilities.

CHAPTER 12

New Ways to Transfer Credit Risk—and Their Implications

Over the last few years, Alan Greenspan, chairman of the U.S. Federal Reserve, has talked of a "new paradigm of active credit management." He and other commentators argue that the U.S. banking system weathered the last credit downturn, which included a spectacular rash of bankruptcies of very large corporations such as WorldCom, partly because banks had transferred and dispersed their credit exposures using new credit instruments such as credit default swaps and collateralized debt obligations.[1]

This chapter takes a look at how leading global banks are learning to manage their credit portfolios using the new credit markets and credit-risk transfer instruments. We explore how these new ideas might affect the way in which banks organize their credit function, and we examine the different kinds of credit derivatives and wholesale credit securitizations that have become available in the market.

Innovation in credit-risk transfer is clearly important for banks, but it will also have a significant effect in the wider world. Although the following discussion is framed in terms of the banking industry, much of it is relevant to the management of credit risks borne by leasing companies and large nonfinancial corporations in the form of account receivables and so on. This is particularly true for producers of capital goods, which very often provide their customers with long-term credits. Furthermore, active credit portfolio management and risk transfer by banks will radically alter not only the nature and amount of credit risk borne by the banking system, but also the amount borne by private and institutional investors such as insurance companies. As the new credit instruments enhance the efficiency of the credit markets, bank loans to corporations will be priced

---

1. Alan Greenspan, "The Continued Strength of the U.S. Banking System," speech, October 7, 2002.

more sharply, and the source of funds to finance corporate loans is likely to expand.

WHY ARE THE NEW BANK TECHNIQUES AND INSTRUMENTS SO REVOLUTIONARY?

Over the years, banks have developed various "traditional" techniques to mitigate credit risk, such as bond insurance, netting, marking to market, collateralization, termination, or reassignment (see Box 12-1). Banks also typically syndicate loans to spread the credit risk of a big deal (as we describe in Box 12-2) or sell off a portion of the loans that they have originated in the secondary loan market.

BOX 12-1

"TRADITIONAL" CREDIT-RISK ENHANCEMENT TECHNIQUES

In the main text, we talk about new instruments for managing or insuring against credit risk. Here, let's remind ourselves about the many traditional approaches to credit protection:

Bond insurance. In the U.S. municipal bond market, insurance is purchased by the issuer to protect the purchaser of the bond (in the corporate debt market, it is usually the lender who buys default protection). Approximately one-third of new municipal bond issues are insured, helping municipalities to reduce their cost of financing.

Guarantees. Guarantees and letters of credit are really also a type of insurance. A guarantee or letter of credit from a third party of a higher credit quality than the counterparty reduces the credit-risk exposure of any transaction.

Collateral. A pledge of collateral is perhaps the most ancient way to protect a lender from loss. The degree to which a bank suffers a loss following a default event is often driven largely by the liquidity and value of any collateral securing the loan; collateral values can be quite volatile, and in some markets they fall at the same time that the probability of a default event rises (e.g., the collateral value of real estate can be quite closely tied to the default probability of real estate developers).

Early termination. Lenders and borrowers sometimes agree to terminate a transaction by means of a mid-market quote on the occurrence of an agreed-upon event, such as a credit downgrade.

(continued on following page)

BOX 12-1 *(Continued)*

Reassignment. A reassignment clause conveys the right to assign one's position as a counterparty to a third party in the event of a ratings downgrade.

Netting. A legally enforceable process called netting is an important risk-mitigation mechanism in the derivative markets. When a counterparty has entered into several transactions with the same institution, some with positive and others with negative replacement values, then, under a valid netting agreement, the net replacement value represents the true credit-risk exposure.

Marking to market. Counterparties sometimes agree to periodically make the market value of a transaction transparent, and then transfer any change in value from the losing side to the winning side of the transaction. This is one of the most efficient credit enhancement techniques, and, in many circumstances, it can practically eliminate credit risk. However, it requires sophisticated monitoring and back-office systems.

Put options. Many of the put options traditionally embedded in corporate debt securities also provide investors with default protection, in the sense that the investor holds the right to force early redemption at a prespecified price, e.g., par value.

BOX 12-2

PRIMARY SYNDICATION

Loan syndication is the traditional way for banks to share the credit risk of making very large loans to borrowers. The loan is sold to third-party investors (usually other banks or institutional investors) so that the originating or lead banks reach their desired holding level for the deal (set by the bank's senior credit committee) at the time the initial loan deal is closed. Lead banks in the syndicate carry the largest share of the risk and also take the largest share of the fees.

Each syndicated loan deal is structured to accommodate both the risk/return appetite of the banks and investors that are involved in the deal and the needs of the borrower. Syndicated loans are often called leveraged loans when they are issued at LIBOR plus 150 basis points or more.

As a rule, loans that are traded by banks on the secondary loan market begin life as syndicated loans. The pricing of syndicated loans is becoming

(continued on following page)

BOX 12-2 *(Continued)*

more transparent as the syndicated market grows in volume, and as the secondary loans market and the market for credit derivatives become more liquid.

Under the active portfolio management approach that we describe in the main text, the retained part of syndicated bank loans is generally transfer-priced at par to the credit portfolio management group.

These traditional mechanisms reduce credit risk by mutual agreement between the transacting parties, but they lack flexibility. Most importantly, they do not separate or "unbundle" the credit risk from the underlying positions so that it can be redistributed among a broader class of financial institutions and investors.

Credit derivatives, the newest credit-risk management tool, are specifically designed to deal with this problem. Recall that credit derivatives are off-balance-sheet arrangements that allow one party (the beneficiary) to transfer the credit risk of a reference asset to another party (the guarantor) without actually selling the asset. They allow users to strip credit risk away from market risk, and to transfer credit risk independently of funding and relationship management concerns. (In the same way, the development of interest-rate and foreign exchange derivatives in the 1980s allowed banks to manage market risk independently of liquidity risk.)

Nevertheless, the credit derivative revolution arrives with its own unique set of risks. Counterparties must make sure that they understand the amount and nature of risk that is transferred by the derivative contract, and that the contract is enforceable. Meanwhile, regulators have expressed concern about the relatively small number of institutions—mainly large banks such as JP Morgan Chase—that currently create liquidity in the credit derivatives market. They fear that this immature market might be disrupted if one or more of these players ran into trouble.

In a related development, *securitization* gives institutions the chance to extract and segment a variety of potential risks from a pool of portfolio credit-risk exposures, and to sell these risks to investors. In the United States, as we discussed in Chapter 9, the securitization of credit card receivables and mortgages has already developed into a comparatively mature market. Similar credit restructuring techniques are being rapidly developed in the corporate credit sector to enable lenders to repackage corporate loans into notes, securities, or credit derivatives with a variety of credit-risk features. These specially engineered securities will allow commercial banks to transfer credit risk off their books in the same way that securitization has helped U.S. retail banks transfer their credit risk. The securities can then be sold to a wide pool of investors, most of which would not have been interested in purchasing bundles of bank loans.

Bankers are particularly excited about credit derivatives and securitization markets because these are contributing to the "price discovery" of credit. That is, they make clear how much economic value the market attaches to a particular type of credit risk. This should lead to improved liquidity, more efficient market pricing, and more rational credit spreads (i.e., the different margins over the bank's cost of funds charged to customers of different credit quality) for *all* credit-related instruments.

The traditional corporate bond markets perform a somewhat similar price discovery function, but corporate bonds are an asset that blends together interest-rate and credit risk, and corporate bonds offer a limited lens on credit risk because only the largest public companies tend to be bond issuers. By contrast, credit derivatives can, potentially at least, reveal a pure market price for the credit risk of high-yield loans that are not publicly traded, and for whole portfolios of loans.

In these newly transparent credit markets, credit risk is not simply the risk of potential default. It is the risk that credit premiums will change, affecting the relative market value of the underlying corporate bonds, loans, and other derivative instruments. In effect, the "credit risk" of traditional banking is evolving into the "market risk of credit risk" for certain liquid credits.

The concept of credit risk as a variable with a value that fluctuates over time is apparent, to a degree, in the traditional bond markets. For example, if a bank hedges a corporate bond with a Treasury bond, then the spread between the two bonds will rise as the credit quality of the corporate bond declines. But this is a concept that will become increasingly critical in bank risk management as the new credit technologies and markets make the price of credit ever more transparent across the credit spectrum.

CREDIT MARKETS ARE DRIVING CHANGE IN BANKS

New technologies aren't the only thing that's driving change in the banking industry. Over the last decade or so, the portfolios of loans and other credit assets held by banks have become increasingly more concentrated in less creditworthy obligors. This situation has made some banks more vulnerable during economic downturns, such as in 2001 and 2002, when some banks experienced huge credit-related losses in sectors such as telecommunications, cable, energy, and utilities.

The period 2001 to 2002 saw defaults reaching levels that had not been experienced since the early 1990s. Default rates for speculative-grade corporate bonds were 9.2 percent and 9.5 percent in 2001 and 2002, respectively, versus 8 percent and 11 percent in 1990 and 1991, respectively. In terms of volume, the default record was much worse than in the early 1990s: it reached the unprecedented peak of $190 billion in 2002, according to Standard & Poor's, compared with approximately $20 billion in 1990 and 1991.[2] At the same time that default rates were high, recovery rates were also abnormally low, producing large credit-related losses at most major banks.

Two forces have combined to lead to a concentration of low-quality credits in loan portfolios:

- First, there is the "disintermediation" of banks that started in the 1970s and continues today. This trend means that large investment-grade firms are more likely to borrow from investors by issuing bonds in the efficient capital markets, rather than borrowing from individual banks;
- Second, current regulatory capital rules make it more economical for banks on a risk-adjusted return basis to extend credit to lower-credit-quality obligors.

As a consequence, banks have found it increasingly difficult to earn adequate economic returns on credit extensions, particularly those to investment-grade borrowers. Lending institutions, primarily commercial banks, have determined that it is no longer profitable to simply make loans and then hold them until they mature.

But we can put a positive spin on this story, too. Banks are finding it more and more profitable to concentrate on the origination and servicing of loans because they have a number of natural advantages in these activities. Banks have built solid business relationships with business clients over the years through lending and other banking services. Banks have hugely complex back offices that facilitate the efficient servicing of loans. The major banks also now have a solid distribution network that allows them to dispose of financial assets to retail and institutional investors, either directly or through structured products. Finally, banks have developed a strong expertise in analyzing and structuring credits (see Chapter 10).

---

2. Standard & Poor's, *Annual Global Corporate Default Study,* January 2005.

Banks will be better able to leverage these advantages as they move away from the traditional "originate and hold" business model toward the new "underwrite and distribute" business model. Under this new model, the bank services the loans, but the funding of the loan is sourced out to investors and, to some extent, the risk of default is shared with outside parties.

To this end, the credit function is undergoing a critical review at many financial institutions, and many banks are changing the way in which they manage credit risk.

HOW EXACTLY IS ALL THIS CHANGING THE BANK CREDIT FUNCTION?

In the traditional model, the bank lending business unit holds and "owns" credit assets such as loans until they mature or until the borrowers' creditworthiness deteriorates to unacceptable levels. The business unit manages the quality of the loans that enter the portfolio, but after the lending decision is made, the credit portfolio remains basically unmanaged.

Let's remind ourselves here of some credit terminology and work out how it relates to the evolution of bank functions.

In modern banking, exposure is measured in terms of the notional value of a loan, or exposure at default (EAD) for loan commitments. The risk of a facility is characterized by

- The external and/or internal rating attributed to each obligor, usually mapped to a probability of default (PD)
- The loss given default (LGD) and EAD of the facilities

The expected loss (EL) for each credit facility is a straightforward multiplicative function of these variables:

$$EL = PD \times EAD \times LGD$$

Expected loss, as defined here, is the basis for the calculation of the institution's allowance for loan losses, which should be sufficient to absorb both specific (i.e., identified) and more general credit-related losses.[3]

---

3. When a loan has defaulted and the bank has decided that it won't be able to recover any additional amount, the actual loss is written off and the EL is adjusted accordingly, i.e., the written-off loan is excluded from the EL calculation. Once a loan is in default, special provisions come into effect, in addition to the general provisions in anticipation of the loss given default (LGD) that will be incurred by the bank once the recovery process undertaken by the workout group of the bank is complete.

EL can be viewed as the cost of doing business. That is, on average, over a long period of time and for a well-diversified portfolio, the bank will incur a credit loss amounting to EL. However, actual credit losses may differ substantially from EL for a given period of time, depending on the variability of the bank's actual default experience. The potential for variability of credit losses beyond EL is called unexpected loss (UL) and is the basis for the calculation of economic and regulatory capital using credit portfolio models (as discussed in Chapter 11).

In the traditional business model, risk assessment is mostly limited to EL and ignores UL, which is the basis not only for modern techniques of capital attribution but also for risk-sensitive pricing of loans. EL, meanwhile, is usually priced into the loan in the form of a spread charged to the borrower above the funding cost of the bank. To limit the risk of default resulting from to unexpected credit losses, i.e., actual losses beyond EL, banks hold capital, although traditionally they did not employ rigorous quantitative techniques to link their capital to the size of UL. (The topic of new techniques of economic capital attribution is addressed in Chapter 15.)

Under the traditional business model, risk management is limited to a binary approval process at origination. The business unit compensation for loan origination is based, in many cases, more on volume than on a pure risk-adjusted economic rationale. Likewise, the pricing of the loans by the business unit is driven by the strength of competition in the local banking market rather than by risk-based calculations. To the extent that traditional loan pricing reflects risk at all, this is generally in accordance with a simple grid that relates the price of the loan to its credit rating and to the maturity of the facilities.

By contrast, in the underwrite and distribute business model, loans are divided into core loans that the bank holds over the long term (often for relationship reasons) and noncore loans that the bank would like to sell or hedge. Core loans are managed by the business unit, while noncore loans are transfer-priced to the credit portfolio management group. For noncore loans, the credit portfolio management unit is the vital link between the bank's origination activities (making loans), and the increasingly liquid global markets in credit risk, as we can see in Figure 12-1.

Economic capital is the key to assessing the performance of a bank under this new model. Economic capital is allocated to each loan based on the loan's contribution to the risk of the portfolio. At origination, the spread charged to a loan should produce a risk-adjusted return on capital

FIGURE 12-1

Underwrite and Distribute Model

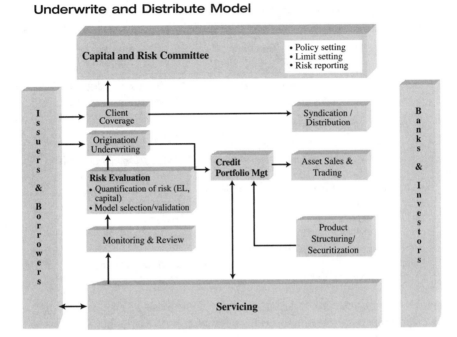

that is greater than the bank's hurdle rate. Table 12-1 notes how all this changes the activities of a traditional credit function, and helps to make clear how the move to active portfolio management is linked to improved credit-market pricing and the kind of risk-adjusted performance measures we discuss in Chapter 15.

In part, the credit portfolio management group must work alongside traditional teams within the bank such as the loan workout group. The workout group is responsible for "working out" any loan that runs into problems after the credit standing of the borrower deteriorates below levels set by bank policy. The workout process typically involves either restructuring the loan or arranging for compensation in lieu of the value of the loan (e.g., receiving equity or some of the assets of the defaulted company).

But managing risk at the portfolio level also means monitoring the kind of risk concentrations that influence bank solvency—and help to determine the amount of expensive risk capital the bank must set aside. Banks commonly have strong lending relationships with a number of large com-

TABLE 12-1

Changes in the Approach to Credit Risk Management

	Traditional Credit Function	Portfolio-Based Approach
Investment strategy	Originate and hold	Underwrite and distribute
Ownership of the credit assets	Business unit	Portfolio management or business unit/portfolio mgmt
Risk measurement	Use notional value of the loan	Use risk-based capital
	Model losses due only to default	Model losses due to default and risk migration
Risk management	Use a binary approval process at origination	Apply risk/return decision-making process
Basis for compensation for loan origination	Volume	Risk-adjusted performance
Pricing	Grid	Risk contribution
Valuation	Held at book	Marked-to market (MTM)

panies, which can create significant concentrations of risk in the form of overlending to single names. Banks are also prone to concentrations as a function of their geography and industry expertise. In Canada, for example, banks are naturally heavily exposed to the oil and gas, mining, and forest products sectors.

Some credit portfolio strategies are therefore based on defensive actions. Loan sales, credit derivatives, and loan securitization are the primary tools used by banks to deal with local regional, country, and industry concentration. Increasingly, however, banks are interested in reducing concentration risk not only for its own sake, but also as a means of managing earnings volatility—the ups and downs in their reported earnings caused by their exposure to the credit cycle.

The credit portfolio management group also has another important mandate: to increase the velocity of capital, that is, to free capital that is tied up in low-return credits and to reallocate this capital to more profitable opportunities. An effective credit portfolio management group actively utilizes superior risk management and capital management approaches to increase the bank's return on economic capital. Nevertheless, the credit portfolio management group should not be a profit center but be run on a budget that will allow it to meet its objectives. Even so, the group must trade in the credit markets in order to carry out its strategies—an activity that could potentially lead to accusations of insider trading if the bank trades credits of firms with which it also has some sort of confidential banking relationship.

For this reason, the credit portfolio management group must be subject to specific trading restrictions monitored by the compliance group. In particular, the bank has to establish a "Chinese wall" that separates credit portfolio management, the "public side," from the "private side" or insider functions of the bank (where the credit officers belong). The issue is somewhat blurred in the case of the loan workout group, but here, too, separation must be maintained. This requires new policies and extensive reeducation of the compliance and insider functions to develop sensitivity to the handling of material nonpublic information. The credit portfolio management team may also require an independent research function.

Counterparty risk in credit derivatives is also a major component of credit risk in banks. In some institutions, both credit risk related to the extension of loans and counterparty credit risk arising from trading activities are managed centrally by new credit portfolio management groups. The credit portfolio management group also advises deal originators on how best to structure deals and mitigate credit risks. Figure 12-2 summarizes the various functions of the credit portfolio management group.

FIGURE 12-2

Credit Portfolio Management

Credit Portfolio Group	
Credit Portfolio Management	• Increases the velocity of capital • Reduces concentration and event risk • Increase return on economic capital • Responsible for financials, but not a profit center
Counterparty Exposure Management	• Hedges and trades retained credit portfolio • Houses "public-side" research analysts, portfolio managers, traders
Credit Portfolio Solutions	• Manages counterparty risk of derivatives exposures • Provides advice to orginators on structuring and credit-risk mitigation

LOAN PORTFOLIO MANAGEMENT

In terms of broad strategy, there are really four primary ways for the bank credit portfolio team to manage a bank credit portfolio:

- Distribute large loans to other banks by means of primary syndication at the outset of the deal, so that the bank retains only the desired "hold level" (see Box 12-2).
- Reduce loan exposure by selling down or hedging concentrated loan positions (e.g., by means of credit derivatives or loan securitization).
- Focus first on high-risk obligors, particularly those that are leveraged in market value terms and that experience a high volatility of returns.
- Simultaneously, sell or hedge low-risk, low-return loan assets to free up bank capital.

In pursuit of these ends, the credit portfolio management group can combine traditional and modern tools to optimize the risk/return profile of the portfolio. At the traditional end of the spectrum, banks can manage an exit from a loan through negotiation with their customer. This is potentially the cheapest and simplest way to reduce risk and free up capital, but it requires the borrower's cooperation.

The bank can also simply sell the loan directly to another institution in the secondary loan market. This requires the consent of the borrower and/or the agent, but in many cases modern loan documentation is designed to facilitate the transfer of loans. (In the secondary loan market, *distressed loans* are those trading at 90 percent or less of their nominal value.)

Securitization is a more sophisticated way to transfer credit exposures. It consists of selling the loans (direct sale) or transferring the credit exposure through credit default swaps (synthetic securitization) to a third-party asset manager. The manager puts these assets into a securitization vehicle that is leveraged and financed by third-party investors. The cash flows from the securitization vehicle are given various levels of priority (and therefore risk) commensurate with the returns that they offer investors. These securitization structures are generally known as collateralized debt obligations (CDOs), or collateralized loan obligations (CLOs) in the special case of securitizations of large portfolios of corporate loans.

Credit derivatives are the latest tool in dynamic portfolio management. Credit derivatives and other risk-transfer techniques can be used to redistribute and repackage risk within the banking sector and outside it, notably to the insurance sector, investment funds, and hedge funds. Credit derivatives can also be used to express a view on credit risk.

In the rest of this chapter, we'll take a more detailed look at the securitization and credit derivative markets and at the range of instruments that are available.

CREDIT DERIVATIVES—OVERVIEW

Credit derivatives such as credit default swaps (CDSs), spread options, and credit-linked notes are over-the-counter financial contracts that have their payoffs contingent on changes in the credit quality of a specified entity.

Both the pace of innovation and the volume of activity in the credit derivative markets are heating up: the triennial survey of the global over-the-counter (OTC) derivatives markets conducted by the Bank for International Settlements reports that by June 2004 the notional amount of credit derivatives outstanding had reached a total of $4.5 trillion (Figure 12-3). This is an impressive number, although notional amounts can be a misleading indicator in derivative markets. Of the $4.5 trillion market notional value in the figure, only perhaps $100 billion represents a transfer of credit risk from banks' lending and trading activities to other market

FIGURE 12-3

Global Credit Derivatives Market—Trading Volume

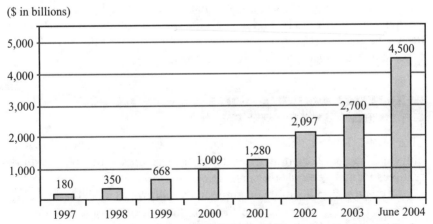

($ in billions)

Sources: British Bankers Association, 2001–2002 Credit Derivatives Surveys and Bank for International Settlements. *Triennal and Semiannual Surveys on Positions in Global Over-the-Counter (OTC) Derivatives markets,* end June 2004, December 2004.

participants. The remainder represents the dealing books of the 15 dealing banks that dominate the business and, to a much lesser extent, investment in credit risks by banks, hedge funds, and insurance companies. In any case, the \$4.5 trillion number pales before the aggregate size of the loan and bond portfolios of the global banking system, which total approximately \$29 trillion and \$5.5 trillion, respectively.

Today, risks that can be protected with credit derivative swaps are largely limited to investment-grade names. In the shorter term, using credit derivative swaps might therefore have the effect of shifting the remaining risks in the banking system further toward the riskier, non-investment-grade end of the spectrum. For the market to become a significant force in moving risk away from banks, the non-investment-grade market in credit derivatives needs to become much deeper and more liquid than it is today. There is some evidence that this is occurring, at least in the United States.

Through 2003, insurance companies were reputed to be the end providers of credit protection, to the extent that some industry commentators began to worry that banks were simply shifting their key risk (credit risk) to another, less credit-savvy, financial sector. However, while insurance companies are indeed net providers of credit protection through CDSs, most of their exposures tend to be in the form of CDOs and basket trades. Furthermore, insurer CDO investment is almost exclusively in the AAA or so-called super-senior tranches of these structures or the second-loss positions; monoline insurers, meanwhile, provide insurance wrap protection on the senior tranches. As we explain later, such tranches cannot be said to absorb much credit risk—indeed, they are specifically designed to sidestep most of the credit risk generated by the underlying assets. Finally, market statistics through 2004 suggest that the role of insurers in the credit derivative market may have become less important, while that of hedge funds and other institutions may have grown.

END-USER APPLICATIONS
OF CREDIT DERIVATIVES

Like any flexible financial instrument, credit derivatives can be put to many purposes. Table 12-2 summarizes some of these applications of credit derivatives from an end user's perspective.

Let's develop a simple example to explain why banks might want to use credit derivatives to reduce their credit concentrations. Imagine two banks, one of which has developed a special expertise in lending to the airline industry and has made \$100 million worth of AA-rated loans to air-

TABLE 12-2

End-User Applications of Credit Derivatives

Investors	▪ Access to previously unavailable markets (e.g., loans, foreign credits, and emerging markets)
	▪ Unbundling of credit and market risks
	▪ Ability to borrow the bank's balance sheet, as the investor does not have to fund the position and also avoids the cost of servicing the loans
	▪ Yield enhancement with or without leverage
	▪ Reduction in sovereign risk of asset portfolios
Banks	▪ Reduce credit concentrations
	▪ Manage the risk profile of the loan portfolio
Corporations	▪ Hedging trade receivables
	▪ Reducing overexposure to customer/supplier credit risk
	▪ Hedging sovereign credit–related project risk

line companies, while the other is based in an oil-producing region and has made $100 million worth of AA-rated loans to energy companies.

In our example, the banks' airline and energy portfolios make up the bulk of their lending, so both banks are very vulnerable to a downturn in the fortunes of their favored industry segment. It's easy to see that, all else equal, both banks would be better off if they were to swap $50 million of each other's loans. Because airline companies generally benefit from declining energy prices, and energy companies benefit from rising energy prices, it is relatively unlikely that the airline and energy industries would run into difficulties at the same time. After swapping the risk, each bank's portfolio would be much better diversified.

Having swapped the risk, both banks would be in a better position to exploit their proprietary information, economies of scale, and existing business relationships with corporate customers by extending more loans to their natural customer base.

Let's also look more closely at another end-user application noted in Table 12-2 with regard to investors: yield enhancement. In an economic environment characterized by low (if rising) interest rates, many investors have been looking for ways to enhance their yields. They might consider high-yield instruments or emerging market debt and asset-backed vehicles. This implies that the investors are willing to accept lower credit quality and longer maturities. At the same time, however, most institutional investors are subject to regulatory or charter restrictions that limit their use of non-investment-grade instruments, or that limit the maturities they can deal in for certain kinds of issuer. Credit derivatives provide investors with ready, if indirect, access to these high-yield markets by combining traditional investment products with credit derivatives. Structured products can be customized to the clients' individual specifications regarding maturity and the degree of leverage. For example, as we discuss later, a total return swap can be used to create a seven-year structure from a portfolio of high-yield bonds with an average maturity of 15 years.

Even when institutional investors can access high-yield markets directly, credit derivatives may offer a cheaper way for them to invest. This is because, in effect, such instruments allow unsophisticated institutions to piggyback on the massive investments in back-office and administrative operations made by banks.

Credit derivatives may also be used to exploit inconsistent pricing between the loan and the bond market for the same issuer, or to take advantage of any particular view that an investor has about the pricing (or mispricing) of corporate credit spreads. However, users of credit derivatives must remember that as well as transferring credit risk, these contracts create an exposure to the creditworthiness of the counterparty of the credit derivative itself—particularly with leveraged transactions.

TYPES OF CREDIT DERIVATIVES

Credit derivatives are mostly structured or embedded in swap, option, or note forms and normally have tenures that are shorter than the maturity of the underlying instruments. For example, a credit default swap may specify that a payment be made if a 10-year corporate bond defaults at any time during the next two years.

Figure 12-4 offers a breakdown of the market by instrument type. Single-name CDSs remain the most popular instrument type of credit derivative, commanding 73 percent of the market in terms of their notional outstanding value. The demand for single-name CDSs has been driven in recent years by the demand for hedges for synthetic single-tranche collateralized debt obligations (as we discuss later) and by hedge funds that use credit derivatives as a way to exploit capital structure arbitrage opportunities. The next most popular instruments are portfolio/correlation products such as CDS instruments based on a group of names rather than a single name—known as "basket CDSs"—and single-tranche CDOs.

FIGURE 12-4

Types of Credit Derivatives—Market Breakdown by Instrument Type

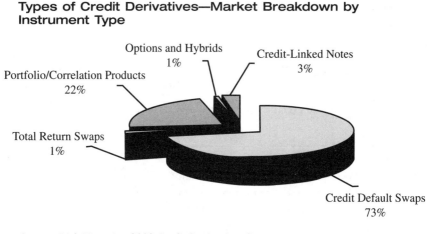

Source: Risk Magazine 2003 Credit Derivatives Survey.

Credit Default Swaps

Credit default swaps can be thought of as insurance against the default of some underlying instrument or as a put option on the underlying instrument.

In a typical CDS, as shown in Figure 12-5, the party selling the credit risk (or the "protection buyer") makes periodic payments to the "protection seller" of a negotiated number of basis points times the notional amount of the underlying bond or loan. The party buying the credit risk (or the protection seller) makes no payment unless the issuer of the underlying bond or loan defaults. In the event of default, the protection seller pays the protection buyer a default payment equal to the notional amount minus a prespecified recovery factor. The recovery factor is there to account for the money that the bank would expect to recover from the defaulted obligation through traditional means (collateral, and so on), which therefore does not need to be "insured" by means of the credit derivative contract.

Since a credit event, usually a default, triggers the payment, this event should be clearly defined in the contract to avoid any litigation when the contract is settled. Default swaps normally contain a "materiality clause" requiring that the change in credit status be validated by third-party evidence. However, Box 12-3 explores some recent difficulties in defining

FIGURE 12-5

Typical Credit Default Swap

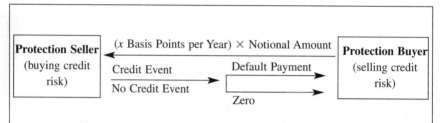

Credit Events
- Bankruptcy, insolvency, or payment default.
- Obligation acceleration, which refers to the situation where debt becomes due and repayable prior to maturity. This event is subject to a materiality threshold of $10 million unless otherwise stated.
- Stipulated fall in the price of the underlying asset.
- Downgrade in the rating of the issuer of the underlying asset.
- Restructuring; this is probably the most controversial credit event (see the Canseco case in Box 12-3).
- Repudiation/moratorium; this can occur in two situations. First, the reference entity (the obligor of the underlying bond or loan issue) refuses to honor its obligations. Second, a company could be prevented from making a payment because of a sovereign debt moratorium (City of Moscow in 1998).

Default Payment
- Par, minus post-default price of the underlying asset as determined by a dealer poll.
- Par, minus stipulated recovery factor, equivalent to a predetermined amount (digital swap).
- Payment of par by seller in exchange for physical delivery of the defaulted underlying asset.

appropriate credit events and makes clear some of the potential implications for institutions buying or selling credit derivatives.

The payment made following a legitimate credit event is sometimes fixed by agreement, but a more common practice is to set it at par minus the recovery rate. (For a bond, the recovery rate is determined by the market price of the bond after the default.) The protection buyer stops paying the regular premium following the credit event. CDSs provide major

BOX 12-3

"RESTRUCTURING" AND "CHEAPEST TO DELIVER"—THE CONSECO CASE

The new credit derivatives market has struggled to define the kind of credit events that should trigger a payout under a credit derivative contract. One of the most controversial aspects of the debate is whether the restructuring of a loan—which can include changes such as an agreed-upon reduction in interest and principal, postponement of payments, or changes in the currencies of payment—should count as a credit event.

The Conseco case famously highlighted the problems that restructuring can cause. Conseco is an insurance company, headquartered in suburban Indianapolis, that provides supplemental health insurance, life insurance, and annuities. In October 2000, a group of banks led by Bank of America and Chase granted to Conseco a three-month extension of the maturity of approximately $2.8 billion of short-term loans, while simultaneously increasing the coupon and enhancing the covenant protection. The extension of credit might have helped prevent an immediate bankruptcy,[1] but as a significant credit event, it also triggered potential payouts on as much as $2 billion of CDSs.

The original sellers of the CDSs were not happy, and they were annoyed further when the CDS buyers seemed to be playing the "cheapest to deliver" game by delivering long-dated bonds instead of the restructured loans; at the time, these bonds were trading significantly lower than the restructured bank loans. (The restructured loans traded at a higher price in the secondary market because of the new credit-mitigation features.)

In May 2001, following this episode, the International Swaps and Derivatives Association (ISDA) issued a Restructuring Supplement to its 1999 definitions concerning credit derivative contractual terminology. Among other things, this document requires that for a restructuring to qualify as a credit event, it must occur to an obligation that has at least three holders, and at least two-thirds of the holders must agree to the restructuring. The ISDA document also imposes a maturity limitation on deliverables—the protection buyer can deliver only securities with a maturity of less than 30 months following the restructuring date or the extended maturity of the restructured loan—and it requires that the delivered security be fully transferable. Some key players in the market have now dropped restructuring from their list of credit events.

---

[1] Conseco filed a voluntary petition to reorganize under Chapter 11 in 2002 and emerged from Chapter 11 bankruptcy in September 2003.

TABLE 12-3

Benefits of Using CDSs

- CDSs act to divorce funding decisions from credit-risk-taking decisions. The purchase of insurance, letters of credit, guarantees, and so on are relatively inefficient credit-risk-transfer strategies, largely because they do not separate the management of credit risk from the asset associated with the risk.
- CDSs are unfunded, so it's easy to make leveraged transactions (some collateral might be required). This is an advantage for institutions with a high funding cost. CDSs also offer considerable *flexibility* in terms of leverage; the user can define the required degree of leverage, if any, in a credit transaction. This makes credit an appealing asset class for hedge funds and other nonbank institutional investors. In addition, investors can avoid the administrative cost of assigning and servicing loans.
- CDSs are customizable, e.g., their maturity may differ from the term of the loan.
- CDSs improve flexibility in risk management, as banks can shed credit risk more easily than by selling loans. There is no need to remove the loans from the balance sheet.
- CDSs are an efficient vehicle for banks to free up capital.
- CDSs can be used to take a spread view on a credit. They offer the first mechanism by which short sales of credit instruments can be executed with any reasonable liquidity and without the risk of a "short squeeze."
- Dislocations between the cash and CDS markets present new "relative value" opportunities (e.g., trading the default swap basis).
- CDSs divorce the client relationship from the risk decision. The reference entity whose credit risk is being transferred does not need to be aware of the CDS transaction. This contrasts with any reassignment of loans through the secondary loan market, which generally requires borrower/agent notification.
- CDSs are bringing liquidity to the credit market, as they have lured nonbank players into the syndicated lending and credit arena.

benefits for both buyers and sellers of credit protection (see Table 12-3) and are very effective tools for the active management of credit risk in a loan portfolio.

First-to-Default CDS

A variant of the credit default swap is the *first-to-default* put, as illustrated in the example in Figure 12-6. Here, the bank holds a portfolio of four high-yield loans rated B, each with a nominal value of $100 million, a maturity of five years, and an annual coupon of LIBOR plus 200 basis points (bp). In such deals, the loans are often chosen such that their default correlations are very small, i.e., there is a very low probability at the time the deal is struck that more than one loan will default over the time until the expiration of the put in, say, two years. A first-to-default put gives the bank the opportunity to reduce its credit-risk exposure: it will automatically be compensated if one of the loans in the pool of four loans defaults at any time during the two-year period. If more than one loan defaults during this period, the bank is compensated only for the first loan that defaults.

If default events are assumed to be uncorrelated, the probability that the dealer (protection seller) will have to compensate the bank by paying it par, that is, $100 million, and receiving the defaulted loan is the sum of the default probabilities, or 4 percent, This is approximately, at the time, the probability of default of a loan rated B for which the default spread was 400 bp, or a cost of 100 bp per loan, i.e., half the cost of the protection for each individual name.

Note that, in such a deal, a bank may chose to protect itself over a two-year period, even though the loans might have a maturity of five years.

FIGURE 12-6

First-to-Default Put

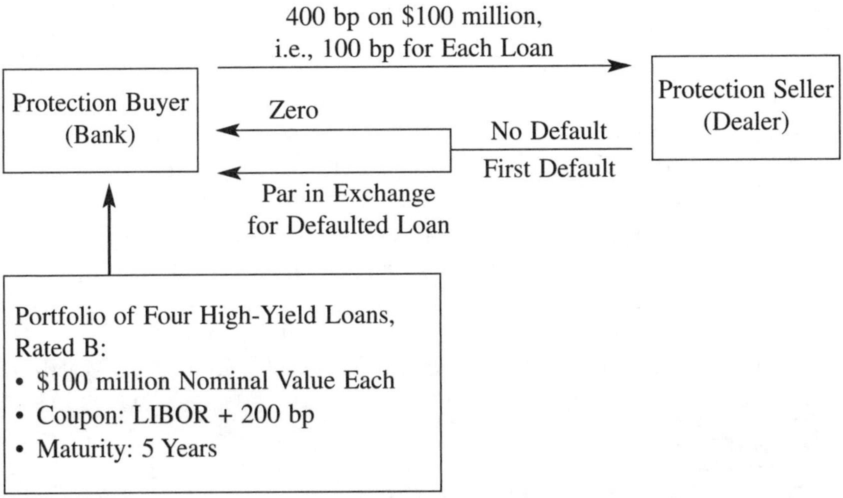

Probability of Experiencing Two Defaults $= (1\%)^2\, 4 \times 3/2 = 0.0006 = 0.06\%$[1]

---

1. The probability that more than one loan will default is the sum of the probabilities that two, three, or four loans will default. The probability that three loans or four loans will default during the same period is infinitesimal and has been neglected in the calculation. Moreover, there are six possible ways of pairing loans in a portfolio of four loans.

First-to-default structures are, in essence, pairwise correlation plays. The yield on such structures is primarily a function of

- The number of names in the basket
- The degree of correlation between the names

The first-to-default spread will lie between the spread of the worst individual credit and the sum of the spreads of all the credits—closer to the latter if correlation is low, and closer to the former if correlation is high.

A generalization of the first-to-default structure is the *nth-to-default* credit swap, where protection is given only to the *nth* facility to default as the trigger credit event.

Total Return Swaps

Total return swaps (TRSs) mirror the return on some underlying instrument, such as a bond, a loan, or a portfolio of bonds and/or loans. The benefits of TRSs are similar to those of CDSs, except that for a TRS, in contrast to a CDS, both market and credit risk are transferred from the seller to the buyer.

TRSs can be applied to any type of security—for example, floating-rate notes, coupon bonds, stocks, or baskets of stocks. For most TRSs, the maturity of the swap is much shorter than the maturity of the underlying assets, e.g., 3 to 5 years as opposed to a maturity of 10 to 15 years.

The purchaser of a TRS (the total return receiver) receives the cash flows and benefits (pays the losses) if the value of the reference asset rises (falls). The purchaser is synthetically long the underlying asset during the life of the swap.

In a typical deal, shown in Figure 12-7, the purchaser of the TRS makes periodic floating payments, often tied to LIBOR. The party selling

FIGURE 12-7

Generic Total Return Swap (TRS)

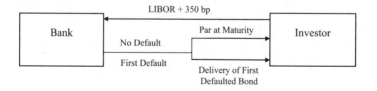

the risk makes periodic payments to the purchaser, and these are tied to the total return of some underlying asset (including both coupon payments and the change in value of the instruments). We've annotated these periodic payments in detail in the figure.

Since in most cases it is difficult to mark-to-market the underlying loans, the change in value is passed through at the maturity of the TRS. Still, it may be difficult to estimate the economic value of the loan at that time, which may still be remote from the maturity of the loan. This is why in many deals the buyer is required to take delivery of the underlying loans at a price P_0, which is the initial value.

At time T, the buyer should receive $P_T - P_0$ if this amount is positive, and pay $P_0 - P_T$ otherwise. By taking delivery of the loans at their market value P_T, the buyer makes a net payment to the bank of P_0 in exchange for the loans.

In some levered TRSs, the buyer holds the explicit option to default on its obligation if the loss in value $P_0 - P_T$ exceeds the collateral accumulated at the expiration of the TRS. In that case, the buyer can simply walk away from the deal, abandon the collateral to the counterparty, and leave the counterparty to bear any loss beyond the value of the collateral.

A total return swap is equivalent to a synthetic long position in the underlying asset for the buyer. It allows for any degree of leverage, and therefore it offers unlimited upside and downside potential. There is no exchange of principal, no legal change of ownership, and no voting rights.

In order to hedge both the market risk and the credit risk of the underlying assets of the TRS, a bank that sells a TRS typically buys the underlying assets. The bank is then exposed only to the risk of default of the buyer in the total return swap transaction. This risk will itself depend on the degree of leverage adopted in the transaction. If the buyer fully collateralizes the underlying instrument, then there is no risk of default and the floating payment should correspond to the bank's funding cost. If, on the contrary, the buyer leverages its position, say, 10 times by putting aside 10 percent of the initial value of the underlying instrument as collateral, then the floating payment is the sum of the funding cost and a spread. This corresponds to the default premium and compensates the bank for its credit exposure with regard to the TRS purchaser.

Asset-Backed Credit-Linked Notes

An asset-backed credit-linked note (CLN) embeds a default swap in a security such as a medium-term note (MTN). A CLN is a debt obligation with a coupon and redemption tied to the performance of a loan. It is an on-balance-sheet instrument, with exchange of principal; there is no legal change of ownership of the underlying assets.

Unlike a TRS, a CLN is a tangible asset and may be leveraged by a multiple of 10. Since there are no margin calls, it offers its investors limited downside and unlimited upside. Some CLNs can obtain a rating that is consistent with an investment-grade rating from agencies such as Fitch, Moody's, or Standard & Poor's.

Figure 12-8 presents a typical CLN structure. The bank buys the assets and locks them into a trust. In the example, we assume that $105

FIGURE 12-8

Asset-Backed Credit-Linked Note (CLN)

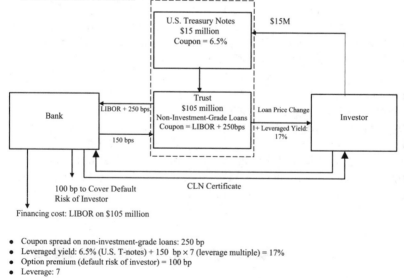

Structure:

- Investor seeks $105 million of exposure with a leverage ratio of 7, i.e., while investing only $15 million in collateral
- Investor purchases $15 million of CLN issued by a trust
- Trust receives $105 million of non-investment-grade loans that are assumed to yield LIBOR + 250 bps on average
- $15 million CLN proceeds are invested in U.S. Treasury notes that yield 6.5%
- Bank finances the $105 million loans at LIBOR and receives from the trust LIBOR + 100 bps on $105 million to cover the investor's default risk

- Coupon spread on non-investment-grade loans: 250 bp
- Leveraged yield: 6.5% (U.S. T-notes) + 150 bp × 7 (leverage multiple) = 17%
- Option premium (default risk of investor) = 100 bp
- Leverage: 7

million of non-investment-grade loans with an average rating of B, yielding an aggregate LIBOR + 250 bp, are purchased at a cost of LIBOR, which is the funding rate for the bank. The trust issues an asset-backed note for $15 million, which is bought by the investor. The proceeds are invested in U.S. government securities, which are assumed to yield 6.5 percent and are used to collateralize the basket of loans. The collateral in our example is 15/105 = 14.3 percent of the initial value of the loan portfolio. This represents a leverage multiple of 7 (105/15 = 7).

The net cash flow for the bank is 100 bp—that is, LIBOR + 250 bp (produced by the assets in the trust), minus the LIBOR cost of funding the assets, minus the 150 bp paid out by the bank to the trust. This 100 bp applies to a notional amount of $105 million and is the bank's compensation for retaining the risk of default of the issue above and beyond $15 million.

The investor receives a yield of 17 percent (i.e., 6.5 percent yield from the collateral of $15 million, plus 150 bp paid out by the bank on a notional amount of $105 million) on a notional amount of $15 million, in addition to any change in the value of the loan portfolio that is eventually passed through to the investor.

In this structure there are no margin calls, and the maximum downside for the investor is the initial investment of $15 million. If the fall in the value of the loan portfolio is greater than $15 million, then the investor defaults and the bank absorbs any additional loss beyond that limit. For the investor, this is equivalent of being long a credit default swap written by the bank.

A CLN may constitute a natural hedge to a TRS in which the bank receives the total return on a loan portfolio. Different variations on the same theme can be proposed, such as compound credit-linked notes where the investor is exposed only to the first default in a loan portfolio.

Spread Options

Spread options are not pure credit derivatives, but they do have creditlike features. The underlying asset of a spread option is the yield spread between a specified corporate bond and a government bond of the same maturity. The striking price is the forward spread at the maturity of the option, and the payoff is the greater of zero or the difference between the spread at maturity and the striking price, times a multiplier that is usually the product of the duration of the underlying bond and the notional amount.

Spread options are used by investors to hedge price risk on specific bonds or bond portfolios. As credit spreads widen, bond prices decline (and vice versa).

Credit-Risk Securitization for Loans and High-Yield Bonds

Collateralized loan obligations (CLOs) and collateralized bond obligations (CBOs) are simply securities that are collateralized by means of high-yield bank loans and corporate bonds. (CLOs and CBOs are also sometimes referred to generically as collateralized debt obligations, or CDOs.) Banks often use these instruments to free up regulatory capital and thus leverage their intermediation business.

A CLO (CBO) is an efficient securitization structure because it allows the cash flows from a pool of loans (or bonds) rated at below investment grade to be pooled together and prioritized, so that some of the resulting securities can achieve an investment-grade rating. This is a big advantage because a wider range of investors, including insurance companies and pension funds, are able to invest in such a "senior class" of notes. The main differences between CLOs and CBOs are the assumed recovery values for and the average life of the underlying assets. Rating agencies generally assume a recovery rate of 30 percent to 40 percent for unsecured corporate bonds, while the rate is around 70 percent for well-secured bank loans. Also, since loans amortize, they have a shorter duration and thus present a lower risk than their high-yield bond counterparts. It is therefore easier to produce notes with investment-grade ratings from CLOs than it is from CBOs.

Figure 12-9 illustrates the basic structure of a CLO. A special-purpose vehicle (SPV) or trust is set up, which issues, say, three types of securities: senior secured class A notes, senior secured class B notes, and subordinated notes or an "equity tranche." The proceeds are used to buy high-yield notes that constitute the collateral. In practice, the asset pool for a CLO may also contain a small percentage of high-yield bonds (usually less than 10 percent). The reverse is true for CBOs: they may include up to 10 percent of high-yield loans.

A typical CLO might consist of a pool of assets containing, say, 50 loans with an average rating of, say, B1 (by reference to Moody's rating system). These might have exposure to, say, 20 industries, with no industry concentration exceeding, say, 8 percent. The largest concentration by

FIGURE 12-9

Typical Collateralized Loan Obligation (CLO) Structure

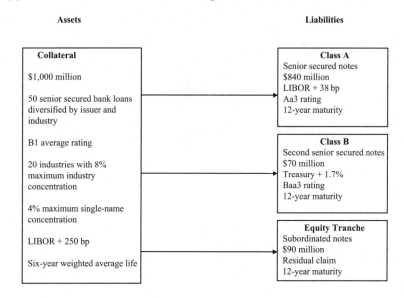

Assets	Liabilities
Collateral	**Class A**
$1,000 million	Senior secured notes
	$840 million
50 senior secured bank loans	LIBOR + 38 bp
diversified by issuer and	Aa3 rating
industry	12-year maturity
B1 average rating	**Class B**
	Second senior secured notes
20 industries with 8%	$70 million
maximum industry	Treasury + 1.7%
concentration	Baa3 rating
	12-year maturity
4% maximum single-name	
concentration	**Equity Tranche**
	Subordinated notes
LIBOR + 250 bp	$90 million
	Residual claim
Six-year weighted average life	12-year maturity

issuer might be kept to, say, under 4 percent of the portfolio's value. In our example, the weighted-average life of the loans is assumed to be six years, while the issued notes have a stated maturity of 12 years. The average yield on these floating-rate loans is assumed to be LIBOR + 250 bp.

The gap in maturities between the loans and the CLO structure requires active management of the loan portfolio. A qualified high-yield loan portfolio manager must be hired to actively manage the portfolio within constraints specified in the legal document. During the first six years, which is called the reinvestment or lockout period, the cash flows from loan amortization and the proceeds from maturing or defaulting loans are reinvested in new loans. (As the bank originating the loans typically remains responsible for servicing the loans, the investor in loan packages should be aware of the dangers of moral hazard and adverse selection for the performance of the underlying loans.) Thereafter, the three classes of notes are progressively redeemed as cash flows materialize.

The issued notes consist of three tranches: two senior secured classes with an investment-grade rating, and an unrated subordinated class or equity tranche. The equity tranche is in the first-loss position and does not have any promised payment; the idea is that it will absorb default losses before they reach the senior investors.[4]

In our example, the senior class A note is rated Aa3 and pays a coupon of LIBOR + 38 bp, which is more attractive than the sub-LIBOR coupon on an equivalent corporate bond with the same rating. The second senior secured class note, or mezzanine tranche, is rated Baa3 and pays a fixed coupon of Treasury + 1.7 percent for 12 years. Since the original loans pay LIBOR + 250 bp, the equity tranche offers an attractive return as long as most of the loans underlying the notes are fully paid.

The rating enhancement for the two senior classes is obtained by prioritizing the cash flows. Rating agencies such as Fitch IBCA, Moody's, and Standard & Poor's have developed their own methodology for rating these senior class notes.

There is no such thing as a free lunch in the financial markets, and this has considerable risk management implications for banks issuing CLOs and CBOs. The credit enhancement of the senior secured class notes is obtained by simply shifting the default risk to the equity tranche. According to simulation results, the returns from investing in this equity tranche can vary widely—from –100 percent, with the investor losing everything, to more than 30 percent, depending on the actual rate of default on the loan portfolio. Sometimes the equity tranche is bought by investors with a strong appetite for risk, such as hedge funds, either outright or more often by means of a total return swap with a leverage multiple of 7 to 10. But most of the time, the bank issuing a CLO retains this risky first-loss equity tranche.

The main motivation for banks that issue CLOs is thus to arbitrage regulatory capital: it is less costly in regulatory capital terms to hold the equity tranche than it is to hold the underlying loans themselves. However, while the amount of regulatory capital the bank has to put aside may fall, the economic risk borne by the bank may not be reduced at all. Paradoxically, credit derivatives, which offer a more effective form of economic hedge, have so far received little regulatory capital relief. This form of regulatory arbitrage won't be allowed under the new Basel Accord.

---

4. This equity tranche is also half-jokingly called "toxic waste" in industry circles, because it is in such an exposed position if the credit quality of the underlying portfolio deteriorates.

Synthetic CDOs

In a traditional CDO, as described in Figure 12-9, the credit assets are fully cash funded with the proceeds of the debt and equity issued by the SPV, and with the repayment of the obligations directly tied to the cash flows of the assets. A synthetic CDO, by contrast, effects a risk transfer without affecting the legal ownership of the credit assets. This is accomplished by a series of CDSs. The sponsoring institution transfers the credit risk of the portfolio of credit assets to the SPV by means of the CDSs, while the assets themselves remain on the balance sheet of the sponsor. In the example in Figure 12-10, the right-hand side is equivalent to the cash CDO structure presented in Figure 12-9, except that it applies to only 10 percent of the pool of reference assets. The left-hand side shows the credit protection in the form of a "super senior swap" provided by a highly rated institution (usually an insurance monoline company).

The SPV typically provides credit protection for 10 percent or less of the losses on the reference portfolio. The SPV, in turn, issues notes in the capital markets to cash collateralize the portfolio default swap with the originating entity. The notes issued can include a nonrated equity piece, mezzanine debt, and senior debt, creating cash liabilities. Most of the default risk is borne by the investors in these notes, with the same risk hierarchy as for cash CDOs, i.e., the equity tranche holders retain the risk of the first set of losses, and the mezzanine tranche holders are exposed to credit losses once the equity tranche has been wiped out. The remainder of the risk, 90 percent, is usually distributed to a highly rated counterparty via a senior swap. Reinsurers and insurance monoline companies, which typically have an AAA credit rating, have traditionally had a healthy appetite for this type of senior risk and are the largest participants in this part of the capital structure, often referred to as super-senior AAAs. The initial proceeds of the equity and notes are invested in highly rated liquid assets.

If an obligor in the reference pool defaults, the trust liquidates investments in the trust and makes payments to the originating entity to cover the default losses. This payment is offset by a successive reduction in the equity tranche, and then the mezzanine tranche; finally, the super-senior tranches are called to make up the losses.

Single-Tranche CDOs

The terms of a single-tranche CDO are similar to those of a tranche of a traditional CDO. However, in a traditional CDO, the entire portfolio may be ramped, and the entire capital structure may be distributed to multiple

FIGURE 12-10

Capital Structure of a Synthetic CDO

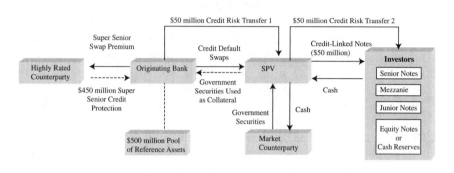

investors. In a single-tranche CDO, only a particular tranche, tailored to the client's needs,[5] is issued, and there is no need to build the actual portfolio, as the bank will hedge its exposure by buying or selling the underlying reference assets according to hedge ratios produced by its proprietary pricing model.

In the structure described in Figure 12-11, for example, the client has gained credit protection for a mezzanine or middle-ranking tranche of credit risk in its reference portfolio, but continues to assume both the first-loss (equity) risk tranche and the most senior risk tranche. The biggest advantage of this kind of instrument is that it allows the client to tailor most of the terms of the transaction. The biggest disadvantage tends to be the limited liquidity of tailored deals. Dealers who create single-tranche CDOs have to dynamically hedge the tranche they have purchased or sold as the quality and correlation of the portfolio change.

Credit Derivatives on Credit Indices

Credit trading based on indices ("index trades") has become popular over the last few years. The indices are based on a large number of underlying credits, and portfolio managers can therefore use index trades to hedge the credit-risk exposure of a diversified portfolio. Index trades are also increasingly popular with holders of CDO tranches and CLNs who need to hedge their credit-risk exposure.

---

5. The client can be a buyer or a seller of credit protection. The "Bank" is on the other side of the transaction.

FIGURE   12-11

Single-Tranche CDOs

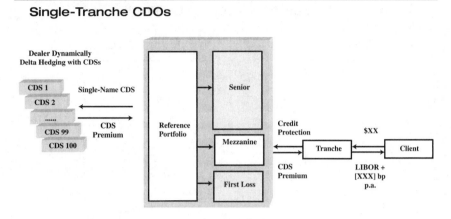

In 2004 the competing TRAC-X and iBoxx families of credit indices merged to create a new family of credit indices and related structured products. There is now a European index of investment-grade names called Dow Jones iTraxx (DJ iTraxx) and a U.S. investment-grade index called Dow Jones CDX (DJ CDX.NA.IG). There is also a high-yield index in the United States named "High Boxx" (HY CDX).

Like CDOs, iTraxx and CDX are tranched, with each tranche absorbing losses in a predesignated order of priority. The tranching is influenced by the nature of the respective geographic markets. For example, CDX.NA.IG tranches have been broken down according to the following loss attachment points: 0–3 percent (equity tranche), 3–7 percent, 7–10 percent, 10–15 percent, 15–30 percent, and 30–100 percent (the most senior tranche), as illustrated in Figure 12-12. For iTraxx, the corresponding tranches are 0–3 percent, 3–6 percent, 6–9 percent, 9–12 percent, 12–22 percent, and 22–100 percent. The tranching of the European and U.S indices is adjusted so that tranches of the same seniority in both indices receive the same rating. The tranches of the U.S. index are thicker because the names that compose the U.S. index are on average slightly more risky than the names in the European index.

There is currently an active broker market in tranches of both the DJ iTraxx and the DJ CDX.NA.IG, with 5- and 10-year tranches actively quoted on both indices. There is also activity in the 5- and 10-year tranches of the DJ HY CDX.

Each tranche is quoted in basis points per annum (bp) of the notional amount of the underlying index. At the end of March 2005, for example,

FIGURE 12-12

Tranched U.S. Index of Investment Grade Names
(CDX.NA.IG)

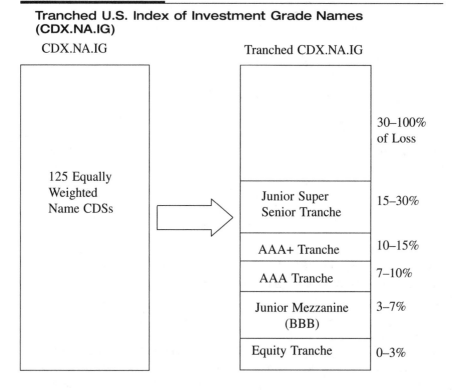

the junior mezzanine tranche for the iTraxx index was quoted at
142.5–146.5 bp. An investor who sold the junior mezzanine tranche of a
$1 billion iTraxx portfolio at 142.5 bp would receive 142.5 bp annually
on $30 million (3 percent of $1 billion), and in return would pay the buyer
for any and all losses between $30 and $60 million of the $1 billion un-
derlying iTraxx portfolio (representing the 3–6 percent tranche).

Options have been traded on iTraxx and CDX to meet the demand
from hedge funds and proprietary trading desks looking to trade credit
volatility and take views on the direction of credit using options.

Trading tranches of iTraxx and CDX offers a number of potential advantages over trading synthetic CDOs in terms of liquidity (they have large
issue sizes and traded with bid/offer spreads of between 5 and 75 bp in
2004), transparency, and cost (CDOs are expensive to execute). However,
synthetic CDOs may have an advantage over tranched iTraxx and CDX
for customers looking for customized risk and return profiles and for portfolio characteristics that are not offered by iTraxx and CDX.

CONCLUSION

Credit derivatives are a key tool of dynamic portfolio management, and one that is growing in importance in the global banking industry.

Over time, the increased use of credit derivatives and other risk-transfer techniques will redistribute and repackage credit risk within the banking system, as well as redistributing credit risk outside the banking system (notably to the insurance sector, investment funds, and hedge funds). Credit derivatives can also be used to express a view on credit risks. For institutions that assume credit risk, the liquidity and convenience of these new markets—as well as the way they help put a price on credit risk—are powerful attractions.

On the supply side, banks benefit by being able to hedge their credit-risk exposure and, more importantly, by being able to break the linkage between the client relationship and lending. On the buy side, investors are able to obtain credit products that are structured closely to their specific needs (together with an increase in transparency and the option of employing a third-party asset manager).

The development of the CDS and CDO markets will facilitate a more efficient allocation of credit risk in the economy and reduce systemic risk during economic recessions (when default rates increase dramatically, as was the case during the 2001–2002 economic downturn). Currently, one of the main reasons for using the new credit instruments is regulatory arbitrage. Basel II should align regulatory capital requirements more closely to economic risk and provide more incentives to use credit instruments to manage the "real" underlying credit quality of a bank's portfolio. Nevertheless, opportunities for regulatory arbitrage will remain. In the case of retail products such as mortgages, the very different regulatory capital treatment for Basel II-compliant banks, compared to the treatment of banks that will continue to remain compliant with the current Basel rules, will itself give rise to an arbitrage opportunity.

So far, it's really only large banks that have benefited much from the type of credit protection provided by CDSs, as only a few names, corresponding to clients of the money-center banks, are traded in the CDS markets. Regional banks, which tend to lend money to local companies, still don't have access to credit derivatives to hedge most of their credit-risk exposures.

There is another kind of downside, however: risks assumed by means of credit derivatives are largely unfunded and undisclosed, which could allow players to become leveraged in a way that is difficult for outsiders (or even senior management) to spot. So far, we've yet to see a major financial disaster caused by the complexities of credit derivatives and the new opportunities they bring for *both* transferring and assuming credit risk. But such a disaster will surely come, particularly if the boards and senior managers of banks do not invest the time to understand exactly how these new markets and instruments work—and how each major transaction affects their institution's risk profile.

CHAPTER 13

Operational Risk

Operational risk is both the oldest and the newest threat faced by financial institutions. Banks have always had to protect themselves from key threats to their operations such as bank robbery and white-collar fraud. But, until recently, the management of these threats focused on practical techniques for minimizing the chance of loss, whether this meant putting a security guard on the door, establishing the independence of the internal audit team, or building robust computer systems. Few banks attempted to either put a specific economic number on the size of the operational risks they faced or manage these risks systematically as a risk class.

Times have changed. Today, banks are putting significant energy into wide-ranging frameworks for managing enterprisewide operational risk and are trying to relate operational risk directly to the risk capital that they set aside to cover unexpected losses—the topics that we will focus on in this chapter.

Attitudes toward operational risk have begun to change over the last few years partly because of the trend toward managing banks in terms of their risk-adjusted performance and stakeholders' demand for this kind of information. As banks began to try to adjust the apparent profits from a business activity in line with the risks the activity generates, often using economic capital calculations, they realized that it made little sense to leave a whole class of operational risks out of the calculation. Also, as banks have begun to bring together their chief credit and market-risk officers under the command of overarching risk committees and chief risk officers, it has become logically difficult to ignore the potential impact of operational risks for the bank as a whole. The problem has been pointed up by a series of catastrophic rogue trader scandals, from the destruction of

Barings Bank in 1995 to the A$360 million currency options loss that shocked National Australia Bank in January 2004.

Industry trends are also pushing operational risks onto the management agenda. While technology helps banks to push down costs as well as to open up new financial markets, it is a double-edged sword. The increasing complexity of financial instruments and information systems increases the potential for an operational risk event. A lack of familiarity with new financial instruments may lead to their misuse and raises the chances of either mispricing or ineffective hedging. Operational errors in data feeds may also distort the bank's assessment of its risks.

A prime example of a historical operational risk event that led to enormous investments to reduce its possible impact was the so-called Y2K event. Y2K was the acronym for the end of the millennium, when it was feared that computer programs might not function properly because of the common use of two digits to specify the calendar year. Programmers were worried that computer systems might interpret 05 as 1905 rather than 2005—or simply crash. Banks and other corporations invested many billions of dollars to avert the problem.

But perhaps the most important force in changing attitudes to operational risk is new bank regulation that, after 2007, for the first time in the banking industry's history, will oblige many banks to set aside specific risk capital for operational risk. In order to specify this capital charge within the new Basel Capital Accord, regulators and the financial industry have converged on a formal definition of operational risk. This, in turn, has facilitated the measurement of operational risk as a risk class, and has made it easier to compare the operational risk profiles of firms.

The regulators have defined operational risk as "the risk of loss resulting from inadequate or failed internal processes, people and systems or from external events." These failures include computer breakdowns, a bug in a key piece of computer software, errors of judgment, deliberate fraud, and many other potential mishaps; Table 13–1 sets this out more formally. This definition from the Basel Committee includes legal risk (exposure to fines, penalties, and punitive damages resulting from supervisory actions as well as private settlements), but it excludes business and reputation risk.

Now let's take a look at how the clearer definitions of operational risk are helping managers to build a coherent approach to operational risk measurement, capital allocation, and operational risk management; we'll then examine the key problem of operational risk measurement in more detail.

TABLE 13-1

Types of Operational Failure

1. People risk:	■ Incompetency ■ Fraud ■ Etc.
2. Process risk: A. Model risk*	■ Model/methodology error ■ Mark-to-model error ■ Etc.
B. Transaction risk	■ Execution error ■ Product complexity ■ Booking error ■ Settlement error ■ Documentation/contract risk ■ Etc.
C. Operational control risk	■ Exceeding limits ■ Security risks ■ Volume risk ■ Etc.
3. Systems and technology risk	■ System failure ■ Programming error ■ Information risk ■ Telecommunications failure ■ Etc.

*See Chapter 14

EIGHT KEY ELEMENTS IN BANK OPERATIONAL RISK MANAGEMENT

In the authors' experience, eight key elements are necessary to successfully implement a bankwide operational risk management framework and the associated operational risk models (Figure 13–1). They involve setting policy and identifying risk on the basis of an agreed-upon terminology, constructing business process maps, building a best-practice measurement methodology, providing exposure management, installing a timely reporting capability, performing risk analysis (inclusive of stress testing), and allocating economic capital as a function of operational risk. These key elements are consistent with the sound operational risk management practices that, according to the Basel Committee,[1] should be adopted by all banks, regardless of their size, level of sophistication, and nature of their activities. These principles are summarized in Box 13–1.

---

1. Basel Committee on Banking Supervision, *Sound Practices for the Management and Supervision of Operational Risk* (Basel: Bank for International Settlements, February 2003).

FIGURE 13-1

Eight Key Elements to Achieve Best-Practice
Operational Risk Management

BOX 13-1

EIGHT SOUND PRACTICES FOR THE MANAGEMENT
OF OPERATIONAL RISK

The Basel Committee has published eight sound principles for the internal
management and supervision of operational risk, organized around three
themes.

DEVELOPING AN APPROPRIATE RISK
MANAGEMENT ENVIRONMENT

Principle 1. The board of directors should be aware of the major
aspects of the bank's operational risks as a distinct risk category
that should be managed, and it should approve and periodically
review the bank's operational risk management framework. The
framework should provide a firmwide definition of operational
risk and lay down the principles for how operational risk is to be
identified, assessed, monitored, and controlled or mitigated.

Principle 2. The board of directors should ensure that the bank's
operational risk management framework is subject to effective
and comprehensive internal audit by operationally independent,
appropriately trained, and competent staff. The internal audit
function should not be directly responsible for operational risk
management.

(continued on following page)

BOX 13-1 *(Continued)*

Principle 3. Senior management should have responsibility for implementing the operational risk management framework approved by the board of directors. The framework should be implemented throughout the whole banking organization, and all levels of staff should understand their responsibilities with respect to operational risk management. Senior management should also have responsibility for developing policies, processes, and procedures for managing operational risk in all of the bank's products, activities, processes, and systems.

RISK MANAGEMENT: IDENTIFICATION, ASSESSMENT, MONITORING, AND MITIGATING OR CONTROLLING

Principle 4. Banks should identify and assess the operational risk inherent in all material products, activities, processes, and systems. Banks should also ensure that before new products, activities, processes, and systems are introduced or undertaken, the operational risk inherent in them is subject to adequate assessment procedures.

Principle 5. Banks should implement a process to regularly monitor risk profiles and material exposure to losses. There should be regular reporting of pertinent information to senior management and the board of directors that supports the proactive management of operational risk.

Principle 6. Banks should have policies, processes, and procedures to control or mitigate material operational risks. Banks should assess the feasibility of alternative risk limitation and control strategies and should adjust their operational risk profile using appropriate strategies, in light of their overall risk appetite.

Principle 7. Banks should have contingency and business continuity plans in place to ensure their ability to operate as going concerns and minimize losses in the event of severe business disruption.

ROLE OF DISCLOSURE

Principle 8. Banks should make sufficient public disclosure to allow market participants to assess their approach to operational risk management.

Let's look at these elements in more detail. The first element is to develop *well-defined operational risk policies*. Banks need to establish clear guidelines for practices that control or reduce operational risk. For example, in the case of an investment bank that runs trading desks, the bank needs to establish policies on trader/back-office segregation, out-of-hours trading, off-premises trading, legal document vetting, the vetting of the pricing models that underpin trading decisions, and so on. Some of these practices will have been defined, and either required or encouraged, by regulators. But many others represent best-practice standards identified through tracking the findings from industry working groups, or best practices that seem to be prevalent in the bank's peer group. Other practices might have to be developed by the bank itself in response to new products and innovative business lines.

The second element is to establish a *common language of risk identification*. For example, the term *people risk* would include a failure to deploy skilled staff, *process risk* would include execution errors, *technology risk* would include system failures, and so on. This common language can be used during either qualitative self-assessments executed by business management (and validated by the risk management function) or statistical assessment.

The third element is to develop *business process maps* for each business. For example, a risk officer might map the business process associated with the bank's dealings with a broker, so that this becomes transparent to management and auditors. The same officer might extend this description to create a full "operational risk catalogue" for all the bank's businesses. This catalogue categorizes and defines the various operational risks arising from each organizational unit in terms of people, process, and systems and technology risks (as in Table 13–1). It would include analyzing the products and services that each organizational unit offers and the actions that the bank needs to take to manage operational risk.

The fourth element is to develop a *comprehensible set of operational risk metrics*. Later in this chapter we discuss in more detail how risk measurement should be carried out by operational risk managers, using a quantitative methodology based on both historical loss experience and scenario analysis, to derive loss frequency and loss severity distributions. These distributions can be combined to calculate the economic capital required to support the activity's operational risk.

The fifth element is to decide *how to manage operational risk exposures* and take appropriate action to hedge the operational risk. The bank should address the cost-benefit trade-offs of insuring against a given risk (for those operational risks that can be insured against, which is far from all of them).

The sixth element is to decide *how to report exposures*. The bank will have to decide which operational risk numbers are the most useful for senior management and the board when tracking the bank's firmwide operational risk profile. The bank will also have to put in place an appropriate infrastructure to provide reporting to the relevant committees (e.g., the operations and administration committee as well as the capital and risk committee).

The seventh element is to develop *tools for risk analysis* and procedures for when these tools should be deployed. The bank must develop appropriate measures for exposure, up-to-date databases of internal and industrywide operational loss data, well-designed scenario analyses, and a deep knowledge of the key risk drivers in its business lines. Figure 13–2 shows how these tools feed into the calculation of operational value-at-risk, a calculation that we discuss in more detail later on. The frequency of risk assessment should be a function of the degree to which operational risks are expected to change over time as businesses undertake new initiatives or as business circumstances evolve. Operational risk analysis is typically performed as part of a new product process. The bank should reassess its approach whenever its operational risk profile changes signifi-

FIGURE 13-2

From Tools for Risk Analysis to OpVaR

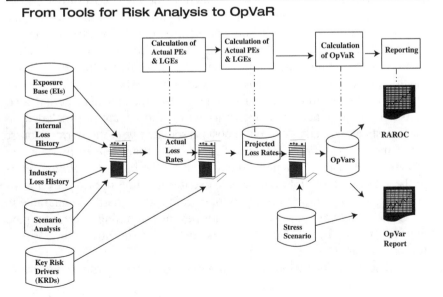

cantly, e.g., after the implementation of a new system or the offering of a new service.

The eighth element is to ensure *appropriate attribution of operational risk capital* to every business.

HOW CAN WE DEFINE AND CATEGORIZE OPERATIONAL LOSSES?

It's clear that quantifying operational risk represents a key challenge in implementing the framework that we've described. But before we try to attach a number to a particular operational risk, we must think through how we define and classify the operational losses that might arise from that risk. If the bank's approach to this problem is not rigorous, it will find that relating internal and external data on losses to the problem of putting a number against operational risk is impossible.

A loss arising from an operational risk takes the form either of a direct external cost or of a write-down associated with the resolution of an operational risk event, net of recoveries (mitigation benefits should be recorded separately). When the loss is deemed probable and estimable, it is likely to be recognized as a profit and loss (P&L) event for accounting purposes, and can also become part of the bank's recorded internal loss history (i.e., be entered into its loss database).

The definition of operational losses should be as specific as possible. For example, an external cost should include the gross cost of compensation and/or penalty payments made to third parties, legal liability, regulatory taxes or fines, or loss of resources. Here we can define three key terms: cost to fix, write-down, and resolution. The *cost-to-fix* statistic is best defined to include only external payments that are directly linked to the incident. For example, legal costs, consultancy costs, or costs of hiring temporary staff would be included in the cost-to-fix statistic. Internal costs associated with general management and operations are not included, as these costs are already covered in costs associated with the normal course of business. *Write-down* refers to the loss or impairment in the value of any financial or nonfinancial assets owned by the bank. *Resolution* refers to the act of correcting the individual event (including out-of-pocket costs and write-downs) and returning to a position (or standard) comparable to the bank's original state before the loss event (including restitution payments to third parties). Note that these definitions do not include lost or forgone revenue.

In sum, losses include payments to third parties, write-downs, resolutions, and cost to fix. Losses do not include the cost of controls, preventive action, and quality assurance. Losses also do not usually include investment in upgrades or new systems and processes.

In building up internal loss histories, risk managers must ensure that the boundaries between separate types of risk (e.g., market, credit, and operational risk) are clearly defined so as to avoid double counting.

One of the most frustrating problems for bankers who are trying to record and measure operational risks is the endless number of ways in which any particular risk might be classified in terms of both its nature and its underlying cause. For example, if a loan officer approves a loan contrary to the bank's guidelines (he or she might even have been given a bribe), any loss arising from this action should ideally be classified as an operational failure, not a credit loss. Typically, loans that default because of third-party fraud are classified as loan losses, whereas loans that default because of internal fraud are classified as operational risk losses.

A list of the sources that give rise to the main categories of operational risk exposure should be developed so that a common taxonomy of the drivers of risks can be established.

The new Basel Capital Accord helpfully considers seven loss event types:[2]

1. *Internal fraud.* Losses caused by acts of a type intended to defraud, misappropriate property, or circumvent regulations, the law, or company policy. For example, intentional misreporting of positions, employee theft, and insider trading on an employee's own account.

2. *External fraud.* Losses caused by acts of a third party of a type intended to defraud, misappropriate property, or circumvent the law. For example, robbery, forgery, check kiting, and damage from computer hacking.

3. *Employment practices and workplace safety.* Losses arising from acts inconsistent with employment, health, or safety laws or agreements, from payment of personal injury claims, or from discrimination events. For example, violation of organized labor activities.

4. *Clients, products, and business practices.* Losses arising from an unintentional or negligent failure to meet a professional

---

2. Basel Committee on Banking Supervision, *International Convergence of Capital Measurement and Capital Standards*, A Revised Framework, June 2004.

obligation to specific clients (including fiduciary and suitability requirements), or from the nature or design of a product. For example, misuse of confidential customer information.

5. *Damage to physical assets.* Losses arising from loss or damage to physical assets from natural disaster or other events. For example, terrorism, vandalism, earthquakes, fire, and floods.

6. *Business disruption and system failures.* Losses arising from disruption of business or system failures. For example, hardware and software failures, telecommunication problems, and utility outages.

7. *Execution, delivery, and process management.* Losses arising from failed transaction processing or process management, or from relations with trade counterparties and vendors. For example, data entry errors, collateral management failures, incomplete legal documentation, and unapproved access to client accounts.

WHAT KIND OF OPERATIONAL RISK SHOULD ATTRACT OPERATIONAL RISK CAPITAL?

In most banks, the methodology for translating operational risk into capital is developed by the group responsible for making risk-adjusted return on capital (RAROC) calculations in partnership with the operational risk management group (see Chapter 15).

Mechanisms for attributing capital to operational risk should be risk-based, transparent, scalable, and fair. Specifically, capital requirements should vary directly with levels of verifiable risk and should provide incentives to manage operational risk so as to improve operational decisions and increase the risk-adjusted return on capital.

But it does not make sense to attribute risk capital to all kinds of operational loss, as Figure 13–3 makes clear. To understand this diagram, remember that operational risks can be divided into those losses that are expected and those that are unexpected. Management knows that in the ordinary course of business, certain operational activities will fail. There will be a "normal" amount of operational loss (resulting from error corrections, minor fraud, and so on) that the business is willing to absorb as a cost of doing business. These failures are explicitly or implicitly budgeted for in the annual business plan and are covered by the pricing of the product or service, so we should not try to allocate risk capital against them.

FIGURE   13-3

Distribution of Operational Losses

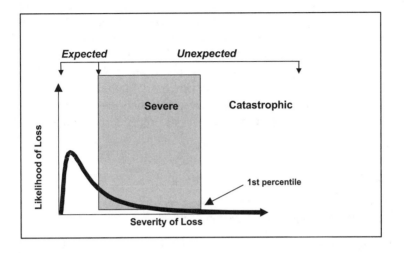

Instead, risk capital makes sense only for unexpected losses, as shown in Figure 13–3. However, as the figure suggests, unexpected failures can themselves be further subdivided into

- *Severe but not catastrophic losses.* Unexpected severe operational failures should be covered by an appropriate allocation of operational risk capital. These losses are covered by the measurement processes described in the following section.
- *Catastrophic losses.* These are the most extreme but also the rarest operational risk events—the kind that can destroy the bank entirely. VaR and RAROC models are not meant to capture catastrophic risk, since they consider potential losses only up to a certain confidence level (say 1 percent), and catastrophic risks are by their very nature extremely rare. Banks may tighten procedures to protect themselves against catastrophic events, or use insurance to hedge catastrophic risk. But risk capital cannot protect a bank against these risks.

Given this, how can we begin to put a number to the severe but not catastrophic risk of operational loss that a bank faces through its business activities?

VaR FOR OPERATIONAL RISK

Operational risk is notoriously difficult to measure. But, in principle at least, the classic loss distribution approach to measuring risk seen in Figure 13–3 can be deployed. This approach corresponds to the Advanced Measurement Approach (AMA) proposed in the new Basel Capital Accord and is based on analytical techniques that are widely used in the insurance industry to measure the financial impact of an operational failure. Box 13–2 reviews the three approaches proposed in the new Basel Capital Accord. Only the AMA is risk-sensitive; the others are somewhat arbitrary and will not produce the right incentives to reduce operational risk.

BOX 13-2

REGULATORY APPROACHES TO OPERATIONAL RISK MODELS

The banking industry's new Basel Capital Accord proposes a spectrum of three increasingly risk-sensitive approaches for measuring operational risk.

BASIC INDICATOR APPROACH

The least risk-sensitive of these approaches is the Basic Indicator Approach, in which capital is a multiple (capital factor = 15 percent) of a single indicator (base), which is the average annual gross income, where positive, over the previous three years for which gross income was positive. The regulators have postulated that gross income serves as a proxy for the scale of operational risk exposure. Gross income is defined as the sum of net interest and noninterest income.

STANDARDIZED APPROACH

The Standardized Approach divides banks' activities into eight lines of business, or LOB_i (see the discussion that follows). Each line of business is then assigned an exposure indicator EI_i, which is, as in the Basic Indicator Approach, the average annual gross income for that line of business, where positive, over the previous three years for which gross income was positive. Each business line is assigned a single multiplier (capital factor β_i) to reflect its relative riskiness. The total capital requirement is defined as the sum of the products of the exposure and the capital factor for each of the N business lines:

(continued on following page)

BOX 13-2 *(Continued)*

$$\text{Capital requirement (OpVaR)} = \sum_{i=1}^{N} EI_i * \beta_i \qquad (13\text{-}1)$$

The Basel Committee has set the betas to the following values:

Business Line	Beta Factor
Corporate finance (β_1)	18%
Trading and sales (β_2)	18%
Retail banking (β_3)	12%
Commercial banking (β_4)	15%
Payment and settlement (β_5)	18%
Agency Services (β_6)	15%
Asset management (β_7)	12%
Retail brokerage (β_8)	12%

ALTERNATIVE STANDARDIZED APPROACH (ASA)

The standardized approach has been criticized because it can lead to double counting for high-default-rate businesses, such as subprime lending. For these activities, the business is hit twice: first, on the credit side, with high regulatory capital because of the high probability of default of the borrowers, and second, on the operational risk side, with high regulatory capital because of high margins (to the extent that expected loss is priced in).

As an alternative to the standardized approach just described, national supervisors can choose to allow banks to employ an alternative standardized approach (ASA). Under the ASA, the operational risk capital framework is the same as for the standardized approach except in the case of two business lines: retail banking and commercial banking. For these business lines, the exposure indicator EI is replaced by

$$EI = m \times LA$$

where $m = 0.035$ and LA is the total outstanding retail loans and advances (non-risk-weighted and gross of provisions), averaged over the past three years.

ADVANCED MEASUREMENT APPROACH (AMA)

Under the AMA, the regulatory capital requirement is the risk measure produced by the bank's internal operational risk model. The loss distribution approach described in the main text is likely to form a core plank of any such model, but individual banks will have to meet some strict qualitative standards before they are allowed by regulators to adopt the AMA approach. The regulators say that any operational risk measurement system must have

(continued on following page)

BOX 13-2 *(Continued)*

certain key features, including "the use of internal data, relevant external data, scenario analysis and factors reflecting the business environment and internal control systems." Under the AMA, the Basel II regulators have not set out exactly how these ingredients should be used. Instead, the regulators say that a bank needs to have a "credible, transparent, well-documented and verifiable approach for weighting these fundamental elements in its overall operational risk measurement system."

The loss distribution approach is analogous to the VaR techniques developed to measure market risk in banking, and therefore we will call it operational value-at-risk (OpVaR). Our aim is to determine the expected loss from operational failures, the worst-case loss at a desired confidence level, the required economic capital for operational risk, and the concentration of operational risk. We should aim to employ the same confidence level as for market- and credit-risk capital.

The firm's activities should be divided into lines of business (LOB), with each line of business being assigned an exposure indicator (EI). The primary foundation for this analysis is the historical experience of operational losses. Where there are no loss data, inputs have to be based on judgment and scenario analysis.

For example, a measure of EI for *legal liability* related to client exposure could be the number of clients multiplied by the average balance per client. The associated probability of an operational risk event (PE) would then be equal to the number of lawsuits divided by the number of clients. The loss given an event (LGE) would equal the average loss divided by the average balance per client.

A measure of EI for *employee liability* could be the number of employees multiplied by the average compensation. The PE for employee liability would then be the number of lawsuits divided by the number of employees, and the LGE would be the average loss divided by the average employee compensation.

A measure of EI for *regulatory, compliance, and taxation penalties* could be the number of accounts multiplied by the balance per account. The PE would then be the number of penalties (including cost to comply) divided by the number of accounts, and the LGE would be the average penalty divided by the average balance per account.

A measure of EI for *loss of or damage to assets* could be the number of physical assets multiplied by their average value. The associated PE would be the number of damage incidents divided by the number of physical assets; the LGE would be the average loss divided by the average value of physical assets.

A measure of EI for *client restitution* could be the number of accounts multiplied by the average balance per account. The PE would then be the number of restitutions divided by the number of accounts, and the LGE would be the average restitution divided by the average balance per account.

A measure of EI for *theft, fraud, and unauthorized activities* could be the number of accounts multiplied by the balance per account (or the number of transactions multiplied by the average value per transaction). The corresponding measures for PE would be the number of frauds divided by the number of accounts or the number of frauds divided by the number of transactions. The respective LGEs would be the average loss divided by the average balance per account or the average loss divided by the average value per transaction.

A measure of EI for *transaction-processing risk* could be the number of transactions multiplied by the average value per transaction. The PE would then be the number of errors divided by the number of transactions. The LGE would be the average loss divided by the average value per transaction.

If we use measures such as these, then we can begin to calculate the OpVaR for the risks associated with particular business lines, as we discuss in detail for credit card fraud in Box 13–3.

BOX 13-3

OpVaR FOR CREDIT CARD FRAUD

To work out the OpVaR number for a bank's risk of credit card fraud, the bank needs first to identify an exposure index. The exposure index (EI) chosen to measure credit card fraud might be the total dollar amount of the transactions, i.e., the product of the number of transactions and the average value of a transaction. For simplicity, let's assume that the average value of a credit card transaction is US$100.[1]

The expected probability of an operational risk event, PE, can be calculated by dividing the number of loss events due to fraud by the number of transactions. If we assume that there are 1.3 fraud loss events per 1,000 transactions, then PE is equal to 0.13 percent.

(continued on following page)

BOX 13-3 *(Continued)*

Assume that the average loss rate given a fraud event (LGE) is US$70. Accordingly, the LGE is calculated by dividing the average loss by the average value of a transaction; in our example, this comes to 70 percent.

Assume further that the statistical worst-case loss set at the appropriate loss tolerance for the industry is US$97 (on an average transaction of US$100) and that the expected loss or loss rate LR is

$$LR = PE \times LGE = 0.13\% \times \$70 = 9 \text{ cents}$$

Figure 13B-1 summarizes the components of our OpVaR calculation for credit card fraud losses.

FIGURE 13B-1

Loss Event Probability plus Loss Severity Gives Rise to Loss Distribution

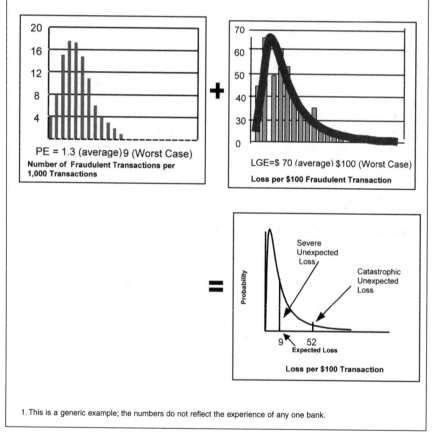

1. This is a generic example; the numbers do not reflect the experience of any one bank.

THE ROLE OF KEY RISK DRIVERS

The OpVaR number for a line of business or bank activity can provide an important indication of that business line or activity's riskiness. But because quantifying operational risk is still in its infancy, and therefore is a very inexact science, most banks make use of a number of techniques to try to understand their levels of exposure.

In any bank activity, there are likely to be a number of identifiable factors that tend to drive operational risk exposure and that are also relatively easy to track. For example, in the case of system risk, these key risk drivers (KRDs) might include the age of computer systems, the percentage of downtime as a result of system failure, and so on. Ideally, KRDs would be entirely objective measures of some risk-related factor in a bank activity. However, we might also think of the audit score awarded to an activity or business line by the bank's internal audit team as a general example of a KRD.

Although KRDs are not a direct measure of operational risk, they are a kind of proxy for it. KRDs can be used to monitor changes in operational risk for each business and for each loss type, providing red flags that alert management of a rise in the likelihood of an operational risk event. Unwelcome changes in KRDs can be used to prompt remedial management action, or tied to incentive schemes so that managers are given an incentive to manage their businesses in a way that is sensitive to operational risk exposures.

KRDs are an important management information tool in themselves. But once they have been established, the bank is likely to want to map changes in a driver to the corresponding changes in OpVaR, so that the KRD and OpVaR approaches offer consistent feedback to the bank's business lines. For example, as shown in Table 13-2, if the KRD score falls by 20 percent, OpVaR might be reduced by 15 percent.

TABLE 13-2

Example of Linkage of a Key Risk Driver to OpVaR

	Δ KRD (%)	Δ Op VaR (%)
	+20	+25
	+10	+15
Base	0	0
	-10	-10
	-20	-15

MITIGATING OPERATIONAL RISK

Many banks and other financial institutions are presently struggling to rationalize how they decide which operational risks should be mitigated, and at what cost.

The process of operational risk assessment should include a review of the likelihood, or frequency, of a particular operational risk, as well as a review of that risk's possible magnitude or severity.

For example, risk managers can publish graphs displaying the potential severity of a risk set against its frequency, as shown in Figure 13–4. This diagram allows managers to visualize the trade-off between severity and likelihood. All risks along the curve exhibit the same expected loss, i.e., likelihood multiplied by severity. Point A5, for example, represents a low likelihood and a medium level of severity. Given an acceptable level of expected loss, management should take appropriate action to mitigate risks located above the curve—here, A7 and A8. A7 has a medium likelihood and medium severity, while A8 has a medium severity but a high likelihood. For both of these risks, the expected level of loss is above the acceptable level.

FIGURE 13-4

Operational Risk Severity versus Frequency

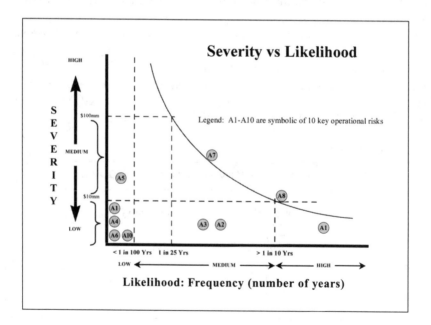

One major factor distinguishes operational risk from both market risk and credit risk. In making risk/reward decisions, a bank can often expect to gain a higher rate of return on its capital by assuming more market risk or credit risk, i.e., with these types of risk, there is a trade-off between risk and expected return. However, a bank cannot generally expect to gain a higher expected return by assuming more operational risk; operational risk destroys value for all claimholders.

This might suggest that banks should always try to minimize or mitigate operational risk. However, trying to reduce exposure to operational risk is costly.

For example, a bank can install better IT systems with more security devices, and also a state-of-the-art backup system. But this investment in new technology is likely to cost the bank millions, or even tens of millions, of dollars. So should the bank spend this amount of money to reduce its exposure? There is often no easy answer to this question. But banks are increasingly looking at the cost of risk capital (as indicated by OpVaR calculations) when assessing such operational risk mitigation decisions. They also compare the economic benefits and costs of many different kinds of risk mitigants, from system investments to risk capital to insurance.

INSURING AGAINST OPERATIONAL RISK

Well before banks began to develop ways of measuring operational risks, they employed insurance contracts to mitigate the effects of key operational risk events. It is common for a bank to purchase insurance to protect itself from large single losses arising from acts of employee dishonesty (e.g., fictitious loans or unauthorized activities), robbery and theft, loans made against counterfeit securities, and various forms of computer crime.

Insurance protection for low-probability but highly severe losses such as these is available through contractually written insuring agreements included in an insurance vehicle known as the "financial institution bond and computer crime policy." Policies are also available in the insurance marketplace for catastrophic exposures associated with lawsuits (e.g., liability exposures arising from allegations of misrepresentation, breach of trust and fiduciary duty, or negligence) and for property damage resulting from major disasters such as fire or earthquake.

However, in essence, insurance is a mechanism for pooling and transferring common loss exposures within the industry or across economies. The availability of insurance for specific risks therefore depends on the ability of an insurer or group of insurers to generate sufficient premium volume and an adequate dispersion of risk to "make a market" and enable them to take on the risk of others. It also depends upon the insurer's being able to avoid the problem of *moral hazard*; that is, the insurer needs to make sure that the insured institution retains a strong interest in preventing any costly event. As a result, limits of up to US$500/600 million per loss occurrence for large financial institutions are common, and banks often have to pay a "first loss" amount on operational risk insurance.

There also remains the danger that the insurance company will fail to pay out on an insurance policy that the bank is depending on for protection. The bank's overall methodology for operational risk measurement and management needs to capture, through discounts and haircuts in the amount of insurance recognition, residual risks such as the remaining life of the insurance policy (e.g., less than one year), chance of policy cancellation and nonrenewal, uncertainty of payment, and mismatches in coverage of insurance policies.

In devising the regulatory capital charge for operational risks under the new Basel Accord, one of the most contentious points proved to be the extent to which regulators will acknowledge the offsetting effects of insurance on a bank's operational risks. The most advanced methodology put forward by the regulators (AMA) will recognize the risk-mitigation impact of insurance in the measures of operational risk used for minimum regulatory capital requirements. But the benefit will be limited to 20 percent of the total operational capital charge.

Many in the banking and insurance industry believe that the 20 percent limitation is a rather conservative reflection of the risk mitigation offered by operational risk insurance. Even so, the regulators' stance underlines the fact that insurance is now an important weapon for banks to examine. The insurance industry has a significant opportunity to tailor new contracts to capitalize on the Basel II rules. Nevertheless, insurance cannot offer a complete answer to the problem of operational risk, since it is simply one weapon in an armory that also must contain a commitment to best-practice internal controls, operational risk measurement, and risk capital.

CONCLUSION

The developments discussed in this chapter are helping institutions to select the appropriate operational risk model and to manage their portfolios of operational risk more effectively. Increasingly, an institution will be able to gain a competitive advantage by monitoring and managing its operational risks on a global basis, although in order to achieve this, it is likely to have to confront some fundamental infrastructure issues.

Measuring operational risk in absolute terms is important, but it is still work in progress at an industry level. A more basic management objective is simply to make operational risk increasingly transparent when the bank is taking key decisions. For example, the approaches we've described in this chapter can be used to answer these key questions more clearly and explicitly:

- What is our largest operational risk in broad terms?
- Might the risk be large enough to threaten our solvency?
- What drives the risk?
- How is the risk changing over time?
- What risks are on the horizon?
- How does our risk level compare to that of our peer group?

Another obvious objective is to provide better management of operational risk through specific action plans and rigorous implementation schedules. All too often, industry inquiries following an operational risk disaster, such as a rogue trader incident, reveal a trail of red flags leading up to the event. The trail often begins months or even years before the loss incident itself, and the red flags often include smaller losses with the same cause, "near misses" that should have alerted the bank to the risk of a large loss, or concerns raised by auditors or regulators that were not properly addressed by management.

Operational risk should be managed as a partnership between business units, business infrastructure groups, and corporate governance units such as internal audit and risk management. To this end, senior management must foster a risk-aware business culture. How personnel behaves is ultimately dependent on how senior management select, train, and reward them.

Arguably the greatest single challenge for senior management is to harmonize the behavior patterns of business units, infrastructure units, corporate governance units, internal audit, and risk management to create an environment in which all sides "sink or swim" together in terms of managing operational risk.

CHAPTER 14

Model Risk

Market prices are normally the best indicator of the value of an asset. However, in the absence of liquid markets and price discovery mechanisms, theoretical valuation models have to be used to value (or "mark-to-model") financial positions. Models are also used to assess risk exposure and to derive an appropriate hedging strategy, as we've discussed in detail in earlier chapters. All this leads to a fast-emerging type of risk in the financial industry: *model risk*.

For simple instruments, such as stocks and straight bonds, model risk is relatively insignificant. It becomes a compelling issue, however, for institutions that trade over-the-counter (OTC) exotic derivative products and for institutions that execute complex arbitrage strategies.

Since 1973, with the publication of the Black-Scholes and Merton option-pricing models, there has been a relentless increase in the complexity of valuation theories used to support financial innovations such as caps, floors, swaptions, spread options, credit derivatives, and other exotic derivative instruments—and a parallel rise in the threat from model risk.

Today, we can liken the trader and the risk manager of a financial institution to the pilot and copilot of a plane that is almost totally dependent upon instruments to land safely. Any error in the electronics on board combined with one heavy storm will be fatal to the plane. Computers are now so powerful that there is a temptation to develop ever more complex models that are less and less understood by management. The technology that is available has substantially increased the chance of creating losses (as well as profits). In the financial world, not a single market crisis passes (e.g., the crisis in the Asian markets in the late 1990s) without several large trading losses that are the direct result of a faulty model appearing in the financial media. Some of these losses are so large that they force institutions to disappear, to restructure, or to accept a takeover by a rival firm.

HOW WIDESPREAD A PROBLEM IS MODEL RISK?

The short answer is that in a modern financial system, model risk is everywhere. A Bank of England survey conducted in 1997 highlighted the variation in models that existed among 40 major derivative-trading firms based in London. Vanilla foreign exchange instruments showed a relatively low level of variation in both value and sensitivities. However, some of the exotic derivatives displayed large variations not only in value, but also in some of the sensitivity measures: 10 to 20 percent for swaptions and up to 60 percent for exotic foreign exchange instruments. (The authors of this book know from experience that even within the same financial institution, different groups might come up with different valuations for similar instruments.)

In another study in the same year, Marshall and Siegel (1997) presented an identical asset portfolio to a number of commercial vendors of software for value-at-risk (VaR) calculations.[1] Each was asked to use the same volatility inputs, obtained from JP Morgan's RiskMetrics, and to report the aggregate VaR for the entire portfolio and the VaR figure for each type of instrument (such as swaps, caps and floors, and swaptions). The variation among vendors was striking, given that in this case they were supposed to be analyzing the same position (in relatively simple instruments), using the same methodology, and using the same market parameter values. For the whole portfolio, the estimates ranged from $3.8 million to $6.1 million, and for the portion containing options, the VaR estimates varied from $747,000 to $2,100,000.

It is therefore not surprising that trading firms experience substantial trading losses in stormy market environments, and sometimes even when things are calm. While most of these losses are the result of an accident or carelessness, there is also the danger that a trader or other interested party might knowingly make a "mistake" that offers him or her beneficial results (in the short term, at least). Because models are used for valuation, a faulty model can make a strategy seem very profitable on paper, even though the bank is incurring economic losses—perhaps for several years. By the time the fault is corrected, a big hole might have appeared underneath the bank's accounts

---

1. C. Marshall and M. Siegel, "Value-at-Risk: Implementing a Risk Measurement Standard," Journal of Derivatives 4(3), 1997, pp. 91-111.

In the rest of this chapter we'll look more closely at the main causes of model risk:

- *Model error.* The model might contain mathematical errors or, more likely, be based on simplifying assumptions that are misleading or inappropriate.
- *Implementing a model wrongly.* The model might be implemented wrongly, either by accident or as part of a deliberate fraud.

Model Error

Derivatives trading depends heavily on mathematical models that make use of complex equations and advanced mathematics. In the simplest sense, a model is incorrect if there are mistakes in the analytical solution (in the set of equations, or in the solution of a system of equations).

But a model is also said to be incorrect if it is based on wrong assumptions about the underlying asset price process—and this is perhaps both a more common and a more dangerous risk. The history of the financial industry is littered with examples of trading strategies based on shaky assumptions (see Box 14-1), and some model risks are really just a

B O X   1 4 - 1

WRONG ASSUMPTIONS—THE NIEDERHOFFER PUT OPTIONS EXAMPLE

A well-established hedge fund run by Victor Niederhoffer, a star trader on Wall Street, was wiped out in November 1997.[1] The fund had been writing a large quantity of naked (i.e., uncovered), deeply out-of-the-money put options on the S&P 500 stock index, and collecting small amounts of option premium in return. Niederhoffer's trading strategy was based on the premise that the market would never drop by more than 5 percent on a given day. On October 27, 1997, the stock market fell by more than 7 percent in reaction to the crisis brewing in the Asian markets. (Such a fall would be virtually impossible if market returns were indeed normally distributed.) Liquidity, or rather the disappearance of liquidity after the market shock, brought the fund to its knees, and it found itself unable to meet margin calls for more than $50 million. As a consequence, Niederhoffer's brokers liquidated the positions at fire-sale prices, and the entire equity of the fund was lost.

1. See *Derivatives Strategy* 3(1), 1998, pp.38–39.

formalization of this kind of mistake. For example, a model of bond pricing might be based on a flat and fixed term structure, at a time when the actual term structure of interest rates is steep and unstable.

The most frequent error in model building is to assume that the distribution of the underlying asset is stationary (i.e., unchanging), when, in fact, it changes over time. The case of volatility is particularly striking. Derivatives practitioners know very well that volatility is not constant. The ideal solution would be to acknowledge that volatility is stochastic and to develop an option-pricing model that is consistent with this, but option valuation models become difficult computationally when any sort of stochastic volatility is included. (Moreover, introducing new unobservable parameters associated with the volatility process into the valuation model makes the estimation problem even more severe.)

Instead, derivative practitioners find themselves engaged in a continual struggle to find the best compromise between complexity (to better represent reality) and simplicity (to improve the tractability of their modeling).

While traders know that they are making simplifying assumptions about price behavior, it is not easy for them (or for risk managers) to assess the impact of this kind of simplifying assumption on any given position or trading strategy. For example, practitioners often assume that rates of return are normally distributed, i.e., that they have a classic "bell-shaped" distribution. However, empirical evidence points to the existence of "fat tails" in distributions; in these distributions, unlikely events are in fact much more common than would be the case if the distribution were normally distributed. Where possible, therefore, empirical distributions rather than theoretical distributions should be used to help alleviate the danger of an unrecognized fat tail. However, such fat tails are not accounted for in the theoretical distributions that lie behind many classic models, such as the Black-Scholes option-pricing model.

Another way to oversimplify a model is to underestimate the number of risk factors that it must take into account. For simple vanilla investment products, such as a callable bond, a one-factor term structure model, where the factor represents the spot short-term rate, may be enough to produce accurate prices and hedge ratios. For more complex products, such as spread options or exotic structures, a two- or three-factor model may be required, where the factors are, for example, the spot short-term and long-term rates for a two-factor model.

Another problem is that models are almost always derived under the assumption that perfect capital markets exist. In reality, many markets, especially those in less-developed countries, are far from perfect. Meanwhile, even in developed markets, over-the-counter derivative products are not traded publicly and usually cannot be perfectly hedged.

As a practical example, most derivative-pricing models are based on the assumption that a delta-neutral hedging strategy can be put in place for the instruments in question, i.e., that the risk of holding a derivative can be continually offset by holding the underlying asset in an appropriate proportion (hedge ratio). In practice, a delta-neutral hedge of an option against its underlying asset is far from being completely risk-free, and keeping such a position delta-neutral over time often requires a very active rebalancing strategy. Banks rarely attempt the continuous rebalancing that pricing models assume. For one thing, the theoretical strategy implies the execution of an enormous number of transactions, and trading costs are too large for this to be feasible. Nor is continuous trading possible, even disregarding transactions costs: markets close at night, national holidays, and on weekends.

Liquidity, or rather the absence of liquidity, may also be a major source of model risk. Models assume that the underlying asset can be traded long or short at current market prices, and that prices will not change dramatically when the trade is executed.

A model can be found to be mathematically correct and generally useful, and yet be misapplied to a given situation. For example, some term structure models that are widely used by practitioners to value fixed-income instruments depend upon the assumption that forward rates are "log normal," that is, that their rates of change are normally distributed. This model seems to perform relatively well when applied to most of the world's markets—except for Japan. In recent years, Japanese markets have been characterized by very low interest rates, for which different statistical tools (e.g., Gaussian and square root models) for interest rates work much better.

In the same way, models that are safe to use for certain kinds of product might not perform well at all on subtly different instruments. Many OTC products have options embedded within them that are ignored in the standard option-pricing model. For example, using a model to value warrants may yield biased results if the warrant is also extendable. Other common errors include using the Black-Scholes option-valuation model to price equity options, while adjusting for dividends by subtracting their present value from the stock price. This ignores the fact that the options can be exercised early. Applying the wrong model is also easy if the researcher is not clear about whether the underlying instrument is a primary asset or is itself a contingent asset on another underlying asset (or basket of assets).

Implementing a Model Wrongly

Even if a model is correct and is being used to tackle an appropriate problem, there remains the danger that it will be wrongly implemented. With complicated models that require extensive programming, there is always a chance that a programming "bug" may affect the output of the model. Some implementations rely on numerical techniques that exhibit inherent approximation errors and limited ranges of validity. Many programs that seem error-free have been tested only under normal conditions, and so may be error-prone in extreme cases and conditions.

In models that require a Monte Carlo simulation, large inaccuracies in prices and hedge ratios can creep in if not enough simulation runs or time steps are implemented. In this case, the model might be right, and the data might be accurate, but the results might still be wrong if the computation process is not given the time it needs.

For models evaluating complex derivatives, data are collected from many different sources. The implicit assumption is that for each time period, the data for all relevant assets and rates pertain to exactly the same time instant, and thus reflect simultaneous prices. Using nonsimultaneous price inputs may be necessary for practical reasons, but, again, it can lead to wrong pricing.

When implementing a pricing model, statistical tools are used to estimate model parameters such as volatilities and correlations. An important question, then, is, how frequently should input parameters be refreshed? Should the adjustment be made on a periodic basis, or should it be triggered by an important economic event? Similarly, should parameters be adjusted according to qualitative judgments, or should these adjustments be based purely on statistics? The statistical approach is bound to be in some sense "backward looking," while a human adjustment can be forward looking, that is, it can take into account a personal assessment of likely future developments in the relevant markets. All statistical estimators are subject to estimation errors involving the inputs to the pricing model. A major problem in the estimation procedure is the treatment of "outliers," or extreme observations. Are the outliers really outliers, in the sense that they do not reflect the true distribution? Or are they important observations that should not be dismissed? The results of the estimation procedure will be vastly different depending on how such observations are treated. Each bank, or even each trading desk within a bank, may use a different estimation procedure to estimate the model parameters. Some may use daily closing prices, while others may use transaction data. Whether the researcher uses calendar time (i.e., the actual number of days elapsed), trading time (i.e., the number of days on which the underlying instrument is traded), or economic time (i.e., the number of days during which significant economic events take place) affects the calculation.

Finally, the quality of a model depends heavily on the accuracy of the inputs and parameter values that feed the model. It's easy for traders to make mistakes (Box 14-2). This is particularly true in the case of relatively new markets, where best-practice procedures and controls are still evolving. The old adage "garbage in, garbage out" should never be forgotten when implementing models that require the estimation of several parameters. Volatilities and correlations are the hardest input parameters to judge accurately. For example, an option's strike price and maturity are fixed, and asset prices and interest rates can easily be observed directly in the market—but volatilities and correlations must be forecast. This gives rise to many opportunities for both genuine mistakes and deliberate tampering that can be countered only through robust control procedures and independent vetting (see Box 14-3).

The most frequent problems in estimating values, on the one hand, and assessing the potential errors in valuation, on the other hand, are

- *Inaccurate data.* Most financial institutions use internal data sources as well as external databases. The responsibility for data accuracy is often not clearly assigned. It is therefore very common to find data errors that can significantly affect the estimated parameters.

- *Inappropriate length of sampling period.* Adding more observations improves the power of statistical tests and tends to reduce the estimation errors. But, the longer the sampling period, the more weight is given to potentially stale and obsolete information. Especially in dynamically changing financial markets, "old" data can become irrelevant and may introduce noise into the estimation process.

- *Problems with liquidity and the bid/ask spread.* In some markets, a robust market price does not exist. The gap between the bid and ask prices may be large enough to complicate the process of finding a single value. Choices made about the price data at the time of data selection can have a major impact on the output of the model.

HOW CAN WE MITIGATE MODEL RISK?

One important way to mitigate model risk is to invest in research to improve models and to develop better statistical tools, either internally at the bank or externally at a university (or at an analytically oriented consulting organization).

An even more vital way of reducing model risk is to establish a process for independent vetting of how models are both selected and constructed. This should be complemented by independent oversight of the profit and loss (P&L) calculation.

The role of vetting is to offer assurance to the firm's management that any model for the valuation of a given security proposed by, say, a trading desk is reasonable. In other words, it provides assurance that the model offers a reasonable representation of how the market itself values

---

B O X   1 4 - 2

WRONG RATE INPUT—THE MERRILL LYNCH EXAMPLE

In the mid 1970s, the Wall Street investment firm Merrill Lynch began to break down (or "strip") 30-year government bonds into their building-block components: coupon annuities and zero-coupon principal payments. It then offered these components to the market as "interest only" (IO) and "principal only" (PO) instruments.

Merrill used the 30-year par yield to price the IOs and the POs. The par yield curve was higher than the annuity yield curve, but lower than the zero-coupon curve. Therefore, by using the par rate rather than the annuity rate, the firm undervalued the IOs, and by using the par rate rather than the zero-coupon rate it overvalued the POs, although the sum of the two valuations did add up to the bond's true value. Merrill sold $600 million of the undervalued IOs and none of the overvalued POs.

Meanwhile, the Merrill Lynch trader hedged the 30-year bonds using a duration of approximately 13 years. This was the correct decision for the bonds as long as the entire bond remained intact on the books of Merrill Lynch. However, even after all the IO components of the bonds were sold, the trader maintained the hedge at 13 years, whereas the correct duration of a 30-year PO instrument is 30 years. When interest rates rose, the firm incurred severe losses. In combination with the misvaluations, this hedging mistake resulted in the firm's booking a $70 million loss.

B O X   1 4 - 3

IMPLEMENTATION RISK—THE NATWEST OPTION PRICING EXAMPLE

In 1997 it was discovered that certain traders at NatWest in London had been selling caps and swaptions in sterling and deutsche marks at the wrong price since late 1994, and had been hedging their short position by buying options priced at too high a volatility vis-à-vis the volatility implied by the swaption premiums. When these discontinuities, especially for long maturities, were removed from the volatility curves in 1997, the downward revisions of NatWest's portfolio value resulted in a loss of $80 million. For risk managers around the world, verifying volatility estimates and, more generally, all the other principal inputs to a pricing model that are handed to them by a trader is a critical issue.

---

the instrument, and that the model has been implemented correctly. Vetting should consist of the following phases:

1. *Documentation.* The vetting team should ask for full documentation of the model, including both the assumptions underlying the model and its mathematical expression. This should be independent of any particular implementation, such as a spreadsheet or a C++ computer code, and should include:
   - The term sheet or, equivalently, a complete description of the transaction.
   - A mathematical statement of the model, which should include:
     - An explicit statement of all the components of the model: stochastic variables and their processes, parameters, equations, and so on.
     - The payoff function and/or any pricing algorithm for complex structured deals.
     - The calibration procedure for the model parameters.
     - The hedge ratios/sensitivities.
   - Implementation features, i.e., inputs, outputs, and numerical methods employed.
   - A working version of the implementation.

2. *Soundness of model.* An indepedent model vetter needs to verify that the mathematical model is a reasonable representation of the instrument that is being valued. For example, the manager might reasonably accept the use of a particular model (e.g., the Black model) for valuing a short-term option on a long-maturity

bond, but reject (without even looking at the computer code) the use of the same model to value a two-year option on a three-year bond. At this stage, the risk manager should concentrate on the finance aspects and not become overly focused on the mathematics.

3. *Independent access to financial rates.* The model vetter should check that the bank's middle office has independent access to an independent market-risk management financial rates database (to facilitate independent parameter estimation).

4. *Benchmark modeling.* The model vetter should develop a benchmark model based on the assumptions that are being made and on the specifications of the deal. Here, the model vetter may use a different implementation from the implementation that is being proposed. A proposed analytical model can be tested against a numerical approximation technique or against a simulation approach. (For example, if the model to be vetted is based on a "tree" implementation, one may instead rely on the partial differential equation approach and use the finite-element technique to derive the numerical results.) Compare the results of the benchmark test with those of the proposed model.

5. *Health-check and stress-test the model.* Also, make sure that the model possesses the basic properties that all derivatives models should possess, such as put-call parity and other nonarbitrage conditions. Finally, the vetter should stress-test the model. The model can be stress-tested by looking at some limit scenario in order to identify the range of parameter values for which the model provides accurate pricing. This is especially important for implementations that rely on numerical techniques.

6. *Build a formal treatment of model risk into the overall risk management procedures, and periodically reevaluate models.* Also, reestimate parameters using best-practice statistical procedures. Experience shows that simple, but robust models tend to work better than more ambitious, but fragile models. It is essential to monitor and control model performance over time.

LTCM AND MODEL RISK: HOW A HEDGE BECAME INEFFECTIVE DURING A LIQUIDITY CRISIS

The failure of the hedge fund Long Term Capital Management (LTCM) in September 1998 provides the classic example of model risk in the financial industry. The failure shocked the financial community, not only because of the reputation of LTCM's principals (including two Nobel laureates along with seasoned and star traders from the legendary bond arbitrage desk at Salomon Brothers), but also because of the unprecedented amounts of capital represented by the firm's positions. LTCM employed $125 billion in total assets with an equity base (before the crisis) of $4.8 billion, that is, it had a leverage ratio of more than 25.

LTCM's crisis was triggered on August 17, 1998, when Russia devalued the ruble and declared a debt moratorium. LTCM's portfolio value fell 44 percent, giving it a year-to-date decline of 52 percent (a loss of almost $2 billion). The hedge fund's positions in the market were so great that the Federal Reserve Bank of New York took the unprecedented step of facilitating a bailout of the fund to avoid any risk of a meltdown in the world markets.

How could a market event, however serious, have affected LTCM so badly? LTCM's arbitrage strategy was based on "market-neutral" or "relative-value" trading, which involves buying one instrument and simultaneously selling another. These trades are designed to make money whether prices rise or fall, as long as the spread between the two positions moves in the appropriate direction.

LTCM, like other hedge funds in early 1998, had positioned its portfolios on the basis of particular bets, albeit bets that seemed pretty safe at first sight. For example, LTCM bet that the spreads between corporate bonds and government Treasuries in different countries, such as the United States and the United Kingdom, were too large and would eventually return to their normal range (as they had always done before). Such strategies are based on intensive empirical research and advanced financial modeling. A trade to capture the relative-value opportunities uncovered by such modeling might consist of buying corporate bonds and selling the relevant government bonds short. Other positions involved betting on convergence in the key European bond markets by selling German government bonds against the sovereign debt of other countries, such as Spain and Italy, which were due to sign up for European economic and monetary union (EMU). When the spread in yields narrows, such positions make money whether the price level goes up or down.

The return on such apparently low-risk strategies tends to be quite small, and it becomes smaller and smaller as more players enter the market to take advantage of the "opportunity." As a result, hedge funds are obliged to use leverage aggressively to boost their absolute performance. LTCM, for example, was trying to earn a 1 percent return on its assets, leveraged 25 times, which would yield a 25 percent return. LTCM was able to obtain huge loans, collateralized by the bonds that it had invested in, because its strategy was widely viewed as safe by the institutions that were its lenders.

LTCM failed because both its trading models and its risk management models failed to anticipate the vicious circle of losses during an extreme crisis when volatilities rose dramatically, correlations between markets and instruments became closer to 1, and liquidity dried up. Let us take a closer look at both of these aspects.

Trading Models

Price relationships that hold during normal market conditions tend to collapse during market crises such as that of August 1998. The crisis in Russia made many investors fear that other nations might follow Russia's lead and that there would be a general dislocation of the financial markets. This triggered a "flight to quality" or "flight to safety," as investors exited the emerging markets and any risky security, and fled to the liquid and safe haven of the U.S. and German government bond markets.

These trends ultimately pushed the yield of U.S. 30-year government bonds to as low as 5 percent and caused the price of riskier bonds, including those of emerging markets, U.S. mortgage-backed securities, high-yield bonds, and even investment-grade corporate bonds, to sink. The same phenomena affected the relative yields of German and Italian bonds: yields started to diverge because German bonds were regarded as safer than Italian bonds. Credit spreads widened as prices for Treasury bonds increased and prices for lower-quality bonds sank—again, in an unprecedented fashion.

When spreads widened, the gains that a trader might make on short positions were not always enough to offset the losses on the long positions. Lenders therefore started to demand more collateral, forcing many hedge funds either to abandon their arbitrage plays or to raise money for the margin calls by selling other holdings at fire-sale prices. Most markets around the world, especially emerging markets, became less liquid and highly volatile.

Most of the losses incurred by LTCM were the consequence of the breakdown of the correlation and volatility patterns that had been observed in the past. Several mechanisms came into play during this market turmoil as a consequence of the "flight to quality" and the disappearance of liquidity:

1. Interest rates on Treasuries and stock prices fell in tandem, because investors deserted the stock market and purchased U.S. government bonds in a flight to quality. In normal markets, stock returns and interest rates are negatively correlated, i.e., when interest rates fall, stock prices rise.

2. When liquidity dries up in many markets simultaneously, it becomes impossible to unwind positions. Portfolios that seem to be well diversified across markets start to behave as if they were highly concentrated in a single market, and market-neutral positions become directionally exposed (usually to the wrong side of the market).

For all these reasons, LTCM found itself losing money on many of its trading positions and looked in danger of becoming insolvent. The fact that the fund was highly leveraged contributed to its problems. First, LTCM ran out of cash and was unable to meet margin calls in a timely fashion. Second, with excessive leverage amplifying its funding risk, LTCM was obliged to liquidate securities at fire-sale prices. At some point, the firm's liabilities threatened to exceed its assets; to keep the firm solvent, a number of major financial institutions were obliged to inject considerable sums.

Risk Measurement Models
and Stress Testing

Risk control at LTCM relied on a VaR model. As discussed in Chapter 8, VaR represents the worst-case loss that can result from a firm's portfolio under normal market conditions, at a given confidence level, and over a given period of time. By themselves, a $1 trillion notional amount, or even a figure of $125 billion in assets, does not say much about the levels of risk that the LTCM positions involved. What matters is the overall volatility of the marked-to-market value of the fund, that is, its VaR.

According to LTCM, the fund was structured so that the risk of investing in it should have been no greater than that of investing in the S&P 500. Based on the volatility of the S&P, and with equity of $4.7 billion, the expected daily volatility of LTCM should have been $44 million, and its 10-day VaR should have been approximately $320 million (at a confidence level of 99 percent). This number is calculated under the assumption that the portfolio returns are normally distributed.

However, some assumptions that are usual in regulatory VaR calculations are not realistic for a hedge fund:

1. The time horizon for economic capital should be the time it takes to raise new capital or the period of time over which a crisis scenario will unfold. Based on the experience of LTCM, 10 days is clearly too short a time horizon for the derivation of hedge fund VaR.
2. Liquidity risk is not factored into traditional static VaR models. VaR models assume that normal market conditions prevail and that these exhibit perfect liquidity.
3. Correlation and volatility risks can be captured only through stress testing. This was probably the weakest point of LTCM's VaR system.

After the crisis, William McDonough, president of the Federal Reserve Bank of New York, told the Committee on Banking and Financial Services of the U.S. House of Representatives:

> We recognize that stress testing is a developing discipline, but it is clear that adequate testing was not done with respect to the financial conditions that precipitated Long-Term Capital's problems. Effective risk management in a financial institution requires not only modeling, but models that can test the full range of financial transactions across all kinds of adverse market developments.

Instead of the envisaged $44 million daily volatility, the fund eventually experienced a $100 million and higher daily volatility. While the 10-day VaR was approximately $320 million, LTCM suffered losses of over $1 billion from mid-August. LTCM's risk modeling had let it down.

CONCLUSION

Models are an inevitable feature of modern finance, and model risk is inherent in the use of models. The most important thing is to be aware of the dangers. Firms must avoid placing undue faith in model values, and must hunt down all the possible sources of inaccuracy in a model. In particular, they must learn to think through situations in which the failure of a model might have a significant impact.

In this chapter, we've stressed the technical elements of model risk, but we should also be wary of the human factor in model risk losses. Large trading profits tend to lead to large bonuses for senior managers, and this creates an incentive for these managers to believe the traders who are reporting the profits (rather than the risk managers or other critics who might be questioning the reported profits). Often, traders use their expertise in formal pricing models to confound any internal critics, or they may claim to have some sort of informal but profound insight into how markets behave. The psychology of this behavior is such that we are tempted to call it the "Tinkerbell" phenomenon, after the scene in *Peter Pan* in which the children in the audience shout, "I believe, I believe" in order to revive the poisoned fairy Tinkerbell (see Box 14-4). The antidote is for senior managers to approach any model that seems to record or deliver above-market returns with a healthy skepticism, to insist that models are made transparent, and to make sure that all models are independently vetted.

B O X   1 4 - 4

"TINKERBELL RISK"—BARINGS, 1995

The infamous destruction of Barings Bank by Nick Leeson in 1995 shows why large profits should act as a red flag for risk—and should prompt as much curiosity as happiness. After moving to Singapore in June 1993 as local head of operations, Leeson started to execute trades for Barings' clients on Simex. He then received permission to implement an arbitrage strategy that was designed to exploit any differences between the prices for the Nikkei futures contract in Singapore and Osaka. Since he still controlled the Singapore back office, he was able to use a reconciliation account, #88888 (which he arranged to be excluded from the reports sent to London), to convert an actual loss of £200 million in 1994 into a sizable reported profit.

Leeson's reported profit was so large that it attracted the attention of Barings' London-based risk controllers in late 1994. However, their enquiries to his superiors were rebuffed with the comment, "Barings had a unique ability to exploit this arbitrage." After he reported a £10 million profit for one week in January 1995, risk control concerns were again summarily dismissed with the comment, "Nick is a turbo-arbitrageur." Simple calculations show that, in order to make this profit, Leeson would have had to trade more than four times the total volume in the Nikkei futures contract in both Singapore and Osaka that week.

The main lesson drawn from the Barings collapse was that trading and control should be separated: reporting and monitoring of positions and risks must be separated from trading. But a more general conclusion is that great success stories should always be independently checked and monitored tightly, to verify that the reported profits are for real—and continue to be for real.

CHAPTER 15

Risk Capital Attribution and Risk-Adjusted Performance Measurement

Our final chapter takes a look at the purpose of risk capital, and at how risk capital can be attributed to business lines as part of a risk-adjusted performance measurement system. This problem brings together many of the themes we've discussed earlier in the book and represents a key challenge for financial institutions around the world today. Only by forging a connection between risk measurement, risk capital, risk-based pricing, and performance measurement can firms ensure that the decisions they take reflect the interests of stakeholders such as bondholders and shareholders.

WHAT PURPOSE DOES RISK CAPITAL SERVE?

Risk capital is the cushion that provides protection against the various risks inherent in a corporation's business, so that the firm can maintain its financial integrity and remain a going concern even in the event of a near-catastrophic "worst-case" scenario. Risk capital gives essential confidence to the corporation's stakeholders, such as suppliers, clients, and lenders (for an industrial firm), or claimholders, such as depositors and counterparties in financial transactions (for a financial institution).

In banking, risk capital is also often called *economic capital*, and in most instances the generally accepted convention is that risk capital and economic capital are identical (although later in this chapter we introduce a slight wrinkle by defining economic capital as risk capital plus strategic capital).

We should be careful not to confuse the concept of risk capital, which is intended to capture the economic realities of the risks a firm runs, and regulatory capital. Regulatory capital performs something of the same function as risk capital in the regulators' eyes. However, because it is calculated according to a set of industrywide rules and formulas as well as is intended to set only a *minimum* required level of capital adequacy, it rarely succeeds in capturing the true level of risk in a firm. The gap between a firm's regulatory capital and its risk capital can therefore be quite wide.

Risk capital measurement is based on the same concepts as the value-at-risk (VaR) calculation methodology that we discussed in Chapter 7. Indeed, risk capital numbers are often derived from sophisticated internal VaR models. However, the choice of the confidence level and risk time horizon when using VaR to calculate risk capital are key policy parameters that should be set by senior management (or the senior risk management committee). Usually, these decisions should be endorsed by the board.

For risk capital to fulfill its purpose, it must be calculated in such a way that the institution can absorb unexpected losses up to a level of confidence in line with the requirements of the firm's various stakeholders. No firm can offer its stakeholders a 100 percent guarantee (or confidence level) that it holds enough risk capital to ride out any eventuality. Instead, risk capital is calculated at a confidence level set at less than 100 percent— say, 99.9 percent for a firm with conservative stakeholders. This means that there is a probability of around 1/10 of 1 percent that actual losses will exceed the amount of risk capital set aside by the firm over the given time horizon (generally one year). The exact choice of confidence level is typically associated with some target credit rating from a rating agency such as Moody's or Standard & Poor's, as these ratings are themselves explicitly associated with a likelihood of default.

EMERGING USES OF RISK CAPITAL NUMBERS

Risk capital is traditionally used to answer the question, "How much capital is required for our firm to remain solvent, given our risky activities?" As soon as a firm can answer this question, it can move on to solve many other management problems. Recently, therefore, risk capital numbers have been used to answer more and more questions, particularly in banks and other financial institutions. (Box 15–1 explains why risk-based calculations are so important for financial institutions.) These new uses include

- *Performance measurement and incentive compensation at the firm, business unit, and individual levels.* Once risk capital has been calculated, it can be plugged into risk-based capital attribution systems, often grouped together under the acronyms RAPM (risk-adjusted performance measurement) or RAROC (risk-adjusted return on capital). These systems, a key focus of this chapter, provide a uniform risk-adjusted measure of performance of various businesses that both management and external stakeholders can use to compare the economic profitability, as opposed to the accounting profitability (such as return on book equity). In turn, RAROC numbers can be used as part of scorecards to compensate the senior management of particular business lines, as well as the infrastructure group, for their contribution to shareholder value.

- *Active portfolio management for entry/exit decisions.* The decision to enter or exit a particular business should be based on both risk-adjusted performance measurement and the "risk diversification effect" of the decision. For example, a firm that is focused on corporate lending in a particular region is likely to find that its returns fluctuate in accordance with that region's business cycle. Ideally, the firm might diversify its business geographically or in terms of business activity. Capital management decisions seek an answer to the question, "How much value will be created if the decision is taken to allocate resources to a new or existing business, or alternatively to close down an activity?"

- *Pricing transactions.* Risk capital numbers can be used to calculate risk-based pricing for individual transactions. Risk-based pricing is attractive because it ensures that a firm is compensated for the economic risk generated by a transaction. For example, common sense tells us that a loan to a non-investment-grade firm that is in relatively fragile financial condition must be priced higher than a loan to an investment-grade firm. However, the *amount* of the differential can be determined only by working out the amount of expected loss and the cost of the risk capital that has to be set aside for each transaction. Increasingly, trading and corporate loan desks in banks are relying on the "marginal economic capital requirement" component in the RAROC calculation to price deals in advance—and to decide whether those deals will increase shareholder value rather than simply add to the volume of transactions.

One problem is that a single measure of risk capital cannot accommodate the four different purposes that we have just described. We'll look at the solution to this later on.

BOX 15-1

WHY IS ECONOMIC CAPITAL SO IMPORTANT TO FINANCIAL INSTITUTIONS?

Allocating risk capital using new economic capital approaches is important for financial institutions for at least four reasons.

First, capital is primarily used in a financial institution not only to provide funding for investments (as for a manufacturing corporation), but also to absorb risk. The fundamental reason for this is that financial institutions can leverage themselves to a much higher degree than other corporations at a much lower cost without raising equity, by means of taking retail deposits or issuing debt securities. (Their debt-to-equity ratio might be as high as 20 to 1, compared to perhaps 2 to 1 for an industrial corporation.) Moreover, many activities undertaken by financial institutions, such as derivatives trading, writing guarantees, issuing letters of credit, and other contingent commitments, do not require significant financing. Yet all these activities draw to some extent on the bank's stock of risk capital, and therefore a risk capital cost must be imputed to each activity.

This brings us to the second reason: a bank's target solvency is a vital part of the product the bank is selling. In contrast to an industrial company, the primary customers of banks and other financial institutions are also their primary liability holders, e.g., depositors, derivatives counterparties, insurance policy holders, and so on. These customers are concerned about default risk on contractually promised payments. Customers make deposits with the expectation that the safety of their deposits does not depend on the economic performance of the bank. In over-the-counter markets, institutions are concerned about counterparty risk: a bank with a poor credit rating will find itself excluded from many markets. Maintaining good creditworthiness is therefore an ongoing cost of doing business for a bank.

Third, although bank creditworthiness is critical, banks are also highly opaque institutions. Banks use proprietary technology for pricing and hedging financial instruments, especially complex financial transactions. A typical bank's balance sheet is relatively liquid and can change very quickly. Any outside assessment of the creditworthiness of a bank is therefore difficult to develop and rapidly becomes obsolete (as the risk profile of the bank keeps on changing). Maintaining enough risk capital and implementing a strong risk management culture allows the bank to reduce these "agency costs" by convincing external stakeholders, including rating agencies, of the bank's financial integrity.

(continued on following page)

B O X   1 5 - 1 *(C o n t i n u e d)*

Fourth, as a result of deregulation of the banking sector, banks now operate in highly competitive financial markets. Increasingly, this makes bank profitability very sensitive to the bank's cost of capital. Banks don't want to carry too much risk capital, because risk capital has to be kept in liquid, safe, low-return investments—it can't be put to work to raise the level of the bank's returns. But banks can't carry too little risk capital, for reasons we've already made clear. So understanding the dynamic balance between the capital the bank carries and the riskiness of its activities is very important.

RAROC—RISK-ADJUSTED RETURN ON CAPITAL

RAROC is an approach—simple at the conceptual level—that is used by practitioners to allocate risk capital to business units and individual transactions for the purpose of measuring economic performance.

Originally proposed by Bankers Trust in the late 1970s, the approach makes clear the trade-off between risk and reward for a unit of capital and, therefore, offers a uniform and comparable measure of risk-adjusted performance across all business activities. If a business unit's RAROC is higher than the cost of the bank's equity (the minimum rate of return on equity required by the shareholders), then the business unit is deemed to be adding value to shareholders. Senior management can use this measure to evaluate performance for capital budgeting purposes, and as an input to the compensation for managers of business units.

The generic RAROC equation is really a formalization of the trade-off between risk and reward. It reads

$$RAROC = \frac{after-tax \ expected \ risk \ adjusted \ net \ income}{economic \ capital}$$

We can see that the RAROC equation employs economic capital as a proxy for risk and after-tax expected risk-adjusted net income as a proxy for reward. Later, we elaborate on how to measure both the numerator and the denominator of the RAROC equation, and on how to tackle the "hurdle-rate" issue—that is, once we know our RAROC number, how do we know if this number is good or bad from a shareholder's perspective?

Before beginning this discussion, however, we must acknowledge that the generic RAROC equation is one of a family of approaches, all with strengths and weaknesses. The definition of RAROC that we've just offered corresponds to industry practice and can be thought of as the traditional RAROC definition. Box 15-2 presents several variants of risk-adjusted performance measures, grouped under the label RAPM (risk-adjusted performance measures).

BOX 15-2

RAPM (RISK-ADJUSTED PERFORMANCE MEASUREMENT) ZOOLOGY

It's long been recognized that traditional accounting-based measures of performance at the consolidated level and for individual business units, such as return on assets (ROA) or return on book equity (ROE), fail to capture the risk of the underlying activity. The amounts of both book assets and book equity, which are accounting measures, are poor proxies for risk measures. Furthermore, accounting income also misses some critical risk adjustments, such as expected loss. The following risk-based measures remedy this shortcoming, although they are not fully consistent with one another.

RAPM (risk-adjusted performance measurement) is a generic term describing all the techniques used to adjust returns for the risk incurred in generating those returns. It encompasses many different concepts, risk adjustments, and performance measures, with RAROC being the form that is most widely used in the banking sector. These RAPM measures are not fully consistent with one another. In the main text, we propose an adjusted RAROC measure that is consistent with the capital asset pricing model (CAPM) and, therefore, with the NPV measure defined here.

- *RAROC (risk-adjusted return on capital)* = *risk-adjusted expected net income/economic capital.* RAROC makes the risk adjustment to the numerator by subtracting a risk factor from the return, e.g., expected loss. RAROC also makes the risk adjustment to the denominator by substituting economic capital for accounting capital.
- *RORAC (return on risk-adjusted capital)* = *net income/economic capital.* RORAC makes the risk adjustment solely to the denominator. In practical applications,

$$\text{RORAC} = \frac{\text{P \& L(profit and loss)}}{\text{VaR}}$$

- *ROC (return on capital)* =
  RORAC. It is also called ROCAR (return on capital at risk).
- *RORAA (return on risk-adjusted assets)* = *net income/risk-adjusted assets.*

(continued on following page)

B O X   1 5 - 2 *(C o n t i n u e d)*

- *RAROA (risk-adjusted return on risk-adjusted assets) = risk-adjusted expected net income/risk-adjusted assets.*
- *S (Sharpe ratio) = (expected return − risk-free rate)/volatility.* The expost Sharpe ratio, i.e., that based on actual returns rather than expected returns, can be shown to be a multiple of ROC.[1]
- *NPV (net present value) = discounted value of future expected cash flows,* using a risk-adjusted expected rate of return based on the beta derived from the CAPM, where risk is defined in terms of the covariance of changes in the market value of the business with changes in the value of the market portfolio (see Chapter 15). In the CAPM, the definition of risk is restricted to the systematic component of risk that cannot be diversified away. For RAROC calculations, the risk measure captures the full volatility of earnings, systematic and specific. NPV is particularly well suited for ventures where the expected cash flows over the life of the project can be easily identified.
- *EVA (economic value added), or NIACC (net income after capital charge),* is the after-tax adjusted net income less a capital charge equal to the amount of economic capital attributed to the activity, times the after-tax cost of equity capital. The activity is deemed to add shareholder value, or is said to be EVA positive, when its NIACC is positive.[2] An activity whose RAROC is above the hurdle rate is also EVA positive.

---

1. See David Shimko, "See Sharpe or Be Flat," *Risk* 10(6), 1997, p. 33.
2. EVA is a registered trademark of Stern Stewart & Co.

RAROC for Capital Budgeting

The decision to invest in a new project or a new business venture, or to expand or close down an existing business line, has to be made before the true performance of the activity is known—no manager has a crystal ball. When implementing the generic after-tax RAROC equation for capital budgeting, industry practice therefore interprets it as meaning

$$= \frac{\text{expected revenues} - \text{costs} - \text{expected losses} - \text{taxes} + \text{return on risk capital} + / - \text{transfers}}{\text{economic capital}}$$

where

- *Expected revenues* are the revenues that the activity is expected to generate (assuming no losses).

- *Costs* are the direct expenses associated with running the activity (e.g., salaries, bonuses, infrastructure expenses, and so on).
- *Expected losses,* in a banking context, are primarily the expected losses from default; they correspond to the loan loss reserve that the bank must set aside as the cost of doing business. Because this cost, like other business costs, is priced into the transaction in the form of a spread over funding cost, there is no need for risk capital as a buffer to absorb this risk. Expected losses also include the expected loss from other risks, such as market risk and operational risk.
- *Taxes* are the expected amount of taxes imputed to the activity using the effective tax rate of the company.
- *Return on risk capital* is the return on the risk capital allocated to the activity. It is generally assumed that this risk capital is invested in risk-free securities, such as government bonds.
- *Transfers* correspond to transfer-pricing mechanisms, primarily between the business unit and the treasury group, such as charging the business unit for any funding cost incurred by its activities and any cost of hedging interest-rate and currency risks; it also includes overhead cost allocation from the head office.
- *Economic capital* is the sum of risk capital and strategic capital where
  strategic risk capital = goodwill + burned-out capital

Our last bullet point deserves some explanation. Risk capital is the capital cushion that the bank must set aside to cover the worst-case loss (minus the expected loss) from market, credit, operational, and other risks, such as business risk and reputation risk, at the required confidence threshold (e.g., 99 percent). Risk capital is directly related to the value-at-risk calculation at the one-year time horizon and at the institution's required confidence level—all topics we've covered in earlier chapters of this book.

Strategic risk capital refers to the risk of significant investments about whose success and profitability there is high uncertainty. If the venture is not successful, then the firm will usually face a major write-off, and its reputation will be damaged. Current practice is to measure strategic risk capital as the sum of burned-out capital and goodwill. It should be viewed as an allocation of capital to account for the risk of strategic failure of recent acquisitions or other strategic initiatives built organically. This capital is amortized over time as the risk of strategic failure dissipates. The goodwill element corresponds to the investment premium, i.e., the amount paid above the replacement value of the net assets (assets – liabilities) when acquiring a company. (Usually, the acquiring company is prepared to pay a premium above the fair value of the net assets because it places a high value on intangible assets that are not recorded on the target's balance sheet.) Goodwill is also depreciated over time.

Some banks also allocate risk capital for unused risk limits, because risk capacity that can be tapped at any moment by the business units represents a potentially costly facility (in terms of the adjustments to risk capital the firm as a whole might have to make if the credit line were drawn upon).

Figure 15–1 shows the linkage between the kind of risk loss distribution that we describe in many other chapters of this book and the RAROC calculation. We show both the expected loss, in this example 15 basis points (bp), and the worst-case loss, 165 bp, at the desired confidence level (in this example, 99 percent) for the loss distribution derived over a given horizon, say one year. The unexpected loss is, therefore, the difference between the total loss and the expected loss, that is, 150 bp at the 99 percent confidence level, over a one-year horizon. The unexpected loss corresponds to the risk capital allocated to the activity.

Now that we understand the trickiest part of the RAROC equation, unexpected loss, we can look at a practical example of how to plug numbers into the RAROC equation.

Let us assume that we want to identify the RAROC of a $1 billion corporate loan portfolio that offers a headline return of 9 percent. The bank has an operating direct cost of $9 million per annum, and an effective tax rate of 30 percent. We'll assume that the portfolio is funded by $1 billion of retail deposits with an interest charge of 6 percent. Risk analysis of the unexpected losses associated with the portfolio tells us that we need to set economic capital of around $75 million (i.e., 7.5 percent of the loan amount) against the portfolio. We know that this economic capital must be invested in risk-free securities rather than being used to fund risky activities, and that the risk-free interest rate on government securities is 7 percent. The expected loss on this portfolio is assumed to be 1 percent per annum (i.e., $10 million).

If we ignore transfer price considerations, then the after-tax RAROC for this loan is

$$RAROC = \frac{(90 - 9 - 60 - 10 + 5.25)(1 - 0.3)}{75} = 0.152 = 15.2\%$$

where $90 million is the expected revenue, $9 million is the operat-

FIGURE 15-1

The RAROC Equation

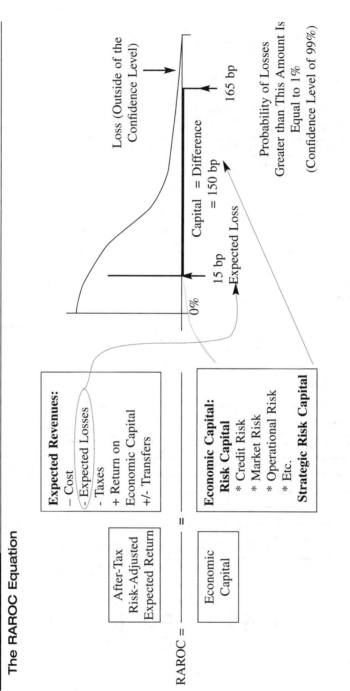

ing cost, $60 million is the interest expense (6 percent of the $1 billion in borrowed funds), $10 million is the expected loss, and $5.25 million is the return on economic capital.

The RAROC for this loan portfolio is 15.2 percent. This number can be interpreted as the annual after-tax expected rate of return on equity needed to support this loan portfolio.

RAROC for Performance Measurement

We should emphasize at this point that RAROC was first suggested as a tool for capital allocation on an anticipatory or ex ante basis. Hence, *expected* revenues and losses are plugged into the numerator of the RAROC equation for capital budgeting purpose. When RAROC is used for performance evaluation, we can use realized revenues and realized losses in our calculation, rather than expected revenues and losses.

RAROC Horizon

All of the quantities that we plug into the RAROC equation must be calculated on the basis of a particular time horizon. Box 15–3 discusses one problem that this brings up: how to harmonize the different time horizons used to measure credit, market, and operational risk. Practitioners usually adopt a one-year time horizon, as this corresponds to the business planning cycle and is also a reasonable approximation of the length of time it might take to recapitalize the bank if it were to suffer a major unexpected loss.

However, the choice of a risk horizon for RAROC is somewhat arbitrary. One could choose to measure the volatility of risk and returns over a longer period of time, say five or ten years, in order to capture the full effect of the business cycle in measuring risk. Calculating economic capital over a longer period of time does not necessarily increase capital, as the level of confidence in any firm's solvency that we require decreases as the time horizon is extended. (If this seems surprising, consider the probability of default of an AA-rated firm to be around 3 basis points over a one-year period; while this probability of default naturally increases if we look at the same firm over a two-year or five-year period, this increase clearly does not affect the one-year credit rating of the firm.) However, from a practical standpoint, it is not reasonable to select a time horizon much beyond one year, as the quality and accuracy of the risk and return data beyond one year become highly questionable.

BOX 15-3

RISK TYPES AND TIME HORIZONS

Risk capital can be characterized as the one-year value-at-risk exposure of the firm, at a confidence level consistent with the firm's target credit risk rating. But how does the time horizon in this characterization relate to the risk measurement approaches we describe in Chapter 7 for market risk, Chapter 10 for credit risk, and Chapter 13 for operational risk?

For credit risk, there is a straightforward equivalence between the one-year VaR produced by credit portfolio models, such as CreditMetrics or KMV, and risk capital. The same is also true for operational risk: most internal models used by institutions have a one-year horizon. Therefore, for both credit risk and operational risk, there is no need for any adjustment in the one-year VaR to determine risk capital.

However, this is not the case for market risk. For trading businesses, market risk is measured using only short-term horizons—one day for risk monitoring on a daily basis, and 10 days for regulatory capital. So how do we translate a one-day risk measure into one-year risk capital attribution?

One approach might be to use what is commonly called the "square root of time" rule. That is, the risk analyst might approximate the one-year VaR by multiplying the one-day VaR by the square root of the number of business days in one year, e.g., 252 days. If we did this, however, we'd be missing the point of risk capital. Risk capital is there to limit the risk of failure during a period of crisis, when the bank has suffered huge losses. As a worst-case scenario unfolds, the bank will naturally reduce its risk exposures in any way that it can. In the case of a proprietary trading desk, with highly liquid positions and no clients to service, this risk reduction can take place very quickly indeed. For other activities, risk can often be reduced only to a *core risk level* for the remainder of the year, defined as the minimum realistic size at which the business can be considered to be a going concern (i.e., can maintain its franchise).

Thus, to work out a meaningful one-year economic capital allocation, we need to analyze the business in question so that we can understand the *time to reduce* from the current risk position to the core risk level, which, in turn, reflects the relative liquidity of positions during adverse market conditions. It doesn't assume a fire sale, but rather assumes a relatively orderly unwinding of positions.

Figure 15B-1 illustrates the calculation of risk capital when the core risk level is lower than the current risk position.

(continued on following page)

BOX 15-3 *(Continued)*

FIGURE 15B-1

Risk Capital Calculation for Market Risk

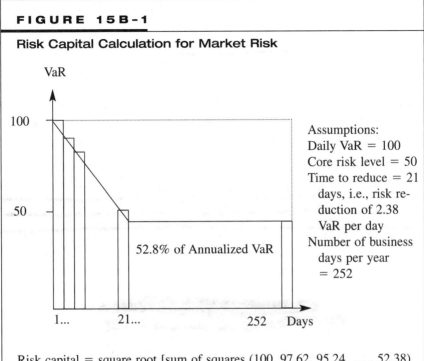

Assumptions:
Daily VaR = 100
Core risk level = 50
Time to reduce = 21 days, i.e., risk reduction of 2.38 VaR per day
Number of business days per year = 252

Risk capital = square root [sum of squares (100, 97.62, 95.24, ... , 52.38) + 50^2 × 231]
= 839
= 52.8% × annualized VaR
where annualized VaR = 100 × square root (252)

Across every bank, there are many other activities that must be allocated capital in a way that is sensitive to time horizons. For example, the bank should allocate capital to cover the risk of options that are embedded in many of its products. The option to prepay a mortgage is one obvious example, but there are many subtle twists on the risks generated by different types of products. For example, mortgage portfolios in Canada often incur commitment risks. These arise because the consumer automatically receives the lowest mortgage rate looking backward over a prescribed commitment period, as a function of the specific type of mortgage. In effect, the consumer has what derivatives practitioners call a "look-back option." The seriousness of the commitment risk is governed by the length of the commitment period; it represents the component that cannot be entirely eliminated by delta hedging (e.g., the basis risk between the wholesale rates and the mortgage rate). All these considerations need to be taken into account in determining the risk capital needed to support a Canadian mortgage business.

Confidence Level

We mentioned earlier that the confidence level in the economic capital calculation should be consistent with the firm's target credit rating. Most banks today hope to obtain a AA credit rating from the agencies for their debt offerings, which implies a probability of default of 3 to 5 basis points. This, in turn, corresponds to a confidence level in the range of 99.95 to 99.97 percent. We can think of this confidence level as the quantitative expression of the "risk appetite" of the firm.

Setting a lower confidence level may significantly reduce the amount of risk capital allocated to an activity, especially when the institution's risk profile is dominated by operational risk, credit risk, and settlement risk (for which large losses occur only with great rarity). Therefore, the choice of the confidence level can materially affect risk-adjusted performance measures and the resulting capital allocation decisions of the firm.

Hurdle Rate and Capital Budgeting Decision Rule

Most firms use a single hurdle rate for all business activities: the after-tax weighted-average cost of equity capital. Box 15–4 explains in more tech-

BOX 15-4

TECHNICAL DISCUSSION: CALCULATING THE HURDLE RATE

Most firms use a single hurdle rate, h_{AT}, for all business activities, based on the after-tax weighted-average cost of equity capital:

$$h_{AT} = \frac{CE \times r_{CE} + PE \times r_{PE}}{CE + PE}$$

where CE and PE denote the market value of common equity and preferred equity, respectively, and r_{CE} and r_{PE} are the cost of common equity and preferred equity, respectively.

The cost of preferred equity is simply the yield on the firm's preferred shares. The cost of common equity is determined via a model such as the capital asset pricing model:

$$r_{CE} = r_f + \beta_{CE} (\overline{R}_M - r_f)$$

where r_f is the risk-free rate, $\overline{R}_M$ is the expected return on the market portfolio, and β_{CE} is the firm's common equity market beta.

nical detail how this hurdle rate is calculated. The hurdle rate should be reset periodically, say every six months, or when it has changed by more than 10 percent.

When a firm is considering investing in a business or closing down an activity, it computes the after-tax RAROC for the business or activity and compares it to the firm's hurdle rate. In theory, the firm can then apply a simple decision rule:

- If the RAROC ratio is greater than the hurdle rate, the activity is deemed to add value to the firm.
- In the opposite case, the activity is deemed to destroy value to the firm and should, in theory, be closed down or the project rejected.

However, one can show that applying this simple rule can lead to the firm's accepting high-risk projects that will lower the value of the firm, and rejecting low-risk projects that will increase the value of the firm.[1] High-risk projects, such as oil exploration, are characterized by very volatile returns, while low-risk projects, such as retail banking, produce steady revenues with low volatility.

To overcome this, we need to make an important adjustment to the RAROC calculation so that the systematic riskiness of the returns from a business activity is fully captured by the decision rule (see Box 15–5).

Diversification and Risk Capital

The risk capital for a particular business unit within a larger firm is usually determined by viewing the business on a stand-alone basis, using the

---

BOX 15-5

ADJUSTING RAROC FOR THE RISK OF RETURNS

Ideally, we would like to adjust the traditional RAROC calculation to obtain a RAROC measure that takes into account the systemic riskiness (beta risk, discussed in Chapter 5) of returns, and for which the hurdle rate (the critical benchmark above which a business adds value) is the same across all business lines. To correct the inherent limitations of the traditional RAROC measure, let's adjust the RAROC ratio as follows:

(continued on following page)

---

1. See Michel Crouhy, Stuart Turnbull, and Lee Wakeman, "Measuring Risk-Adjusted Performance," *Journal of Risk* 2(1), pp. 5–35.

BOX 15-5 *(Continued)*

$$Adjusted\ RAROC \equiv RAROC\ -\ \beta_E(R_M\ -\ r_f)$$

where R_M is the expected rate of return on the market portfolio, r_f denotes the risk-free interest rate, say the interest rate paid on three-month Treasury bills, and β_E is the beta of the equity of the firm. The new decision rule is:

> Accept (reject) projects whose adjusted RAROC is greater (smaller) than r_f.

The risk adjustment, $\beta(R_M - r_f)$, is the excess return above the risk-free rate required in order to compensate the shareholders of the firm for the nondiversifiable systematic risk they bear when investing in the activity, assuming that the shareholders hold a well-diversified portfolio. When the returns are thus adjusted for risk, the hurdle rate becomes the risk-free rate.

top-of-the-house hurdle rate that we discussed earlier. However, intuition suggests that the risk capital for the firm should be significantly less than the sum of the stand-alone risk capital of the individual business units, because the returns generated by the various businesses are unlikely to be perfectly correlated.

Measuring the true level of this "diversification effect" is extremely problematic. As of today, there is no fully integrated VaR model that can produce the overall risk capital for a firm, taking into account all the correlation effects between market risk, credit risk, and operational risk across all the business units of a company. Instead, banks tend to adopt a bottom-up decentralized approach, under which distinct risk models are run for each portfolio or business unit.

For capital adequacy purpose, running these business-specific models at the confidence level targeted at the top of the house. For example, 99.97 percent produces an unnecessarily large amount of overall risk capital, precisely because it neglects diversification effects (across both risk types and business activities). It is therefore common practice to adjust for the diversification effects by lowering the confidence level used at the business level to, say, 99.5 percent or lower—an adjustment that is necessarily more of an educated guess than a strict risk calculation.

If this sounds unsatisfactory, we can at least put some boundaries around the problem. The aggregate VaR figure obtained by this approach should fall in between the two extreme cases of perfect correlation and zero correlation between risk types and across businesses. For example, ignoring business and reputation risks for illustrative purpose, suppose that we've calculated the risk capital for each type of risk as follows:

Market risk   = $200
Credit risk   = $700
Operational risk = $300

Then aggregate risk capital at the top of the house is either

Simple summation of the three risks (perfect correlation) = $1,200

Square root of the sum of squares of the three risks (zero correlation) = $787

We can say with some confidence, therefore, that any proposed approach for taking diversification effects into account should produce an overall VaR figure in the range of $787 to $1,200.

While the simple logic of our boundary setting makes sense, these boundaries are pretty wide! They also leave us with the reverse problem: how do we allocate any diversification benefit that we calculate for the business as a whole back to the business lines? The allocation of the diversification effect can be important for certain business decisions, e.g., about whether to enter or continue a business line.

Logically, a business whose operating cash flows are strongly correlated with the earnings of the other activities in the firm should require more risk capital than a business with the same volatility whose earnings move in a countercyclical fashion. Bringing together countercyclical business lines produces stable earnings for the firm as a whole; the firm can then operate to the same target credit rating with less risk capital.

In truth, institutions continue to struggle with the problem of attributing capital back to business lines, and there are diverging views as to the appropriate approach. For the moment, as a practical solution, most institutions allocate the portfolio effect pro rata with the stand-alone risk capital.

Diversification effects also complicate matters *within* business units. Let's look at this and other issues in relation to an example business unit, BU, which comprises two activities, X and Y (Figure 15-2). When calculating the risk capital of the business unit, let's assume that the firm's risk analysts have taken into account all the diversification effects created by combining activities X and Y and that the risk capital for BU is $100. The complication starts when we try to allocate risk capital at the activity

FIGURE 15-2

Diversification Effect

Combination of Businesses	Economic Capital		Marginal Business	Marginal Economic Capital
X+Y	$100			
X	$60		X	$30
Y	$70		Y	$40
Diversification effect	$30		Total	$70

level within the business unit. There are three different measures of risk capital:

- *Stand-alone capital* is the capital used by an activity taken independently of the other activities in the same business unit, that is, risk capital calculated without any diversification benefits. In our example, the stand-alone capital for X is $60 and that for Y is $70. The sum of the stand-alone capitals of the individual constituents of the business unit is generally higher than the stand-alone risk capital of the business unit itself (it is equal only in the case of perfectly correlated activities X and Y).

- *Fully diversified capital* is the capital attributed to each activity X and Y, taking into account all diversification benefits from combining them under the same leadership. In our example, the overall portfolio effect is $30 ($60 + $70 - $100). Allocating the diversification effect is an issue here. Following our earlier discussion, we'll allocate the portfolio effect pro rata with the stand-alone risk capital, $30 × 60/130 = $14 for X and $30 × 70/130 = $16 for Y, so that the fully diversified risk capital becomes $46 for X and $54 for Y.

- *Marginal capital* is the additional capital required by an incremental deal, activity, or business. It takes into account the full benefit of diversification. In our example, the marginal risk capital for X (assuming that Y already exists) is $30 (= $100 - $70), and the marginal risk capital for Y (assuming that X already exists) is $40 (= $100 - $60). In the case where more than two activities are included in the business unit BU, marginal capital is calculated by subtracting the risk capital required for the BU without this business from the risk capital required for the full portfolio of businesses. Note that the summation of the marginal risk capital, $70 in our example, is less than the full risk capital of the BU.

As this example shows, the choice of capital measure depends on the desired objective. Fully diversified measures should be used for assessing the solvency of the firm and minimum risk pricing. Active portfolio management or business mix decisions, on the other hand, should be based on marginal risk capital, taking into account the benefit of full diversification. Finally, performance measurement should involve both perspectives: stand-alone risk capital for incentive compensation, and fully diversified risk capital to assess the extra performance generated by the diversification effects.

However, we must be cautious about how generous we are in attributing diversification benefits. Correlations between risk factors drive the extent of the portfolio effect, and these correlations tend to vary over time. During market crises, in particular, correlations sometimes shift dramatically toward either 1 or −1, reducing or totally eliminating portfolio effects for a period of time.

RAROC IN PRACTICE

Economic capital is increasingly a key element in the assessment of business line performance, in the decision to exit or enter a business, and in the pricing of transactions. It also plays a critical role in the incentive compensation plan of the firm. Adjusting incentive compensation for risk in this way is important, because managers tend to align their performance to maximize whatever performance measures are imposed on them.

Needless to say, in firms in which RAROC has been implemented, business units often challenge the risk management function about the fairness of the amount of economic capital attributed to them. The usual complaint is that their economic capital attribution is too high (never that it is too low!). Another complaint is that economic capital attribution is sometimes too unstable—the numbers can move up and down in a way that is disconcerting for a business trying to hit a target.

The best way to defuse this debate is for the RAROC group to be transparent about the methodology used to assess risk, and to institute forums where the issues related to the determination of economic capital can be debated and analyzed. From our own experience, the VaR methodologies for measuring market risk and credit risk that underpin RAROC calculations are generally well accepted by business units (although this is not yet true for operational risk). It's the setting of the parameters that feed into these models, and that drive the size of economic capital, that causes acrimony.

Here are a number of recommendations for implementing a RAROC system:

1. *Senior management commitment.* Given the strategic nature of the decisions steered by a RAROC system, the marching orders must come from the top management of the firm. Specifically, the CEO and his or her executive team should sponsor the implementation of a RAROC system, and should be active in the diffusion, within the firm, of a new culture in which performance is measured in terms of contribution to shareholder value. The message to push down to the business lines is this: What counts is not how much income is generated, but how well the firm is compensated for the risks that it is taking on.

2. *Communication and education.* The RAROC group should be transparent and should explain the RAROC methodology not only to the business's heads, but also to the business line managers and the CFO's office, in order to gain acceptance of the methodology throughout all the management layers of the firm.

3. *Ongoing consultation.* Institute a forum such as a "parameter review group" that periodically reviews the key parameters that drive risk and economic capital. This group, composed of key representatives from the business units and the risk management function, will bring legitimacy to the capital allocation process. For credit risk, the parameters that should be reviewed include probabilities of default, credit migration frequencies, loss given default, and credit line usage given default. These parameters evolve over the business cycle and should be adjusted as more data become available. An important issue to settle is the choice of a historical period over which these parameters are calibrated, i.e., should this be the whole credit cycle (in order to produce stable risk capital numbers) or a shorter period of time to make capital more pro-cyclical (capital goes down when the credit environment improves and goes up when it deteriorates). For market risk, volatility and correlation parameters should be updated at least every month, using standard statistical tech-

niques. Other key factors, such as the core risk level and time to reduce (see Box 15-3) should be reviewed on an annual basis. For operational risk, the approach is currently more judgmental and, as such, more open to heated discussions!

4. *Maintaining the integrity of the process.* As with other risk calculations, the validity of RAROC numbers depends critically on the quality of the data about risk exposures and positions collected from the management systems (e.g., in a trading business, the front- and back-office systems). Only a rigorous process of data collection and centralization can ensure accurate risk and capital assessment. The same rigor should also be applied to the financial information needed to estimate the adjusted-return element of the RAROC equation. Data collection is probably the most daunting task in risk management. But the best recipe for failure in implementing a RAROC system is to base calculations on inaccurate and incomplete data. The RAROC group should be accountable for the integrity of the data collection process, the calculations, and the reporting process. The business units and the finance group should be accountable for the integrity of the specific data that they produce and feed into the RAROC system.

5. *Combine RAROC with qualitative factors.* Earlier in this chapter, we described a simple decision rule for project selection and capital attribution, i.e., accept projects where the RAROC is greater than the hurdle rate. In practice, other qualitative factors should be taken into consideration. All the business units should be assessed in the context of the two-dimensional strategic grid shown in Figure 15-3. The horizontal axis of this figure corresponds to the RAROC return calculated on an ex ante basis. The vertical axis is a qualitative assessment of the quality of the earnings produced by the business units. This measure takes into consideration the strategic importance of the activity for the firm, the growth potential of the business, the sustainability and volatility of the earnings in the long run, and any synergies with other critical businesses in the firm. Priority in the allocation of balance-sheet resources should be given to the businesses in the upper right quadrant. At the other extreme, the firm should try to exit, scale down, or fix the activities of businesses that fall into the lower left quadrant. The businesses in the category "managed growth," in the lower right quadrant, are high-return

FIGURE 15-3

Strategic Grid

Quality of Earnings: Strategic Importance/Long-Term Growth Potential

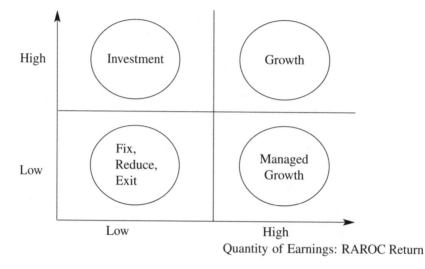

activities that have low strategic importance for the firm. On the contrary, businesses in the category "investment," in the upper left quadrant, are currently low-return activities, but have high growth potential and high strategic value for the firm.

6. *Put an active capital management process in place.* Balance-sheet requests from the business units, such as economic capital, footings, and risk-weighted assets, should be channeled to the RAROC group every quarter. (*Footings* is the numerator of a leverage ratio employed by bank regulators; it includes all on-balance-sheet assets plus financial guarantees and standby letters of credit.) Limits are then set for economic capital, footings, and risk-weighted assets based on the kind of analysis we've discussed in this chapter. Footings limits are also reviewed by the treasury group to ensure that they are consistent with funding limits. This limit-setting process is a collaborative effort, with any disagreements about the amount of balance-sheet resources attributed to a business put to arbitration by the senior executive team.

CONCLUSION

RAROC systems, developed first by large financial institutions, are now also being implemented in small banks and other trading firms, such as energy trading companies. Wherever risk capital is an important concern, RAROC balances the divergent desires of the various external stakeholders, while also aligning them with the incentives of internal decision makers (Figure 15-4). When business units (or transactions) earn returns in excess of the hurdle rate, shareholder value is created, while the allocated risk capital indicates the amount of capital required to preserve the desired credit rating.

RAROC information allows senior managers to better understand where shareholder value is being created and where it is being destroyed. It promotes strategic planning, risk-adjusted profitability reporting, proactive allocation of resources, better management of concentration risk, and better product pricing.

Because RAROC is not just a common language of risk, but a quantitative technique, we can also think of a RAROC-based capital budgeting process as akin to an internal capital market in which businesses are competing with one another for scarce balance-sheet resources—all with the objective of maximizing shareholder value.

FIGURE 15-4

How RAROC Balances the Desires of Various Stakeholders

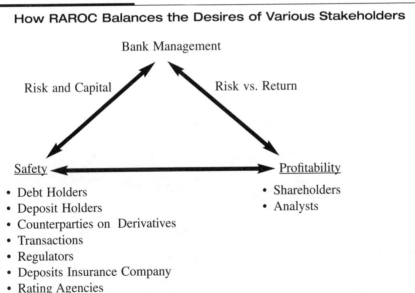

Bank Management

Risk and Capital   Risk vs. Return

Safety   Profitability

- Debt Holders
- Deposit Holders
- Counterparties on Derivatives
- Transactions
- Regulators
- Deposits Insurance Company
- Rating Agencies

- Shareholders
- Analysts

Trends in Risk Management

Several trends will shape risk management over the next decade, but one starting point is particularly clear: External bodies, such as rating agencies, regulators, and public officials, will hold boards and senior executives increasingly accountable and legally liable for their failures in risk management. Pleading ignorance will no longer prove to be a reliable defense.

It follows that board members will want to improve their knowledge and understanding of risk management in order to meet their fiduciary responsibilities and, in turn, will press for more effective collaboration between risk and business management as well as among the firm's corporate governance activities.

There will be increasing demands on firms to make the significant investments necessary to comply with a new generation of risk regulation (notably Basel II) and corporate governance regulation (such as the Sarbanes-Oxley Act). Accordingly, the need for economies of scale in risk management infrastructure, along with the potential for more effective use of capital, will prove to be an important driver in the consolidation of the financial services industries.

Boards are likely to press for the introduction of a more integrated risk management approach that encompasses market risk, credit risk, and operational risk across all operating units. That is, they will push for the introduction of an enterprise risk management (ERM) approach, as we discussed in Chapter 1.

Today, ERM largely exists in name only. In truth, most firms have neither a truly integrated set of risk measures nor a harmonized set of policies, methodologies, and infrastructure. Over the next few years, however, we will see a steadily increasing integration of corporate compliance, corporate governance, capital management, and risk management activities.

There are also likely to be significant efforts to integrate the management of business risk, reputation risk, and strategic risk in a more formal manner at the top of the firm. Banks are likely to continue to lead the way in this evolution, but other industries (such as the insurance industry) will want, or be obliged, to follow. A missing piece of the risk and corporate governance jigsaw puzzle at the moment is a meaningful discussion about how a "risk culture" can be inculcated not just at the top of the firm, but across the entire firm.

Furthermore, there will still be many firms that fail to comprehend the value of superior risk management and that, therefore, will not achieve best-practice standards. Shocking financial failures will continue to hit the headlines, reminding the public of the millennial corporate governance scandals and, perhaps, putting stress on risk-transfer markets (e.g., the credit derivatives market). This won't signal that risk management as a discipline has "failed," but simply that a new challenge has to be met.

A performance gap will develop and grow between those firms that are benefiting from the tremendous investment they have made in risk management (e.g., from an improved credit ratings process) and those that have not made such investments. Over time, the market will punish those firms that fail to invest wisely.

Chief risk officers (CROs) in well-run firms will use the backing of the board and senior management to make sure that their firm adopts best-of-breed risk management approaches. The good news for CROs is that they will be empowered to invest significant amounts of the firm's resources to develop best-practice risk policies, risk methodologies, and risk infrastructure.

The bad news for CROs is that they will ultimately be subject to formal legal liabilities. The mixed news for CROs is that while they are likely to earn more and more, they will also come under pressure to prove objectively how much value they are adding to the way the firm is managed.

To conclude this book, let's take a brief look at 10 possible extensions and ramifications of an ambitious conception of risk management in areas such as national policy, insurance, pensions, and risk education.

1. COUNTRYWIDE RISK MANAGEMENT

The discipline of risk management has so far concentrated on developing new ways to manage risk within the firm. It is our view that, within five to ten years, national governments will spend significantly more time, attention, and resources on innovative ways to manage the risks of their economies.

It's interesting to consider how far this kind of macro risk management might advance. Nobel Laureate Robert Merton has suggested that a country with exposure to a few concentrated industries might diversify its current exposure by swapping these risks for the risks of other industries to which it is not currently exposed.[1] He suggests that a simple country swap might be used to improve the national risk profile. For example, a country without an automobile industry might diversify its national industry portfolio by participating in a swap that creates a long position in an automobile industry index while shorting, say, the electronics industry. By using swaps, countries can pursue comparative advantage in their industrial strategies and remove the risk of any concentrated dependence on a few industries. It's a visionary idea, but then so was a market in credit derivatives not so long ago.

There are many other potential macroapplications of risk management concepts. Countries will be able to improve the management of their social security obligations by taking into account the potential returns and risks associated with the monies set aside from the social security investments of their citizens. Countries will also be able to hedge the risks to which their economy is exposed in order to support their entitlement programs. Risk management tools could also help countries to manage sovereign debt more efficiently (in the same manner as risk-literate professional portfolio managers manage bond portfolios). For example, a country might issue bonds with an interest rate that is related to the country's success in tax collection or is a function of the growth rate of its GDP. Further, as indicated earlier, cross-country swaps of various kinds might be developed to assist countries in managing their sovereign debt exposures and reduce the cost of external debt. According to a Moody's assessment in 2002, about 50 countries have defaulted on a portion of their external debt since 1980.

2. THE SPREAD OF BANK RISK MANAGEMENT TO OTHER FINANCIAL SECTORS

Banks are the most regulated of both financial services and nonfinancial firms with respect to their risk exposures. Over the next decade, more industries, especially in the financial services sector, will find themselves subject to dramatically increased regulation of their risk exposures. For

---

1. See Robert C. Merton, "On Financial Innovation and Economic Growth," *Harvard China Review,* Spring 2004.

example, there will be tremendous pressure on the insurance regulatory community to introduce regulatory reforms similar to those of banking and security regulators (especially Basel II). We predict that the insurance industry will ultimately upgrade its regulatory capital regulation and move toward a three-pillar framework, like that of Basel II. We also foresee a dramatic effort by insurance companies to adapt the ERM practices and techniques that are under development in the banking industry.

Insurers have long struggled with effectively managing their risk. On the one hand, the industry has struggled with overcapitalization, leading to weak returns. On the other hand, as we know all too well, insurers and reinsurers can become insolvent in very short periods of time. Both problems have the same root cause: insurers have historically had a very difficult time relating their risks to the economic capital that should support their businesses.

We expect that the insurance market will learn from its mistakes and develop new approaches and risk products that protect it against financial and nonfinancial risk. For example, the management of reinsurance risk has been poorly controlled by insurance companies, and therefore we predict that securitization vehicles and credit derivative style products will be developed and tailored for reinsurance risk. The evolution of standardized documentation and more effective operational risk controls will help to control the documentation risk associated with insurance products.

In the past, the insurance industry has lost out on several significant opportunities to benefit from the dramatic evolution in risk management. In particular, insurance companies failed to capitalize on the demand from banks that needed to find some way of insuring against their credit risk in the late 1990s. Banks developed their own market for laying off credit risk after failing to convince insurers to write protection for them. Credit derivatives now fuel a highly lucrative $5 trillion credit-risk-transfer market that is growing fast.

3. RISK MANAGEMENT AND PENSION PLANS[2]

The potential for crises in the private and public pension fund sector is already apparent. But one aspect of the problem, overreliance on returns from equity markets, is less remarked upon.

---

2. This section is based on Z. Bodie, "An ERM Perspective on Company Pension Plans," November 29, 2004. The accounting standard for pension plans in the United States is SFAS 87.

A firm that sponsors a defined-benefit pension plan can provide its employees with assurance against default risk by fully funding the plan and investing the assets in a matched portfolio of high-grade bonds and other fixed-income securities. This is called a strategy of *immunizing* the pension liability. However, in reality, pension immunization is rare. The vast majority of corporate plan sponsors invest a large fraction of their pension fund in stocks.

The practitioner literature on pension fund investment strategy explains why this is so. Since there is a positive risk premium on stocks versus bonds, many investment consultants and pension actuaries advise companies to invest in stocks in order to lower their pension expense, the rationale being that since pension obligations are long-term, stocks are not really riskier than bonds. Therefore, the returns need only match the stock market historical averages to reduce pension costs.

But this reasoning is fallacious. The ups and downs of the stock market do not necessarily cancel out over time, no matter how long the time period. Instead of the value of the stock portfolio going up after it has just gone down, it can continue to go down and move even further away from the value of the promised pension benefit. Contrary to the traditional actuarial reasoning, the risk of falling short of the target is actually *greater* in the long run than in the short run. From an ERM perspective, the risk exposure of the owners of a company that invests its pension assets in stocks is higher than the risk exposure of a hypothetical twin company that invests in a matched portfolio of bonds.

The rules allow companies that invest in stocks to book an expected return on assets in the plan that is greater than the interest rate charged on accrued pension liabilities. Discrepancies between the actual and assumed rate of return on the assets in the plan are eventually recognized after a period of time and are "smoothed" by averaging them.

The result of this procedure is that if a company should choose to immunize its pension liabilities by investing in bonds, in the short run it would have to report higher pension expenses and lower profits than would its identical twin company that invests in stocks. The difference in reported net pension expenses and profits can be quite large.

Companies whose plans invest in equities overstate their earnings and understate the volatility of their earnings and net worth. Companies that invest in fixed-income instruments are punished by higher reported costs without visible benefits from risk reduction. Thus, when it comes to pension asset allocation, the illusory arbitrage opportunity created by generally accepted accounting principles is a major barrier to sound risk management decisions.

As long as accounting rules diverge from economic reality and values, we can expect that pension plan managers will fail to take future uncertainties fully into account. Managers often prefer to demonstrate smooth financial performance, even when this is not really the case, and even when the strategy destroys value for members of the plan.

4. RISK TRANSPARENCY

Regulation and market forces are combining to demand more disclosure by corporations about their risks and risk management practices. We are likely to see increasingly lucid and comprehensive external quantitative disclosure (e.g., using value-at-risk, stress tests, sensitivity analysis, and back testing) at both the business division and enterprise levels. The disclosures will encompass market risk, credit risk, and operational risk, and will eventually include sophisticated qualitative disclosures about business risk, reputation risk, and strategic risk.

In particular, in risk-intensive industries, the market will expect increasing disclosure of how much can be lost in extreme markets. The results of applications of extreme value theory (EVT) and other models will help to provide an objective and transparent assessment of very rare, but very extreme, forms of risk.

The market (e.g., rating agencies and equity analysts) as well as stakeholders (e.g., shareholders and bondholders) will become increasingly negative and impatient with firms that do not demonstrate superior risk disclosure. Rating agencies are likely to be pressed to transparently rate enterprises on the quality of their risk management. Financial services industries that lack sophisticated regulatory capital rules (such as the insurance sector) will be significantly influenced by rating agency views on appropriate levels of capital. For example, in the United States, each state has its own regulatory body to manage insurance risk, and it is generally agreed that the insurance regulatory framework has not yet evolved toward a meaningful risk-sensitive set of regulatory minimum required capital rules.

Equity analysts will place an increased emphasis on the need to examine a firm's risk-adjusted performance. In particular, metrics will evolve to incorporate systematic risk measures (as opposed to measures of specific risk) that allow stakeholders to understand the degree to which investments in a specific firm are vulnerable to macroeconomic shocks. Equity analysts will also demand increased disclosure of strategic risk, business risk, and reputation risk.

The hedge fund industry will be obliged to become much more transparent about risk. For example, beginning in February 2006, the UCITS (Undertakings for the Collective Investment of Transferable Securities) III Act will oblige asset management companies in the euro zone to manage their exposure to risk. UCITS III is a European regulation (directive), issued by the Committee of European Securities regulators, that aims to protect investors by ensuring that asset management companies are suitably capitalized, and that they have appropriate measures in place for risk management and reporting. But the directive does not specify how to manage risks and leaves the companies themselves to determine the details of any procedures.

In the United States, regulators are also considering whether to require hedge funds to report on their risk exposures and on their policies for monitoring and managing risks, in response to the increasing appeal of hedge funds to retail clients (who are mostly unaware of the risks inherent in the multitude of investment strategies followed by hedge funds).

5. RISK MANAGEMENT EDUCATION

We have already seen the emergence of dedicated graduate courses on financial risk management at leading universities in the United States, such as Harvard, University of California at Berkeley, University of California at Los Angeles, Carnegie Mellon, New York University, and Columbia, among others. Similar initiatives have been pioneered in Europe, such as in France at the HEC School of Management and in the United Kingdom at the London Business School. From now on, offering degrees in risk management and financial engineering will become routine. Universities will also start to offer specialized executive education programs in risk management.

Less visibly, but perhaps more importantly, there will be a significant growth in demand for "down to earth" (nonanalytic) education on the essentials of risk management, driven by a variety of stakeholders. Formalized risk education will become a common component of corporate education programs. Nonanalytic education about risk will include topics such as legal risk, reputation risk, business ethics, and compliance risk. A premium will be placed on formal certification programs in the spirit of a CPA (Certified Public Accountant) or CFA (Chartered Financial Analyst). Global risk associations such as PRMIA (Professional Risk Managers' International Association) and GARP (Global Association of Risk Professionals) have developed an international presence and offer certification programs with evaluation exams leading to diplomas that are already well recognized in the financial services industry.

6. STANDARDIZATION OF RISK METHODOLOGIES AND RISK LANGUAGE

We will see the emergence of a formalized set of generally accepted risk principles (GARP) that will standardize the most commonly used risk methodologies. This standardization, in addition to being important in itself, will help risk principles to become part of the lexicon of the accounting profession. Furthermore, we will also see increasing portions of the balance sheet placed under fair-value accounting as a way of increasing balance-sheet transparency.

International accounting standards that deal with reporting on derivatives and other risky positions are being constantly modified and amended, in response to the concerns of accountants, financial institutions, and other global corporations. IAS 32 and IAS 39 are the two major international accounting standards dealing with reporting requirements and measurement issues, respectively. We can expect a movement toward convergence of the international standards with American accounting standards (e.g., SFAS 133). This process will contribute to the standardization of risk measurement methodologies on a global basis.

The classic risk methodologies and the associated language of risk (such as value at risk) will become part of the public business lexicon. For example, it will become common to use risk-adjusted measures of performance at the business division level, and these will be published in the normal course of business disclosure. The risk concepts and language of risk adopted and promoted by the Basel II banking regulators with regard to risk classes and risk factors (e.g., definitions of probability of default, loss given default, and so on) will also help to regularize how financial risks are assessed and discussed.

7. INTEGRATION OF RISK MEASURES

For the moment, there is still an awkward gulf between different *types* of risk discussion. Over the next few years, we will see the introduction and use of "all-source" business intelligence risk measurement techniques. These techniques will integrate risk management's classic statistically based approaches with nonclassic approaches such as expert judgment and structured ways to discuss plausible risk scenarios as well as causal relationships. Causal relationship techniques, meanwhile, will benefit from significant advances in the mathematics of Bayesian belief networks.

We will also see the integration of advanced retail-related customer relationship management (CRM)/marketing tools with risk management analytics (e.g., sophisticated acquisition, cross-selling, and retention analytics). These tools will be applied at the level of individual transactions and at the level of whole portfolios, and will be augmented by better ways of forecasting human behavior, such as a customer's propensity to take up the offer of a product. These new methodologies will help institutions to price their products more efficiently as a combined function of risk, cost, and behavioral factors.

8. OPERATIONAL RISK-TRANSFER MARKETS

Risk-mitigation methodologies will evolve in order to facilitate risk transfer for operational risk. For example, we may see an evolution toward an internal operational risk treasury function, following the recent trend toward internal credit-risk treasury functions (which, in turn, exhibit many of the same features as traditional interest-rate treasury functions). An internal operational risk treasury function would centralize the management of operational risk. The transfer pricing of these operational risks will benefit from the kind of risk-neutral operational techniques currently applied in other aspects of the financial markets.[3]

Operational risk transfer techniques will transform the nature of the insurance markets. For example, a major challenge for property/casualty insurance companies is to manage the risk that they might not be paid money owed to them by reinsurers. A properly packaged operational risk securitization vehicle, with appropriately designed tranches of operational risk, could provide additional price discovery and offer another venue through which to lay off operational risk.

We would expect that the market for operational risk transfer might turn out to be as big as the market for credit-risk mitigation.

9. BASEL II WILL AFFECT THE WORLD, AND THE WORLD WILL AFFECT IT

Basel II is intended to align regulatory capital requirements more closely with the economic risks borne by financial institutions. The original 1988

---

3. The authors have published a technical paper on how to price operational risk based on risk-neutral pricing in the *Journal of Derivatives*, November 2003.

Basel Accord, as described in Chapter 3, is a "one size fits all" approach that is not very risk sensitive; it is based on a rough proxy for credit risk, and it does not differentiate other forms of risk. Furthermore, the paradigm underpinning the capital requirement is not explicit. The new Basel II rules are based on a broader coverage of market, credit, and operational risk, and therefore should help to improve ERM practices. They also offer institutions a menu of increasingly sophisticated approaches that are more closely aligned and harmonized with economic capital.

But Basel II will also produce some unexpected surprises. In particular, regulatory capital arbitrage will be accelerated with the advent of Basel II. For example, in the United States, more sophisticated banks opting for the Basel II regime will be charged less capital for certain products, such as residential mortgages, than less sophisticated banks (which, on the whole, will remain compliant with the original 1988 Basel Capital Accord). The fact that the same asset will carry two different capital charges as a function of different regulatory schemes is bound to encourage arbitrage. The Basel II rules will also drive further consolidation in the financial industry as a result of the huge fixed cost of upgrading information-gathering infrastructures to become Basel II–compliant, and may lead to substantial competitive imbalances in the banking industry.

This kind of unexpected consequence will oblige regulators to make significant modifications as the industry works to implement the new rules, perhaps initially with regard to operational risk. The Basel II approach to operational risk is too simplistic at the standardized and foundation levels, and too unspecified at the advanced level. As banks try to build up their modeling techniques, they will petition regulators to introduce improved methods.

The refinement introduced by Basel II in assessing an obligor's credit risk will put added pressure on corporations to better manage their risks (as their borrowing costs will depend on their rating). Better risk management at the corporate level will lead to reduced borrowing costs.

10. INFRASTRUCTURE

Leading banks in Europe are expected to each invest, on average, 100 million euro to become compliant with Basel II—most of it on infrastructure. Basel II puts a big emphasis on the quality of the transaction and market data used as inputs to regulatory risk calculations. As other industries are required to formally manage their risks and/or report on their risk exposures, these industries too will have to invest in improved infrastructure (including data warehousing and system interfaces).

The good news is that we will see the evolution of increasingly practical and affordable infrastructure risk solutions and specialized computational technologies that are capable of facilitating the rapid computation and distribution of risk information (including massively fast cluster computing networks). We will also see more effective and lower-cost risk solutions provided by external suppliers, together with a movement toward implementing ERM systems. Institutions will increasingly move toward consolidating their suppliers of risk services. In particular, we will see a further consolidation of ERM software providers as well as a complementary evolution of unique and highly specialized boutiques (e.g., credit risk and operational risk database providers).

The bad news is that most institutions will continue to struggle to fully integrate data, software, and analytics into their overarching ERM frameworks. In ERM, as elsewhere in the world of risk management, there is an inevitable trade-off between completeness and accuracy, on the one hand, and cost and timeliness, on the other.

Combining analytical and advanced statistical methods with extensive integrated databases should allow the industry to create increasingly reliable and useful risk management systems. As this book has stressed, however, a well-designed risk infrastructure is a necessary, but not a sufficient, condition for superior risk management.

INDEX

Dr. Michel Crouhy is head of research and development and financial engineering at IXIS Corporate and Investment Bank (Groupe Caisse d'Epargne). He has the bankwide oversight on all quantitative research and the development of new products and applications supporting the trading and structuring businesses. He was formerly Senior Vice President, Business Analytic Solutions, in the Treasury Balance Sheet and Risk Management Division at CIBC (Canadian Imperial Bank of Commerce). His responsibilities included the approval of all pricing, balance sheet, risk and capital related models, the development of risk measurement methodologies and models for market, credit (corporate and retail) and economic capital attribution, as well as customer behavior analytics.

Prior to his current position at CIBC, Michel Crouhy was a professor of finance at the HEC School of Management in Paris, where he was also director of the M.S. HEC in international finance. He has been a visiting professor at the Wharton School and at UCLA. Dr. Crouhy holds a Ph.D. from the Wharton School and is Doctoris Honoris Causa from the University of Montreal.

He is coauthor of *Risk Management* (McGraw-Hill), *The Essentials of Risk Management* (forthcoming, McGraw-Hill), and has published extensively in academic journals in the areas of banking, options, risk management, and financial markets. He is also associate editor of the *Journal of Derivatives*, the *Journal of Credit Risk*, the *Journal of Banking and Finance*, *Asia-Pacific Financial Markets*, the *Journal of Operational Risk*, and is on the editorial board of the *Journal of Risk*.

Professor Dan Galai is the Abe Gray Professor of Finance and Business Administration at the School of Business Administration, the Hebrew University in Jerusalem. He was a visiting professor of finance at INSEAD and at the University of California, Los Angeles. He has also taught at the University of Chicago and at the University of California, Berkeley. Dr. Galai holds a Ph.D. from the University of Chicago and undergraduate and graduate degrees from the Hebrew University.

He has served as a consultant for the Chicago Board of Options Exchange and the American Stock Exchange, as well as for major banks. He had coinvented the volatility index based on the prices of traded index options.

He has published numerous articles in leading business and finance journals on options, financial assets, and corporate finance, and serves on the boards of a few academic journals. He is a coauthor of *Risk Management*, McGraw-Hill (2000) and of *The Essentials of Risk Management*, McGraw-Hill (2005). He was a winner of the First Annual Pomeranze Prize for excellence in options research presented by the CBOE.

Dr. Galai is a principal in Sigma P.C.M. Ltd., which is engaged in portfolio management and corporate finance. In the company he is responsible for risk management consulting to financial institutions as well as nonbank corporations. He is a cofounder of MutualArt Inc., a financial services company, which provides pensionlike benefits to selected artists worldwide.

Dr. Robert M. Mark is the CEO of Black Diamond, which provides corporate governance, risk management consulting, and transaction services. He also serves on several corporate boards, and has worked in a variety of senior corporate positions. He was awarded the Financial Risk Manager of the Year by the Global Association of Risk Professionals (GARP). He serves on the board of The Professional Risk Managers' International Associations (PRMIA), and is also the chairperson of the Blue Ribbon Panel of PRMIA. He served on the board of ISDA and was also the chairperson of the National Asset/Liability Management Association (NALMA).

Prior to his current position, he was the Senior Executive Vice-President and Chief Risk Officer (CRO) at the Canadian Imperial Bank of Commerce (CIBC). Dr. Mark was a member of the Management Committee. His global responsibility covered all credit, market, and operating risks for all of CIBC as well as for its subsidiaries. Prior to his CRO position, he was the Corporate Treasurer at CIBC.

Prior to CIBC, he was the partner in charge of the Financial Risk Management Consulting practice at Coopers & Lybrand (C&L). Before his position at C&L, he was a managing director in the Asia, Europe, and Capital Markets Group (AECM) at Chemical Bank. His responsibilities within AECM encompassed risk management, asset/liability management, quantitative analysis, strategic planning, and analytical systems. He was a senior officer at HongKongShanghaiBank (HKSB), where he headed the technical analysis trading group within the Capital Markets Sector.

He earned his Ph.D. from New York University and is a graduate of the Harvard Business School Advanced Management Program. He is an adjunct professor, and coauthor of *Risk Management* (McGraw-Hill), published in October 2000.